Retirement Planning for High Net Worth Individuals

Seventh Edition

Retirement Planning for High Net Worth Individuals

Seventh Edition

by

Alec Ure

Self-employed Pensions Consultant

Tottel Publishing Ltd, Maxwelton House, 41–43 Boltro Road, Haywards Heath, West Sussex, RH16 1BJ

A CIP Catalogue record for this book is available from the British Library.

ISBN 13 978 1 84592 266 5
ISBN 10 1 84592 266 2

Typeset by Kerrypress Ltd, Luton, Beds

Printed and bound in Great Britain by Antony Rowe, Chippenham, Wilts

Preface

This book primarily concerns high earners, and it replaces the 6th edition of SSAS-SIPPS-FURBS which was published in September 2003 and was followed by a supplement of recent changes the following year. There have been major changes since the last publications, with the advent of the new tax simplification regime from A-Day (6 April 2006).

The acronyms SSAS's and SIPPS are likely to fall away and be replaced by new terminology in the future. The status of pensioneer trustee has gone, although such persons are being retained by many schemes in the role of independent trustees in order to assist in scheme administration and/or guidance. The Government has been focussing strongly on small schemes with influential members with regard to their investment activity. Several new terms have appeared, including 'self-directed' (by the HMRC – previously the Inland Revenue), and 'small schemes' as referred to in the *Directive of the European Parliament and the Council on the activities and supervision of institutions for occupational retirement provision* (the Pensions Directive). The Pensions Directive places specific emphasis on new investment rules, although small schemes (being schemes with fewer than 100 members) are exempt from most requirements with the main exception of the need for diversification of assets. The Government has also been introducing new rules on taxable and moveable property and inheritance tax.

The above matters are considered in detail in this book. Chapters 4 and 5 concentrate on the effect of the new tax regime on SSAS's and SIPPS, and list the pre A-Day criteria which will be needed in connection with transitional considerations and finalising pre A-Day accounts for some time to come. Greater detail of the pre A-Day rules was given in the 6th edition of SSAS-SIPPS-FURBS should the reader require more information. The remainder of this book describes the new tax regime in some detail, the main rules being contained in Chapter 2 under clearly identifiable headings. The only move away from a single tax regime has been the Government's deliberations on self-directed schemes referred to above. Otherwise, tax simplification is what it says, for future pension accrual and new schemes. However, it has been imperative to ensure that people do not retrospectively lose their expectations and entitlements as a result of the new changes from A-Day. This book therefore covers the transitional protections for those rights and entitlements under the relevant subjects. Full details of these far-reaching protections can be found in Chapter 9 of the 7th edition of Tottel's Taxation of Pensions Benefits, which is to be published shortly.

In keeping with the spirit of the Pensions Directive, the new regime offers much freer transferability of pension rights, both at home and abroad. There are specific rules to be met, and the main aspects of those rules are described in Chapter 7. There have also been major changes to the treatment of schemes which are not tax-advantaged. These schemes were previously referred to as FURBS and UURBS. Such schemes are not recognised from A-Day, and existing and new schemes are re-designated 'Employer Financed Retirement Benefits Schemes' (EFRBS). There is a high degree of protection for accrued rights and entitlements under FURBS as at A-Day (although not total), but it must be said that the investment in such products from A-Day as a tax-efficient means of pension-saving has ceased to be attractive. In particular, the ability to pay out the scheme benefit in full as a tax-free lump sum has been removed, and the inheritance tax shelter of a discretionary trust is no longer effective. As many high earners who entered employment from 1989 were capped on their pensionable earnings, the FURBS had become a popular means of topping-up income to pre 1989 level. For the first time since that date, persons who were not capped will find that their pension savings are capped (by the new 'Lifetime Allowance'). In view of these matters, Chapter 6 describes the new rules which apply.

The new tax regime brings in a new reporting regime, and the use of the self-assessment system in order to control pensions and lump sum payments by relation to the tax-relievable ceilings on contributions and pension fund size (the 'Annual Allowance' and the Lifetime Allowance). Failure to comply with the new rules, or the making of unauthorised payments, attracts new penalties and it is important that these are fully understood. Accordingly these matters are explained in chapter 2.

As the new tax regime is the most important date in pensions legislation in 50 years or more, members, advisers, providers, employers and trustees will need to be familiar with the implications of these considerable changes. The removal of the complex eight tax regimes that were in place prior to A-Day is most welcome. However, there are areas of some complication under the new regime, albeit that, in general, it should lead to much more efficient administration in the future. It is hoped that, in buying this book, the reader will be much better prepared for decision-making whether on his or her own behalf or that of clients or scheme members or employees according to the role he or she fills. The book covers the issues which most affect high earners in the UK. A fuller digest of the changes for the main category of members in UK tax-advantaged ('registered') schemes is contained in the 7th edition of Tottel's Taxation of Pensions Benefits.

Finally I wish to thank my associates for their support, Teresa Sienkiewicz of KPMG and John Hayward for their valuable contributions in chapter 8. John has added the VAT and IPT information and Teresa, with the assistance of her colleague Barbara Griessner, has provided an essential update to the accounting and auditing requirements of registered schemes. I am also indebted to the HMRC for the use of its published legislation and practice, in particular the extracts taken from its comprehensive Registered Pension Schemes Manual.

Alec Ure

Alec Ure & Associates

Contents

List of Abbreviations

AVC(s)	–	Additional Voluntary Contribution(s)
CAA	–	Capital Allowances Act 2001
CGT	–	Capital Gains Tax
EC	–	European Commission
ECJ	–	European Courts of Justice
EFRBS	–	Employer-financed retirement benefits scheme
ESC	–	Extra Statutory Concession by the Inland Revenue
EU	–	European Union (formerly European Community)
FA	–	Finance Act
FSA	–	Financial Services Authority–the single regulator from 28 October 1997
FSAVC	–	Free-Standing Additional Voluntary Contributions
FSMA	–	Financial Services and Markets Act 2000
FURBS	–	Funded Unapproved Retirement Benefit Scheme
GAD	–	Government Actuary's Department
GMP	–	Guaranteed Minimum Pension as described in the Pension Schemes Act 1993
GN	–	Actuarial Guidance Note
HMRC	–	Her Majesty's Revenue and Customs
HMRC NICO	–	HMRC National Insurance Contributions Office (formerly Contributions Agency and later NICO)
ICTA 1988	–	Income and Corporation Taxes Act 1988
IHT	–	Inheritance Tax
IHTA 1984	–	Inheritance Tax Act 1984
IORPs	–	Institutions for Occupational Retirement Provision
IPT	–	Insurance Premium Tax
IR SPSS	–	HMRC Savings, Pensions, Share Schemes; including the former PSO (Pension Schemes Office)
ITEPA	–	Income Tax (Earnings and Pensions) Act 2003
MFR	–	Minimum Funding Requirement
NAPF	–	National Association of Pension Funds
NIC(s)	–	National Insurance Contribution(s)
NICO	–	National Insurance Contributions Office

NISPI	–	National Insurance Services to Pensions Industry
OEIC	–	Open-ended Investment Company
PA 1995	–	Pensions Act 1995
PA 2004	–	Pensions Act 2004
PN(s)	–	Practice Notes issued by the Pension Schemes Office (IR 12). The current version is PN(2001), but PN(1979) is still extant for some schemes.
PSA 1993	–	Pensions Schemes Act 1993
RAS	–	Relief at Source
RPI	–	The Government's Index of Retail Prices
s	–	section
ss	–	Sub-section
Sch	–	Schedule
SERPS	–	State Earnings – Related Pension Scheme
SI	–	Statutory Instrument
SIPPS(s)	–	Self–Invested Personal Pension Scheme(s)
SP	–	Inland Revenue Statement of Practice
SPA	–	State Pension Age (65 for men, 60 for women)
SSA	–	Social Security Act(s)
SSAS(s)	–	Small Self-Administered Scheme(s)
S2P	–	The State Second Pension, which replaced SERPS as a second tier state pension from 6 April 2002
TCGA	–	Taxation of Chargeable Gains Act 1992
TUPE	–	Transfer of Employment (Pension Protection) Regulations 2005 (SI 2005/649)
TMA	–	Taxes Management Act 1970
UK	–	United Kingdom
UURBS	–	Unapproved Unfunded Retirement Benefit Scheme
VAT	–	Value Added Tax
VATA	–	Value Added Tax Act 1994

Table of Cases

Table of Statutes

References at the right-hand side of the column are to paragraph numbers.

Table of Statutory Instruments

References at the right-hand side of the column are to paragraph numbers.

Chapter 1

Introduction

1.1 This is the seventh edition of SSAS-SIPPS-FURBS. The sixth edition was published in September 2003, and it was updated by a supplementary booklet in the following year. Such is the speed of change in UK pension law, both for approved schemes and non-approved schemes, that this edition is, by necessity, a complete restructure of the previously updated version.

We are now in the era of a new single tax regime. This is a major change of direction, and it is the result of many years of debate and consultation in the UK. The changes also go some way towards accommodating overseas developments in the area of pension provision. Directive 2003/41/EC of the European Parliament and the Council on the activities and supervision of institutions for occupational retirement provision (IORPs) which was adopted on 3 June 2003 (the European (IORPS) Pension Directive). Its objective was to allow pension funds to benefit from the Internal Market principles of free movement of capital and free provision of services.

These important matters are described respectively in Chapters 2 and 7 of this book. The tax changes took effect from 6 April 2006 (A-Day). A full description of the new tax regime for all types of pension schemes can be found in the fourth edition of Tottel's *Taxation of Pension Benefits*.

This book continues to give emphasis to small self-administered schemes (SSASs), self-invested personal pension schemes (SIPPs) and funded unapproved retirement benefits schemes (FURBS). Such schemes are effectively now classified as self-directed schemes (occupational and personal) and employer-financed retirement benefits schemes (EFRBS). The need for compliance with the European Directive has introduced the term small scheme, which includes the existing terms SSASs and SIPPs, as described in Chapter 4. The imposition of the new simplified tax regime may seem to have removed most of the relevance of past law and practice for such schemes. However, special conditions still apply to small schemes under the new regime. This means that they retain much of their flexibility but must comply with separate rules from other schemes of a larger nature in certain areas. Also of great significance are the transitional arrangements which apply under the new regime. All of these matters are explained in Chapter 3 (transitional arrangements between the new and old tax regimes), Chapter 4 (small self-administered schemes), Chapter 5 (self-invested personal pension schemes) and Chapter 6 (unapproved schemes (non-registered EFRBS from 6 April 2006).

A separate Chapter 8 has now been included, which considers some wider tax considerations for registered schemes.

Transitional arrangements

1.2 Because of the importance of the transitional arrangements, the above-named chapters contain tables and summaries of the most important criteria with which the reader will need to be acquainted. For fully comprehensive details of the pre A-Day rules, the reader is referred to the updated version of the sixth edition of SSAS-SIPPS-FURBS. The pre A-Day changes which have taken place since that version was published are summarised in the relevant chapters of this book. A full detailed explanation of the transitional arrangements for all registered schemes can be found in Chapter 9 of the fourth edition of Tottel's *Taxation of Pension Benefits*.

It seems most likely that SSASs and SIPPs will remain attractive to many in their existing form. This is not only because they can still operate in accordance with the rules that applied before A-Day with regard to their undisturbed investments, in most cases, but also because the new tax regime offers many incentives to such type of pension provision for the future.

The position for existing FURBS and UURBS is not so attractive. Indeed, they are considered by many to be very stringent. In future, funded schemes which are not treated as 'registered' schemes under the new legislation (that is, tax-advantaged schemes resembling pre-A-Day approved and exempt-approved schemes) are classified as EFRBS. The previously available tax advantages for such schemes are effectively lost, subject to some important transitional protection for pre-A-Day rights. High networth individuals are already seeking alternative provision in the form of cash options, share options, overseas provision etc, dependent on their individual circumstances and tax and domicility status.

Summary of the new tax regime

1.3 Although the basic concept of the new tax regime is simple, namely to replace all existing pension tax regimes with a single one, the existing regimes were a formidable mixture of legislation, practice, precedents, concessions and guidance notes. The removal of the discretionary powers of HMRC (see (*a*) below) has meant that the new legislation, HMRC guidance manuals and codes of practice must be clear in their effect. This called for a comprehensive review of all aspects of tax-advantaged pension provision, some of which has still not been finalised. By way of example, the HMRC publication 'Registered Pension Scheme Manual' (RPSM) is still not fully finalised, although nearly so, and HMRC guidance on FURBS/ UURBS and EFRBS is still awaited.

In view of the above, it is considered that a list of the main subjects which are covered by the new tax regime will be a less daunting method of familiarisation with the new rules than a full read-through of the main text of the book. Such a list is provided below, and it is hoped that it will also provide the reader with an easy source of ready-reference to the main issues in the future.

The primary features of the new tax regime are:

(*a*) HMRC no longer has any discretionary powers when granting tax advantages to pension schemes, or to advise in advance on the appropriateness of scheme management and investment activity.

(*b*) From A-Day there must be strict compliance with the legislative requirements and published codes of practice and guidelines.

(*c*) Tax charges, penalties and sanctions may be incurred in the event of non-compliance (see 2.109 to 2.134 and 2.135 to 2.137 concerning tax avoidance schemes).

(*d*) New compliance requirements extend (variously) to trustees, managers, administrators, fund managers, pension scheme promoters and scheme advisers.

(*e*) Membership of registered pension schemes is now permitted for most individuals, including migrants/non-residents (see 2.86 below).

(*f*) Multiple-employer schemes are permitted, whether or not the employers are connected (see 2.86 below).

(*g*) Members may be concurrent members of any number or type of scheme (see 2.86 below).

(*h*) All existing approved or exempt-approved schemes as at A-Day will be classified as registered schemes (see 2.88 below) unless they choose to opt out of the new tax regime.

(*i*) All new schemes set up on or after A-Day must apply to HMRC if registration is required, otherwise they will be treated as EFRBS (see 6.13 below).

(*j*) Nearly all limits on benefits have been removed, and there is no limit on pension provision.

(*k*) Most tax-free lump sums are limited to 25% of the lifetime allowance (see (*l*) below, and 2.36 below).

(*l*) In place of benefit limits, there is a tax-free aggregate lifetime pension fund ceiling (the 'lifetime allowance') for registered schemes (see 2.23 to 2.26 below).

(*m*) In place of existing limits on tax-relievable contributions, there is an annual aggregate tax allowable input limit ('annual allowance') for registered schemes (see 2.13 to 2.21 below).

(*n*) Tax-relievable contributions may be paid at much higher levels than pre-A-Day limits by most members and employers (see 2.103 to 2.105 below).

(*o*) Full reliefs are available on employers' contributions, subject to spreading rules (see 2.105 below).

(*p*) Any amounts which exceed the allowances in (*l*) and (*m*) above will be subjected to tax charges (see 2.22 and 2.27 below).

(*q*) New reporting procedures are in place (see 2.91 to 2.100 below, and Appendix 4).

(*r*) The self-assessment procedure must be used to manage the allowances in (*l*) and (*m*) above and the tax due (see 2.101 below and Chapter 7).

(*s*) The investment income and capital gains of registered schemes are generally exempt from tax (see 2.106 below).

(*t*) A 35% tax charge will be imposed on certain death benefit lump sums (see 2.62 and 2.63 below).

(*u*) Existing FURBS and non-registered/opted-out schemes are classified as EFRBS and enjoy no special tax privileges (see Chapter 6).

(*v*) There are transitional protections for benefit entitlements which were in place as at A-Day under either 'primary protection' or 'enhanced protection' (see Chapter 3).

(*w*) New drawdown provisions are available, including whilst in service, and secured, alternatively secured and unsecured pensions facilitate flexible retirement provision (see 2.51 to 2.53 below).

(*x*) Transfers may be made freely between registered schemes (see 2.138 (*a*) below).

(*y*) Transfers may generally be made from UK registered schemes to overseas schemes, which are regulated as pension funds in their country of establishment, if they undertake to comply with information-reporting requirements (see 2.138 below).

(*z*) Many of the pre-A-Day investment restrictions have been removed, but there are special rules for small schemes – see 2.73 to 2.85 below and Chapters 4 and 5).

(*aa*) In keeping with the EU developments, and on a wider overseas platform, there are significant relaxations for overseas members. For example, migrants who come to the UK will be given tax reliefs on their contributions in place of the old corresponding relief provisions (see 7.9 to 7.11 below).

(*bb*) Registration, reporting, payments and returns are mainly provided for, and will all ultimately be provided for, on the internet. For most actions this will become compulsory.

(*cc*) Employer-sponsored occupational schemes can be provided on a defined benefits, a money purchase or a hybrid basis, and registered personal pension schemes and stakeholder pension schemes on a money purchase basis.

Chapter 2

Details of the new tax regime

Introduction

2.1 Chapter 1 of this book contains a list of the main subjects which are covered by the new simplified tax regime from 6 April 2006 (A-Day). Schemes which were designated as approved schemes and exempt-approved schemes prior to that date have been re-designated as registered schemes unless they have opted out of registration or lost their tax-exempt status. This is explained in 2.112, 6.5 and 6.11 below. An in-depth description of the rules of the new regime and their application can be found in the 4th edition of Tottel's *Taxation of Pension Benefits*, which contains many worked examples.

The purpose of this comprehensive chapter is primarily to provide details of the effect of the new legislation on members of registered schemes who are covered by this book, namely senior directors and high networth individuals. It is hoped that this will lead to an easier understanding of the impact on the three categories of scheme which are covered by Chapters 4, 5 and 6 of this book, which formed the earlier title of this work, as explained in 1.1 above. Overseas considerations, VAT, IPT and accounting matters are dealt with in Chapters 7 and 8 respectively.

Structure of this chapter and HMRC examples

2.2 This chapter covers the main subjects of simplification. Some extracts from the Registered Pensions Schemes Manual (RPSM) on Her Majesty's Revenue and Customs' (HMRC) website have been included in boxes at the end of each subject, where this is likely to be helpful in understanding how the new rules work in individual cases. Emphasis has been put on those matters which are most likely to affect high earners. In view of the potential interest in the rules which affect the greater flexibility to make transfer payments, an Annex has been included at the end of this chapter which contains extracts from the RPSM specific guidance on this wide-ranging matter.

Clear headings

2.3 The chapter has been broken down under the clear headings shown below for ease of reference:

- Background
- The main considerations for high earners
- Administration expenses
- Amending existing rules
- Annual allowance
- Annual allowance charge
- Lifetime allowance
- Lifetime allowance charge, and transitional protection
- Benefits, and transitional protection
- Benefit crystallisation events
- Investments, and transitional protection
- Membership of schemes
- Registration
- Reporting
- Tax reliefs and charges
- Transfers.

Background

The main legislation

2.4 The removal of the existing tax regimes which applied to tax-advantaged pension schemes up until A-Day was a result of many years of consultation. At the same time as the consultations were taking place, legislative rewrites of other tax law were undertaken. These rewrites resulted in the coming into force of *CAA 2001* and *ITEPA 2003*. *CAA 2001* restated the existing capital allowances legislation, and *ITEPA 2003* restated certain enactments relating to income tax on employment income, pension income and social security income. Both Acts made relatively minor changes to existing legislation.

The *Finance Act 2004*, by way of a complete contrast, totally replaced the great majority of the extant tax legislation which applied to pension schemes under the old regimes with effect from A-Day. *Subsections 149* to *284* of that Act cover pension simplification, *ss 306* to *319* concern the disclosure of tax avoidance schemes and *Schs 28* to *36* cover other pension rules, including transitional provisions and savings.

The first *Finance Bill 2005* was published on 24 March 2005. The Bill received many delays in its process through both Houses of Parliament. Accordingly, with a general election approaching, a shorter *Finance* (*No.2*) *Bill* was published on 6 April 2005. This Bill was enacted on 7 April 2005 as the *Finance Act 2005*. A new Bill was published on 26 May 2005 and was later enacted as the *Finance* (*No.2*) *Act 2005*. The Act brought in some of the provisions of the first Bill which were omitted from the later Bill, together with some new provisions (in particular concerning capital gains tax avoidance by temporary non-residents and trustees and matters involving the disposal of assets overseas by residents and non-residents).

Earlier reviews

2.5 The reviews of the many tax regimes which had applied to tax-advantaged UK schemes began some 15 years prior to the enactment of the *Finance Act 2004*. The main purpose was to encourage private pension provision for all, whilst providing an opportunity to reduce the administrative costs that fell on HMRC staff and the trustees, managers, administrators and employers of tax-advantaged UK pension schemes.

High earners

2.6 There was little concern shown for the high networth earner, the general opinion being that such persons were able to organise their own savings without added tax incentives. This led to some strong exchanges between various consultative committees, HMRC and pension representative bodies over the years. Whereas the *Finance Act 1989* had introduced the earnings cap on high earners from 1 June 1989, the new tax regime has capped all members from 6 April 2006 (A-Day). For the first time, this includes high earners who previously had pre-1989 protected rights. There are transitional protections, but a review of future pension planning of such individuals, and their long-term savings plans, is paramount. It has been observed by some that the new rules will accelerate the drive to overseas investment and pension provision by high earners in the future.

Others

2.7 For the bulk of UK individuals, and many migrants, the new simplified regime does offer far more attractive pension provision for the future. The new opportunities which are summarised in this chapter will be of interest to those family members of high earners whose pension entitlements fall within the new lifetime allowance.

Chronology

2.8 The main pension reviews which led to the new rules are described in chapter 1 of the 4th edition of Tottel's *Taxation of Pension Benefits*. In brief, they were:

- 1993: the Goode Report, by Professor Roy Goode, was published by the Pension Law Committee in September 1993.
- 1998: the National Association of Pension Funds ('NAPF') report on its ongoing review of UK pension provision, accompanied by proposals which had been put forward by the Department of Social Security (now the DWP).
- 2000: Paul Myners' report into institutional investment.
- 2001: the Sandler Review which recommended a simplification of products and advice, and significant reductions in costs and overheads, with FSA support.
- 2002: the Pickering Report into UK pension provision.
- 2002: The HMRC/Treasury Simplification Team report entitled *Simplifying the Taxation of Pensions: Increasing Choice and Flexibility for All* was published on 17 December 2002 (on the same date, the DWP published a report entitled *Simplicity, Security and Choice: Working and Saving for Retirement*).
- 2003 to date: The HMRC/Treasury Simplification Team successor report dated 10 December 2003 and entitled *Simplifying the Taxation of Pensions: The Government's Proposals*.
- The *Finance Act 2004* and the subsequent developments which are described in this book.

During the simplification consultative process it had been estimated by the National Audit Office (NAO) that between 5,000 and 10,000 people would be adversely affected by the simplification proposals. Following this statement the lifetime allowance (see **2.23** below) was raised from £1.4 million pounds to £1.5 million, which is the current level.

The main considerations for high earners

Overall impact

2.9 The main change which affects high earners is the new lifetime allowance limit on aggregate tax-relievable lifetime funds (see 2.23 to 2.26

below). This does not have a great impact on those individuals who were previously subject to the earnings cap, but it does have an adverse effect on future pension savings for those who enjoyed transitional protection from that limit.

A major decision for individuals who already have funds and entitlements which exceed the lifetime allowance is whether to opt for primary protection or enhanced protection (see 2.28 and 2.29 below). The decision is a critical one, and it is likely that most will opt for enhanced protection as the fund yield will remain tax free. For those persons who are already subject to the earnings cap, the withdrawal of the tax advantages which could be gained from FURBS and UURBS (see Chapter 6) means that alternative high earner provision should be considered. The new EFRBS seem far from tax-attractive.

The lifetime allowance is accompanied by the annual tax-relievable input into registered schemes. This is known as the annual allowance (see 2.13 to 2.21 below). In some cases this will provide greater investment opportunities on a tax-efficient basis, but it must be remembered that future contributions, most transfers and/or benefit accrual will cause enhanced protection to be lost, and any amount in excess of the lifetime allowance will attract the lifetime allowance charge (see 2.27 below).

Decisions made before A-Day

2.10 It will be necessary for trustees and managers to review any decisions which were made before A-Day which affect entitlements and funds after that date. Their considerations are likely to include some of the following:

- whether registration for enhanced protection or for primary protection from the standard lifetime allowance has already been made;
- if registration for enhanced protection has been made, or is intended, no further accrual or contributions should be made;
- whether member contributions to any retirement annuities have been maximised (carry-back reliefs cease on 31 January 2007 and the carry-forward facility for unused reliefs was abolished from A-Day);
- whether any AVC arrangements are still in place;
- whether death benefits have been restructured, perhaps as lump sums;
- whether limited price indexation cap of 2.5% for future benefit accrual for defined benefits schemes has been adopted, and indexation removed for money purchase schemes;
- any changes to employment terms, including flexible retirement and early retirement;

- details of the result of investment reviews and testings for the lifetime allowance;
- what investment decisions were made in readiness for A-Day, and the transitional protection rules for existing holdings;
- whether the scheme rules are to retain benefit limits;
- details of any legal review of the scheme documentation, and the likely impact of the overriding legislation on entitlements and trustee decisions.

Administration expenses

2.11 The administration expenses of the scheme must not exceed those which might be expected to be paid to a person at arm's length.

Amending existing rules

2.12 There are modification powers under the *Finance Act 2004* for the purpose of providing transitional protection for schemes if their documentation has not been amended to comply with the new tax rules. The transitional protection ends on 6 April 2011, but it is particularly important for high earners to ensure that their documentation is reviewed by a pensions lawyer at the earliest opportunity. This is most advisable in order to ensure that the existing rules are not over-restrictive, confer unnecessary powers or place unintended responsibilities on trustees. The *Pension Schemes (Modification of Rules of Existing Schemes) Regulations 2006 (SI 2006/364)* contain overrides to existing scheme documentation. They include, amongst other things, a rule of construction and they give trustees discretion over whether or not to make a payment which would otherwise fall to be treated as an unauthorised payment.

Annual allowance

2.13 The new aggregate annual allowance for tax relievable contributions offers greater scope to pay contributions for many. This is particularly relevant in the later years of members' lives when loans and debts are often paid off, children have grown up and inheritances are received. However, for the high earner it will be necessary to consider the effect of the lifetime allowance charge if the fund is already at a high level.

Exemptions

2.14 It is not necessary to count the following towards the annual allowance:

- any transfers between registered funds, and recognised and regulated overseas schemes;
- member contributions in excess of earnings;
- AVCs for the purpose of securing added years.

Also, no test is required in a year when the allowance has already been tested and the pension has vested in full, or where the individual died before the end of the tax year concerned.

The level of the allowance, and the methods of calculation

2.15 The allowance will increase steadily from £215,000 to £255,000 by the year 2010, as shown below:

- Tax year 2006/2007– £215,000
- Tax year 2007/2008– £225,000
- Tax year 2008/2009– £235,000
- Tax year 2009/2010– £245,000
- Tax year 2010/2011– £255,000.

Thereafter five-yearly reviews will be carried out, and the allowance will not decrease.

There are different methods of calculation for the increase in the annual allowance for defined benefits schemes and money purchase schemes. These are described in detail in Chapter 2 of the 4th edition of Tottel's *Taxation of Pension Benefits*. The increases are referred to as the 'pension increase amount' and they are measured over the 'pension increase period'. The method of calculating the pension increase amount for a defined benefits arrangement is based on the increase in the capital value of an individual's rights over the applicable pension input period (for example, an increase in the amount of the member's pensionable service and/or pensionable earnings under the scheme provisions, and an augmentation of a member's benefit entitlement under the scheme). These increases are converted by using a factor of 10:1 to give an increased capital value, as shown under the relevant heading below. For money purchase arrangements a factor of 1:1 is applied to the contributions which are received by the scheme. There are other categories of arrangement described below.

Pension input period

2.16 There must be a pension input period in every tax year. The commencement of the first period will be the day that the member begins to accrue his pension rights under the scheme. However, there is wide flexibility in the choice of an end date, under *s 238, Finance Act 2004*. This may be determined as the end of the scheme accounting period, the end of the tax year or any other chosen date. Detailed working examples are given in Chapter 2 of the 4th edition of Tottel's *Taxation of Pension Benefits*, which has drawn examples from the HMRC's registered pension schemes manual (RPSM).

Pension input amount

2.17 There are four types of arrangement for the purpose of calculating the pension input amount. These are summarised below. A detailed explanation is given in Chapter 2 of the 4th edition of Tottel's *Taxation of Pension Benefits*. The main methods of calculation are summarised below under the relevant headings.

Cash balance arrangement

2.18 In a cash balance arrangement the pension increase amount is the increase in the value of an individual's rights within the pension input period in the tax year concerned. This means that the pension value at the beginning of that period is compared with the pension value at the end of that period.

In order to determine the value at the two relevant dates, the opening value and the closing value must be determined:

(*a*) the opening value is the amount which would have been available to provide benefits on the assumption that an entitlement to their payment arose at the beginning of the pension input period. The amount is increased by RPI or 5%, whichever is higher, unless another amount is laid down in regulations;

(*b*) the closing value is the amount which would be available to provide benefits on the assumption that an entitlement to their payment arose at the end of the period.

The following additional rules apply:

- pension debits which occur in the period are added back;
- pension credits which occur in the period are deducted;
- the amount of transfers to registered, or qualifying recognised overseas, schemes, together with the market value of the assets is added back;
- the amount of transfers in from registered, or qualifying recognised overseas, schemes, together with the market value of the assets is discounted;

- benefits which have crystallised are added back, unless the member has become entitled to the whole benefit, or died;
- any minimum payments under the *Pension Schemes Act 1993* are subtracted;
- there are special provisions for employer contributions which are paid during the period 6 April 2006 to 7 July 2006 (see 2.20 below).

Other money purchase arrangements

2.19 In money purchase arrangements which are not cash balance arrangements, the amount of the increase within the pension input period in the tax year concerned is:

- the total tax-relievable contributions paid by or on behalf of the individual; and
- the contributions paid in respect of the individual under the arrangement by an employer of the individual.

Additionally, s *233* (*3*), *Finance Act 2004,* states:

> 'when at any time contributions paid under a pension scheme by an employer otherwise than in respect of any individual become held for the purposes of the provision under an arrangement under the pension scheme of benefits to or in respect of an individual, they are to be treated as being contributions paid at that time in respect of the individual under the arrangement'.

As for cash benefit schemes:

- any minimum payments under the *Pension Schemes Act 1993* are deducted;
- there are special provisions for employer contributions paid during the period 6 April 2006 to 7 July 2006 (see 2.20 below).

Defined benefits arrangement

2.20 In a defined benefits arrangement the pension increase amount is the increase in the value of an individual's rights within the pension input period in the tax year concerned. This means that the pension value at the beginning of that period is compared with the pension value at the end of that period.

To assist in determining the opening value and the closing value, *ss 234* (*4*),(*5*), *Finance Act 2004*, contains the following wording:

'(4) The opening value of the individual's rights under the arrangement is:

(10 × PB) + LSB

where

PB is the annual rate of the pension which would, on the valuation assumptions (see *section 277*), be payable to the individual under the arrangement if the individual became entitled to payment of it at the beginning of the pension input period, and

LSB is the amount of the lump sum to which the individual would, on the valuation assumptions, be entitled under the arrangement (otherwise than by commutation of pension).

(5) The closing value of the individual's rights under the arrangement is:

(10 × PE) + LSE

where

PE is the annual rate of the pension which would, on the valuation assumptions, be payable to the individual under the arrangement if the individual became entitled to payment of it at the end of the pension input period, and

LSE is the amount of the lump sum to which the individual would, on the valuation assumptions, be entitled under the arrangement (otherwise than by commutation of pension) if the individual became entitled to the payment at that time'.

There are special provisions for employer contributions which were paid during the period 6 April 2006 to 7 July 2006 for the purpose of discharging previously unfunded contractual obligations incurred by them before 6 April 2006 (*s 227(7), and para 48, Sch 36, Finance Act 2004*). The amount of the relevant consolidated contribution should be deducted from the closing value.

The following additional rules apply:

- pension debits which occur in the period are added back;
- pension credits which occur in the period are deducted;
- the amount of transfers to registered, or qualifying recognised overseas, schemes together with the market value of the assets is added back;

- the amount of transfers in from registered, or qualifying recognised overseas, schemes together with the market value of the assets is discounted;
- benefits which have crystallised are added back, unless the member has become entitled to the whole benefit or died;
- any minimum payments under the *Pension Schemes Act 1993* are deducted.

There are special provisions for the valuation of deferred benefits. *The Registered Pension Schemes* (*Defined Benefits Arrangements – Uprating of Opening Value*) *Regulations 2006* (*SI 2006/130*) prescribe an alternative percentage. This is the greatest of 5%; the RPI increase and any percentage prescribed by regulations.

Hybrid arrangement

2.21 In a hybrid arrangement the pension increase amount is the greater or greatest of such of input amounts **A, B** and **C** as are relevant input amounts:

- **A** is what would be the pension input amount under *ss 230–232, Finance Act 2004,* if the benefits provided to or in respect of the individual under the arrangement were cash balance benefits
- **B** is what would be the pension input amount under *s 233, Finance Act 2004,* if the benefits provided to or in respect of the individual under the arrangement were other money purchase benefits
- **C** is what would be the pension input amount under *ss 234* to *236, Finance Act 2004,* if the benefits provided to or in respect of the individual under the arrangement were defined benefits.

Annual allowance charge

2.22 If the annual allowance is exceeded, a freestanding charge of 40% is applied to the excess. The member is liable to pay the charge, and must inform HMRC if he has not been issued with a personal tax return. The charge is incurred whatever the residence or domicility of the administrator or member. The net balance of the excess may remain in the scheme, subject to the ultimate application of the lifetime allowance. The excessive amount is not treated as pension income (or any other income) for the purposes of UK bilateral double taxation conventions.

Lifetime allowance

2.23 The new aggregate lifetime allowance for tax relievable contributions is regulated by the self-assessment return. For high earners it imposes a cap on their aggregate tax-free lifetime pensions savings. In the case of individuals who were not subject to the 1989 earnings cap this means that they will need to consider how best to save in the future. The option chosen by many 'capped' employees before A-Day was a FURBS or an UURBS. However, such products are no longer tax-viable for most, and the rules for funded schemes have been replaced by the new employer-financed retirement benefits scheme (EFRBS) rules (see Chapter 6 for details of these matters). Nevertheless, there are wider opportunities for individuals to join registered pension schemes from A-Day and they are likely to be an attractive first level of benefit provision for the high earner who was previously ineligible for any savings through an approved scheme.

There are new opportunities in the areas of transfers (see 2.138 to 2.171 below), and overseas considerations (see Chapter 6 and 2.172 to 2.210 below), which may well be of interest to some, particularly the internationally mobile. However, it is likely that high earners and the employers of key personnel will have looked at the attractiveness of cash, share options and different types of investment trusts amongst other incentives.

Many small schemes do, of course, have family members who will not be caught by the new lifetime allowance. This is likely to be of particular benefit to them as they grow older, pay off loans and debts, their children leave home and inherited monies are received. The annual allowance limit (see 2.15 above) allows for accelerated savings for such individuals compared with the past regimes.

The lifetime allowance will increase steadily from £1.5 million to £1.8 million by the year 2010, as shown below:

- Tax year 2006/2007–£1,500,000
- Tax year 2007/2008–£1,600,000
- Tax year 2008/2009–£1,650,000
- Tax year 2009/2010–£1,750,000
- Tax year 2010/2011–£1,800,000.

Thereafter five-yearly reviews will be carried out, and the allowance will not decrease.

Testing for the lifetime allowance

2.24 As is the case for the annual allowance (see 2.15 to 2.21 above), the method of testing the lifetime allowance depends on the nature of the scheme or arrangement:

- money purchase schemes should be measured at market value;
- a factor of 20:1 should be used for defined benefits schemes (or a special factor where benefit increases exceed RPI, or a fixed 5% per annum, or for survivors' benefits which in aggregate exceed the member's pension);
- a factor of 25:1 should be applied to pensions in payment at A-Day if further benefits are provided later;
- where pensions are payable as income withdrawal, the pension should be assumed to be the maximum permitted annual income.

The rules that apply

2.25 The following rules apply:

- where the value of benefits exceeds the lifetime allowance at A-Day, the protections to entitlements described in Chapter 3 apply (which may include a protected tax-free lump sum);
- notification procedures apply to HMRC, administrators and members etc (see 2.91 to 2.101 below);
- a member must certify that he has sufficient allowance available before his benefits vest;
- tests must be made where pensions increases exceed RPI or the assumed rate, on transfers to overseas schemes; at age 75; on cessation of corresponding approval or a change to, or cessation of, a double taxation agreement;
- if pension-splitting orders were already in place at A-Day the recipient's allowance may be increased by an appropriate pension credit factor to reflect the increased benefits;
- where pension-splitting orders are made after A-Day, pension credits count against the recipient's allowance, pension debits do not count against the donor's allowance (if a pension credit is received that relates to a pension in payment, and the credit relates to both crystallised and uncrystallised rights, only the crystallised element is taken into account);
- discretionary augmentations may be given across the board without testing if they apply to all pensions payable and there are at least 50 such persons in the scheme;
- transfers from recognised overseas pension schemes do not count against the allowance to the extent they have not previously received tax reliefs in the UK;
- partnership retirement annuities are not included, but excluding other retirement annuities must be included;

- transfers to other registered schemes are not included;
- if a member dies before his benefits are fully vested, any cash sum paid in lieu of pension will not be taxable to the extent that it is within the member's own lifetime allowance.

Administrator's responsibility

2.26 The administrator has responsibility for the following actions in connection with the lifetime allowance:

(*a*) establishing whether a chargeable amount arises at a benefit crystallisation event (BCE – see 2.71 to 2.72 below);

(*b*) accounting quarterly to HMRC for the lifetime allowance charge (see 2.101 below); and

(*c*) providing the member with a statement of the total level of the member's lifetime allowance that has been used up (and, if a chargeable amount arose, a notice confirming the level of chargeable amount, the lifetime allowance charge due and whether or not accounted for/to be accounted for by the administrator).

Lifetime allowance charge and transitional protection

2.27 If the lifetime allowance is exceeded, a lifetime allowance charge is imposed on the excess. The charge is 25% if the balance is paid as a pension, or 55% if it is taken as a lump sum, and it falls jointly and severally on the member and the administrator, or on the recipient in the case of a lump sum death benefit. The member is liable for the charge, but the administrator shall withhold it and remit it to HMRC. The member must declare it in his self-assessment return. The charge is incurred whatever the residence or domicility of the administrator or member.

The following formula is provided in *s 218, Finance Act 2004,* for the purpose of calculating the lifetime allowance at the benefit crystallisation date where one or more lifetime allowance enhancement factors apply. The formula is:

SLA + (SLA x LAEF)

where:

SLA is the standard lifetime allowance at that date; and

LAEF is the lifetime allowance enhancement factor which operates at that date with regard to the event and the member.

It is important for high earners to be aware of the two types of available protection from the charge. Members must decide by 5 April 2009 to choose which form of protection suits them better, but decisions are best made before or shortly after A-Day if the opportunity for enhanced protection is not to be lost. Full details are given in Chapter 9 of the 4th edition of Tottel's *Taxation of Pension Benefits*. Records relating to the protection notification must be kept for at least six years.

If the option form is completed by someone else on the individual's behalf, the individual must still sign the form unless he is physically or mentally incapable of doing so. An individual's personal representative may also sign the form if the individual has died. Once HMRC have processed the form they will issue a certificate showing the enhanced lifetime allowance. In brief, the choice of method of protection falls under the two following headings.

Primary protection

2.28 Primary protection applies to the value of relevant pension rights in excess of the lifetime allowance at A-Day. It allows further benefits to accrue post A-Day. The individual's lifetime allowance is increased by an enhancement factor based on the amount of pension rights already accrued at A-Day. The disadvantage for high earners is that future accrual will attract the lifetime allowance charge to the extent that the fund increase exceeds the equivalent progression of the lifetime allowance shown in 2.23 above. The enhancement factor is the percentage by which the value of rights on 5 April 2006 exceeds £1,500,000 and is expressed in the following formula:

(RR – SLA) / SLA

Where:

RR is the value of pension rights on 5 April 2006

SLA is the standard Lifetime Allowance for the 2006/07 tax year (£1,500,000)

[if the value of an individual's total pension rights on 5 April 2006 was £1,830,000, his lifetime allowance enhancement factor would be 0.22, calculated as:

(1,830,000 – 1,500,000) / 1,500,000 = 0.22].

Relevant pension rights derive from one or more of the following:

(*a*) a retirement benefit scheme approved under *Ch I, Part XIV, ICTA 1988*;

(*b*) a scheme formerly approved under *s 208, ICTA 1970*;

(*c*) a relevant statutory scheme;

(*d*) a *s 32* policy;

(*e*) a Parliamentary pension fund;

(*f*) a retirement annuity contract ('*s 226* annuity'); or

(*g*) a personal pension scheme approved under *Ch IV, Part XIV, ICTA 1988.*

If an individual's pension rights are decreased by a pension debit, the enhancement factor needs to be recalculated by reference to the value of rights that remain after the pension debit is deducted. If this reduces the value of rights below £1,500,000 then primary protection is lost and the individual will be subject to the standard £1,500,000 lifetime allowance.

Enhanced protection

2.29 Enhanced protection applies to all benefits for members who cease active membership at A-Day, provided they do not join another registered scheme (whether or not they exceed the lifetime allowance). The effect of enhanced protection is to ensure that scheme members are able to protect their accrued rights and avoid the new lifetime and annual allowance charges completely. However, there must be no further relevant benefit accrual from A-Day. Relevant benefit accrual means the following:

for a money purchase arrangement (*but not a cash balance arrangement*): where a contribution is paid which is:

(*a*) a tax relievable contribution paid by or on behalf of the individual;

(*b*) a contribution in respect of the individual by his employer;

(c) any other contribution which becomes held for the benefit of the individual

for a cash balance or defined benefits arrangement: where, at the time when a benefit payment is made (or on making a permitted transfer to a money purchase arrangement), the crystallised value of the benefit exceeds the higher of:

(*a*) the value of an individual's rights on 5 April 2006, increased to the date of payment by the highest of:

- % compound;
- the increase in the Retail Prices Index;

- an increase specified in statutory order applicable to contracted-out rights.

(*b*) the benefit derived by using pensionable service to 5 April 2006, the scheme's accrual rate, and the amount of pensionable earnings at the actual date of payment, which may be some time after A-Day (the elements included in earnings must be the same elements that were pensionable prior to A-Day).

The elements in (*b*) above are:

(*a*) if the member was subject to the post-'89 regime (see Chapter 4) on 5 April 2006, his earnings are limited to the highest earnings in any consecutive 12-month period in the three years before retirement, or 7.5% of the standard lifetime allowance if that is lower;

(*b*) if the member was not subject to the post-'89 regime on 5 April 2006, his earnings are similarly calculated as the highest earnings in any consecutive 12-month period in the three years before retirement, but if they exceed 7.5% of the standard lifetime allowance they must be restricted to a three-year average or to 7.5% of the standard lifetime allowance, whichever is greater.

Defined benefits may continue to accrue post A-Day under enhanced protection as long as the eventual amount crystallised on retirement does not exceed the appropriate limit set out above. This allows for modest pay rises to the date of retirement, but, more importantly, it allows for normal accrual to continue and for early retirement to be taken where the early retirement reduction factor takes the value of the actual benefit paid under the appropriate limit.

Transfers: there are exceptions whereby transfers are permitted without loss of protection:

(*a*) where all the sums and assets or all pension rights of the individual under the arrangement are transferred;

(*b*) where the sums and assets or pension rights are transferred to form all or part of the assets of one or more money purchase arrangements under a registered pension scheme or recognised overseas pension scheme (if the transfer is in connection with the winding up of a scheme under which the individual has defined benefit or cash balance rights, his rights can be transferred to another cash balance or defined benefits arrangement for the individual – provided that the receiving arrangement is a registered pension scheme or recognised overseas pension scheme relating to the same employment as the wound-up arrangement;

(*c*) where defined benefit or cash balance pension rights are transferred to a money purchase arrangement, and the value of the sums and assets received by the money purchase arrangement are actuarially equivalent to the rights being transferred.

A transfer of rights which is made to a scheme for an ex-spouse following a pension sharing order is a permitted transfer.

How to value pre-A-Day rights for protection

2.30 The methods of valuing rights that have accrued at A-Day are complex. They are described in detail in Chapter 9 of the 4th edition of Tottel's *Taxation of Pension Benefits*. The value of benefits is not based on one of the traditional actuarial methods, e g transfer value, but on the standard HMRC valuation factor.

Rights not yet in payment

2.31 Different methods of valuation apply to money purchase, cash balance, defined benefit or hybrid schemes:

Money purchase arrangements: the value of uncrystallised rights is the sum of any cash held and the market value of the other assets held to provide the member's benefits on 5 April 2006.

Cash balance scheme: the value of uncrystallised rights is the amount that would be available for the provision of immediate benefit if the member had been entitled to receive it on 5 April 2006 (it is assumed that the member is in good physical and mental health and has reached either age 60 or a different protected age).

Defined benefits arrangement: the value of uncrystallised rights is calculated as follows (it is assumed that the member is in good physical and mental health and has reached either age 60, or, a different protected age):

(RVF x ARP) + LS

where:

RVF is the relevant valuation factor (i e 20)

ARP is the annual rate of pension the member would be entitled to if he acquired an actual rather than a prospective right to receive it on 5 April 2006

LS is the amount of lump sum the member would have received otherwise than by commutation (i e only applicable for schemes that provide separate pension and lump sum).

Hybrid arrangement: the value of uncrystallised rights is calculated on whichever of the bases produces the highest result.

The value of uncrystallised rights must be restricted to comply with pre-A-Day HMRC limits where those rights derive from one of the following occupational pension schemes:

(*a*) a retirement benefit scheme approved for the purpose of *Ch I, Pt XIV, ICTA 1988*;

(*b*) a scheme formerly approved under *s 208, ICTA 1970;*

(*c*) a relevant statutory scheme as defined in *s 611A, ICTA 1988*, or a pension scheme treated by HMRC as such; or

(*d*) a deferred annuity contract securing benefits under any of the three types of scheme above.

The formula is:

20 x MPP

where **MPP** is the maximum permitted pension that could be paid to the individual on 5 April 2006 under the arrangement without giving HMRC grounds for withdrawing tax approval (it is assumed that the member is in good physical and mental health and has reached either age 60 or if a different protected age).

Rights in payment

2.32 Where rights have come into payment, they are valued as 25 times the annual rate of pension that is being paid. Rights in payment in the form of income drawdown are valued as 25 times the maximum annual rate of drawdown that could be received on 5 April 2006.

Lump sums

2.33 The value of lump sum rights on 5 April 2006 is calculated by the formula:

(¼ x VCPR) + VULSR

where:

VCPR is the value of relevant crystallised pension rights

VULSR is the value of relevant uncrystallised lump sum rights

VCPR is calculated as 25 times the annual rate at which any existing pension (or the sum if more than one) is currently payable on 5 April 2006 from one or more of the arrangements under which relevant pension rights may be payable, including a right to make income withdrawals under *s 634A of ICTA 1988*.

For members of occupational pension schemes the value of the lump sum is restricted by reference to the HMRC limits which applied before A-Day. For a member still in service on 5 April 2006, it is assumed that he left employment on that date.

If lump sum rights are valued at more than £375,000 they may be included in the notification to HMRC to rely on primary and/or enhanced protection.

Benefits, and transitional protection

2.34 The benefit rules under the new tax regime are described in detail in Chapter 3 of the 4th edition of Tottel's *Taxation of Pension Benefits*. A summary of the main rules is given below, with particular emphasis on those matters which affect high earners. There are general benefits rules which apply:

Scheme pension:

(*a*) a limit of 25% of the capital value of the pension applies to tax-free lump sums;

(*b*) payment of benefits must commence by age 75 and normally be paid for life in at least annual instalments;

(*c*) with certain exceptions, benefits must not normally commence before age 55;

(*d*) pensions are taxable as earnings under *ITEPA 2003* and must be non-assignable, except where otherwise permitted;

(*e*) pensions must not normally be guaranteed for more than 10 years, and schemes must not offer a capital guarantee of more than value protection up to age 75.

A defined benefits scheme may only pay a scheme pension. There is much greater flexibility for money purchase schemes (see 2.51 to 2.55 below). This will be of particular interest to most high earners as it is common for their scheme benefits to accrue on a money purchase basis.

Recipients of death benefits:

The rules are:

(*a*) children's pensions must cease at age 23 unless dependency continues by reason of disability (some transitional arrangements apply);

(*b*) adult's dependants pensions may be paid for life;

(*c*) a dependant may include a person financially dependent on the member; mutually dependent, or dependent because of physical or mental impairment;

(*d*) own right pensions do not need to be restricted to the member's pension level, but must not be value protected or guaranteed; and

(*e*) non-assignment and non-surrender rules apply (except where a pensions sharing order is in point) and non-commutation rules apply except in cases of triviality.

Pensions

2.35 There is no monetary limit on the level of pension which may be paid.

Lump sums

2.36 Lump sums must come into payment before the member's lifetime allowance has been fully used up, by age 75 and normally within three months of the entitlement arising. The calculation of lump sums is complex, although the general rule is that the maximum tax-free lump sum which may be paid is 25% of the capital value of the pension which comes into payment.

The permitted maximum lump sum is calculated using a divider of 25% of the standard lifetime allowance after the deduction of any crystallised benefits. An applicable amount of one-third of the market value of the assets underlying the member's unsecured fund on income withdrawal, or one-third of the annuity purchase price if the lump sum is linked to the lifetime allowance, is used in appropriate cases.

Subject to the provisions of the governing scheme documentation, it is envisaged that many members of defined benefit schemes will enjoy a higher level of tax-free lump sums. However, high earners are most likely to be members of small money purchase schemes and are less likely to benefit from the 25% limit. Nevertheless, the transitional protections in 2.40 to 2.50 below will be of interest to some members. Members of personal pension schemes already have a tax-free limit of 25% of their fund values.

The formula for the 25% test is:

VULSR / VUR x 100

Where:

VULSR is the value of uncrystallised lump sum rights on 5 April 2006

VUR is the value of uncrystallised rights on 5 April 2006

For retirement annuity contracts (*'s 226'* policies), the value is 25% of the funds under the arrangement on 5 April 2006, whether or not a higher percentage could have been paid.

For arrangements other than retirement annuity contracts, the lump sum is calculated as if the member had become entitled to payment of the benefit on 5 April 2006. It should be assumed that the member is in good physical and mental health and had reached either age 60, or any earlier age which was specified at 10 December 2003 as the minimum age at which benefits could be paid without reduction.

Certified lump sums

2.37 Existing lump sum certificates can be ignored once post-A-Day valuations for transitional protection have taken place. However, for personal pension schemes which received a transfer from an occupational pension scheme the lump sum must not exceed that shown on the certificate.

Excessive lump sums

2.38 Excessive lump sums which are repaid will be charged to tax at a rate of 55%.

Lump sum transitional protection

2.39 There are two main protections from the new limits for existing rights as at A-Day:

(*a*) lump sum entitlements which exceed £375,000 at A-Day;

(*b*) uncrystallised rights that are greater than 25% of the standard lifetime allowance.

It is most important that the trustees/managers of the scheme retain the required data to enable them to calculate and evidence their members' lump sum entitlements when they become payable.

Lump sum entitlements which exceed £375,000 at A-Day

2.40 In the case of an individual who has applied for primary protection and has registered lump sum rights greater than £375,000 (under 2.39 (*a*) above), the pension commencement lump sum is calculated as the amount registered at A-Day increased by the rise in the standard lifetime allowance between A-Day and the year in which benefits are vested.

If lump sums are taken from two different schemes at two different times, the protected lump sum amount will have to be adjusted to take account of the first lump sum paid, by increasing the first lump sum in line with increases in the standard lifetime allowance, and then deducting it from the increased protected lump sum amount at the second payment date.

The pension commencement lump sum is calculated as the same percentage of rights being crystallised at the vesting date as the percentage arrived at by dividing uncrystallised lump sum rights at A-Day by the value of uncrystallised rights at A-Day and multiplying by 100. If an individual had more than one pension arrangement, then the maximum lump sum that could be taken from each arrangement would be limited by the percentage derived from the total uncrystallised lump sum rights at A-Day divided by the total uncrystallised rights and multiplied by 100. This means that if one arrangement paid a lump sum less than this percentage, the excess could not be taken from another arrangement.

Where the protected lump sum is greater than 25% (see 2.45 to 2.50 below), a member who does not register for primary or enhanced protection may continue to have a lump sum entitlement greater than £375,000 if that entitlement was greater than 25% of the value of his rights at A-Day (the formulae in *paras 31* to *34, Sch 36, Finance Act 2004* apply).

The following numbered boxes from the RPSM contain some helpful examples of the different scenarios which can apply.

BOX 1

2.41 RPSM03105160 – Protection of lump sums with primary protection: taking benefits at more than one time – some lump sum benefits are not tax-free

Sally has lump sum rights of £1 million on 5 April 2006 and has primary protection on pension rights of £5 million. She has rights in two arrangements. Her lump sum rights are payable by commuting pension rights.

She takes benefits on 3 April 2011 from the smaller of the two arrangements.

The standard Lifetime Allowance in 2010–2011 is £1.8 million. The amounts of her protected pension and lump sum have increased in line with the increase in the standard Lifetime Allowance to £6 million and £1.2 million (each amount being multiplied by £1.8 million/£1.5 million).

As the smaller arrangement, a money purchase arrangement, is valued at £600,000 she chooses to take all her benefit as a lump sum.

Sally takes benefits from her second arrangement in 2017 when the standard Lifetime Allowance is £2.1 million. The amounts of her protected pension and lump sum have increased in line with the increase in the standard Lifetime Allowance to £7 million and £1.4 million (each being multiplied by £2.1million/£1.5 million).

Sally has taken benefits previously so the amounts of benefits currently protected must be reduced by the value of the earlier benefits. The value of the earlier benefits must be increased in line with the increase in the standard Lifetime Allowance from its value when the benefits were taken to its current value.

In this example, the standard Lifetime Allowance has increased from £1.8 million to £2.1 million. The value of the £600,000 lump sum taken in 2011 is therefore £700,000 (£600,000 x £2.1/1.8 million).

Sally's available protected pension and lump sum are therefore £6.3 million (£7 million – £700,000) and £700,000 (£1.4 million – £700,000) respectively.

Her second arrangement is a money purchase arrangement worth £8.3 million. She takes a pension commencement lump sum of £700,000 and uses the remainder of her protected pension rights, £5.6 million, to buy a lifetime annuity.

The residue of £2 million in the arrangement (£8.3 million less protected pension rights of £6.3 million) is liable to the Lifetime Allowance charge. From this residue she takes a lump sum of £900,000 after tax of £1.1 million.

BOX 2

2.42 RPSM03105170 – Protection of lump sums with primary protection: taking benefits at more than one time – some lump sum benefits are not tax-free

Jane has primary protection for her pension rights, and her lump sum rights on 5 April 2006 exceeded £375,000. She has already taken some benefits after 5 April 2006 under primary protection. Her remaining rights are in a money purchase arrangement, which are valued at £1 million.

Her available protected pension rights are valued at £600,000, which means her available personal Lifetime Allowance is £600,000.

The amount of protected lump sum is £700,000 – her protected lump sum rights are greater than her available personal Lifetime Allowance.

Jane decides to take all of her benefits as a lump sum. She takes a pension commencement lump sum of £700,000, using up all of her available Lifetime Allowance.

She takes the balance of the £1 million (£300,000), as a Lifetime Allowance excess lump sum.

£600,000 of her pension commencement lump sum is free of income tax, but £100,000 is liable to the Lifetime Allowance charge under *section 215, Finance Act 2004*.

So she receives £600,000 tax-free and £180,000 after tax under the Lifetime Allowance Charge.

Jane cannot take all of her protected lump sum amount tax-free because the maximum amount of pension commencement lump sum exceeds the amount of her available Lifetime Allowance.

Because Jane took too little lump sum when she took her earlier benefits, the full aggregate lump sum available under protection was not paid entirely free of income tax.

BOX 3

2.43 RPSM03105180 – Protection of lump sums with primary protection: taking benefits at more than one time, some lump sum benefits are not tax-free

Dean had registered pension rights of £3 million and lump sum rights of £800,000 by commutation under primary protection on 5 April 2006. £3 million was the equivalent of the standard Lifetime Allowance (£1.5 million) plus an additional factor of 1.

In 2011, Dean took pension rights worth £3 million plus a lump sum of £600,000. In 2011 the standard Lifetime Allowance was £1.8 million. So Dean's personal Lifetime Allowance is £3.6 million (this being the standard lifetime allowance of £1.8 million at the time plus a factor of 1) and his maximum protected lump sum is £960,000 (£800,000 x £1.8million/£1.5 million).

Dean has now used up all of his personal Lifetime Allowance.

In 2013, Dean took further benefits including a lump sum, and paid a Lifetime Allowance Charge on the whole of the benefits that he took.

Although Dean originally had a lump sum right of £800,000, he did not use this up whilst he had some personal Lifetime Allowance remaining. The result is that any lump sum taken after his personal Lifetime Allowance has been used up in full is subject to the Lifetime Allowance Charge. The lump sum paid after his personal Lifetime Allowance had been used up is a lifetime allowance excess lump sum.

BOX 4

2.44 RPSM03105210 – Protection of lump sum rights with enhanced protection

Sally has uncrystallised lump sum rights of £400,000 and uncrystallised pension rights of £2 million on 5 April 2006. This gives (**VULSR ÷ VUR**) of 20%.

She takes benefits from three schemes on different dates whilst retaining enhanced protection.

Sally takes benefits from the first scheme, which are worth £1 million, by taking unsecured pension using income withdrawal. She designates assets valued at £800,000 for the payment of her unsecured pension and takes a lump sum benefit of £200,000. This is the maximum permitted by (**VULSR ÷ VUR**) multiplied by the value of the funds designated for the payment of unsecured pension plus the lump sum (*para 29(2), Sch 36, Finance Act 2004*).

Sally takes benefits from the second scheme worth £750,000 in the form of a lifetime annuity bought for £600,000 and a lump sum benefit of £150,000. This is the maximum permitted by (**VULSR ÷ VUR**) multiplied by the value of the annuity purchase price plus the lump sum (*para 29(2), Sch 36, Finance Act 2004*).

Sally takes benefits from the third scheme as a scheme pension of £20,000 plus a lump sum benefit of £100,000. The scheme pension is valued at £400,000 (20 x the annual pension of £20,000). And the lump sum is the maximum permitted by (**VULSR ÷ VUR**) multiplied by the value of the scheme pension plus the lump sum (*para 29(2), Sch 36, Finance Act 2004*).

If one of Sally's schemes paid her a lump sum of 15% of the combined value of her lump sum and pension benefits (because scheme rules did not permit a larger lump sum) her other schemes could not pay her a lump sum greater than 20% to make up the 'shortfall'.

Uncrystallised rights that are greater than 25% of standard lifetime allowance

2.45 Where a lump sum entitlement as at A-Day exceeds 25% of existing rights, the entitlement to the lump sum is retained. Schemes must keep the required data to give effect to members' lump sum entitlements when they come to retire. However, protection is subject to:

- the member becoming entitled to all pensions under the scheme on the same date;
- the pension scheme must have been an approved occupational pension scheme;
- the value of the member's uncrystallised lump sum rights on 5 April 2006 must have exceeded 25% of the value of his or her uncrystallised rights on 5 April 2006;
- if the lump sum entitlement at A-Day exceeded £375,000, the member must not have given notice to HMRC of his intention to rely on either primary or enhanced protection;
- the member's benefits must not have been transferred out of the scheme at his or her request on or after A-Day.

The following numbered boxes from the RPSM contain some helpful examples of the different scenarios which can apply. There are many other worked examples in the RPSM which the reader will find helpful in the appropriate case:

BOX 5

2.46 RPSM03105560 – Technical Pages: Protecting pension rights from tax charges: Protection of lump sum rights: Example of valuing lump sum rights where lump sum is over HMRC limit

Valuing lump sum benefits exceeding 25%: lump sum benefits on 5 April 2006 exceed 'HMRC limits': example

Asif has pension and lump sum rights for a single employment on 5 April 2006. His total pension rights are £210,000 and total lump sum rights are £60,000. These rights are held in three schemes. His rights are held in a single arrangement under each scheme.

Asif's 'maximum permitted lump sum' for the employment under 'HMRC limits' was calculated as £54,000. His 'maximum permitted pension' under 'HMRC limits' was greater than £210,000.

Therefore VULSR must be adjusted whilst VUR remains the same.

The position before adjustment was as follows:

- Scheme 1 – pension rights of £60,000; lump sum £15,000; lump sum percentage 25%
- Scheme 2 – pension rights of £60,000 ; lump sum £20,000; lump sum percentage 33.33%
- Scheme 3 – pension rights of £90,000; lump sum £25,000; lump sum percentage 27.78%.

The reduction in Asif's lump sum rights from £60,000 to £54,000 must be apportioned amongst the three schemes. In scheme 1 the lump sum rights are adjusted as follows, £15,000 – (£6,000 x £15,000 ÷ £60,000) which gives a figure of £13,500.

After adjustment, Asif's lump sum percentage from each of the three schemes becomes:

- Scheme 1 – pension rights of £60,000; lump sum £13,500; scheme percentage 22.5%
- Scheme 2 – pension rights of £60,000; lump sum £18,000; scheme percentage 30%
- Scheme 3 – pension rights of £90,000; lump sum £22,500; scheme percentage 25%.

So after the required adjustment, only the rights in scheme 2 qualify for protection as the lump percentage exceeds 25% of the uncrystallised pension rights in that scheme.

Rights in schemes 1 and 3 may be taken at 25% because the normal rules for **pension commencement lump sums** in *Schedule 29, Finance Act 2004* apply to the rights under those two schemes.

BOX 6

2.47 RPSM03105570 – Technical Pages: Protecting pension rights from tax charges: Protection of lump sum rights: Example of valuing lump sum rights where pension is over HMRC limit

Valuing lump sum benefits exceeding 25%: pension benefits on 5 April 2006 exceed 'HMRC limits': example

An adjustment to the value of an individual's uncrystallised pension rights also triggers a re- calculation of the lump sum percentage available in multiple schemes.

Lesley has pension and lump sum rights in two schemes for a sole employment on 5 April 2006. She has total pension rights of £200,000 and her lump sum rights are £44,000. Her rights are held in a single **arrangement** under each scheme. The £44,000 is less than her 'maximum permitted lump sum' under 'HMRC limits' but her 'maximum permitted pension' under 'HMRC limits' is valued at £160,000.

The position before adjustment was as follows:

- Scheme A – pension rights of £80,000; lump sum £20,000; lump sum percentage 25%
- Scheme B – pension rights of £120,000; lump sum £24,000; lump sum percentage 20%.

The reduction in Lesley's pension rights from £200,000 to £160,000 must be apportioned between the two schemes. In scheme A, the value of the pension rights is adjusted as follows, £80,000 – (£40,000 x £80,000 ÷ £200,000) which gives a figure of £64,000.

After adjustment, Lesley's lump sum percentages from the two schemes become:

- Scheme A – pension rights of £64,000; lump sum £20,000; lump sum percentage 31.25%
- Scheme B – pension rights of £96,000; lump sum £24,000; lump sum percentage 25%.

So after the required adjustment, the rights in scheme A qualify for protection, as the lump sum percentage exceeds 25% of Lesley's uncrystallised pension rights in that scheme.

BOX 7

2.48 RPSM03105580 – Technical Pages Protecting pension rights from tax charges: Protection of lump sum rights: How to pay protected 25% plus lump sum benefits

How to pay protected lump sum benefits exceeding 25%

Where an individual does have lump sum rights that exceed 25% of their uncrystallised pension rights in a scheme, *paragraph 34, Schedule 36, Finance Act 2004* modifies *paragraphs 2* and *3* of *Schedule 29, Finance Act 2004*. The modification allows the payment of a **pension commencement lump sum** with a value greater than 25% of the combined value of the lump sum itself plus the value of any connected pension.

When benefits come into payment from the scheme, the amount of the lump sum payable as a pension commencement lump sum is as follows:

- where the payment of the lump sum benefit will not use up all of the individual's available personal lifetime allowance (which may be greater than the **standard lifetime allowance**), the lump sum will be either:
  - the amount of 'VULSR' on 5 April 2006 increased in line with increases in the standard lifetime allowance (see example in rpsm03105590), if there has been no 'relevant benefit accrual' (see rpsm03104080 which defines this) for the individual under the scheme, or
  - the amount of 'VULSR' on 5 April 2006 increased in line with increases in the standard lifetime allowance plus an additional lump sum which relates to the further benefit accrual after 5 April 2006 (see example in rpsm03105600 and example in rpsm03105610 which show the calculation process), where there has been 'relevant benefit accrual' for the individual under the scheme.
- where the value of the proposed lump sum benefit is greater than the available amount of the individual's lifetime allowance, the proposed lump sum benefit should be calculated in the same way as lump sums under the previous bullet point. If all of the proposed lump sum benefit is paid, part of it will be subject to the **lifetime allowance charge** under *section 215, Finance Act 2004* (see example in rpsm03105620).
- where the individual has already used all of their available personal lifetime allowance before the payment of benefits from the scheme, no pension commencement lump sum may be paid. Protection for the lump sum rights in the scheme has no effect.

BOX 8

2.49 RPSM03105560 – Technical Pages: Protecting pension rights from tax charges: Protection of lump sum rights: Example of valuing lump sum rights where lump sum is over HMRC limit

Valuing lump sum benefits exceeding 25%: lump sum benefits on 5 April 2006 exceed 'HMRC limits': example

Asif has pension and lump sum rights for a single employment on 5 April 2006. His total pension rights are £210,000 and total lump sum rights are £60,000. These rights are held in three schemes. His rights are held in a single arrangement under each scheme.

Asif's 'maximum permitted lump sum' for the employment under 'HMRC limits' was calculated as £54,000. His 'maximum permitted pension' under 'HMRC limits' was greater than £210,000.

Therefore VULSR must be adjusted whilst VUR remains the same.

The position before adjustment was as follows:

- Scheme 1 – pension rights of £60,000; lump sum £15,000; lump sum percentage 25%
- Scheme 2 – pension rights of £60,000 ; lump sum £20,000; lump sum percentage 33.33%
- Scheme 3 – pension rights of £90,000; lump sum £25,000; lump sum percentage 27.78%.

The reduction in Asif's lump sum rights from £60,000 to £54,000 must be apportioned amongst the three schemes. In scheme 1 the lump sum rights are adjusted as follows, £15,000 – (£6,000 x £15,000 ÷ £60,000) which gives a figure of £13,500.

After adjustment, Asif's lump sum percentage from each of the three schemes becomes:

- Scheme 1 – pension rights of £60,000; lump sum £13,500; scheme percentage 22.5%
- Scheme 2 – pension rights of £60,000; lump sum £18,000; scheme percentage 30%
- Scheme 3 – pension rights of £90,000; lump sum £22,500; scheme percentage 25%.

So after the required adjustment, only the rights in scheme 2 qualify for protection as the lump percentage exceeds 25% of the uncrystallised pension rights in that scheme.

Rights in schemes 1 and 3 may be taken at 25% because the normal rules for pension commencement lump sums in *Schedule 29, Finance Act 2004* apply to the rights under those two schemes.

BOX 9

2.50 RPSM03105570 – Technical Pages: Protecting pension rights from tax charges: Protection of lump sum rights: Example of valuing lump sum rights where pension is over HMRC limit

Valuing lump sum benefits exceeding 25%: pension benefits on 5 April 2006 exceed 'HMRC limits': example

An adjustment to the value of an individual's uncrystallised pension rights also triggers a re- calculation of the lump sum percentage available in multiple schemes.

Lesley has pension and lump sum rights in two schemes for a sole employment on 5 April 2006. She has total pension rights of £200,000 and her lump sum rights are £44,000. Her rights are held in a single arrangement under each scheme. The £44,000 is less than her 'maximum permitted lump sum' under 'HMRC limits' but her 'maximum permitted pension' under 'HMRC limits' is valued at £160,000.

The position before adjustment was as follows:

- Scheme A – pension rights of £80,000; lump sum £20,000; lump sum percentage 25%
- Scheme B – pension rights of £120,000; lump sum £24,000; lump sum percentage 20%.

The reduction in Lesley's pension rights from £200,000 to £160,000 must be apportioned between the two schemes. In scheme A, the value of the pension rights is adjusted as follows, £80,000 – (£40,000 x £80,000 ÷ £200,000) which gives a figure of £64,000.

After adjustment, Lesley's lump sum percentages from the two schemes become:

- Scheme A – pension rights of £64,000; lump sum £20,000; lump sum percentage 31.25%
- Scheme B – pension rights of £96,000; lump sum £24,000; lump sum percentage 25%.

So after the required adjustment, the rights in scheme A qualify for protection, as the lump sum percentage exceeds 25% of Lesley's uncrystallised pension rights in that scheme.

Annuity purchase, income withdrawal etc

2.51 There is much greater flexibility to draw income from a money purchase scheme under the new regime. However, it is a condition of registration of a money purchase scheme that it must offer an open market option to a member before an annuity is purchased for that member.

The following general rules apply:

- monetary limits are no longer required to be endorsed on purchased annuity policies, and a tax-free lump sum of up to 25% of policy value may be paid;
- buy-out policies must be provided through a registered scheme, and not be freestanding;
- money purchase contracts must use a factor of 20:1 to determine limits (pre-A-Day bought-out benefits are subject to the limits that were written into those contracts);
- only insurance companies are able to offer deferred annuity contracts for a registered scheme;
- existing bridging pensions may remain in place, but the amount by which the scheme pension is reduced is limited to the amount of the state pension;
- policies securing benefits must not be freestanding.

A defined benefits scheme must pay a scheme pension, as described in pension rule 3, *s 165, Finance Act 2004*. The general benefit rules apply to such a pension (see 2.34 above). Although a money purchase scheme may also pay a scheme pension, the following alternative methods of payment are now available:

- securing a lifetime annuity with an insurance company of the member's choice; or
- paying an unsecured pension by way of income withdrawal and/or a short-term annuity up to age 75 maximum; or
- paying alternatively secured pension from age 75.

In order to understand the way in which the different methods work, it is necessary to know what these terms mean. An explanation is given below:

- secured pension: an entitlement under a registered scheme which is backed by an employer or has been guaranteed by an annuity purchase;
- alternatively secured pension: an entitlement under a registered scheme which is limited by income limits and annual reviews from being depleted too rapidly – the general rule it that this will represent 70% of the amount that could be generated from applying an annuity rate for the member's age and sex up to age 75;
- unsecured pension: the returns on designated or widely-invested funds which deliver growth rather than security up to age 75 – the maximum

annual income withdrawal is 120% of the flat-rate single life annuity which could be bought out of the member's credit with five-yearly reviews.

Any existing income drawdown arrangements are unsecured pensions. They are treated as having commenced on A-Day and having been valued at that date in order to establish the maximum that may be drawn. There is a two-year period from A-Day for providers to review their arrangements.

Secured pension

2.52 The payment of a lifetime annuity is within benefit crystallisation Event 4 (see 2.72 below). A secured pension may be provided even if a chargeable amount arises. Either the excess benefits can be reduced to cover the lifetime allowance charge or a payment may be made as a lifetime allowance excess lump sum. The charge incurred is 25%.

Alternatively secured pension

2.53 The amount of alternatively secured pension which can be drawn is calculated on the initial sums and assets together with investment growth and any assets which are acquired to replace disposals. Benefits must be tested annually; and:

- an annuity must be purchased on a scheme wind up;
- the income must be applied on death firstly to secure dependants' pensions, and in the absence of dependants shall be returned to the scheme with the exception of lump sum benefits to charities;
- value protection may be provided for secured pensions (this provides a return of the balance of the pension's initial capital value of the pension, subject to a tax charge of 35%);
- by way of an alternative to value protection, a guaranteed pension for a period not exceeding ten years may be provided and existing ten year guarantees will be allowed to continue.

The matter of potential inheritance tax charges on death was announced by the Chancellor in the Budget 2005. With effect from 6 April 2006, monies held in an alternatively secured pension by an investor aged 75 or over are subject to inheritance tax at 40% as part of the deceased person's chargeable estate. This applies to assets over the nil rate band of £285,000. The tax must be deducted from the scheme's fund by the administrator. The charge is based on the value of the taxable property at the time the charge arises, calculated by reference to the assets over the nil rate band and the rate of tax at the time. There will be provision to cover two instances where the tax charge on alternatively secured pension funds overlap. Any monies paid to charities will avoid the tax. Funds paid to provide pension benefits for a spouse, civil partner or financial dependant will not be chargeable until the entitlement to the benefit ceases.

Under the draft *Finance Bill 2006*, there will be provision to cover the 1992 concessionary practice in relation to an IHT charge. This charge can arise when a person aged under 75 exercises a choice which reduces his chargeable estate and increases that of another (unless on an arms' length basis, and so excepted as a transfer of value). The exemption can apply in a pension scheme where the member exercised his right not to take pension. An example would be where the member was in good health when the decision was made, but subsequently his life expectancy was seriously impaired and an enhanced death benefit is paid. Whereas exemptions continue to apply to payments made to a spouse, civil partner or financial dependant, funds could be subject to IHT if HMRC considers that a person had deliberately avoided purchasing an annuity in an attempt to avoid the tax.

Tax will be payable on trusts when they are set up if the value of the trust is higher than the nil IHT band (see above). A further tax charge will be levied on the tenth anniversary after they are set up. These measures apply to trusts set up in the future and to existing ones from 2008. The main impact will be on Accumulation and Maintenance Trusts and Interest in Possession Trusts. All transfers into new trusts are taxable at 20% above the nil rate band plus a further 6% charge every ten years. However, existing trusts will only be charged at 6% – the ten yearly charge. The new restrictions also apply to certain circumstances of divorce.

Additionally, the following is an extract from the RPSM.

BOX 10

2.54 RPSM09103010 – Technical Pages: Member benefits: An alternatively secured pension: Payment after age 75

Payment of an alternatively secured pension after age 75

[s165(1), 'Pension rules 6 and 7'][Paras 11 to 14, Sch 28]

Once a member reaches the age of 75 a pension may only be provided for the life of that member, either through the purchase or provision of a secured pension or, if benefits are from a money purchase arrangement, as an alternatively secured pension.

An alternatively secured pension is the continuation of income withdrawal beyond the member's 75th birthday. It will be subject to more restrictive rules on the maximum pension that can be paid and a more rigid and frequent review of that limit. There are also more stringent rules on what benefits can be paid on the death of the member where in receipt of an alternatively secured pension (see rpsm09103170).

Alternatively secured pension fund and fund designation

[Para 11(1) to (4), Sch 28][Para 20(2) and (3), Sch 10, FA 2005]

The funds used to generate an alternatively secured pension for the member are referred to as the alternatively secured pension fund. Unless a secured pension is being provided all funds held within a money purchase arrangement at the member's 75th birthday will become alternatively secured pension fund at that point. The effective date of this switch will be the point the member reaches age 75, which is immediately after midnight (00:01 hrs) on their 75th birthday.

There are limited circumstances where the initial entitlement to an alternatively secured pension will arise after the member's 75th birthday. These circumstances are detailed in rpsm09103100. rpsm09103160 deals with the position on transfers.

Once sums or assets have been 'designated' into a member's alternatively secured pension fund any capital growth or income is treated as being part of that alternatively secured pension fund. Similarly, where assets are purchased at a later date from such funds those replacement assets also fall as part of the member's alternatively secured pension fund (as do any future growth or income generated by those assets). Any sums generated by the sale of assets held in those funds also form part of the alternatively secured pension fund. This is because that growth or income and those replacement assets are derived from that alternatively secured pension fund.

Any funds that are subsequently applied to purchase a lifetime annuity contract from an insurance company, or are applied to provide a scheme pension, will cease to be part of the alternatively secured pension fund.

rpsm09103020 gives an example of payment of an alternatively secured pension.

Unsecured pension

2.55 The amount of unsecured pension which can be drawn is calculated on the initial sums and assets together with investment growth and any assets which are acquired to replace disposals. Payments may be made directly out of the scheme, or from a short-term annuity contract which has been purchased from a money purchase scheme.

Death benefits

2.56 Despite the clear simplification which pervades most of the new pensions tax regime, the tax rules for death benefits are far from straightforward. The general rule that pensions must be payable for life remains, with the following exceptions (which are subject to the scheme rules permitting the change in terms, where appropriate):

- on recovery from ill-health (subject to the rules of the scheme);
- for compliance with pension sharing orders;
- for bridging pensions, whereby a member's pension is reduced by the amount of state pension when it comes into payment;
- in compliance with a court order (for example, an attachment of earnings order);
- by an abatement provision of a public service pension scheme;
- on forfeiture, subject to HMRC regulations;
- where the reduction is applied to all the pensions which are being paid under the scheme to or in respect of its members.

Dependants' pensions no longer need to be payable for life, and a spouse may include a person to whom the member had been married when the benefit came into payment.

Otherwise, the main features are:

Commutation

2.57 A dependant's pensions may be commuted, but the amount will count towards the lifetime allowance of the member.

Commutation involving contracted-out rights will be subject to the relevant legislation (although commutation on grounds of triviality is permitted).

Funeral benefits – one-off payments on death

2.58 Some schemes provide a capital payment on the death of a member in retirement for the purpose of assisting with the payment of funeral benefits.

Where this is in place at A-Day it may continue. This is only available in circumstances where the right would have been a member right if he had joined the scheme on 10 December 2003 and retired before A-Day. No such benefit must be provided for members who are age 75 or over at the date of death.

Guarantees

2.59 Five-year guarantees may continue on a tax-free basis. For defined benefits schemes the legislation provides that tax-free payments may be made to the extent that the lump sum is within the lifetime allowance (*Sch 5, ss 216* and *217, Sch 2, para 16, Finance Act 2004*). This is a transitional provision. Payments must be made before age 75 in respect of persons with pensions in payment pre A-Day (*Sch 36, Pt 3, para 36, Finance Act 2004*). Money purchase schemes have been included in the concession. As an alternative, value protection may be in place.

Ten-year guarantees may be provided on date of vesting, where income has been secured. However, a guarantee is not permissible if income is not secured before the end of the ten-year period.

Payment date

2.60 Benefits are payable on the death of a member before the age of 75. After age 75, a member will normally already be in receipt of his benefits and so no further capital payments are permitted. Unvested pensions which have not already been paid may be paid to a dependant or dependants. If the member has not yet reached age 75 they may be paid as a lump sum.

Recipients of lump sum death benefits

2.61 Except in the cases of triviality commutation and winding up, lump sum benefits may be paid to any person. In these two exceptions, they must be paid to dependants (*s 168* and *Sch 29, Pt 2, Finance Act 2004*). A dependant may include a person who was married to the member when the pension commenced but divorced before the member's death – subject to the scheme rules permitting). Lump sum death benefits may be made on a tax-free basis to charities where a member or dependant dies on or after age 75. This facility is only available where the member or dependant had an alternatively secured pension and no dependants.

Dependants' benefits may be restricted if it appears there is a device to avoid the lifetime allowance. If the member dies after attaining age 75 the aggregate of all dependants' benefits must not exceed the amount of the member's pension at death. Future pension increases must be restricted in order to avoid evading this initial limit.

If the lump sum death payments are not paid directly to the legal personal representative, that person must be notified of the payment. It is also a requirement that the amount of the lifetime allowance used up is declared, and a charge of 55% on any excess will fall on the beneficiary. However, there will be no additional charge on any pension payments made.

Tax position

2.62 A tax charge does not arise on a money purchase uncrystallised funds lump sum death benefit if it does not exceed the amount of the uncrystallised funds. Dependant's benefits which are commuted before the member's benefits have vested are not taxable. Lump sums paid after vesting will be taxed at 35%. The following detailed rules apply:

Taxable at 35% (*s 206, Finance Act 2004*):

- value protection (a pension protection lump sum death benefit from a defined benefit, or an annuity protection lump sum death benefit from a money purchase benefit);
- an unsecured pension fund lump sum death benefit (a return of fund under income drawdown by a member or a dependant of a money purchase scheme).

If the rules permit, the tax may be recovered from the payment. The lump sum may be paid to a deceased member's nominee. The administrator must deduct the tax charge in order to cover payments made by insurance companies.

Tax exempt: A tax charge does not arise on a defined benefit lump sum death benefit if:

- the benefit is paid in respect of a defined benefits arrangement;
- the member had not reached age 75 at his date of death;
- the benefit is paid before the end of two years from date of death;
- the benefit is not a pension protection lump sum death benefit, a trivial commutation lump sum death benefit, or a winding-up lump sum death benefit.

Unsecured income

2.63 Whilst income is unsecured, pensions may be payable to dependants in similar form until they attain age 75. At age 75, the pension must be secured or any undrawn funds repaid. Lump sums will be taxed at 35%. If value protection is in place, any lump sums must be paid before the recipient attains age 75.

Early retirement

2.64 Early retirement is still permitted. However, the lifetime allowance is abated by 2.5% per annum on taking benefits before normal 'minimum pension age'. This applies in respect of individuals who have a protected pension age lower than 50 (age 55 from 2010).

Protected pension age means the age from which the individual had an actual or prospective right to receive payment of benefits as at A-Day. Such a right may also be protected on making a block transfer into a scheme. Generally, any age lower than 55 must have been in place on 10 December 2003. The *Finance Act 2004* does not have effect so as to give a member a protected pension age of more than 50 at any time before 6 April 2010.

Ill-health pensions

2.65 The ill-health and incapacity provisions under the pre-A-Day rules largely remain, with little change. A member must have left the employment to which the pension relates (either now or at a previous date) and the administrator must obtain proper medical evidence that the member is incapable of continuing in his or her current occupation. If a scheme permits, it may temporarily suspend a pension if the member recovers sufficiently to return to his or her original job.

Pension sharing on divorce

2.66 If a pension splitting order was in place at A-Day:

- rights to benefits which existed before A-Day will be protected, and an additional lifetime allowance may be made available;
- where the credit relates both to crystallised and uncrystallised rights, and the pension is already in payment, only the crystallised element is taken into account.

If pension splitting orders are made after A-Day, any pension credit will count against the recipient's lifetime allowance. Any pension debit will not count against the donor's lifetime allowance or towards the annual allowance of that person.

Refunds of contributions, and compensation payments

2.67 Refunds of member contributions are permitted on leaving pensioned employment or on winding up the scheme, where a member has less than two years' qualifying service. The amount will be taxed at 20% on £10,800 and at 40% on any excess. Compensation payments may be made to authorised employers in respect of a criminal, fraudulent or negligent act or omission by a scheme member.

Retained benefits

2.68 Retained benefits need not be taken into account when testing for HMRC limits if members' earnings (that is, P60 plus P11d) are less than £50,000 in the tax year which preceded A-Day.

Serious ill-health

2.69 It is still permitted to pay serious ill-health commutation. The payment should be made out of any uncrystallised benefits. The administrator must obtain written medical evidence and must notify HMRC if a benefit becomes payable. There will be no tax liability on the payment if the lifetime allowance is not exceeded.

Triviality commutation

2.70 Trivial commutation is a 'once only' option, not available before age of 65, and only where no other trivial commutation is paid. Tax is charged on 75% of the commuted value, but there is an exception for low aggregate value pensions, whereby 100% may be commuted between age 60 and 75 in a 12-month period. The payment must extinguish all of the member's entitlement to benefits under the pension scheme, and the maximum limit is 1% of the lifetime allowance disregarding any non trivial tax-free lump sums already taken, or to be taken, in that year. Payments do not count towards the lifetime allowance.

Where a scheme is winding up, trivial commutation is permitted if the employer ceases all contributions to registered schemes and scheme benefits do not exceed 1% of the lifetime allowance. This option does not affect a member's rights to voluntarily commute or a member's lifetime allowance.

Dependants' pensions may be commuted, but they count towards the lifetime allowance. Where contracted-out rights are involved, it will only be possible to commute on grounds of triviality. If dependants' benefits are commuted before a member's benefit has vested they will be tax free. If a lump sum is paid after vesting, tax will be charged at 35%.

Benefit crystallisation events

2.71 Benefit crystallisation events (BCEs) are a new concept under the simplification regime, and they are described in 2.72 below.

The events

2.72 There are eight events when a test must be made. These are listed *in s 216, Finance Act 2004*. The events are triggered as shown below:

Event 1: By the designation of sums or assets held for the purposes of a money purchase arrangement under any of the relevant pension schemes as available for the payment of unsecured pension to the individual.

The amount crystallised is the aggregate of the amount of the sums and the market value of the assets designated.

Event 2: By the individual becoming entitled to a scheme pension under any of the relevant pension schemes.

The amount crystallised is RVF × P.

Event 3: By the individual, having become so entitled, becoming entitled to payment of the scheme pension, otherwise than in excepted circumstances, at an increased annual rate which exceeds by more than the permitted margin the rate at which it was payable on the day on which the individual became entitled to it.

The amount crystallised is RVF × XP.

Event 4: By the individual becoming entitled to a lifetime annuity purchased under a money purchase arrangement under any of the relevant pension schemes.

The amount crystallised is the aggregate of the amount of such of the sums, and the market value of such of the assets, representing the individual's rights under the arrangement as are applied to purchase the lifetime annuity (and any related dependants' annuity).

Event 5: By the individual reaching the age of 75 when prospectively entitled to a scheme pension or a lump sum (or both) under a defined benefit arrangement under any of the relevant pension schemes.

The amount crystallised is (RVF × DP) + DSLS.

Event 6: By the individual becoming entitled to a relevant lump sum under any of the relevant pension schemes.

The amount crystallised is the amount of the lump sum (paid to the individual).

Event 7: By a person being paid a relevant lump sum death benefit in respect of the individual under any of the relevant pension schemes.

The amount crystallised is the amount of the lump sum death benefit.

Event 8: By the transfer of sums or assets held for the purposes of, or representing accrued rights under, any of the relevant pension schemes so as to become held for the purposes of or to represent rights under a qualifying recognised overseas pension scheme in connection with the individual's membership of that pension scheme.

The amount crystallised is the aggregate of the amount of any sums transferred and the market value of any assets transferred.

The following terms have the following meanings:

P is the amount of the pension which will be payable to the individual in the period of 12 months beginning with the day on which the individual becomes entitled to it (assuming that it remains payable throughout that period at the rate at which it is payable on that day);

RVF is the relevant valuation factor;

XP is (subject to the above) the amount by which the increased annual rate of the pension exceeds the rate at which it was payable on the day on which the individual became entitled to it, as increased by the permitted margin;

DP is the annual rate of the scheme pension to which the individual would be entitled if, on the date on which the individual reaches 75, the individual acquired an actual (rather than a prospective) right to receive it;

DSLS is so much of any lump sum to which the individual would be entitled (otherwise than by way of commutation of pension) as would be paid to the individual if, on that date, the individual acquired an actual (rather than a prospective) right to receive it.

Investments, and transitional protection

2.73 The HMRC investment rules under the new regime are greatly simplified. Nevertheless, there are still certain criteria to follow. The new rules are described in detail in Chapter 6 of the 4th edition of Tottel's *Taxation of Pension Benefits*. The general rules are summarised in 2.74 to 2.85 below, and the special requirements for small schemes and high earners are described in Chapters 4 and 5 of this book for SSASs and SIPPs respectively.

It was not intended that HMRC would impose special rules on small schemes under UK legislation, but the government has identified certain schemes as being 'self-directed'. It has stated (see 5.4 below) that such schemes must follow special rules, particularly with regard to investment in residential property and second homes.

UK legislation and practice has needed to take the impact of the *European Union Pensions Directive* (*2003/41/EC*) on IORPS into consideration (see 4.4 below). Investments must be made on a prudent basis, and consideration must be given to an appropriate level of scheme liquidity. Disposals and acquisitions by registered schemes must be transacted at commercial rates, and must be permitted by the scheme rules. The *Occupational Pension Schemes* (*Investment*) *Regulations 2005* (*SI 2005/3378*) revoked the *Occupational Pension Schemes* (*Investment*) *Regulations 1996* (*SI 1996/3127*). Regulation 12, states as follows (importantly, it contains an exemption from the following requirement for schemes with fewer than 12 members):

- not more than five per cent of the current market value of the resources of a scheme may at any time be invested in employer-related investments; and
- none of the resources of a scheme may at any time be invested in any employer-related loan.

Schemes with fewer than 100 active and deferred members are exempted from many of the requirements of the regulations.

Transitional rules, and HMRC guidance

2.74 The general rule is that investments which were held under the rules which applied to approved schemes before A-Day may be retained unless the terms which apply to the investment are changed (for example, a loan is extended beyond its permitted repayment period, or payment of loan interest is deferred). The investment rules which otherwise apply from A-Day are described below. Further details are contained in the HMRC registered pension schemes manual.

Borrowing

2.75 Registered schemes may borrow monies from any source on commercial terms. *Section 163, Finance Act 2004*, defines the meaning of borrowing under the Act. The aggregate amount of borrowing by a scheme must not exceed 50% of the fund value of the scheme.

Loans

2.76 Loans are permitted at commercial rates, other than member loans. They may be made to the sponsoring employer or any party which is unconnected with the member. There are restrictions on the permitted level of employer-related investments under regulations which reflect the terms of the *EU Pensions Directive* (see 4.4 below).

The specific rules which apply to loans under the *Finance Act 2004* are:

- aggregate loans must not exceed 50% of total fund value, and they must be secured against assets of at least equal value;
- loan periods are permissible to extend to five years' duration;
- if a loan cannot be repaid within the period under the agreement if may be rolled over once for a further period not exceeding five years;
- under the *Pension Schemes* (*Prescribed Interest Rates for Authorised Employer Loans*) *Regulations 2005* (*SI 2005/3449*) a loan reference rate must be charged;
- the loan reference rate is 1% more than the relevant interest rate, which is an average of the base rates of a specified group of banks on the sixth working day of the month which follows the start of the period.

Investment in land and buildings

2.77 There are no specific restrictions on investment in land and buildings. Transactions must be conducted at commercial rates and any associated tax charges on acquisitions and disposals met by the appropriate party.

Trustees should, of course, continue to be aware of the requirements of the *Control of Asbestos at Work Regulations 2002* (*SI 2002/2675*) with regard to property. The 'duty holder' under a tenancy agreement has a 'duty to manage' asbestos in all non-domestic properties, and could be liable to criminal prosecution if he or she fails to do so. It can be desirable to appoint the tenant as the duty holder. There is also a duty on the employer to prepare procedures, provide information and establish warning systems to deal with an emergency in the workplace related to the use of asbestos in a work process or the removal or repair of asbestos-containing materials.

Investment in property including in some circumstances residential property

2.78 A registered scheme may invest in property. However, any asset which a scheme member or his family or household use will be taxed as if it were an unauthorised payment. Any fair rent etc) paid may be discounted against the charge. Some exemptions exist for spouses who owned disposed property and where an elderly parent retains some enjoyment on use of the property of a domestic nature following a part disposal. As from April 2004 benefit-in-kind charges have been imposed on individuals who have sought to avoid inheritance tax by way of home loan schemes (that is, schemes whereby the owner of the house disposes of it to a trust; receives an IOU in return which he bequests to his heirs through a further trust and continues to live in the house).

The meaning of a member of family for the purposes of any charge includes:

- a member's spouse;
- a member's children and their spouses;
- a member's parents;
- a member's dependants.

The meaning of members of a household is:

- a member's domestic staff;
- a member's guests.

With regard to investment in residential property (see also 5.4 below), RPSM 07200030 states as follows.

BOX 11

2.79 RPSM07200030 – Member Pages: Investments: Can my pension scheme invest in residential property?

Can my pension scheme invest in residential property?

The tax rules allow a registered pension scheme to invest in any type of property, including residential property. As with all investments it is the scheme administrator/trustees' decision as to whether or not they will allow residential property to be held as an asset of the scheme.

Using a registered pension scheme to invest in a buy to let residential property or holiday home or any other type of residential property may have the following consequences:

- The property becomes an asset of the pension fund and there is a requirement to put all rental income into the pension fund so it is locked away and cannot be accessed until authorised benefits are paid.
- If the property is made available to a member of the scheme or members of their family it will give rise to a benefits-in-kind tax charge if a market rent is not paid (even if they choose not to use it).
- Any property bought by the pension fund in most cases will need to be sold before the pension can be drawn, to provide a secured income in retirement.
- Only 25% of the capital in the pension arrangement will be able to be extracted as a lump sum, the remainder will be locked in the pension to be drawn out over the period of retirement.
- Borrowing to fund a property purchase cannot exceed 50% of the value of the pension arrangement.
- Although any rental income or capital gains from the disposal of the property will be tax free in the pension fund when the money is paid as a pension it will be taxable at the members marginal rate of tax. Depending on the rate of tax this may well be higher than the rate that would be paid if the disposal were subject to the CGT regime after the property has been held for 7 years.
- Putting any previously-owned property into the pension scheme will trigger any unrealised chargeable gain on the property, and transaction costs such as stamp duty.
- Maximum tax relief on contributions made in any year is 100% of UK chargeable earnings, subject to an annual allowance set initially at £215,000. Tax relieved pension savings are also subject to a lifetime allowance initially set at £1.5 million.

Purchases of assets by scheme members or connected persons from the scheme

2.80 All member transactions must be conducted on a commercial basis. A member's business may purchase assets from the scheme on an arm's-length basis.

Sale of assets by a member to a registered scheme

2.81 All member transactions must be conducted on a commercial basis. A member's business may sell assets to the scheme on an arm's-length basis. The member should check whether capital gains tax is payable, and declare the sale on his self-assessment tax return.

Investment in quoted or unquoted shares

2.82 Investments are permissible in quoted and unquoted shares, and any shares in general. There is a ceiling of 5% of the net value of the fund in respect of shares acquired in the sponsoring employer (or 20% where there is more than one employer).

Trading activities by the trustees or scheme manager

2.83 RPSM07101050 states that there are no restrictions on scheme trading. However, the scheme is liable to pay tax on any income derived from a trading activity, and the income must be returned on a self-assessment tax return.

Transactions between an employer's or member's business and the scheme

2.84 Transactions between an employer's or member's business and a registered scheme must be at commercial rates and on an arm's-length basis; they are not to be treated as unauthorised payments.

Unauthorised activities, and compliance

2.85 Any activity which involves an unauthorised transaction which falls within the meaning of 'payment' under *ss 160* to *163, Finance Act 2004*, is liable to a charge and or penalties and sanctions (see 2.109 to 2.137 below). Transfers of assets or of monies or monies worth are deemed to be payments by the Act. Unacceptable investment activity includes:

- taking value out of a pension scheme for unauthorised reasons;
- pensions liberation;
- value shifting of assets;

- non-commercial transactions;
- acquisition of wasting assets (that is, assets that have an anticipated life of less than 50 years, such as properties with less than 50-year leases, cars, racehorses, plant and machinery etc);
- waivers of debt.

Membership of schemes

2.86 Registered pension schemes will be open to all, whatever the employment or residence status of the individual concerned. Additionally, a member may concurrently be a member of any type or any number of scheme (for example, occupational pension schemes and personal pension schemes). The way is open for non-associated multi-employer schemes which can clearly benefit from economies of scale.

Providers

2.87 An application to register a pension scheme may be made only if the scheme is an occupational pension scheme or has been established by:

- an insurance company;
- a unit trust scheme manager;
- an operator, trustee or depositary of a recognised EEA collective investment scheme;
- an authorised open-ended investment company;
- a building society;
- a bank; or
- an EEA investment portfolio manager.

A scheme need not be established under trust, and there is no requirement that the employers in a multi-employer scheme should be connected.

Registration

2.88 Full details of the registration requirements are contained in Chapter 7 of the 4th edition of Tottel's *Taxation of Pension Benefits*.

In general, schemes which were already approved at A-Day received automatic registration unless they opted-out. New schemes from A-Day must register, if they wish to do so, and the scheme must be an occupational pension scheme or have been established by an acceptable provider (see 2.87 below). Core information must be provided to HMRC, although this refreshingly does not include scheme documentation. *Sections 153* and *154,* and *Sch 36, Pt 1, paras 1* and *2, Finance Act 2004,* refer. Any scheme which opts out or which fails to be accepted for registration incurs a 40% tax charge.

Sections 250 and *251, Finance Act 2004*, explain the compliance procedures and information requirements that apply that is required on registration.

Summary of the main requirements

2.89 It is the responsibility of the administrator to make the application, and HMRC have 12 months in which to raise any queries (except where information is withheld or falsely given, in which case the period can be extended). Over the next year the procedures will appear for online registration, which will become mandatory as each need arises.

The following list contains the main information requirements:

- the legal structure of the arrangement;
- size of the membership (bands of 0, 1–10, 11–50, 51–10,000 and over 10,000 apply – it is still considered by HMRC that small schemes are a higher risk than large schemes);
- the degree of control that a member has over the assets;
- who established the scheme (a connected employer is to carry more risk than an 'off-the-shelf' product);
- the administrator, together with a declaration of compliance and understanding from the administrator or authorised practitioner;
- registration with the Pensions Regulator for schemes with more than one member;
- an election to contract out of S2P, where this is relevant;
- a registration for contributions relief at source where this is applicable;
- registration of a stakeholder plan, where this is relevant.

The main forms

2.90 The main forms which concern registration, and reports under 2.91 to 2.100 below, are:

- Registration for tax relief and exemptions
- Registration for relief at source
- Contracting out (Industry-wide schemes)
- Contracting out (other schemes)
- Event report
- Accounting for tax return
- Registered pension scheme return
- Protection of existing rights
- Enhanced lifetime allowance (pension credit rights)
- Enhanced lifetime allowance (international)
- Declare as a scheme administrator of a deferred annuity contract.

Additionally, some maintenance forms have been published:

- Pre-register as a scheme administrator
- Notify scheme administrator details
- Change of scheme administrator/practitioner details
- Authorising a practitioner
- Add scheme administrator
- Amend scheme details.

[See Appendix 14 for details]

Reporting requirements

2.91 There is a whole new set of reporting procedures from A-Day. These are contained in the *Registered Pension Schemes (Provision of Information) Regulations 2006 (SI 2006/567)*. Full details are provided in Chapter 7 of Tottel's 4th edition of *Taxation of Pension Benefits*. The reporting service will be made available on Pension Schemes Online from April 2006 in stages, according to need. The main forms are listed in 2.90 above. A summary of the requirements is given below.

Failure to provide information can lead to fines normally at a level of £300, plus £60 per day for continued non-compliance. Where fraudulent statements have been made, or there has been negligence in making returns, transfers, statements and information, these fines may be increased up to £3,000. Most reports must be made after 5 April of the year following the relevant event, and before the following 31 January. Generally, records must be kept for a period of six years.

The events which must be reported are summarised below.

Administrator to HMRC

2.92 The administrator must report to HMRC:

- any change in the legal structure of a scheme, the number of members or the rules;
- any change to the rules of pre-commencement schemes treated as more than one scheme;
- benefit crystallisation events, enhanced lifetime allowance or enhanced protection;
- early payment of benefits;
- an overseas event check on the lifetime allowance;
- payment of a lump sum payment after the death of a member aged 75 or over;
- payment of an alternatively secured pension;
- payment of a pension commencement lump sum which, when added to the crystallised amount, exceeds 25% of the total; and is more than 7.5%, but less than 25%, of the current standard lifetime allowance;
- payment of a transfer lump sum death benefit;
- payment of a pension commencement lump sum – primary and enhanced protection, where lump sums exceed £375,000;
- payment of a serious ill-health lump sum;
- suspension of an ill-health pension;
- transfers to a qualified and recognised overseas pension scheme;
- unauthorised payments by members or employers;
- where a member is able to control scheme assets;
- of the termination of his appointment together with the date on which termination took effect, within 30 days of the event;
- of a scheme wind up and the date on which the winding up was concluded – the prescribed time for making the notice is any time on or before:

(*a*) the last day of the period of three months beginning on the day on which the winding up is completed; or

(*b*) the last day otherwise prescribed by the regulations for the purpose of that information

whichever is the earlier.

Administrator to member

2.93 The administrator must report to the member:

- on an events statement, the level of lifetime allowance that individual has used up;
- to each member:

  (*a*) to whom a pension is being paid, at least once in each tax year; or

  (*b*) in respect of whom a benefit crystallisation event has occurred, within three months of that event;
- a statement of the cumulative total percentage of the lifetime allowance crystallised, at the date of statement, by the events in respect of the scheme and any other scheme from which that scheme has received whether directly or indirectly a transfer payment;
- where a scheme has made an unauthorised payment to a member, before 7 July following the tax year in which the event took place, the following information:

  (*a*) the nature of the benefit provided;

  (*b*) the amount of the unauthorised payment which is being treated as being made by the provision of the benefit;

  (*c*) the date on which the benefit was provided;
- where he makes a payment on account of his liability to pay for the lifetime allowance charge, within three months of the crystallisation event, give details of:

  (*a*) the chargeable amount on which the charge arises;

  (*b*) how the chargeable amount is calculated;

  (*c*) the amount of the tax charge; and

  (*d*) whether he has accounted for the tax or intends to do so.

Member to administrator

2.94 The member must report to the administrator, if an enhanced lifetime allowance or enhanced protection is to apply under *s 256(1)* of the *Finance Act 2004*, the reference number given by HMRC under the enhanced lifetime allowance regulations.

Administrator to administrator

2.95 If part or all of a member's pension rights are transferred from one scheme to another (scheme A to scheme B), the administrator of scheme A must provide the administrator of scheme B, within three months of the transfer, a cumulative total percentage of the standard lifetime allowance crystallised by the event in respect of scheme A and any scheme from which that scheme has received directly or indirectly a transfer payment.

Administrator to the personal representatives

2.96 On the death of a member:

- the percentage of the standard lifetime allowance crystallised by, and the amount and date of payment of, a relevant lump sum death benefit by the scheme in relation to the member (no later than the last day of the period of three months beginning with the day on which the final such payment was made);
- the cumulative total percentage crystallised at the date of the statement, by benefit crystallisation events in respect of the deceased member under the scheme or any schemes from which assets have been transferred (whether directly or indirectly), in respect of the deceased member's pension rights, but excluding any amount in respect of any relevant lump sum death benefit payment in respect of the deceased member – the information shall be provided no later than the last day of the period of two months beginning with the day on which a request for it is received from the member's personal representatives.

By the administrator of annuities in payment – provided to and by the administrator, insurance company and annuitant

2.97 If, on the crystallisation of a member's pension rights, an insurance company is provided with funds to provide a lifetime annuity, the scheme administrator shall, within three months of annuity purchase, provide the insurance company with details of the percentage of the standard lifetime allowance crystallised both before and after such a purchase.

At least annually, the insurance company shall provide the annuitant with a statement of the percentage of the standard lifetime allowance crystallised at the date of the statement in respect of the annuity.

By the employer company

2.98 If an unauthorised employer payment is made to a company, that company shall provide the following information:

(*a*) details of the scheme that made the payment;

(*b*) the nature of the payment;

(*c*) the amount of the payment;

(*d*) the date on which the payment was made.

The information must be provided to HMRC no later than the 31 January following the tax year in which the payment was made.

By an insurance company etc to personal representatives on death

2.99 Where an insurance company or similar provider has paid an annuity from the assets of the scheme and the person concerned has died, the provider shall on request provide the following information to the personal representatives:

(*a*) date the annuity was purchased;

(*b*) amount crystallised as a percentage of the standard Lifetime Allowance within two months of the request.

By personal representatives to HMRC

2.100 Where a relevant lump sum death benefit is paid and, either alone or when aggregated with other similar payments, results in a lifetime allowance charge, the following information must be provided:

(*a*) name of the scheme and the name and address of the administrator;

(*b*) name of the deceased member;

(*c*) the amount and date of the payment; and

(*d*) the chargeable amount on which the charge arises

within 13 months of the death of the member, or 30 days from the date that the personal representatives became aware of the event giving rise to the charge.

If a requirement to report arises after expiration of the above period, the information must be provided within 30 months of the death of the member. On the discovery of further information after the expiry of such a period, a report must be made within three months of discovery.

Tax returns

2.101 There is a registered pension scheme return which HMRC may require, by giving notice, to be completed for any year together with the provision of any information which is reasonably required. The subjects covered by the return are, briefly:

(*a*) payments (contributions, transfers, payments out and borrowing);

(*b*) assets/connected party information (shares, property, loans etc);

(*c*) cash/bank balances, non-connected party transactions;

(*d*) declaration signed by the administrator or authorised practitioner.

The normal timescale for submission applies, being 31 January following the relevant tax year (or three months after any notice which is given after 31 October in the relevant tax year, or three months from the completion of the winding up of a scheme which wound up before that date).

An accounting for tax return must be completed by the administrator concerning any lifetime allowance charges, lump sum refunds, death benefits, surplus refunds and de-registration charges. Payment is due quarterly and must be made within 45 days of quarter end. Members must be notified of their fund value at vesting, the percentage of the lifetime allowance used (the P60 form) and any benefits-in-kind by 19 July following the relevant tax year end.

Tax reliefs and charges

Annual allowance and lifetime allowance

2.102 The main tax reliefs are similar to those which applied before A-Day. However, the high earner is likely to be constrained by the new annual allowance and the lifetime allowance. Otherwise, there is much greater scope to make tax-relievable contributions by members and employers, and a high tax-relievable fund limit for most.

Member contributions

2.103 There are no formal limits on member contributions, only on the amount which may enjoy tax relief. Full relief is available on member contributions up to a level of 100% of the individual's annual allowance, or £3,600 if that is the higher figure. The rules mean that persons with minimal UK earnings (that is, below £3,600 per annum) may pay up to that amount in any one year. Third parties may also contribute to a registered pension scheme in respect of a person (for example, a minor or a spouse who is not working).

Employer contributions

2.104 The spreading rules for employer contributions which were in place as at A-Day remain. The relevant statutory references are *ss 197* and *198, Finance Act 2004*. The main criterion is that contributions exceeding 210% of an amount paid in a preceding accounting year must be considered for spreading. Major exceptions are:

- spreading will not apply to any payment which has not exceeded £500,000;
- on a cessation of business, where a period of spread is already in place, the relief may be allowed in an earlier accounting period of the employer choice;
- contributions which are paid to fund cost of living increases for pensioners, or to meet future service liabilities for new entrants, are excluded from spreading.

Period of spread

2.105 Spreading is calculated as follows:

Amount of excess payment	*Period of spread*
Between £500,000 and £1m	Over two years
Between £1m and £2m	Over three years
More than £2m	Over four years

General reliefs

2.106 The other tax reliefs are:

- any increase in pension benefits which are promised in defined benefit arrangements up to the limit of the annual allowance do not attract a charge;
- contributions made by the employer are tax relievable;
- investment income is free of income tax;
- investment gains are free of capital gains tax;
- lump sum benefits, in specified circumstances, are paid free of income tax;
- pension business – such of a company's life assurance business as is referable to contracts entered into for the purposes of a registered pension scheme, or is the re-insurance of such business, is not taxable.

Tax relief on contributions will commence from the date that HMRC acknowledges registration. In effect, tax-efficient contributions and benefit accrual will cease after A-Day once the lifetime allowance is exceeded.

Tax charges and penalties

2.107 Full details of the tax charges, penalties and sanctions which may be incurred under the new regime are contained in Chapters 2, 4 and 5 of the 4th edition of Tottel's *Taxation of Pension Benefits*. This is an important area, and the main features are summarised below.

The main charges and penalties are:

- annual allowance and lifetime allowance charge;
- the general charge of unauthorised payments of 40%;
- the benefit-in-kind charge;
- the charge on deliberately winding up a scheme;
- the de-registration of a scheme charge;
- penalties on failures to provide documents or required particulars;
- failure to provide information;
- fraudulent or negligent statements;
- liberated pension savings;

- charges on RNUKSs;
- charges on false or fraudulent information concerning the lifetime allowance;
- charges on surplus repayments;
- charges on value shifting transactions;
- charges on withholding information;
- the unauthorised payments surcharge;
- the scheme sanction charge.

Annual allowance charge and lifetime allowance charge

2.108 These charges are described in 2.22 and 2.27 above.

Unauthorised payments charge

2.109 A major feature of the new tax regime is the imposition of tax charges on unauthorised payments.

Payments by registered schemes which are not authorised by their rules may incur a tax charge of 40% on the amount which is paid out. The tax is chargeable on the member, the recipient or the sponsoring employer, as appropriate. The circumstances in which a charge can be triggered include:

- where benefits are taken before the permitted age of 50 from A-Day, where permitted by the rules, and age 55 from the year 2010;
- where cash sums exceed the permitted maximum allowable;
- where there have been assignments or surrenders of pension;
- where pensions have been reduced or stopped in contravention of the new rules;
- where lump sum death benefits are paid to a person who did not exist at the date of death of the member;
- where the deceased member's rights are used to increase the rights of a connected person;
- where dependants' pensions exceed the member's pension limit;
- when trivial commutation exceeds the 1% permitted limit;
- where transfers are made to non-registered schemes;
- where unauthorised loans are made;

- where lump sum death benefits are paid on winding up to non-dependants;
- where value shifting has taken place from the registered scheme to a member or sponsoring employer;
- where payments are made to migrant members which have benefited from earlier UK tax relief;
- where debts payable by members to a scheme are not at arm's-length (these include debts payable by a connected person).

The scheme sanction charge is reduced from 40% in cases where the unauthorised payments charge has already been paid. The reduction is the lower of:

- 25% of the scheme chargeable payments on which the tax was paid; and
- the actual amount of tax paid on the unauthorised payment.

There is a further concession where a scheme sanction charge is incurred on funds which have been liberated in the member's pension savings through no fault of the member. Where the funds are repatriated, *s 266, Finance Act 2004,* relieves the scheme sanction charge. However the scheme administrator has to claim the relief within a year of the repatriation taking place.

Benefit-in-kind charge

2.110 There is no provision in the legislation which prohibits payment of benefits-in-kind. However, any non-commercial use of assets by a member or an associate of a member will attract a benefit-in-kind charge on the member. An example would be members or connected parties who occupy residential property or enjoy use of pride in possession assets held by the scheme and charged at less than commercial rates. A tax charge of 40% is levied on the member or other recipient whatever their own marginal rate of tax. The charge is incurred under *s 173, Finance Act 2004.*

Deliberate winding up of scheme

2.111 If a scheme is deliberately wound up in order to secure lump sums to the members or beneficiaries, the administrator may be liable to a penalty not exceeding £3,000 in respect of each transaction. The penalty will be incurred under *s 265, Finance Act 2004*. As a consequence of such action the scheme may lose its registration and accordingly suffer the 40% tax de-registration charge.

De-registration of scheme

2.112 This charge will only be incurred if HMRC decide to withdraw the registration of an existing scheme. The administrator will be liable to a 40% tax charge on the value of the entire fund.

Failure to provide documents or required particulars

2.113 Penalties will be imposed on any person who fails to comply with a notice to provide certain documents or particulars. The penalty is imposed by *s 259 (1), Finance Act 2004*. The initial amount is £300, with a daily penalty for non compliance thereafter of £60 per day (*s 259 (2), Finance Act 2004*). In cases of fraud or negligence penalties may be charged up to £3,000 under *s 259 (4), Finance Act 2004.*

Penalties may be imposed on a scheme administrator who fails to make an accounting return. The penalty is imposed by *s 260, Finance Act 2004.*

In cases of fraud or negligence further penalties may be imposed by *s 260 (6), Finance Act 2004.*

Failure to provide information

2.114 Penalties will be incurred in circumstances where persons have either failed to provide required information or have provided false information. The penalty is imposed by *s 258 (1), Finance Act 2004.* Penalties will also be imposed on a failure to preserve documentation for a prescribed period under *s 258 (2), Finance Act 2004*. The penalty shall not exceed £3,000.

Fraudulent or negligent statements

2.115 If a person makes a fraudulent or negligent statement for the purpose of obtaining tax reliefs a penalty may be incurred under *s 264 (1), Finance Act 2004* not exceeding £3,000. Anyone who assists in the provision of such information may also be liable for a charge under *s 264 (2), Finance Act 2004.* An administrator who does not ensure that transfers which are made to a scheme that invests in insurance policies have been made to the appropriate person may be liable to a penalty of up to £3,000 under *s 266, Finance Act 2004.*

Liberated pensions savings

2.116 In some circumstances a member may have been duped into a situation whereby an unauthorised payment arises as a means of liberating his pension funds. Where these funds are repatriated, *s 266, Finance Act 2004*, relieves the member from the unauthorised payment charge. However, any claim for relief must be made within a year of the repatriation date.

Non-UK schemes (RNUKSs)

2.117 Certain charges may fall on non-UK schemes (RNUKSs), and they may also encompass member payment charges. These schemes are described in *Sch 34, para 1, Finance Act 2004.*

Provision of false or fraudulent information in respect of the enhanced lifetime allowance

2.118 Certain documentation is required to support an application for enhanced lifetime allowance protection. A penalty will be imposed if that information is incorrect or false. The penalty is chargeable under *s 261, Finance Act 2004,* on up to 25% of the excess allowance claimed. Failure to provide information which is required by HMRC for the purpose of verifying registration for enhanced lifetime allowance may incur penalties of up to £3,000 under *s 262, Finance Act 2004.*

If an individual has applied for enhanced protection and recommences accrual of benefits that person must notify HMRC within 90 days. Failure to do so may result in a penalty of up to £3,000 under *s 263, Finance Act 2004.*

Surplus repayments

2.119 *Sections 177* and *207, Finance Act 2004*, provide that surplus monies may be paid to employers under governing scheme rules. There must be compliance with DWP rules and legislation. Although not in strictness a penalty, there is an authorised surplus payment charge to be paid by a registered scheme that makes such a payment to a sponsoring employer. The tax chargeable is 35% of the amount of the surplus, and it is incurred under *s 177, Finance Act 2004.*

RPSM04102020 contains technical pages which describe authorised surplus payments made under the *Registered Pension Schemes (Authorised Surplus Payments) Regulations 2006 (SI 2006/574)*. These regulations, and the technical pages, relate to occupational pension schemes. Of particular note is that a surplus payment will not be regarded as an authorised payment where a deceased member was connected with the sponsoring employer at the date of his death.

Value shifting

2.120 The *Finance Act 2004* describes value shifting as transactions which pass value from a registered scheme to a member without creating a payment. Under *s 174* of the Act, such a transaction may be deemed to be an unauthorised payment and taxable as such. It is also intended to introduce rules to prevent the reallocation of investments and benefits if the purpose is to achieve tax avoidance.

Wide powers concerning provision of information

2.121 *Sections 257* to *266, Finance Act 2004,* empower the HMRC to seek to charge penalties, sometimes of a substantial nature, where information has been withheld or false information has been provided.

Unauthorised payments surcharge

2.122 An unauthorised payment surcharge may become payable in addition to the unauthorised payment charge described in 2.109 above. This charge will be triggered if the unauthorised payment which is made to the member or the employer is 25% or more of the fund value, or if more than one authorised payment is made within a specified period. The rate of the surcharge is 15% of the unauthorised payment. The relevant references under the *Finance Act 2004* are *ss 210*(2), *213*(2), *213*(7) and *227.*

Scheme sanction charge

2.123 A scheme sanction charge will fall on the administrator of any registered scheme which makes one or more scheme chargeable payments in the year. *Section 41, Finance Act 2004*, defines scheme chargeable payments as either unauthorised payments or unauthorised borrowings. The rate of tax payable is 40% of the amount of the scheme chargeable payment and it is incurred under *s 239, Finance Act 2004*.

The scheme administrator must pay the charge, although there may be some mitigation where other charges have already been incurred. The provisions which exempt members from charges where they have been duped into making a chargeable payment or receiving one, are followed through in the legislation for scheme administrators. It is a requirement of the *Finance Act 2004* that, in many circumstances, the administrator must be provided with information from the member (for example, the amount of the lifetime allowance which is available). If the administrator has been given false information, he may seek a discharge under *s 267, Finance Act 2004*. His application must be made to HMRC.

The exemptions are described in *ss 267* and *268, Finance Act 2004*. In the event that HMRC refuses to discharge the administrator he can appeal within 30 days to the General or Special Commissioners under *s 269* of the Act.

General penalty charges

The Accounting for Tax Return

2.124 Failure by an administrator to make a return may attract a penalty under *s 260, Finance Act 2004*. The amount of the penalty will depend on the amount of the tax which should have been paid and the number of people who have been omitted from the return. However, where fraud or negligence is concerned additional penalties may be incurred under *s 260(6), Finance Act 2004*.

Enhanced protection

2.125 If additional benefits have accrued after A-Day and a member has claimed enhanced protection, HMRC must be notified. Failure to notify HMRC within 90 days of the recommencement of benefit accrual can incur a penalty on the individual of up to £3,000 under *s 263*, *Finance Act 2004*.

Fraudulent or negligent statements

2.126 Any individual who makes a fraudulent or negligent claim or representation or order to obtain tax reliefs or repayments or unauthorised payments may attract a penalty of £3,000 under *s 264(1)*, *Finance Act 2004*. Other persons who are implicated in the action, if any, may attract penalties under *s 264*(2), *Finance Act 2004* of the same amount.

Failure to provide information

2.127 There has been a revision to *s 98*, *TMA 1970*, to extend penalties in circumstances where there has been a failure to provide information or false information has been provided. Additionally, failure to preserve documents can incur a penalty not exceeding £3,000 under *s 258*(2), *Finance Act 2004*.

Failure to comply with notices

2.128 Where there is failure to comply with notices regarding documents or particulars penalties may be incurred under *s 259(1), Finance Act 2004*. The penalties shall not exceed £300, plus an additional £60 per day for continuing failure. Where a person fraudulently or negligently produces incorrect documents or particulars the penalty shall not exceed £3,000 under *s 259(4), Finance Act 2004*.

Registration for enhanced protection

2.129 Where incorrect or false documents where information is provided seeking enhanced protection from the lifetime allowance, *s 261, Finance Act 2004*, empowers HMRC to impose a penalty of up to 25% of the excess allowance claimed on the individual return. Where HMRC requests evidence of an individual's registration for enhancement, failure to comply may incur a charge of up to £3,000 on the individual concerned (*s 262, Finance Act 2004*).

Winding up

2.130 Any attempt to deliberately wind up the scheme for the purpose of providing lump sums to members or beneficiaries can attract a penalty on the administrator under *s 265, Finance Act 2004*. The penalty shall not exceed £3,000 in respect of each member to whom a lump sum has been paid. It is also important to note that the scheme may lose its registration and so suffer a 40% tax charge.

Misdirection of transfer payments

2.131 It is a scheme administrator's duty to ensure that transfers to a registered scheme which invests in insurance policies are made to the appropriate person. Failure to do so can attract a penalty of up to £3,000 under *s 266, Finance Act 2004*.

Discharge from liability

2.132 There may be cases where scheme administrators have been provided with false information by scheme members, for example, in connection with the lifetime allowance. Scheme administrators can ask HMRC for discharge under *s 267, Finance Act 2004,* from the lifetime allowance charge if they think it fair and reasonable to do so. This may also apply where the unauthorised payment or scheme sanction charges have been incurred.

Appeals can be made if there is a refusal from HMRC to discharge the scheme administrator. The appeal right is contained in *s 269, Finance Act 2004,* and the appeal should be made to the General Commissioners or Special Commissioners within 30 days of HMRC refusing to discharge the said person.

Right to appeal

2.133 A right to appeal against any action or decision by HMRC may be made to the General Commissioners or Special Commissioners within 30 days of the relevant event taking place. Appeals may be made in the following circumstances where there is a grievance which can be supported by the appellant:

- against failure to register a scheme;
- against de-registration of a scheme;
- against exclusion from a scheme being treated as a recognised overseas pension scheme;
- against notices which call for the release of documents or particulars or other information;
- in respect of the discharge of the lifetime allowance charge.

It will be seen that the A-Day appeals procedures largely are retained.

The general tax avoidance rules

2.134 *Part 7, Finance Act 2004,* covers general tax avoidance. However, it could apply to tax avoidance arrangements in relation to pension schemes, if anything is done in breach of prescribed circumstances. A summary of the main disclosure requirements is given below.

Notifiable overseas arrangements, and promoters

2.135 *Section 306* concerns notifiable arrangements and notifiable proposals under tax avoidance schemes. Such arrangements are those which fall within any description prescribed by the Treasury by regulations. They enable a person to gain a tax advantage by means of the main, or one of the main, benefits of the arrangement. A promoter is described in *s 307* as a person in relation to a notifiable proposal, if, in the course of a trade, profession or business which involves the provision to other persons of services relating to taxation:

(*a*) he is to any extent responsible for the design of the proposed arrangements; or

(*b*) he makes the notifiable proposal available for implementation by other persons

in relation to notifiable arrangements, if he is [*by virtue of paragraph* (*a*)(*ii*)*]* a promoter in relation to a notifiable proposal which is implemented by those arrangements or if, in the course of a trade, profession or business which involves the provision to other persons of services relating to taxation, he is to any extent responsible for:

(*a*) the design of the arrangements; or

(*b*) the organisation or management of the arrangements.

A person is not to be treated as a promoter for the purposes of this Part by reason of anything done in prescribed circumstances. By way of a relaxation, The Government stated on 24 June 2004 that only those at the heart of the scheme or arrangement, who are capable of meeting its obligations, will be treated as the promoter.

Under *s 308*, the promoter must provide information to HMRC within a prescribed period after the date on which he makes a notifiable proposal, or the date on which he first becomes aware of any transaction forming part of the proposed arrangements. This applies under *s 319* to post-17 March 2004 relevant dates and transactions.

Under *s 309* the duty falls on any client who enters into any transaction forming part of any notifiable arrangements in relation to which a promoter is resident outside the UK, and no promoter is resident in the UK. Under *s 310* the duty extends to any other person who enters into any transaction forming part of any notifiable arrangements in similar circumstances. *Sections 309* and *310* apply, by virtue of *s 319,* to post-22 April 2004 transactions.

Penalties for non-compliance

2.136 Under *s 312*, the promoter must provide information to the client within 30 days in relation to the arrangements. There are penalties for non-compliance – *s 315* inserts *s 98C* into the *Taxes Management Act 1970*. A penalty not exceeding £5,000 will be imposed on a promoter, with penalties of £600 a day for continuing non-compliance. Any person who is a party to the arrangement who fails to comply will be fined £100 per scheme, or £500 or £1,000 if he has previously failed to comply during the preceding period of 36 months on one or more occasion (respectively).

Disclosure

2.137 Disclosures must be made on the forms on the HMRC website, which were published on 28 May 2004. These are S292 for UK promoters, S293 for users where there is an overseas promoter and S294 for users where there is no external promoter. Various draft 'tax avoidance' and 'tackling tax avoidance' regulations have been drafted.

The statutory rules are not only very wide, they are almost impossible to understand. The intended meanings of 'avoidance' and 'promoter' in the Act are unclear. It is hoped that clarification will be received at a future date. The new rules potentially impact on employment terms, securities, financial products, premium fees and confidentiality testing – which will widely impact on disclosure rules for employers, advisers and others.

Transfers

New flexibility

2.138 One of the more significant changes which has been introduced by the new tax regime is a freeing up of the payment of transfer values from registered (previously approved or newly registered) pension schemes to other registered schemes. There is also wide flexibility to transfer to recognised overseas pensions schemes, and this matter is addressed in more detail in Chapter 7.

This means is that transfers between registered schemes and recognised overseas schemes may be made with far less complication than existed under the pre-A-Day rules.

Inevitably, there are still some special rules for high earners and these are described in 2.141 (*m*) and the RPSM extracts which apply to protected persons which are contained in the Annex to this chapter. However, special rules were not intended to exist under the single tax regime, and consequently there is generally a welcome added flexibility for the future of pension provision for such persons. The UK legislative change has in no small part been triggered by the *European Union Pensions Directive 2003/41/EC* for IORPS, which requires greater transferability of members' rights under its portability initiatives.

The main rules which now apply are:

(*a*) transfers may be made from registered schemes to other registered schemes freely, and no test will have to be made against the lifetime allowance;

(*b*) transfers may be made to a qualifying recognised overseas pension scheme without restriction.

Information requirements

2.139 There are certain information requirements that must be met in respect of transfers. Any transfers that do not fall within the above categories will be liable to charge as unauthorised payments, although any payment which is made in good faith by a person having placed reliance on false or misleading information should escape penalty by virtue of regulations.

Allowance limits

2.140 With regard to transfers into registered schemes, they can be made under the circumstances described in 2.138 above. In general such transfers are not regarded as pension input payments counting towards the annual allowance, and they also do not count towards the lifetime allowance to the extent they comprise monies on which no UK tax reliefs have previously been given. RPSM14101010 explains how transfers are treated with regard to the annual allowance and lifetime allowance. Recognised transfers are not deemed to be benefit crystallisation events and so do not count towards the lifetime allowance. A benefit crystallisation event will take place when the benefits are taken from the receiving scheme.

For defined benefits schemes the market values of the assets are to be counted at closing value, money purchase arrangements which are cash balance arrangements are treated similarly, and for any other money purchase arrangement the transfer does not count towards the annual allowance – indeed, if it did so, it would be entitled to tax relief.

Detailed rules

2.141 Greater detail of the rules which apply on transfers, plus worked examples, are contained in Chapter 8 of the 4th edition of Tottel's *Taxation of Pension Benefits*. In summary the main principles which apply are:

(*a*) If a transfer is made into an insurance company or to a third party administrator, they must be made directly. Any failure to meet this requirement will mean that the transfer will be deemed to be a contribution and will be counted towards the annual allowance for the period in question. In addition, it will count against the lifetime allowance for the member concerned.

(*b*) The new legislation provides favourable treatment for bulk transfers, provided that members involved were not already members of a receiving scheme prior to the transfer date. In practice this means not having been a member for one year or more before the transfer date.

(*c*) Transfers may be made in specie, in other words, they need not be in cash only form. However, the appropriate cash value must be determined at the point of transfer.

(*d*) If a member has applied for enhanced protection, any transfers which take the form of unvested rights must be certified, stating that the transfer does not contain post A-Day contributions or that the individual has not been actively accruing benefits since A-Day.

(*e*) There are no hard and fast rules concerning fragmenting lump sums. However, HMRC stated in Pensions Update No 147 that any attempt to circumnavigate the lump sum limits under the new regime by fragmentation would be unacceptable and could incur penalties.

(*f*) Schemes which are approved under *ss 647* to *654, ITEPA 2003* (previously *s 615, ICTA 1988* schemes) may transfer into registered schemes. There is no firm statement on this, but *ss 245(5)* and *249(3), Finance Act 2004,* do not impede such transfers.

(*g*) Certain tax charges may be attracted in respect of transfers to relevant non-UK schemes (RNUK Schemes). This is explained more fully in Chapter 7.

(*h*) In some circumstances an 'unauthorised member payment charge' may be incurred under *s 160, Finance Act 2004*. This is described in more detail in 2.109 above.

(*i*) Transfers of contracted-out rights have been opened up by the removal of the residency requirements which previously applied. The *Contracting-out, Protected Rights and Safeguarded Rights* (*Transfer Payment*) *Amendment Regulations 2005* (*SI 2005/555*) came into effect from 6 April 2005. Transfers of contracted-out rights can be made without the need for a member to have permanently emigrated, provided that the transfers are to recognised overseas pensions schemes arrangements or other registered schemes.

(*j*) Where a scheme is in wind up, the transfer may be made to another registered scheme. The availability of protection for lump sums is described in detail in Chapter 9 of the 4th edition of Tottel's *Taxation of Pension Benefits*.

(*k*) Any unauthorised payment will receive a tax charge under the provisions of *s 169(1), Finance Act 2004*. The amount of the charge is 40% on the total payment made. However there are further unauthorised payment charges which may be incurred (see 2.110 to 2.123 above). It is therefore very important that high earners take appropriate advice before moving substantial sums of money out of registered schemes. Further guidance is contained in RPSM14102010.

(*l*) Any transfers out must comply with social security legislation where contracted-out rights are involved (*s 169*(*1*), *Finance Act 2004*). In practice this means that the receiving scheme must be capable of receiving and holding contracted-out rights.

(*m*) Generally transfers in respect of members who have enhanced protection will cause a loss of that protection, unless the transfer is a permitted transfer (see Chapter 8 of the 4th edition of Tottel's *Taxation of Pension Benefits*).

(*n*) Transfers in respect of members who have elected for primary protection will retain that protection in the new scheme (RPSM14105020). The lump sum protection works in a similar way, and is described in RPSM14105030 and RPSM03105000.

(*o*) Where a transfer is not a permissible transfer in respect of a member who had elected for enhanced protection, any lump sum entitlement will either revert to the primary protection lump sum (RPSM03100060) or 25% of the standard lifetime allowance if the only election by the member was enhanced protection. Further details on lump sum limits and transfers are contained in RPSM14105050.

(*p*) A member's entitlement to a low pension age payment may be retained on a transfer (RPSM14105060).

(*q*) Entitlements to low normal retirement ages may be a retained on a block transfer if the rules of the receiving scheme so permit (RPSM14105070).

(*r*) A right to early retirement benefits may be transferred to the receiving scheme (RPSM 14105080) where the transfer is part of a block transfer and the rules of the receiving scheme so permit.

(*s*) In a major change of policy, transfers may now be made whilst persons are in service and also after their pensions have come into payment. The main proviso is there must be no change in the terms which apply to the benefits payable. Transfers may be made in relation to a pension which is already in payment or an unsecured pension where an entitlement to benefits has already arisen. Regulations determine the formal amount of pension that may be paid (RPSM14106010).

(*t*) Where a transfer represents benefits which are already in payment or to which an entitlement has arisen, and that transfer is to an insurance company, the insurance company must not act within a registered scheme and the provision of a pension must comply with the rules which previously applied to the member's pension. (RPSM14106020).

(*u*) Where the pension payment made in the circumstances described in (*t*) above is paid from an annuity certain conditions must be met in order to transfer the annuity from one insurance company to another (RPSM14106030).

(*v*) Where transfers are made in the circumstances described in (*t*) above, and there was previous entitlement to an unsecured pension or alternatively secured pension payment there are certain rules with regards to prohibition of additional pension commencement lump sum payments (RPSM14106040).

(*w*) Transfers from an unsecured fund to another unsecured fund, where a pension is already in payment or entitlement has arisen, may be made but if such a transfer is made within the same registered scheme it would be disregarded. This means that the monies transferred would still be treated as if they were part of the original arrangement in order to counter a circumnavigation of the pension rules. (RPSM14106050).

The transfer boxes from RPSM extracts, which are included in the 4th edition of Tottel's *Taxation of Pension Benefits*, are inserted by way of a separate Annex below.

ANNEX

RPSM transfer extracts

PART A

All transfers except international transfers

2.142 BOX 1: RPSM14101010 – Technical Pages: Transfers: Recognised transfers from registered pension schemes: Transfer to another registered pension scheme.

BOX 2: RPSM14101070 – Technical Pages: Transfers: Recognised transfers from registered pension schemes: Reporting requirements on transfer to a qualifying recognised overseas pension scheme.

BOX 3: RPSM14101080 – Technical Pages: Transfers: Recognised transfers from registered pension schemes: Transfer to a deferred annuity contract or buyout policy.

BOX 4: RPSM14102010 – Technical Pages Transfers: Non-recognised transfers from registered pension schemes: Transfer to a non- registered UK pension scheme.

BOX 5: RPSM14102020 – Technical Pages Transfers: Non-recognised transfers from registered pension schemes: Transfer to a non-registered overseas pension scheme which is not a qualifying recognised overseas pension scheme.

BOX 6: RPSM14103010 – Technical Pages: Transfers: Recognised transfers to registered pension schemes: Transfer from another registered pension scheme.

BOX 7; RPSM14103010 – Technical Pages: Transfers: Recognised transfers to registered pension schemes: Transfer from another registered pension scheme.

BOX 8: RPSM14103020 – Technical Pages: Transfers: Recognised transfers to registered pension schemes: Transfer from a recognised overseas pension scheme.

BOX 9: RPSM14104010 – Technical Pages: Transfers: Non-recognised transfers to registered pension schemes. Transfer received from a non-registered pension scheme which is not a recognised overseas pension scheme.

BOX 10: RPSM14104010 – Technical Pages: Transfers: Non-recognised transfers to registered pension schemes. Transfer received from a non-registered pension scheme which is not a recognised overseas pension scheme.

BOX 11: RPSM14105010 – Technical Pages: Transfers: Transfer of a member's rights where the member has protection from tax charges: Member with enhanced protection.

BOX 12: RPSM14105020 – Technical Pages: Transfers: Transfer of a member's rights where the member has protection from tax charges: Member with primary protection.

BOX 13: RPSM14105030 – Technical Pages: Transfers: Transfer of a member's rights where the member has protection from tax charges: Lump sum protection in transferring scheme: member with primary protection.

BOX 14: RPSM14105040 – Technical Pages: Transfers: Transfer of a member's rights where the member has protection from tax charges: Lump sum protection in transferring scheme: member with enhanced protection.

BOX 15: RPSM14105050 – Technical Pages: Transfers: Transfer of a member's rights where the member has protection from tax charges: Lump sum protection in transferring scheme. Member entitled to lump sum of more than 25% of rights.

BOX 16: RPSM14105060 – Technical Pages: Transfers: Transfer of a member's rights where the member has protection from tax charges: Member has protected low pension age.

BOX 17: RPSM14105070 – Technical Pages: Transfers: Transfer of a member's rights where the member has protection from tax charges: Member has a protected low normal retirement age.

BOX 18: RPSM14105080 – Technical Pages: Transfers: Transfer of a member's rights where the member has protection from tax charges: Entitlement to take pension before normal retirement age.

BOX 19: RPSM14106010 – Technical Pages: Transfers: Transfers of pensions in payment, or rights where there is already an entitlement to benefits: Transfer of crystallised rights.

BOX 20: RPSM14106020 – Technical Pages: Transfers: Transfers of pensions in payment, or rights where there is already an entitlement to benefits: Transfer to an insurance company of pension in payment.

BOX 21: RPSM14106030 – Technical Pages: Transfers: Transfers of pensions in payment, or rights where there is already an entitlement to benefits: Transfer to an insurance company of an annuity in payment.

BOX 22: RPSM14106040 – Technical Pages: Transfers: Transfers of pensions in payment, or rights where there is already an entitlement to benefits: Transfer of rights where previous entitlement to the payment of unsecured pension or alternatively secured pension.

BOX 23: RPSM14106050 – Technical Pages: Transfers: Transfers of pensions in payment, or rights where there is already an entitlement to benefits: Transfer within a registered pension scheme.

BOX 24: RPSM14107010 – Technical Pages: Transfers: General points for transfers: Transfers must be made between pension schemes.

BOX 25: RPSM14107020 – Technical Pages: Transfers: General points for transfers: Form of transferred rights.

BOX 26: RPSM14107030 – Technical Pages: Transfers: General points for transfers: Fragmentation – splitting rights between recipient schemes.

BOX 27: RPSM14107040 – Technical Pages: Transfers: General points for transfers: Partial transfers.

BOX 28: RPSM14107050 – Technical Pages: Transfers: General points for transfers: Reporting transfers to HMRC. Reporting transfers to HMRC. Registered Pension Scheme Return

BOX 1

2.143 RPSM14101010 – Technical Pages: Transfers: Recognised transfers from registered pension schemes: Transfer to another registered pension scheme

Transfer to another registered pension scheme

[Section 169(1)(a)]

A transfer from a registered pension scheme to another registered pension scheme is a 'recognised transfer'. A recognised transfer is a type of authorised payment. No tax charges or sanctions apply to recognised transfers.

Tax relief

[Section 188(5)]

A recognised transfer from one registered pension scheme to another is not a contribution, so no tax relief is due in respect of the transfer. The contributions to the transferring scheme would usually have received tax relief when originally made to that scheme, and the transfer is merely relocating the pension rights represented by those contributions to a different registered pension scheme.

Annual allowance

[Sections 188(5), 230 – 234 & 236]

The treatment of the value transferred for the purpose of the member's annual allowance calculation for the year in which the transfer takes place is as follows.

Defined benefit arrangements

Where the transferring scheme is one under which the member has a defined benefit arrangement, the amounts transferred, and the market values of any assets transferred in the pension input period are to be included in the member's closing value in the arrangement (so they are added back in at their values at the time of the transfer).

Where the receiving scheme is one under which the member has a defined benefit arrangement, the amounts transferred, and the market values of any assets transferred in the pension input period are to be deducted from the member's closing value in the arrangement (so they are subtracted at their values at the time of the transfer).

Money purchase arrangement

cash balance arrangement, as for defined benefit arrangement, see above.

any other money purchase arrangement – the transfer is not a contribution (see above), so no tax relief is due and the transfer value is not to be included in the individual's annual allowance calculation for the receiving arrangement.

Lifetime allowance

A recognised transfer from one registered pension scheme to another is not a benefit crystallisation event for the purpose of applying the lifetime allowance. But if, for example, the transfer is of funds from which the member had not already started to draw benefits, there will be a benefit crystallisation event for the lifetime allowance when the benefits are taken in the receiving scheme.

BOX 2

2.144 RPSM14101070 – Technical Pages: Transfers: Recognised transfers from registered pension schemes: Reporting requirements on transfer to a qualifying recognised overseas pension scheme

Reporting requirements on transfer to a qualifying recognised overseas pension scheme

The scheme administrator of a registered pension scheme must report to HMRC any transfer from their scheme to a qualifying recognised overseas pension scheme. See pages about the Event Report. (The details to be provided on the form are set out in the Registered Pension Schemes (Provision of Information) Regulations 2006 (SI 2006/567)).

Qualifying recognised overseas pension scheme

The scheme manager of a qualifying recognised overseas pension scheme must undertake to contact HMRC when they make a payment to a member in respect of whom there is a relevant transfer fund within the meaning of the Pension Schemes (Application of Charges to UK Tax to non-UK Schemes) Regulations 2006 (SI 2006/567).

Broadly speaking, a member will have a relevant transfer fund within the scheme if they have transferred sums or assets into it that relate to UK tax-relieved contributions. That includes transfers from registered pension schemes and certain transfers from non-UK schemes that are not registered pension schemes. Further details are on page RPSM131.

The scheme manager must provide HMRC with the following information:

- the name and address of the member, and
- the date, amount and nature of the payment.

A payment includes a transfer from the scheme. Where a non-pension payment such as a lump sum or a transfer is made, the scheme manager must provide the information to HMRC by 31 January following the end of the tax year in which each payment is made. Where a pension payment is made, the scheme manager must provide the information by 31 January following the end of the tax year in which the first payment is made, but it is only necessary to do this in respect of the first such payment to any individual.

Exceptionally, HMRC may require the information to be provided within 30 days of the issue of a notice to the scheme. That can happen if HMRC has reasonable grounds for believing that the scheme has failed, or may fail, to comply with any of the information requirements and that such failure is likely to have led, or to lead, to serious prejudice to the proper assessment or collection of tax.

BOX 3

2.145 RPSM14101080 – Technical Pages: Transfers: Recognised transfers from registered pension schemes: Transfer to a deferred annuity contract or buyout policy

Transfer to a deferred annuity contract or buyout policy

A transfer from a registered pension scheme to a deferred annuity contract is a recognised transfer. This is because the deferred annuity contract is automatically treated as a registered pension scheme under the legislation, from the day on which the contract or policy is made. So the transfer is being made between registered pension schemes.

See RPSM14101010 for more about transfers between registered pension schemes.

For an explanation of what a deferred annuity contract is, see RPSM02104000.

Assigning an annuity policy which does not provide for immediate payment of benefits is also a recognised transfer under the tax legislation.

BOX 4

2.146 RPSM14102010 – Technical Pages Transfers: Non-recognised transfers from registered pension schemes: Transfer to a non-registered UK pension scheme

Transfer to a non-registered UK pension scheme

[Section 169(1)]

A transfer to a UK pension scheme that is not a registered pension scheme is not a recognised transfer.

It is therefore an unauthorised member payment.

Tax charges

[Section 160(5)]

Such a transfer incurs a tax charge on the member at a rate of 40% of the payment.

This tax charge – broadly speaking – recoups the tax relief already given in respect of the contributions made by or on behalf of the member, and the income from the investment of those contributions. If the transfer payment and any other unauthorised payments to the member in a 12-month period exceeds 25% of the member's fund, the member is liable to an unauthorised payment surcharge of a further 15% of the payment.

A scheme sanction charge of up to 40% may also apply, for which the scheme administrator is liable. If the scheme administrator has deducted the member's tax charge from the transfer payment and paid the tax charge to HMRC on the member's behalf, the scheme administrator may reduce the amount of the scheme sanction charge by the lesser of 25% and the amount of member's tax charge deducted as a proportion of the transfer payment.

In addition, if the amounts transferred equate to 25% or more of the scheme fund value, HMRC may withdraw the transferring scheme's registration. This involves a de-registration charge of 40% (see RPSM02105050).

Tax relief

[Section 188(5)]

The transfer is not a contribution and no tax relief is due.

Annual allowance

If the transfer was made from a cash balance arrangement, or from a defined benefit arrangement, the amount transferred is not to be included in the closing value when calculating the member's pension input amount for the transferring arrangement. (See RPSM06101020 and RPSM06103010) The closing value is not adjusted where the transfer is not to a registered pension scheme or a qualifying recognised overseas pension scheme.

In a money purchase arrangement that is not a cash balance arrangement, the amount transferred in itself is not included when calculating the member's pension input amount, as only contributions are counted for the pension input amount in such an arrangement.

Lifetime allowance

[Section 216]

The transfer is not a benefit crystallisation event for the purpose of the member's lifetime allowance and so is not taken into account for the member's lifetime allowance either on the occasion of the transfer, or on any future crystallisation of other benefits the member might take from registered pension schemes.

Reporting requirement

The transferring scheme administrator must report such a transfer (as an unauthorised member payment) on the Event Report [RPSM12301010].

BOX 5

2.147 RPSM14102020 – Technical Pages Transfers: Non-recognised transfers from registered pension schemes: Transfer to a non-registered overseas pension scheme which is not a qualifying recognised overseas pension scheme

Transfer to a non-registered overseas pension scheme which is not a qualifying recognised overseas pension scheme

A transfer from a registered pension scheme to a non-UK pension scheme that is not a qualifying recognised overseas pension scheme is not a recognised transfer. Such a transfer is an unauthorised member payment.

See RPSM14101030 and RPSM14101040 for the conditions for a recognised overseas pension scheme.

Tax charges

The member incurs a tax charge of 40% on the amount of the payment.

This tax charge, broadly speaking, recoups the tax relief already given in respect of the contributions made by the member or on their behalf, and the income from the investment of those contributions. If the transfer payment and any other unauthorised payments to the member in a 12-month period exceeds 25% of the member's fund, the member is liable to an unauthorised payment surcharge of a further 15% of the payment.

A scheme sanction charge of up to 40% may also apply for which the scheme administrator is liable. If the scheme administrator has deducted the member's tax charge from the transfer payment and paid the tax charge to HMRC on the member's behalf, the scheme administrator may reduce the amount of the scheme sanction charge by the lesser of 25% and the amount of member's tax charge deducted as a proportion of the transfer payment.

In addition, if the amounts transferred equate to 25% or more of the scheme fund value, HMRC may withdraw the transferring scheme's registration. This involves a de-registration charge of 40% (see RPSM02105050).

Tax relief

[Sections 188(5) & 232]

Tax relief is only given on contributions to registered pension schemes. A transfer is not a contribution. The payment is not being made to a registered pension scheme. No UK tax relief is due to the receiving scheme.

Annual allowance

If the transfer is made from a cash balance arrangement, or from a defined benefit arrangement, the amount transferred is not to be included in the closing value when calculating the member's pension input amount for the transferring arrangement (See RPSM06101020 and RPSM0610310). The closing value is not adjusted where the transfer is not a registered pension scheme or a qualifying recognised overseas pension scheme.

In a money purchase arrangement that is not a cash balance arrangement, the amount transferred in itself is not included when calculating the member's pension input amount, as only contributions are counted for the pension input amount in such a scheme.

Lifetime allowance

The transfer is not a benefit crystallisation event for the purpose of the member's lifetime allowance and is not taken into account for the member's lifetime allowance either on the occasion of the transfer or on any future crystallisation of other benefits the member might take from registered pension schemes.

Reporting requirement

The scheme administrator of the transferring scheme must report the transfer (as an unauthorised member payment) to HMRC on the Event Report [RPSM12301010].

BOX 6

2.148 RPSM14103010 – Technical Pages: Transfers: Recognised transfers to registered pension schemes: Transfer from another registered pension scheme

Transfer from another registered pension scheme

[section 169 (1)(a)]

A transfer of a member's pension rights from a registered pension scheme to another registered pension scheme is a recognised transfer, (see RPSM14101010).

Although a transfer may be a recognised transfer for tax purposes, if there are contracted-out rights involved, Department for Work and Pensions (DWP) legislation provides that the transfer can only go ahead if the receiving scheme is eligible to hold those rights.

BOX 7

2.149 RPSM14103010 – Technical Pages: Transfers: Recognised transfers to registered pension schemes: Transfer from another registered pension scheme

Transfer from another registered pension scheme

[section 169 (1)(a)]

A transfer of a member's pension rights from a registered pension scheme to another registered pension scheme is a recognised transfer, (see RPSM14101010).

Although a transfer may be a recognised transfer for tax purposes, if there are contracted-out rights involved, Department for Work and Pensions (DWP) legislation provides that the transfer can only go ahead if the receiving scheme is eligible to hold those rights.

BOX 8

2.150 RPSM14103020 – Technical Pages: Transfers: Recognised transfers to registered pension schemes: Transfer from a recognised overseas pension scheme

Transfer from a recognised overseas pension scheme

[section 188(5) and sections 224–226]

A transfer to a registered pension scheme from a recognised overseas pension scheme that is not a registered pension scheme is not a recognised transfer. But it is not an unauthorised payment either, because unauthorised payments are payments from registered pension schemes. And the legislation specifically states that an amount received by transfer from another pension scheme is not a contribution, so it does not qualify for tax relief on being received by a registered pension scheme.

Instead, special treatment is given to the lifetime allowance of a member who transfers-in funds from a recognised overseas pension scheme that is not registered, to a pension scheme that is registered (see rpsm 13100010).

No UK tax relief has been received, so it would be unfair if the transferred amount were to use up the member's available lifetime allowance. But, broadly, any part of an amount transferred that relates to UK tax relieved contributions made after 5 April 2006 will count against the member's lifetime allowance.

As explained in RPSM11101050, the member's lifetime allowance is increased, or 'enhanced', by an appropriate factor, from the date of the transfer. The member must claim this enhancement no later than five years after 31 January following the tax year in which the transfer is made, and register the amount with HMRC. This process enables HMRC to verify the amount claimed in appropriate cases.

For the member's annual allowance, the treatment of the transfer value depends on the type of scheme receiving the transfer. If the receiving scheme is either a defined benefit scheme or a cash balance scheme, subtract the transfer value from the closing value. If the receiving scheme is any other type of money purchase scheme, the transfer is not included, as only contributions are included for the annual allowance.

BOX 9

2.151 RPSM14104010 – Technical Pages: Transfers: Non-recognised transfers to registered pension schemes

Transfer received from a non-registered pension scheme which is not a recognised overseas pension scheme

A registered pension scheme may receive a transfer payment from another scheme that is neither a registered pension scheme nor a recognised overseas pension scheme, for example:

- an employer-financed retirement benefits scheme, or
- a pension scheme abroad that does not satisfy the requirements to be treated as a recognised overseas pension scheme.

Tax relief

A transfer payment is not a contribution, because section 188(5) specifically excludes transfer payments between pension schemes from being considered as contributions for tax relief purposes (regardless of whether or not the pension schemes concerned are registered or recognised).

No tax relief is due on the transfer payment on receipt. However, any investment income or gain in relation to the funds in the receiving scheme is free of income tax and capital gains tax.

Member's annual allowance

If the rights are being transferred into a defined benefit arrangement or a cash balance arrangement, the value of the transfer payment should be deducted from the closing value of the member's rights.

If the rights are being transferred into any other type of money purchase arrangement, the transfer payment is not included for the annual allowance. This is because, for annual allowance purposes, in a money purchase arrangement only contributions are counted, and a transfer payment is not a contribution.

Member's lifetime allowance

A transfer into a registered pension scheme is not a benefit crystallisation event (BCE) for lifetime allowance purposes. When the member eventually takes benefits, there will be a benefit crystallisation event at that point, and the lifetime allowance test must be carried out.

Where the transfer to a registered pension scheme has come from a scheme abroad, the member's lifetime allowance should only be enhanced if the transferring scheme is a recognised overseas pension scheme. In any other case, the standard lifetime allowance applies on a BCE, unless the member qualifies for an enhancement due to other special circumstances.

BOX 10

2.152 RPSM14104010 – Technical Pages: Transfers: Non-recognised transfers to registered pension schemes

Transfer received from a non-registered pension scheme which is not a recognised overseas pension scheme

A registered pension scheme may receive a transfer payment from another scheme that is neither a registered pension scheme nor a recognised overseas pension scheme, for example:

- an employer-financed retirement benefits scheme, or
- a pension scheme abroad that does not satisfy the requirements to be treated as a recognised overseas pension scheme.

Tax relief

A transfer payment is not a contribution, because section 188(5) specifically excludes transfer payments between pension schemes from being considered as contributions for tax relief purposes (regardless of whether or not the pension schemes concerned are registered or recognised).

No tax relief is due on the transfer payment on receipt. However, any investment income or gain in relation to the funds in the receiving scheme is free of income tax and capital gains tax.

Member's annual allowance

If the rights are being transferred into a defined benefit arrangement or a cash balance arrangement, the value of the transfer payment should be deducted from the closing value of the member's rights.

If the rights are being transferred into any other type of money purchase arrangement, the transfer payment is not included for the annual allowance. This is because, for annual allowance purposes, in a money purchase arrangement only contributions are counted, and a transfer payment is not a contribution.

Member's lifetime allowance

A transfer into a registered pension scheme is not a benefit crystallisation event (BCE) for lifetime allowance purposes. When the member eventually takes benefits, there will be a benefit crystallisation event at that point, and the lifetime allowance test must be carried out.

Where the transfer to a registered pension scheme has come from a scheme abroad, the member's lifetime allowance should only be enhanced if the transferring scheme is a recognised overseas pension scheme. In any other case, the standard lifetime allowance applies on a BCE, unless the member qualifies for an enhancement due to other special circumstances.

BOX 11

2.153 RPSM14105010 – Technical Pages: Transfers: Transfer of a member's rights where the member has protection from tax charges: Member with enhanced protection

Member with enhanced protection

[Schedule 36 Part 2, Para 12]

A member with enhanced protection is entitled to crystallise their benefits in full from the protected funds without incurring a tax charge, regardless of whether in doing so they exceed the standard lifetime allowance.

When a member applies to transfer benefit rights which have enhanced protection, the enhanced protection will be lost unless the transfer is a permitted transfer (see RPSM03104090).

BOX 12

2.154 RPSM14105020 – Technical Pages: Transfers: Transfer of a member's rights where the member has protection from tax charges: Member with primary protection

Member with primary protection

A scheme member who is entitled to primary protection (see RPSM03100050), but transfers their pension rights out of the pension scheme of which they were a member at 5 April 2006, retains any primary protection obtained in relation to those pension rights. This retention of primary protection also applies on any subsequent transfer.

This means that for such an individual, the standard lifetime allowance (at the time the benefits that have primary protection are crystallised) is increased by the same proportion by which the individual's benefits exceeded £1,500,000 on 5 April 2006.

Example

The value of the member's benefits at 5 April 2006 was £2 million.

This is one third more than £1.5 million, the standard lifetime allowance at the start of the new tax regime for pension schemes.

The member is entitled to primary protection on crystallising benefits of up to one third more than the standard lifetime allowance at any time, even if those benefits have been transferred to other schemes.

If those benefits were eventually paid in 2010–11, when the standard lifetime allowance is £1.8 million, the member's lifetime allowance at that time would be increased by one third, to £2.4 million – regardless of the benefits being paid by a different pension scheme to that which originally calculated the value of the benefits at 5 April 2006.

If the amount being crystallised in 2010–11 was £2.5 million, the lifetime allowance tax charge would apply to only £100,000 of that payment.

If the amount being crystallised in 2010–11 was £2.35 million, no lifetime allowance tax charge would apply on that crystallisation.

BOX 13

2.155 RPSM14105030 – Technical Pages: Transfers: Transfer of a member's rights where the member has protection from tax charges: Lump sum protection in transferring scheme: member with primary protection

Lump sum protection in transferring scheme: member with primary protection

Where a scheme member who is entitled to primary protection (see RPSM03100050) transfers their pension rights out of a pension scheme of which they were a member at 5 April 2006, they retain any primary protection in relation to those pension rights.

The way in which the lump sum protection works is explained in RPSM03105000.

BOX 14

2.156 RPSM14105040 – Technical Pages: Transfers: Transfer of a member's rights where the member has protection from tax charges: Lump sum protection in transferring scheme: member with enhanced protection

Lump sum protection in transferring scheme: member with enhanced protection

Where a member is entitled to enhanced protection (see RPSM03100040), they retain that protection on transfer providing the transfer is a permitted transfer (see RPSM03104090).

If the transfer is not a permitted transfer, the member loses enhanced protection and the member's lump sum entitlement reverts to:

- primary protection, if they have claimed this (see RPSM03100060), or
- 25% of the standard lifetime allowance for the tax year in question, if the member only claimed enhanced protection.

BOX 15

2.157 RPSM14105050 – Technical Pages: Transfers: Transfer of a member's rights where the member has protection from tax charges: Lump sum protection in transferring scheme

Member entitled to lump sum of more than 25% of rights

Where a member's lump sum rights in a registered pension scheme qualify for lump sum protection under the rules at RPSM03105510, the member retains that protection on transferring those rights, providing the conditions set out in RPSM03105520 are met.

If the transfer is made in other circumstances, the protection is lost. The member's lump sum entitlement reverts to a maximum of 25% of the standard lifetime allowance for the tax year in question.

BOX 16

2.158 RPSM14105060 – Technical Pages: Transfers: Transfer of a member's rights where the member has protection from tax charges: Member has protected low pension age

Member has protected low pension age

[paragraph 21 and 23 Schedule 36 Finance Act 2004]

A member may qualify for low pension age protection in their pension scheme. They may also qualify to retain their low pension age after transferring into another scheme if certain circumstances prevail. These are that:

- the transferring scheme, immediately before 6 April 2006, was either:
  - a tax approved personal pension scheme or
  - a tax approved retirement annuity contract, and
- the low pension age which applied to the member on 5 April 2006 was an age under 50, and
- the member's occupation on 5 April 2006 was or had been a prescribed occupation, and
- the transfer is part of a block transfer (transferring from a retirement annuity contract may not satisfy condition if there is only one member at the time of the transfer).

This is also subject to the new scheme's rules allowing payment of benefits at an age earlier than the normal minimum pension age.

When the member crystallises benefits from the scheme they transferred into, the benefit payments will not be treated as unauthorised payments even though they are being paid earlier than normal minimum pension age.

But the member will be treated as receiving an unauthorised payment on crystallisation at the earlier age unless he becomes entitled to all uncrystallised rights under the receiving scheme at the same time.

BOX 17

2.159 RPSM14105070 – Technical Pages: Transfers: Transfer of a member's rights where the member has protection from tax charges: Member has a protected low normal retirement age

Member has a protected low normal retirement age

[paragraph 21 and 22 Schedule 36 Finance Act 2004]

A member may be entitled to low normal retirement age (NRA) protection in the scheme they were a member of on 5 April 2006. They may also qualify to retain this protection after transferring out of that pension scheme.

The member qualifies to retain their low NRA after transfer to another registered pension scheme if:

- the transferring scheme, immediately before 6 April 2006, was either:
    - a tax approved retirement benefits scheme, or
    - a deferred annuity contract, or
    - a former approved superannuation fund, or
    - a statutory pension scheme, or
    - a Parliamentary pension scheme, and
- the member's NRA under that scheme on 5 April 2006 was an age less than 55, and
- that scheme's rules on 10 December 2003 conferred this NRA on at least some members of the scheme, and
- this included the member now transferring from that scheme (or would have done if he had been a scheme member on that date), and
- the transfer is part of a block transfer.

Payment of benefits at the protected age will also depend on the rules of the receiving scheme allowing this.

When the member crystallises benefits from the scheme they transferred into, the benefit payments will not be treated as unauthorised payments even though they are being paid earlier than the normal minimum pension age, providing:

- the member becomes entitled to all benefits under that scheme at the same time, and
- the member is not employed by a sponsoring employer in relation to that scheme after becoming entitled to a pension from that scheme.

BOX 18

2.160 RPSM14105080 – Technical Pages: Transfers: Transfer of a member's rights where the member has protection from tax charges: Entitlement to take pension before normal retirement age

Entitlement to take pension before normal retirement age

[paragraph 21 and 22 Schedule 36 Finance Act 2004]

A member may have been entitled to receive benefits before normal retirement age (NRA) in the scheme they were a member of on 5 April 2006. (For example, they may be entitled to receive benefits at an age up to 10 years before NRA in the scheme, and NRA in the scheme may be age 60). The member may qualify to retain this entitlement after transferring out of that registered pension scheme.

The member qualifies to retain this right after transfer to another registered pension scheme if:

- the transferring scheme, immediately before 6 April 2006, was either:
    - a tax approved retirement benefits scheme, or
    - a deferred annuity contract, or
    - a former approved superannuation fund, or
    - a statutory pension scheme, or
    - a Parliamentary pension scheme, and
- the member was entitled under that scheme on 5 April 2006 to crystallise benefits before age 55, and
- that scheme's rules on 10 December 2003 conferred this right on at least some members of the scheme, and
- this included the member now transferring from that scheme (or would have done if he had been a scheme member on that date), and

- the transfer is part of a block transfer.

Payment of benefits at the earlier age will also depend on the rules of the receiving scheme allowing it.

When the member crystallises benefits from the scheme they have transferred into, the benefit payments will not be treated as unauthorised payments even though they are being paid earlier than the normal minimum pension age, providing:

- the member becomes entitled to all benefits under that scheme at the same time, and
- the member is not employed by a sponsoring employer in relation to that scheme after becoming entitled to a pension from that scheme.

BOX 19

2.161 RPSM14106010 – Technical Pages: Transfers: Transfers of pensions in payment, or rights where there is already an entitlement to benefits: Transfer of crystallised rights

Transfer of crystallised rights

Section 169(1B) to (1E)

It is possible within the tax rules on authorised payments to make a transfer from a registered pension scheme relating to a pension which is already in payment, or in the case of an unsecured or alternatively secured pension fund, where an entitlement to benefits has already arisen.

A pension in payment under a registered pension scheme, is capable of being transferred to another registered pension scheme and being regarded as a recognised transfer. This applies to any of the following:

- member's scheme pension,
- member's unsecured pension,
- member's alternatively secured pension,
- dependant's scheme pension,
- dependant's unsecured pension or,
- dependant's alternatively secured pension.

If the provision of benefits derived from the transfer meet certain conditions, then the benefits paid from the transfer in the receiving registered pension scheme are capable of being within the pension rules and being authorised payments. Any failure to meet the conditions will result in the amount transferred being regarded as an unauthorised payment.

The conditions will be set out in forthcoming regulations.

BOX 20

2.162 RPSM14106020 – Technical Pages: Transfers: Transfers of pensions in payment, or rights where there is already an entitlement to benefits: Transfer to an insurance company of pension in payment

Transfer to an insurance company of pension in payment

Section 169(1A)

Scheme pension

It is possible within the tax rules on authorised payments for a scheme pension in payment under a registered pension scheme to be transferred to an insurance company.

Such a transfer is capable of being a recognised transfer provided certain conditions are met. The main condition is that, although the insurance company is not acting within a registered pension scheme, the transfer as received is nonetheless applied to provide a pension which conforms to the pension rules for a member's scheme pension.

For example, if a registered pension scheme is paying scheme pensions and the scheme is later winding-up, it is possible for the sums and assets representing the rights concerned to be transferred to an insurance company to provide for those pensions. Whereas an insurance company acting outside of a registered pension scheme would not otherwise be able to pay a scheme pension, the continuation of the pension rules on a scheme pension will be possible such that the ongoing pension is capable of being an authorised payment.

Failure to be within the pension rules applying to an ongoing scheme pension will mean that the amount transferred will be regarded as an unauthorised payment.Continuation of the pension rules for a scheme pension by the receiving insurance company means that, for example, the transfer should not be used as an event to stop or reduce the pension other than permitted under the usual pension rules. Forthcoming regulations will set out the precise conditions.

BOX 21

2.163 RPSM14106030 – Technical Pages: Transfers: Transfers of pensions in payment, or rights where there is already an entitlement to benefits: Transfer to an insurance company of an annuity in payment

Transfer to an insurance company of an annuity in payment

Schedule 28 para 3(2B), 6(1B) and para 17(3) and 20(1B)

Where an insurance company is paying a:

- lifetime annuity,
- dependant's annuity,
- short-term annuity or,
- dependant's short-term annuity

  it is not doing so directly under a registered pension scheme but following the application of sums and assets formerly held under a registered pension scheme.

If a transfer of an annuity took place, given that no registered pension scheme is involved, it would not be a recognised transfer. Nor therefore would such a transfer fall within the provisions within the tax rules relating to transfers of pensions in payment under registered pension schemes. Nonetheless, it is possible within the tax rules for authorised payments for a lifetime annuity or dependant's annuity in payment to be transferred from one insurance company to another.

Certain conditions must be met. If they are not, then the amount transferred will be regarded as an unauthorised payment.

The conditions will be specified in regulations.

BOX 22

2.164 RPSM14106040 – Technical Pages: Transfers: Transfers of pensions in payment, or rights where there is already an entitlement to benefits: Transfer of rights where previous entitlement to the payment of unsecured pension or alternatively secured pension

Transfer of rights where previous entitlement to the payment of unsecured pension or alternatively secured pension

Section 169(1D) and (1E)

It is possible within the tax rules on authorised payments for an unsecured pension or an alternatively secured pension under a registered pension scheme (whether payable to the member or a dependant) to be transferred to another registered pension scheme. This also applies where entitlement to an unsecured or alternatively secured pension exists but no payments of pension were actually being drawn under the transferring scheme.

More details will follow when regulations have been laid. The regulations are likely to include conditions that no benefit crystallisation event is regarded as taking place directly as a result of the transfer and no new entitlement to a pension commencement lump sum arises.

BOX 23

2.165 RPSM14106050 – Technical Pages: Transfers: Transfers of pensions in payment, or rights where there is already an entitlement to benefits: Transfer within a registered pension scheme

Pensions in payment or rights where there is already an entitlement to benefits

Schedule 28

It may happen that a scheme administrator of registered pension scheme makes a transfer from one unsecured pension fund of a member to another unsecured pension fund of the same member within the same registered pension scheme.

For the purpose of the tax rules, such a transfer within a registered pension scheme is disregarded. That is, under the tax rules, the sums and assets transferred continue to be treated as part of the original arrangement. This is to counter the use of a transfer as a means of circumventing the pension rules as would have applied if a transfer did not take place.

This condition applies to transfers within a registered pension scheme of:

- member's alternatively secured pension fund (Schedule 28 paragraph 11(5)),
- member's unsecured pension fund (Schedule 28 paragraph 8(4)),
- dependant's unsecured pension fund (Schedule 28 paragraph 22(3)),
- dependant's alternatively secured pension fund (Schedule 28 paragraph 25(4)).

The above applies equally to transfers between funds for the same individual, whether those funds are held in respect of that individual as a member or as a dependant.

BOX 24

2.166 RPSM14107010 – Technical Pages: Transfers: General points for transfers: Transfers must be made between pension schemes

Transfers must be made between pension schemes

[section 266]

A scheme administrator of a registered pension scheme should make sure that the person to whom they are transferring funds is someone with a position of responsibility in the receiving scheme.

A transfer is not a recognised transfer unless it is:

- between registered pension schemes, or
- from a registered pension scheme to a qualifying recognised overseas pension scheme.

Non-recognised transfers incur tax charges.

Where the receiving scheme is an 'insured scheme', but the transfer payment is not made directly to the scheme administrator or an insurance company which issues policies under the receiving scheme, the scheme administrator of the transferring registered pension scheme is liable to a maximum penalty of £3,000.

An 'insured scheme' is a pension scheme where all the income and other assets are invested in policies of insurance.

BOX 25

2.167 RPSM14107020 – Technical Pages: Transfers: General points for transfers: Form of transferred rights

Form of transferred rights

Subject to the rules of the pension schemes concerned, either assets (which includes insurance policies) or cash funds, or a combination of the two, can be transferred provided they represent the full value of the member's rights to be transferred.

BOX 26

2.168 RPSM14107030 – Technical Pages: Transfers: General points for transfers: Fragmentation – splitting rights between recipient schemes

Fragmentation – splitting rights between recipient schemes

If the rules of the schemes involved allow this, and benefits are not yet in payment, a transfer value may be split and each part transferred to separate destination schemes.

Where an individual has enhanced protection, the normal rules on permitted transfers apply (see RPSM03104090). So if the transfer is not a permitted transfer, the member loses enhanced protection.

BOX 27

2.169 RPSM14107040 – Technical Pages: Transfers: General points for transfers: Partial transfers

Partial transfers

A transfer of part of a member's pension rights in a registered pension scheme leaving the remaining rights in the scheme is a recognised transfer providing:

- it is made to either another registered pension scheme or a qualifying recognised overseas pension scheme, and
- the pension rights are uncrystallised.

BOX 28

2.170 RPSM14107050 – Technical Pages: Transfers: General points for transfers: Reporting transfers to HMRC

Reporting transfers to HMRC

Registered Pension Scheme Return

The Registered Pension Scheme Return is for a scheme administrator to complete, but this should only be done at HMRC's request. The Return can be submitted through the Pension Schemes Service Online, which can be found on the HMRC website.

If completing the Registered Pension Scheme Return, the scheme administrator must report the following information concerning transfers to HMRC on it:

- the amount transferred to other pension schemes that tax year'
- the amount received as transfers from other pension schemes that tax year.

The Registered Pension Scheme Return must be received by HMRC by 31 January following the tax year it relates to.

See RPSM12301400 for further guidance on the Registered Pension Scheme Return.

Event Report

A scheme administrator must report to HMRC, using the online Event Report:

- a transfer to a qualifying recognised overseas pension scheme,
- any transfer which is an unauthorised member payment (for example, a transfer to an employer-financed retirement benefits scheme).

The Event Report must be received by HMRC by 31 January following the end of the tax year in which the transfer took place (but see RPSM12301020 where the scheme is wound up).

Unlike the Registered Pension Scheme Return, the Event Report is to be completed in all cases, without HMRC requesting it.

See RPSM123001010 for further guidance on the Event Report.

PART B

International transfers

2.171 BOX 1: RPSM13100040 – Technical Pages: International: Enhancement: General principles. General principles of international enhancement

BOX 2: RPSM13100110 – Technical Pages: International: Enhancement: Non-residence factor

BOX 3: RPSM13100120 – Technical Pages: International: Enhancement: Non-residence factor: Non-residence after 5 April 2006

BOX 4: RPSM13100130 – Technical Pages: International: Enhancement: Non-residence factor: Active membership period

BOX 5: RPSM13100140 – Technical Pages: International: Enhancement: Non-residence factor: Relevant overseas individual

BOX 6: RPSM13100150 – Technical Pages: International: Enhancement: Non-residence factor: Who is not a relevant overseas individual?

BOX 7: RPSM13100160 – Technical Pages: International: Enhancement: Non-residence factor: Pension scheme arrangements

BOX 8: RPSM13100170 – Technical Pages: International: Enhancement: Non-residence factor: Notifications procedure

BOX 9: RPSM13100180 – Technical Pages: International: Enhancement: Non-residence factor: Example of notifying HMRC

BOX 10: RPSM13100190 – Technical Pages: International: Enhancement: Non-residence factor: Separate notifications needed

BOX 11: RPSM13100200 – Technical Pages: International: Enhancement: Non-residence factor: Example of separate notifications

BOX 12: RPSM13100210 – Technical Pages: International: Enhancement: Non-residence factor: Notification and hybrid arrangements

BOX 13: RPSM13100220 – Technical Pages: International: Enhancement: Non-residence factor: After HMRC notified

BOX 14: RPSM13100230 – Technical Pages: International: Enhancement: Non-residence factor: Benefit payment

BOX 15: RPSM13100240 – Technical Pages: International: Enhancement: Non-residence factor: Cash balance arrangement

BOX 16: RPSM13100250 – Technical Pages: International: Enhancement: Non-residence factor: Example for a cash balance arrangement

BOX 17: RPSM13100260 – Technical Pages: International: Enhancement: Non-residence factor: Other money purchase arrangement

BOX 18: RPSM13100270 – Technical Pages: International: Enhancement: Non-residence factor: Example for other money purchase arrangement

BOX 19: RPSM13100280 – Technical Pages: International: Enhancement: Non-residence factor: Defined benefits arrangement

BOX 20: RPSM13100290 – Technical Pages: International: Enhancement: Non-residence factor: Example 1 for a defined benefits arrangement

BOX 21: RPSM13100300 – Technical Pages: International: Enhancement: Non-residence factor: Example 2 for a defined benefits arrangement

BOX 22: RPSM13100310 – Technical Pages: International: Enhancement: Non-residence factor: Hybrid arrangement

BOX 23: RPSM13100410 – Technical Pages: International: Enhancement: Recognised overseas scheme transfer factor

BOX 24: RPSM13100420 – Technical Pages: International: Enhancement: Recognised overseas scheme transfer factor: Post 5 April 2005 transfers

BOX 25: RPSM13100430 – Technical Pages: International: Enhancement: Recognised overseas scheme transfer factor: Not a relevant overseas individual

BOX 26: RPSM13100440 – Technical Pages: International: Enhancement: Recognised overseas scheme transfer factor: Notification procedure

BOX 27: RPSM13100450 – Technical Pages: International: Enhancement: Recognised overseas scheme transfer factor: What happens after HMRC has been notified?

BOX 28: RPSM13100460 – Technical Pages: International: Enhancement: Recognised overseas scheme transfer factor: Benefit payment

BOX 29: RPSM13100470 – Technical Pages: International: Enhancement: Recognised overseas scheme transfer factor: How to calculate the factor

BOX 30: RPSM13100480 – Technical Pages: International: Enhancement: Recognised overseas scheme transfer factor: Examples of how to calculate the factor

BOX 31: RPSM13100490 – Technical Pages: International: Enhancement: Recognised overseas scheme transfer factor: The relevant relievable amount

BOX 32: RPSM13100500 – Technical Pages: International: Enhancement: Recognised overseas scheme transfer factor: Cash balance arrangement relevant relievable amount

BOX 33: RPSM13100510 – Technical Pages: International: Enhancement: Recognised overseas scheme transfer factor: Example of relevant relievable amount for a cash balance arrangement

BOX 34: RPSM13100520 – Technical Pages: International: Enhancement: Recognised overseas scheme transfer factor: Other money purchase arrangement relevant relievable amount

BOX 35: RPSM13100530 – Technical Pages: International: Enhancement: Recognised overseas scheme transfer factor: Example of other money purchase arrangement relevant relievable amount

BOX 36: RPSM13100540 – Technical Pages: International: Enhancement: Recognised overseas scheme transfer factor: Defined benefits arrangement relevant relievable amount

BOX 37: RPSM13100550 – Technical Pages: International: Enhancement: Recognised overseas scheme transfer factor: Example 1 of defined benefits arrangement relevant relievable amount

BOX 38: RPSM13100560 – Technical Pages: International: Enhancement: Recognised overseas scheme transfer factor: Example 2 of defined benefits arrangement relevant relievable amount

BOX 39: RPSM13100570 – Technical Pages: International: Enhancement: Recognised overseas scheme transfer factor: Hybrid arrangement relevant relievable amount.

PART C

International Enhancement: non-residence factors and recognised overseas schemes factors

BOX 1

2.172 RPSM13100040 – Technical Pages: International: Enhancement: General principles

General principles of international enhancement

[s221–226)]

The lifetime allowance is an overall ceiling on the amount of UK tax-relieved pension savings that an individual can draw from registered pension schemes and certain overseas pension schemes. If when a benefit crystallisation event occurs (see example at RPSM11102040) the total value of an individual's benefits exceeds their unused lifetime allowance then that individual will be subject to a lifetime allowance charge (RPSM11103000 refers).

Everyone is entitled to the standard lifetime allowance, which is £1.5million in the 2005/06 tax year and will increase in subsequent years. However, in certain circumstances an individual can notify HMRC that they are entitled to a lifetime allowance that is higher than the standard amount: an 'enhanced' lifetime allowance. If so, a lifetime allowance charge would only arise when a benefit crystallisation event occurred if the total value of that individual's benefits exceeded their unused enhanced lifetime allowance.

An individual can notify HMRC of an entitlement to enhance their lifetime allowance in two international situations in which benefits in a registered pension scheme are built up without UK tax relief. These are:

1 membership of a registered pension scheme whilst a relevant overseas individual (see RPSM13100100 to RPSM13100310), and

2 transfer to a registered pension scheme from a recognised overseas pension scheme (see RPSM13100410 to RPSM13100570).

Even if an individual is entitled to enhance their lifetime allowance they may not need to do so. A notification will be beneficial where the total value of an individual's UK tax relieved pension scheme benefits is likely to exceed the standard lifetime allowance.

BOX 2

2.173 RPSM13100110 – Technical Pages: International: Enhancement: Non-residence factor

Overview

[s221–223]

Generally speaking, where an individual is working abroad they will not receive UK tax relief on contributions to, or the accrual of benefits under, a registered pension scheme.

Sections 221–223 provide broadly for an individual's lifetime allowance to be enhanced for such a period of overseas service after 5 April 2006. That is intended to offset the benefits relating to the unrelieved contributions or accrual for that period and prevents them giving rise to a lifetime allowance charge.

BOX 3

2.174 RPSM13100120 – Technical Pages: International: Enhancement: Non-residence factor: Non-residence after 5 April 2006

Basic principles: non-residence after 5 April 2006

[s221]

An individual who has an arrangement under a registered pension scheme has to be a relevant overseas individual during any part of an active membership period to qualify for a non-residence lifetime allowance enhancement.

The individual's lifetime allowance will be enhanced by a factor that is called a non-residence factor. That is calculated by dividing the amount of contributions to, or accrual under, the individual's pension arrangement during that part-period by the standard lifetime allowance for the tax year in which that part-period ends.

RPSM13100130 sets out what is an active membership period.

RPSM13100140 and RPSM13100150 set out who is and who is not a relevant overseas individual.

It is possible to be a relevant overseas individual during more than one part of an active membership period relating to the same pension arrangement. For example, an individual could work overseas for 5 years, return to the UK for a year and then work overseas for another 5 years. That individual's lifetime allowance will be enhanced by the aggregate of the non-residence factors calculated separately for each of those part-periods under that arrangement.

RPSM13100240 to RPSM13100310 explain how the non-residence factor is calculated for each type of pension arrangement.

BOX 4

2.175 RPSM13100130 – Technical Pages: International: Enhancement: Non-residence factor: Active membership period

Basic principles: active membership period

[s221(4)]

An active membership period is defined in section 221(4) and relates to an individual's membership of an arrangement under a registered pension scheme. It begins on the later of the following dates:

- the date when benefits first began to accrue to or in respect of an individual under the pension arrangement, and
- 6 April 2006.

It ends on the earlier of the following dates:

- immediately before the benefit crystallisation event, and
- the date when benefits ceased to accrue to or in respect of the individual under the pension arrangement.

BOX 5

2.176 RPSM13100140 – Technical Pages: International: Enhancement: Non-residence factor: Relevant overseas individual

Basic principles: who is a relevant overseas individual?

[s221(3)]

A relevant overseas individual is defined in section 221(3) as someone who either is not a relevant UK individual (see RPSM13100430) under section 189 or is a relevant UK individual in specified circumstances.

Not a relevant UK individual

Someone who is not a relevant UK individual:

- does not have relevant UK earnings chargeable to UK income tax,
- is not UK tax resident,
- was not UK tax resident both at any time during the previous five tax years and when they became a member of the scheme, and
- does not have general earnings from overseas crown employment subject to UK tax (and neither does their spouse).

Relevant UK individual in specified circumstances

Someone who is a relevant UK individual in specified circumstances:

- meets all of the above requirements for not being a relevant UK individual except for the third bullet point, and
- is not employed by a UK tax resident employer.

An individual who falls into this specified category will be eligible for UK tax relief on the basic amount (£3,600 in 2006–2007) for up to five years' overseas service if they are a member of a registered pension scheme that operates relief at source (see RPSM05101310). But if they are working abroad for an overseas tax resident company its contributions will not attract UK tax relief.

It is possible to be a relevant overseas individual during more than one part of an active membership period relating to the same pension arrangement. For example, an individual could work overseas for 5 years, return to the UK for a year and then work overseas for another 5 years. That individual's lifetime allowance will be enhanced by the aggregate of the non-residence factors calculated separately for each of those part-periods under that arrangement.

BOX 6

2.177 RPSM13100150 – Technical Pages: International: Enhancement: Non-residence factor: Who is not a relevant overseas individual?

Basic principles: who is not a relevant overseas individual?

An individual will not be a relevant overseas individual for any tax year in which they are a relevant UK individual. So where someone who is resident and working in the UK goes to work overseas on 25 November 2006 they will not be a relevant overseas individual for the 2006–2007 tax year, even if they become non-resident at the time they leave the UK. They will have had relevant UK earnings chargeable to UK income tax up to that date and so will be a relevant UK individual in the 2006–2007 tax year. For a similar reason if they return to work in the UK on 25 May 2009 they will not be a relevant overseas individual in the 2009–2010 tax year.

In these circumstances enhancement by a non-residence factor would not be appropriate in respect of the 2006–2007 and 2009–2010 tax years. That is because the individual is eligible to receive UK tax relief under section 188 on their contributions to a registered pension scheme during those years.

BOX 7

2.178 RPSM13100160 – Technical Pages: International: Enhancement: Non-residence factor: Pension scheme arrangements

Pension scheme arrangements

[s222 to s223]

The non-residence factor (see RPSM13100120) is calculated in one of a number of different ways depending on whether the individual's arrangement under the registered pension scheme is:

- a cash balance arrangement (see RPSM13100240),
- an other money purchase arrangement (see RPSM13100260),
- a defined benefits arrangement (see RPSM13100280), or
- a hybrid arrangement (see RPSM13100310).

Normally there will be only one type of arrangement in a registered pension scheme. If that is the case the basis of calculation of the individual's non-residence factor will be determined by which of the above types of arrangement it is. However, an individual could be accruing benefits under different types of arrangement within a single registered pension scheme that has multiple arrangements. For example, a member of a defined benefits scheme could have two types of arrangement if they were paying additional voluntary contributions, one being a defined benefit arrangement and the other a money purchase arrangement. If that is the case separate non-residence factors will need to be calculated for each of the types of arrangement under which the individual is accruing benefits.

BOX 8

2.179 RPSM13100170 – Technical Pages: International: Enhancement: Non-residence factor: Notifications procedure

Notification procedure

[Reg 7 The Pension Schemes (Enhanced Lifetime Allowance) Regulations 2005]

An individual has to notify HMRC of their entitlement to a non-residence factor in accordance with Regulation 7 of The Pension Schemes (Enhanced Lifetime Allowance) Regulations 2005 – to be laid. Notification should be made on form APSS 202 no later than five years after 31 January following the end of the tax year in which the 'accrual period' ends. That happens when the earliest of the following events occurs:

- immediately before a benefit crystallisation event in relation to the individual's arrangement
- the individual ceases to be a relevant overseas individual (see RPSM13100140), and
- benefits cease to accrue to or in respect of the individual under the arrangement.

RPSM13100180 gives an example.

The form APSS 202 should be used to notify HMRC of an entitlement to a non-residence factor for part of an active membership period relating to a pension arrangement during which the individual was a relevant overseas individual.

Separate APSS 202 notification forms should be submitted to HMRC in the certain circumstances. RPSM13100190 sets out the circumstances where separate notification is required.

A single APSS 202 form can be submitted where an individual has been accruing benefits under different types of arrangement within a single registered pension scheme that has multiple arrangements (see RPSM13100160). Such an individual can notify HMRC of a non-residence factor relating to all of their arrangements under the scheme. They will need to fill in all of the sections of the form that apply to those arrangements.

Special consideration needs to be given to an individual who is a member of a hybrid arrangement (see RPSM13100210 for more details).

Incorrect information supplied

If an individual has received a certificate and realises later that the information provided on the APSS 202 notification form was incorrect they should send another form to HMRC. They should complete all of the relevant boxes as if it was a new notification, but must tick the 'yes' box at 1.5 on the form and enter there the reference number that is shown on the certificate. In addition, if after the certificate was issued there has been a benefit crystallisation event in respect of any of the individual's pension arrangements they must inform HMRC about that in a covering letter.

BOX 9

2.180 RPSM13100180 – Technical Pages: International: Enhancement: Non-residence factor: Example of notifying HMRC

Example of notifying HMRC of entitlement to a non-residence factor

Phillip returned from an overseas secondment with an overseas resident employer on 1 June 2007. He was a relevant UK individual in the 2007–2008 tax year so he ceased to be a relevant overseas individual with effect from 5 April 2007. At that time he was still accruing benefits under the arrangement and had not been paid benefits from it.

To claim an enhancement Phillip must submit a completed form APSS 202 to HMRC no later than five years after 31 January 2008, i e by 31 January 2013.

Phillip was then seconded to work overseas on 1 January 2009. So he became a relevant overseas individual with effect from 6 April 2009 (the start of the following tax year). He returned to work in the UK on 1 January 2011 so he ceased to be a relevant overseas individual on 5 April 2010 as he became a relevant UK individual during the 2010–2011 tax year. On 5 April 2010, Philip was still accruing benefits under his arrangement and had not received benefits from it.

Phillip must submit another completed form to HMRC no later than five years after 31 January 2011, i e by 31 January 2016.

BOX 10

2.181 RPSM13100190 – Technical Pages: International: Enhancement: Non-residence factor: Separate notifications needed

When separate notifications of a non-residence factor are needed

Separate APSS 202 notification forms should be submitted to HMRC in the following circumstances.

Relevant overseas individual during more than one part of an active membership period

Where an individual is a relevant overseas individual during more than one part of an active membership period relating to the same pension arrangement a separate notification should be made for each part-period.

Relevant overseas individual in more than one pension scheme

Where an individual is a relevant overseas individual during part of an active membership period relating to more than one pension scheme a separate notification should be made for each pension scheme.

Benefit crystallisation event occurs in an arrangement whilst the individual is a relevant overseas individual and is still accruing benefits under the arrangement

One APSS 202 form should relate to the part of the active membership period during which the individual was a relevant overseas individual up to the date of that benefit crystallisation event. Another APSS 202 form should relate to the part-period from the same start date to the date of the following benefit crystallisation event. The individual should tick box 1.5 on the second form, to show that it is amending the first notification, and should enter on that form the reference number shown on the certificate issued in response to the first notification. Any figures entered at box 4.1 or box 6.1 on the second form should be calculated by adding the rights or benefit entitlement used up on the first benefit crystallisation event to the rights or benefit entitlement as at the date of the second benefit crystallisation event.

However, if the second benefit crystallisation event occurs before the end of the notification time limit relating to the first benefit crystallisation event, and before the individual has submitted a form APSS 202 in respect of the part-period up to the date of the first benefit crystallisation event, the individual can submit one form instead of two. That form should relate to the same part-period as would be covered by the second form referred to above. Any figures entered at box 4.1 or box 6.1 on the form should be calculated by adding the rights or benefit entitlement used up on the first benefit crystallisation event to the rights or benefit entitlement as at the date of the second benefit crystallisation event. Box 1.5 should not be ticked as this form is not amending an earlier notification. The form must be submitted within the notification time limit relating to the first benefit crystallisation event.

RPSM131002000 gives an example.

BOX 11

2.182 RPSM13100200 – Technical Pages: International: Enhancement: Non-residence factor: Example of separate notifications

Example of when separate notification to HMRC of a non-residence factor is required

On 6 April 2006, Tom was a member of a defined benefits arrangement under a registered pension scheme and was working abroad. His first benefit crystallisation event from the scheme occurred on 19 July 2007 whilst he was still accruing benefits under the scheme and working abroad. His second benefit crystallisation event occurred on 16 October 2012 when he retired.

Following his first benefit crystallisation event Tom should submit a form APSS 202 showing the value of his benefit entitlement as at 6 April 2006 and as at 19 July 2007. He will then receive a certificate giving him a non-residence factor based on the increase in the value of his benefit entitlement from 6 April 2006 to 19 July 2007.

After his second benefit crystallisation event, Tom should submit a second form APSS 202 showing the value of his benefit entitlement as at 6 April 2006 and as at 16 October 2012, and should tick box 1.5 to show that this form is amending the earlier notification. He will then receive a certificate giving him a non-residence factor based on the increase in the value of his benefit entitlement from 6 April 2006 to 16 October 2012 which replaces his earlier certificate.

However, if Tom had not submitted a form APSS 202 relating to the part-period up to his first benefit crystallisation event before the occurrence of his second benefit crystallisation event, he could then have submitted instead a form APSS 202 showing the value of his benefit entitlement as at 6 April 2006 and as at 16 October 2012. He would have received a certificate giving him a non-residence factor based on the increase in the value of his benefit entitlement from 6 April 2006 to 16 October 2012.

BOX 12

2.183 RPSM13100210 – Technical Pages: International: Enhancement: Non-residence factor: Notification and hybrid arrangements

Notifying HMRC of non-residence factor for a hybrid arrangement

If an individual has a hybrid arrangement within a scheme, and also has one or more other arrangements under that scheme, total figures for the hybrid arrangement and for the other arrangements may have to be shown in section 4, 5 or 6 of the APSS 202 form.

This is because the hybrid arrangement is treated as if it were a cash balance arrangement, other money purchase arrangement, or defined benefits arrangement when calculating a non-residence factor (see RPSM1310310).

For example, if the highest amount available under the hybrid arrangement was that calculated on a cash balance basis, and the individual was also claiming in respect of a cash balance arrangement, the total closing values for both the hybrid arrangement and the cash balance arrangement should be shown in box 4.1, and the total opening values for both arrangements should be shown in box 4.2.

BOX 13

2.184 RPSM13100220 – Technical Pages: International: Enhancement: Non-residence factor: After HMRC notified

What happens after HMRC has been notified of entitlement to a non-residence factor

After receiving the APSS 202 notification form HMRC will send the individual a certificate stating the non-residence factor that the individual can use to enhance their lifetime allowance. Each certificate will have a unique reference number, and will also state the type of lifetime allowance enhancement, the individual's National Insurance number (if they have one), the date of issue of the certificate and the date from which it is valid.

Individuals must retain all documents relating to the information submitted to HMRC on form APSS 202 for a period of 6 years beginning with the day on which the notification is given to HMRC. They may wish to keep the documentation for longer than that in case a query arises subsequently. If they do not do so and there is a query then they could ask HMRC for a copy of the certificate and of the backing paperwork. They could also authorise the administrator of their registered pension scheme to view, or receive a copy of, the certificate.

Getting a certificate amended

If an individual has received a certificate and realises later that the information provided on the APSS 202 notification form was incorrect they should send an amended notification to HMRC. They should complete all of the relevant boxes as if it was a new notification, but must tick the 'yes' box at 1.5 on the form and enter there the reference number that is shown on the original certificate. In addition, if after the certificate was issued there has been a benefit crystallisation event in respect of any of the individual's pension arrangements they should inform HMRC about that in a covering letter.

BOX 14

2.185 RPSM13100230 – Technical Pages: International: Enhancement: Non-residence factor: Benefit payment

Notifying details of the non-residence factor when benefits are paid

If an individual intends to rely on a non-residence factor, they will have to notify the scheme administrator of their registered pension scheme when a benefit crystallisation event occurs. The individual will need to provide the administrator with the unique reference number and the enhancement factor details shown on the certificate.

The administrator will have to include information about the benefit crystallisation event on the Event Report that is made to HMRC (see RPSM12300030 [NWL]). The administrator will need also to account for any lifetime allowance charge on the quarterly Accounting for Tax return to HMRC.

If an individual has not notified HMRC of an entitlement to a non-residence factor before a benefit crystallisation event occurs a lifetime allowance charge may arise and the scheme administrator may have paid the tax due. If the individual subsequently provides the administrator of their registered pension scheme with the unique reference number and the enhancement factor details shown on the certificate, the administrator may then send an amended Accounting for Tax return to HMRC and obtain a repayment.

If an individual who is a member of a defined benefits arrangement (see RPSM13100280) thinks that a non-standard factor should be used to value their pension entitlement, they should submit form APSS 202 as normal, together with a covering letter. A certificate will initially be issued using the standard valuation factor of 20. However, if HMRC has agreed a different valuation factor then this can be amended subsequently.

BOX 15

2.186 RPSM13100240 – Technical Pages: International: Enhancement: Non-residence factor: Cash balance arrangement

How to calculate the non-residence factor for a cash balanced arrangement

[s222(3)–(5)] [s277]

For each part of an active membership period (see RPSM13100130) during which the individual is a relevant overseas individual (see RPSM13100140), the cash balance arrangement non-residence factor is established as follows:

(a) obtain the value of the individual's rights under the cash balance arrangement as at the latest of the following dates:
- the date when the individual became a relevant overseas individual,
- the date when benefits first began to accrue to or in respect of the individual under the cash balance arrangement, and
- 6 April 2006.

(b) obtain the value of the individual's rights under the cash balance arrangement as at the earliest of the following dates:
- immediately before the benefit crystallisation event,
- the date when the individual ceased to be a relevant overseas individual, and
- the date when benefits ceased to accrue to or in respect of the individual under the cash balance arrangement.

(c) deduct the value of a. from the value of b.

(d) express the resulting amount in c. as a factor of the standard lifetime allowance as at the earliest date in b.

If there was an earlier part of the active membership period relating to the same arrangement during which the individual was a relevant overseas individual the two factors for the two part- periods should be aggregated.

The individual's rights under the cash balance arrangement are represented by the amount which would be available to provide benefits to or in respect of the individual if they became entitled to the immediate payment of them at the applicable date (as determined under a or b above). The value of the individual's rights is established using the valuation assumptions set out in section 277. These are as follows:

- the individual concerned has reached any designated age as must have been reached to avoid any reduction in their benefits on account of their age, and
- their benefits should be valued on the basis that they are not physically or mentally impaired.

RPSM13100250 gives an example of how to calculate the non-residence factor for a cash balance arrangement.

This page will be updated when The Pension Schemes (Part 4 of the Finance Act 2004: Transitional [and Transitory] Provisions) Order 2005 is laid.

BOX 16

2.187 RPSM13100250 – Technical Pages: International: Enhancement: Non-residence factor: Example for a cash balance arrangement

Example of calculating the non-residence factor for a cash balance arrangement

Lee began to accrue benefits under his cash balance arrangement on 6 April 2004. He was seconded to work overseas on 24 October 2006 so he became a relevant overseas individual on 6 April 2007. The value of his pension rights in his cash balance arrangement as at 6 April 2007 amounted to £500,000.

Lee returned to work in the UK on 6 May 2011 (before a benefit crystallisation event and before he ceased to accrue benefits under the cash balance arrangement). He therefore ceased to be a relevant overseas individual on 5 April 2011. The value of his pension rights in his cash balance arrangement as at 5 April 2011 amounted to £950,000.

£950,000 – £500,000 = £450,000

The cash balance arrangement non-residence factor is therefore 0.25. That is calculated by dividing £450,000 by the standard lifetime allowance for the 2010–2011 tax year (£1.8million).

£450,000/£1.8 million = 0.25

BOX 17

2.188 RPSM13100260 – Technical Pages: International: Enhancement: Non-residence factor: Other money purchase arrangement

How to calculate the non-residence factor for an other money purchase arrangement

[s222(6) & (7)]

For each part of an active membership period (see RPSM13100130) during which the individual is a relevant overseas individual (see RPSM13100140), the other money purchase arrangement non-residence factor is calculated in the following way.

Establish the total amount of contributions made by or in respect of the individual to the other money purchase arrangement between the dates determined under a. and b. below:

(a) the latest of the following dates:

- the date when the individual became a relevant overseas individual,
- the date when benefits first began to accrue to or in respect of the individual under the other money purchase arrangement, and
- 6 April 2006.

(b) the earliest of the following dates:

- immediately before the benefit crystallisation event,
- the date when the individual ceased to be a relevant overseas individual, and
- the date when benefits ceased to accrue to or in respect of the individual under the other money purchase arrangement.

Express the resulting amount as a factor of the standard lifetime allowance as at the date in b. above.

If there was an earlier part of the active membership period relating to the arrangement during which the individual was a relevant overseas individual the two factors for the two part-periods should be aggregated.

RPSM13100270 gives an example of how to calculate the non-residence factor for an other money purchase arrangement.

This page will be updated when The Pension Schemes (Part 4 of the Finance Act 2004: Transitional [and Transitory] Provisions) Order 2005 is laid

BOX 18

2.189 RPSM13100270 – Technical Pages: International: Enhancement: Non-residence factor: Example for other money purchase arrangement

Example of calculating the non-residence factor for an other money purchase arrangement

Marilyn began to accrue benefits under her other money purchase arrangement on 6 January 2006. She was seconded to work overseas on 6 November 2006 and so became a relevant overseas individual on 6 April 2007.

Marilyn returned to work in the UK on 6 May 2010 and so ceased to be a relevant overseas individual on 5 April 2010. That was before a benefit crystallisation event and before she ceased to accrue benefits under the other money purchase arrangement.

The total contributions made by and in respect of Marilyn between 6 April 2007 and 5 April 2010 amounted to £175,000.

The other money purchase arrangement non-residence factor is therefore 0.1. This is calculated by dividing £175,000 by £1.75 million (the standard lifetime allowance for the 2009–2010 tax year).

£175,000/£1.75 million = 0.1

BOX 19

2.190 RPSM13100280 – Technical Pages: International: Enhancement: Non-residence factor: Defined benefits arrangement

How to calculate the non-residence factor for a defined benefits arrangement

[s223(3) & (4)] [s277]

For each part of an active membership period (see RPSM13100130) during which the individual is a relevant overseas individual (see RPSM13100140), the defined benefits arrangement non-residence factor is established as follows:

(a) multiply the individual's pension entitlement under the defined benefits arrangement as at the latest of the following dates by the relevant valuation factor of 20 or a factor greater than 20 as agreed by HMRC (see RPSM11104230):

- the date when the individual became a relevant overseas individual,
- the date when benefits first began to accrue to or in respect of the individual under the defined benefits arrangement, and
- 6 April 2006.

Where the registered pension scheme rules provide for a separate lump sum that is not a commutation of pension it is necessary to take that into account as well. That is done by adding to the amount resulting from the above calculation the separate lump sum entitlement that the individual has under the defined benefits arrangement as at the latest date above. This only applies if the lump sum entitlement is not linked to the individual's pension entitlement so that their prospective pension entitlement is not reduced as a result of taking the lump sum.

(b) multiply the individual's pension entitlement under the defined benefits arrangement as at the earliest of the following dates by the relevant valuation factor of 20 (or a factor greater than 20 as agreed by HMRC):

- immediately before the benefit crystallisation event,
- the date when the individual ceased to be a relevant overseas individual, and
- the date when benefits ceased to accrue to or in respect of the individual under the defined benefits arrangement.

Where the registered pension scheme rules provide for a separate lump sum that is not a commutation of pension it is necessary to take that into account as well. That is done by adding to the amount resulting from the above calculation the separate lump sum entitlement that the individual has under the defined benefits arrangement as at the earliest date above. This only applies if the lump sum entitlement is not linked to the individual's pension entitlement so that their prospective pension entitlement is not reduced as a result of taking the lump sum.

(c) deduct the result of a from the result of b.

(d) express the resulting amount as a factor of the standard lifetime allowance as at the date in b.

If there was an earlier part of the active membership period relating to the arrangement during which the individual was a relevant overseas individual the two factors for the two part-periods should be aggregated.

The individual's pension entitlement under the defined benefits arrangement is the annual rate of pension which would be payable to or in respect of the individual if they became entitled to payment of it at the applicable date (as determined under a or b above). The individual's lump sum entitlement under the defined benefits arrangement is the amount of lump sum which would be payable to or in respect of the individual if they became entitled to payment of it at the applicable date.

(a) Both the pension entitlement and the lump sum entitlement are established using the valuation assumptions set out in section 277. These are as follows:

- the individual concerned has reached any designated age as must have been reached to avoid any reduction in their benefits on account of their age, and
- their benefits should be valued on the basis that they are not physically or mentally impaired.

RPSM13100290 and RPSM13100300 give some examples.

This page will be updated when The Pension Schemes (Part 4 of the Finance Act 2004: Transitional [and Transitory] Provisions) Order 2005 is laid.

BOX 20

2.191 RPSM13100290 – Technical Pages: International: Enhancement: Non-residence factor: Example 1 for a defined benefits arrangement

Example 1 of how to calculate the non-residence factor for a defined benefits arrangement

Vicky began working overseas on 6 December 2006 and so she became a relevant overseas individual on 6 April 2007. She began to accrue benefits under her defined benefits arrangement on 6 November 2006. The latest date for the purposes of step a. on RPSM13100280 is therefore 6 April 2007.

Vicky's pension entitlement as at 6 April 2007 was £40,000 p.a. She had an option under the rules of the registered pension scheme defined benefits arrangement to commute part of her pension entitlement for a lump sum on retirement. She was not entitled to a separate lump sum.

£40,000 x 20 = £800,000

Vicky returned to work in the UK on 6 June 2009 and so she ceased to be a relevant overseas individual on 5 April 2009. That was before a benefit crystallisation event and before she ceased to accrue benefits under the defined benefits arrangement. Her pension entitlement as at 5 April 2009 was £56,500 p.a

£56,500 x 20 = £1.13 million

£1.13 million – £800,000 = £330,000

The defined benefits arrangement non-residence factor is therefore 0.2. That is calculated by dividing £330,000 by £1.65 million (the standard lifetime allowance for the 2008–2009 tax year).

£330,000/£1.65 million = 0.2

BOX 21

2.192 RPSM13100300 – Technical Pages: International: Enhancement: Non-residence factor: Example 2 for a defined benefits arrangement

Example 2 of how to calculate the non-residence factor for a defined benefits arrangement

Anne began to accrue benefits under her defined benefits arrangement on 6 January 2006. She was seconded to work overseas on 6 January 2007 and so became a relevant overseas individual on 6 April 2007. The latest date for the purposes of step a. on RPSM13100280 is therefore 6 April 2007.

Anne's pension entitlement as at 6 April 2007 was £30,000 p.a. She was also entitled to a separate lump sum of £60,000.

(£30,000 x 20) + £60,000 = £660,000

Anne returned to work in the UK on 6 May 2009 and so ceased to be a relevant overseas individual on 5 April 2009. That was before a benefit crystallisation event and before she ceased to accrue benefits under the defined benefits arrangement. Anne's pension entitlement as at 5 April 2009 was £56,500 p.a. She was also entitled to a separate lump sum of £80,000.

(£56,500 x 20) + £80,000 = £1.21 million

£1.21 million – £660,000 = £550,000

The defined benefits arrangement non-residence factor is therefore 0.33. That is calculated by dividing £550,000 by £1.65 million (the standard lifetime allowance for the 2008–2009 tax year).

£550,000/ £1.65 million = 0.33

BOX 22

2.193 RPSM13100310 – Technical Pages: International: Enhancement: Non-residence factor: Hybrid arrangement

How to calculate the non-residence factor for a hybrid arrangement

[s223 (5)–(7)]

A hybrid arrangement is an arrangement that may, at any one time, provide one of two or three types of benefits in the form of cash balance benefits, other money purchase benefits, or defined benefits. There are effectively two or three potential outcomes but they are mutually exclusive so benefits are provided in only one of those ways. They should not be confused with schemes with multiple arrangements (see RPSM13100160) where benefits accrue separately under different types of arrangement within a single scheme.

An example of a hybrid arrangement is one which, on the member's retirement, will provide benefits calculated by reference to a pot of money available to that member, but subject to an underlying defined benefit promise calculated by reference to the member's final salary and length of service. Should the pot of money available provide less than the underlying defined benefit promise the benefits provided will be augmented up to the level promised. Alternatively, if the pot of money provides a greater level of benefits than the underlying defined benefit promise, the individual would receive the money purchase benefits up to the level that the pot of money will provide. So the benefits will be either money purchase benefits or defined benefits, but not both.

For each part of an active membership period (see RPSM13100130) during which the individual is a relevant overseas individual (see RPSM13100140), the hybrid arrangement non-residence factor is established as follows:

(a) if the benefits that may ultimately be provided under the arrangement may be cash balance benefits, calculate what would be the cash balance arrangement non-residence factor as set out in RPSM13100240 if the registered pension scheme were a cash balance arrangement,

(b) if the benefits that may ultimately be provided under the arrangement may be other money purchase benefits, calculate what would be the other money purchase arrangement non-residence factor as set out in RPSM13100260 if the registered pension scheme were any other type of money purchase arrangement,

(c) if the benefits that may ultimately be provided under the arrangement may be defined benefits, calculate what would be the defined benefits arrangement non-residence factor as set out in RPSM13100280 if the registered pension scheme were a defined benefits arrangement,

(d) select the greater or greatest non-residence factor from whichever of a., b., or c. above are relevant.

Example

Glenn's hybrid arrangement can provide either cash balance benefits, other money purchase benefits or defined benefits:

Glenn's potential cash balance arrangement non-residence factor is 0.1, his potential other money purchase non-residence factor is 0.05, and his potential defined benefits arrangement non-residence factor is 0.06.

Glenn's hybrid arrangement non-residence factor is therefore 0.1.

This page will be updated when The Pension Schemes (Part 4 of the Finance Act 2004: Transitional [and Transitory] Provisions) Order 2005 is laid.

BOX 23

2.194 RPSM13100410 – Technical Pages: International: Enhancement: Recognised overseas scheme transfer factor

Overview

[s224–226)]

Where there is a benefit crystallisation event a member of a registered pension scheme must count the value of all of those crystallised benefits against their unused lifetime allowance in order to determine whether or not a lifetime allowance charge arises.

Sections 224–226 provide for an individual's lifetime allowance to be enhanced where a recognised overseas scheme transfer of pension rights that is, a transfer to a registered pension scheme from a recognised overseas pension scheme (RPSM14103020 refers) is made after 5 April 2006 but before the benefit crystallisation event. That broadly offsets the benefits relating to the sums and assets transferred from a pension scheme in an overseas country and prevents them giving rise to a lifetime allowance charge.

It recognises that those sums and assets are likely to have been built up without UK tax relief. However, that will not always be the case. So sections 224–226 restrict the enhancement of the individual's lifetime allowance in such circumstances.

BOX 24

2.195 RPSM13100420 – Technical Pages: International: Enhancement: Recognised overseas scheme transfer factor: Post 5 April 2005 transfers

Transfers after 5 April 2006

[s224]

If after 5 April 2006 there is a recognised overseas scheme transfer of an individual's rights from an arrangement under a recognised overseas pension scheme to an arrangement under a registered pension scheme the individual's lifetime allowance may, on notification to HMRC, be enhanced by a factor which is called a recognised overseas scheme transfer factor.

The recognised overseas scheme transfer factor is calculated by dividing the amount of any sums and assets transferred by the standard lifetime allowance as at the date of the transfer. But if contributions made by or in respect of an individual to, or their accrual of benefits under, the overseas arrangement after 5 April 2006 received UK tax relief the amount transferred has to be reduced by the relevant relievable amount (see RPSM13100490).

The deduction of the relevant relievable amount ensures broadly that the enhancement does not include amounts transferred into the registered pension scheme that have benefited from UK tax relief after 5 April 2006 (for example because the individual has had migrant member relief on contributions to the overseas scheme). The relevant relievable amount relates to any part of the period during which the individual was an active member of the recognised overseas pension scheme and was not a relevant overseas individual.

BOX 25

2.196 RPSM13100430 – Technical Pages: International: Enhancement: Recognised overseas scheme transfer factor: Not a relevant overseas individual

Definition of not a relevant overseas individual

[s189]

An individual is not a relevant overseas individual in a tax year if they are a relevant UK individual by virtue of meeting one or more of the conditions in section 189(1)(a), (b) or (d). Those are:

- they have relevant UK earnings chargeable to UK income tax for that year,
- they are resident in the UK at some time during that year,
- they, or their spouse, have for that year general earnings from overseas Crown employment subject to UK tax.

An individual is also not a relevant overseas individual in a tax year if:

- they are a relevant UK individual only by virtue of meeting the condition in section 189(1)(c) that they were resident in the UK both at some time during the five tax years immediately before that year and when they became a member of the registered pension scheme, and
- they are employed by a UK resident person.

BOX 26

2.197 RPSM13100440 – Technical Pages: International: Enhancement: Recognised overseas scheme transfer factor: Notification procedure

Notification procedure

[Reg 8 The Registered Pension Schemes (Enhanced Lifetime Allowance) Regulations 2006, SI 2006/131]

An individual has to notify HMRC of their entitlement to a recognised overseas scheme transfer factor in accordance with Regulation 8 of The Registered Pension Schemes (Enhanced Lifetime Allowance) Regulations 2006, SI 2006/131. Notification should be made on form APSS 202 no later than five years after the 31 January following the end of the tax year in which the transfer took place.

Example

Beryl transferred funds from her recognised overseas pension scheme to a registered pension scheme on 5 February 2007, during the 2006/2007 tax year. This means that she must submit a completed form APSS 202 to HMRC no later than five years after 31 January 2008, i e by 31 January 2013.

Separate APSS 202 notification forms should be submitted to HMRC in the following circumstances:

- where transfers to a registered pension scheme are made from different recognised overseas pension schemes,
- where transfers to different registered pension schemes are made from one or more recognised overseas pension schemes, and
- where transfers to a registered pension scheme from a recognised overseas pension scheme are made on different dates.

However, a single APSS 202 form can be submitted to HMRC where there have been transfers from more than one arrangement under a recognised overseas pension scheme to the same registered pension scheme at the same time. The total figures for the transfers from those different arrangements should be shown in the boxes at 7.2 and 7.3.

Incorrect information provided

If an individual has received a certificate and later realises that the information provided on the APSS 202 notification form was incorrect they should send another form to HMRC. They should complete all of the relevant boxes as if it was a new notification, but must tick the 'yes' box at 1.5 on the form and enter there the reference number that is shown on the certificate. In addition, if after the certificate was issued there has been a benefit crystallisation event in respect of any of the individual's pension arrangements they must inform HMRC about that in a covering letter.

BOX 27

2.198 RPSM13100450 – Technical Pages: International: Enhancement: Recognised overseas scheme transfer factor: What happens after HMRC has been notified?

What happens after HMRC has been notified?

After receiving an APSS 202 notification form HMRC will send the individual a certificate confirming the recognised overseas scheme transfer factor. Each certificate will have a unique reference number, and will also state the type of lifetime allowance enhancement, the individual's National Insurance number (if they have one), the date of issue of the certificate and the date from which it is valid.

Individuals must retain all documents relating to the information submitted to HMRC on form APSS 202 for a period of 6 years, beginning with the day on which the notification is given to HMRC. They may wish to keep the documentation for longer than that in case a query arises subsequently. If they do not do so and there is a query then they could ask HMRC for a copy of the certificate and of the backing paperwork. They could also authorise the scheme administrator of their registered pension scheme to view, or receive a copy of, the certificate.

Amending a certificate

If an individual has received a certificate and later realises that the information provided on the APSS 202 notification form was incorrect they should send an amended notification to HMRC. They should complete all of the relevant boxes as if it was a new notification, but must tick the 'yes' box at 1.5 on the form and enter there the reference number that is shown on the original certificate. In addition, if after the certificate was issued there has been a benefit crystallisation event in respect of any of the individual's pension arrangements they should inform HMRC about that in a covering letter.

BOX 28

2.199 RPSM13100460 – Technical Pages: International: Enhancement: Recognised overseas scheme transfer factor: Benefit payment

Notifying details of the recognised overseas scheme transfer factor when benefits are paid

If an individual intends to rely on a recognised overseas scheme transfer factor they will have to notify the scheme administrator of their registered pension scheme when a benefit crystallisation event occurs. The individual will need to provide the administrator with the unique reference number and the enhancement factor details shown on the certificate.

The administrator will have to include information about the benefit crystallisation event on the Event Report that is made annually to HMRC (see RPSM12300030 [NWL]). The administrator will need also to account for any lifetime allowance charge on the quarterly Accounting for Tax return to HMRC.

If an individual has not notified HMRC of an entitlement to a recognised overseas scheme transfer factor before a benefit crystallisation event occurs a lifetime allowance charge may arise and the scheme administrator may have paid the tax due. If the individual subsequently provides the administrator of their registered pension scheme with the unique reference number and the enhancement factor details shown on the certificate the administrator may then send an amended Accounting for Tax return to HMRC and obtain a repayment.

BOX 29

2.200 RPSM13100470 – Technical Pages: International: Enhancement: Recognised overseas scheme transfer factor: How to calculate the factor

How to calculate the recognised overseas scheme transfer factor

[s224 (4) & (5)]

Where a transfer is made as described in RPSM13100420, an individual's lifetime allowance is enhanced by a recognised overseas scheme transfer factor, which is established as follows:

(a) Calculate any relevant relievable amount (see RPSM13100490).

(b) Deduct the result of a. from the total amount of sums and assets transferred (including the market value of any assets transferred) from an arrangement under a recognised overseas pension scheme (see RPSM14101040) made after 5 April 2006.

(c) Express the resulting amount in b. as a factor of the standard lifetime allowance as at the date on which the transfer took place.

The recognised overseas scheme transfer factor can be used by the individual in respect of any benefit crystallisation event occurring after the transfer is made.

RPSM13100480 gives some examples.

BOX 30

2.201 RPSM13100480 – Technical Pages: International: Enhancement: Recognised overseas scheme transfer factor: Examples of how to calculate the factor

Examples of how to calculate the recognised overseas scheme transfer factor

Example 1

Ken transferred £200,000 from his arrangement under a recognised overseas pension scheme to a registered pension scheme on 6 April 2007. He doesn't have a relevant relievable amount. The standard lifetime allowance for the 2007/08 tax year is £1.6 million so his recognised overseas scheme transfer factor is calculated by dividing 200,000 by 1.6 million. The resulting factor is 0.125, but that is rounded up to 0.13.

Example 2

Amanda transferred £800,000 from her recognised overseas pension scheme to a registered pension scheme on 6 December 2007. She had a relevant relievable amount of £400,000.

So the amount at step b in RPSM13100470 is

£800,000 – £400,000 = £400,000

The recognised overseas scheme transfer factor is therefore 0.25. That is calculated by dividing £400,000 by £1.6 million (the standard lifetime allowance for the 2007–2008 tax year).

£400,000/£1.6 million = 0.25

BOX 31

2.202 RPSM13100490 – Technical Pages: International: Enhancement: Recognised overseas scheme transfer factor: The relevant relievable amount

How to calculate the relevant relievable amount

[s224] [s225] [s226]]

The relevant relievable amount relates to any part of the overseas arrangement active membership period during which the individual was not a relevant overseas individual (see RPSM13100430). If there is more than one part of the overseas arrangement active membership period where the individual was not a relevant overseas individual then that individual's relevant relievable amount is the total of the amounts relating to each of those part-periods.

The overseas arrangement active membership period is defined in section 224(7) and relates to membership of an arrangement under a recognised overseas pension scheme. It begins on the later of the following dates:

- the date when benefits first began to accrue to or in respect of an individual under the overseas arrangement, and
- 6 April 2006.

It ends on the earlier of the following dates:

- immediately before the transfer was made, and
- the date when benefits ceased to accrue to or in respect of the individual under the overseas arrangement.

The relevant relievable amount is calculated in a number of different ways depending on whether the individual's recognised overseas pension scheme arrangement is:

- a cash balance arrangement (see RPSM13100500),
- an other money purchase arrangement (see RPSM13100520),
- a defined benefits arrangement (see RPSM13100540), or
- a hybrid arrangement (see RPSM13100570).

Normally there will be only one of those types of arrangement in a recognised overseas pension scheme. If that is the case there will be a single transfer and, if applicable, a single calculation of a relevant relievable amount. The basis of the calculation will be determined by the type of arrangement it is.

However, it is possible that an individual could be accruing benefits under different types of arrangement within a single recognised overseas pension scheme that has multiple arrangements. For example, a member of a defined benefits scheme could have two types of arrangement if they were making additional voluntary contributions to the scheme. That is because the additional voluntary contributions would be an other money purchase arrangement. Should that be the case, and if the total amount transferred from the recognised overseas pension scheme related to separate transfers from each of the arrangements, separate calculations of any relevant relievable amounts would need to be made.

BOX 32

2.203 RPSM13100500 – Technical Pages: International: Enhancement: Recognised overseas scheme transfer factor: Cash balance arrangement relevant relievable amount

How to calculate the relevant relievable amount for a cash balance arrangement

[s225(3)–(5)]

Where the individual's arrangement under their recognised overseas pension scheme is a cash balance arrangement, the cash balance relevant relievable amount is established as follows:

(a) obtain the value of the individual's rights in the cash balance arrangement as at the latest of the following dates:

- the date that the individual became someone who is not a relevant overseas individual (see RPSM13100430),
- the date that benefits first began to accrue to or in respect of the individual under the cash balance arrangement, and
- 6 April 2006.

(b) obtain the value of the individual's rights in the cash balance arrangement as at the earliest of the following dates:

- immediately before the transfer was made,
- the date that the individual ceased to be someone who is not a relevant overseas individual, and
- the date that benefits ceased to accrue to or in respect of the individual under the cash balance arrangement.

(c) deduct the result of a. from the result of b.

(d) If the individual had not been a relevant overseas individual during another part of the overseas arrangement active membership period (see RPSM13100490) relating to the same cash balance arrangement then the amount calculated in the same way in respect of that other part-period should be added to the amount at c.

The individual's rights under the cash balance arrangement is the amount which would be available to provide benefits to or in respect of the individual if they became entitled to them at the applicable date (as determined under a or b above). The rights are established using the valuation assumptions set out in section 277. They are as follows:

- the individual concerned has reached any designated age as must have been reached to avoid any reduction in their benefits on account of their age, and
- their benefits should be valued on the basis that they are not physically or mentally impaired.

RPSM13100510 gives an example.

BOX 33

2.204 RPSM13100510 – Technical Pages: International: Enhancement: Recognised overseas scheme transfer factor: Example of relevant relievable amount for a cash balance arrangement

Example of how to calculate the relevant relievable amount for a cash balance arrangement

Joseph transferred £400,000 from his recognised overseas pension scheme that was a cash balance arrangement to a registered pension scheme on 6 June 2007.

Joseph began to accrue benefits under his cash balance arrangement on 6 April 2000. He became resident in the UK on 16 October 2006 so he became someone who is not a relevant overseas individual with effect from 6 April 2006. The value of his rights in his cash balance arrangement as at 6 April 2006 amounted to £250,000.

The value of his rights in his cash balance arrangement immediately before the transfer to his registered pension scheme on 6 June 2007 amounted to £300,000. At that date he was still someone who is not a relevant overseas individual and was still accruing benefits under the cash balance arrangement.

The cash balance relevant relievable amount is therefore £50,000 (£300,000 – £250,000).

Box 34

2.205 RPSM13100520 – Technical Pages: International: Enhancement: Recognised overseas scheme transfer factor: Other money purchase arrangement relevant relievable amount

How to calculate the relevant relievable amount for an other money purchase arrangement

[s225(6) & (7)]

Where the individual's arrangement under their recognised overseas pension scheme is a money purchase arrangement other than a cash balance arrangement, the other money purchase relevant relievable amount is calculated in the following way.

Establish the total amount of contributions made by or in respect of the individual to the other money purchase arrangement between the dates determined under a. and b. below:

(a) the latest of the following dates:

- the date that the individual became someone who is not a relevant overseas individual (see RPSM13100430),
- the date that benefits first began to accrue to or in respect of the individual under the recognised overseas pension scheme other money purchase arrangement, and
- 6 April 2006.

(b) the earliest of the following dates:

- immediately before the transfer was made,
- the date that the individual ceased to be someone who is not a relevant overseas individual, and
- the date that benefits ceased to accrue to or in respect of the individual under the recognised overseas pension scheme other money purchase arrangement.

If the individual had not been a relevant overseas individual during another part of the overseas arrangement active membership period (see RPSM13100490) relating to the same other money purchase arrangement then the amount calculated in the same way in respect of that other part-period should be added to the above amount.

RPSM13100530 gives an example.

BOX 35

2.206 RPSM13100530 – Technical Pages: International: Enhancement: Recognised overseas scheme transfer factor: Example of other money purchase arrangement relevant relievable amount

Example of calculating the relevant relievable amount for an other money purchase arrangement

Kate transferred £350,000 from her recognised overseas pension scheme other money purchase arrangement to a registered pension scheme on 6 June 2012.

Kate began working in France on 19 July 2003 and joined her recognised overseas pension scheme other money purchase arrangement on 6 March 2004. She returned to work in the UK on 1 January 2008 and became someone who is not a relevant overseas individual with effect from 6 April 2007. The latest date under step a. in RPSM13100520 is therefore 6 April 2007.

Kate started working in the USA on 1 June 2010 and ceased to be someone who is not a relevant overseas individual with effect from 6 April 2010. That was before she made the transfer to her registered pension scheme and before she ceased to accrue benefits under the recognised overseas pension scheme other money purchase arrangement.

The total contributions made by or in respect of Kate between 6 April 2007 and 6 April 2010 amounted to £150,000. The other money purchase relevant relievable amount is therefore £150,000.

BOX 36

2.207 RPSM13100540 – Technical Pages: International: Enhancement: Recognised overseas scheme transfer factor: Defined benefits arrangement relevant relievable amount

How to calculate the relevant relievable amount for a defined benefits arrangement

[s226(3) &)4)]

Where the individual's arrangement under their recognised overseas pension scheme is a defined benefits arrangement, the defined benefits relevant relievable amount is established as follows:

(a) multiply the individual's pension entitlement under the defined benefits arrangement as at the latest of the following dates by the relevant valuation factor of 20 (or a factor greater than 20 as agreed by HMRC):

- the date when the individual became someone who is not a relevant overseas individual (see RPSM13100430);
- the date when benefits first began to accrue to or in respect of the individual under the recognised overseas pension scheme defined benefits arrangement; and
- 6 April 2006.

Where the defined benefits arrangement rules provide for a separate lump sum that is not a commutation of pension it is necessary to take that into account as well. That is done by adding to the amount resulting from the above calculation the separate lump sum entitlement that the individual has under the defined benefits arrangement as at the latest date above. This only applies if the lump sum entitlement is not linked to the individual's pension entitlement so that their prospective pension entitlement is not reduced as a result of taking the lump sum.

(b) multiply the individual's pension entitlement under the defined benefits arrangement as at the earliest of the following dates by the relevant valuation factor of 20 (or a factor greater than 20 as agreed by HMRC):

- immediately before the transfer was made,
- the date that the individual ceased to be someone who is not a relevant overseas individual, and
- the date when benefits ceased to accrue to or in respect of the individual under the recognised overseas pension scheme defined benefits arrangement.

Where the defined benefits arrangement rules provide for a separate lump sum that is not a commutation of pension it is necessary to take that into account as well. That is done by adding to the amount resulting from the above calculation the separate lump sum entitlement that the individual has under the defined benefits arrangement as at the earliest date above. This only applies if the lump sum entitlement is not linked to the individual's pension entitlement so that their prospective pension entitlement is not reduced as a result of taking the lump sum.

(c) deduct the result of a. from the result of b.

(d) If the individual had not been a relevant overseas individual during another part of the overseas arrangement active membership period (see RPSM13100490) relating to the same defined benefits arrangement then the amount calculated in the same way in respect of that other part-period should be added to the amount at c.

The individual's pension entitlement under the defined benefits arrangement is the annual rate of pension which would be payable to or in respect of the individual if they became entitled to payment of it at the applicable date (as determined under a or b above). The individual's lump sum entitlement under the defined benefits arrangement is the amount of lump sum which would be payable to or in respect of the individual if they became entitled to payment of it at the applicable date. Both the pension entitlement and the lump sum entitlement are established using the valuation assumptions set out in section 277. They are as follows:

- the individual concerned has reached any designated age as must have been reached to avoid any reduction in their benefits on account of their age, and
- their benefits should be valued on the basis that they are not physically or mentally impaired.

RPSM13100550 and RPSM13100560 give some examples.

BOX 37

2.208 RPSM13100550 – Technical Pages: International: Enhancement: Recognised overseas scheme transfer factor: Example 1 of defined benefits arrangement relevant relievable amount

Example 1 of calculating the relevant relievable amount for a defined benefits arrangement

Shona transferred £1.13 million from her recognised overseas pension scheme defined benefits arrangement to a registered pension scheme on 6 June 2010.

Shona went to work in Germany and joined her recognised overseas pension scheme defined benefits arrangement on 6 May 2002. She returned to work in the UK on 6 May 2007 and so became someone who is not a relevant overseas individual with effect from 6 April 2007. Her pension entitlement as at 6 April 2007 was £40,000 p.a. Shona had an option under the rules of the recognised overseas pension scheme defined benefits arrangement to commute part of her pension entitlement for a lump sum on retirement. She was not entitled to a separate lump sum.

£40,000 x 20 = £800,000

Shona ceased to accrue benefits under the defined benefits arrangement on 6 May 2009. That was before she made the transfer and before she ceased to be someone who is not a relevant overseas individual. Her pension entitlement as at 6 May 2009 was £56,500 p.a.

£56,500 x 20 = £1.13 million

The defined benefits relevant relievable amount is therefore £330,000 (£1.13 million – £800,000).

BOX 38

2.209 RPSM13100560 – Technical Pages: International: Enhancement: Recognised overseas scheme transfer factor: Example 2 of defined benefits arrangement relevant relievable amount

Example 2 of calculating the relevant relievable amount for a defined benefits arrangement

Eric transferred £1.21 million from his recognised overseas pension scheme defined benefits arrangement to a registered pension scheme on 6 June 2008.

Eric was working in France when he joined his recognised overseas pension scheme defined benefits arrangement on 6 March 2000. He came to work in the UK on 6 May 2006 and so became someone who is not a relevant overseas individual with effect from 6 April 2006. His pension entitlement as at 6 April 2006 was £30,000 p.a. He was also entitled to a separate lump sum of £60,000.

(£30,000 x 20) + £60,000 = £660,000

Eric returned to work in France on 6 May 2008 and so ceased to be someone who is not a relevant overseas individual with effect from 6 April 2008 whilst still accruing benefits under the scheme. His pension entitlement as at 6 April 2008 was £56,500 p.a. He was also entitled to a separate lump sum of £80,000.

(£56,500 x 20) + £80,000 = £1.21 million

The defined benefits relevant relievable amount is therefore £550,000 (£1.21 million – £660,000).

BOX 39

2.210 RPSM13100570 – Technical Pages: International: Enhancement: Recognised overseas scheme transfer factor: Hybrid arrangement relevant relievable amount

How to calculate the relevant relievable amount for a hybrid arrangement

[s226(5)–(7)]

A hybrid arrangement is an arrangement that may, at any one time, provide one of two or three types of benefits in the form of cash balance benefits, other money purchase benefits, or defined benefits. There are effectively two or three potential outcomes but they are mutually exclusive so benefits are provided in only one of those ways. They should not be confused with schemes with multiple arrangements where benefits accrue separately under different types of arrangement within a single recognised overseas pension scheme.

An example of a hybrid arrangement is one which, on the member's retirement, will provide benefits calculated by reference to a pot of money available to that member, but subject to an underlying defined benefit promise calculated by reference to the member's final salary and length of service. Should the pot of money available provide less than the underlying defined benefit promise the benefits provided will be augmented up to the level promised. Alternatively, if the pot of money provides a greater level of benefits than the underlying defined benefit promise, the individual would receive the money purchase benefits up to the level that the pot of money will provide. So the benefits will be either money purchase benefits or defined benefits, but not both.

Where the individual's arrangement under their recognised overseas pension scheme is a hybrid arrangement, the hybrid arrangement relevant relievable amount is established as follows:

(a) if the benefits that may ultimately be provided under the arrangement may be cash balance benefits, calculate what would be the cash balance relevant relievable amount as set out in RPSM13100500 if the recognised overseas pension scheme were a cash balance arrangement,

(b) if the benefits that may ultimately be provided under the arrangement may be other money purchase benefits calculate what would be the other money purchase relevant relievable amount as set out in RPSM13100520 if the recognised overseas pension scheme were an other money purchase arrangement,

(c) if the benefits that may ultimately be provided under the arrangement may be defined benefits, calculate what would be the defined benefits relevant relievable amount as set out in RPSM13100540 if the recognised overseas pension scheme were a defined benefits arrangement,

(d) select the greater or greatest relevant relievable amount from whichever of a., b., or c. are relevant.

Example

Natalie's hybrid arrangement can provide either cash balance benefits, other money purchase benefits or defined benefits.

Natalie's potential cash balance relevant relievable amount is £50,000, her potential other money purchase relevant relievable amount is £16,000, and her potential defined benefits relevant relievable amount is £100,000.

Natalie's hybrid arrangement relevant relievable amount is therefore £100,000.

Chapter 3

Transitional arrangements

Modification of scheme rules

3.1 Much has been made of the fact that removal of the existing HMRC benefit restrictions on 6 April 2006, especially the *Finance Act 1989* earnings cap, could leave scheme sponsors exposed to a significant increase in liability. Additionally, phrases such as '... as will not prejudice the tax approved status of the scheme ...' are scattered throughout occupational pension scheme rules concerning payment of benefits or certain other duties or discretions conferred on trustees. And scheme rules may even compel trustees to make a payment which would be unauthorised under the new tax regime.

To address these issues, HMRC published the draft Pension Schemes (Modification of Rules of Existing Schemes) Regulations. These regulations were subsequently brought into force as the *Pension Schemes (Modification of Rules of Existing Schemes) Regulations 2006 (SI 2006/364)*. They are for the purpose of providing transitional protection for schemes whose documentation has not been amended to comply with the new tax rules (see 2.12 above). The general effect is explained below:

1 If the rules of a scheme would require the trustees to make what would be an unauthorised payment, then the trustees have discretion whether or not to make that payment. If, before A-Day, the consent of the sponsoring employer was required before making the payment in question, that consent is still required. Where such payment is made, that part of it relating to pre-A-Day rights will not be a scheme chargeable payment.

2 If any scheme rule limits benefit by reference to the earnings cap (in whatever terms), then that rule should continue to be construed as limiting the benefit post A-Day as if the earnings cap legislation had not been repealed.

3 If the rules provide for a certain pension to be paid and mention that a greater payment may be made subject to not prejudicing approval, then post A-Day the trustees can pay up to the HMRC maximum benefit as if pre-A-Day limits were still in place, but they are prohibited from paying a sum greater than the pre-A-Day maximum benefit. If, before A-Day, the

consent of the sponsoring employer was required before making the augmentation, then it is still required post A-Day.

4 If the rules provide for any payment to be made of such amount as would not prejudice approval, then post A-Day the trustees are prohibited from making a payment which would be greater than HMRC maximum benefits calculated as if pre-A-Day limits were still in place.

5 If the rules do not permit the trustees to recover from a member any lifetime allowance charge for which the trustees are liable, then post A-Day the trustees are able to reduce the member's benefits to reflect the amount of tax paid, such reduction to be determined in accordance with 'normal actuarial practice'.

6 Transfers may be made only to the extent that the payments would have been authorised by the rules immediately before the coming into force of the Regulations, and subject to not prejudicing the scheme's approval.

These modification provisions may continue in effect until 6 April 2011 or, if earlier, until the trustees specifically disapply any particular modification by making an appropriate amendment to the relevant scheme rule.

In addition to these HMRC regulations, the *Occupational Pension Schemes (Modification of Schemes) Regulations 2006* (*SI 2006/759*) give trustees power to make a permanent modification by resolution to give effect to most of the above (if they do not already have the power) and to exempt certain modifications from *s 67, PA 1995* by disapplication. They also explain the qualifications or experience required to calculate the actuarial value of subsisting rights.

Transitional protection

3.2 One of the most important aspects of the new pension tax regime is that it will be retrospective in effect. This means that many people with accrued pension rights already greater than the 2006/07 lifetime allowance of £1,500,000 could find themselves facing a significant tax bill.

The *Finance Act 2004* therefore introduces a range of measures to protect various rights of individuals accrued up to 5 April 2006. For details of the protections available to individuals, please refer to Chapter 9 of *Taxation of Pension Benefits*. For transitional provisions relating to investments held within SSAS, SIPPs and FURBS arrangements, please refer to Chapters 4, 5 and 6 of this volume.

Explanatory note extract

3.3 In addition to the primary and enhanced protections which are available under the *Finance Act 2004* (see 2.28 and 2.29 above) and the lump sum protections under that Act (see 2.39 to 2.50 above), the *Taxation of Pension Schemes (Transitional Provisions) Order 2006 (SI 2006/572)* provides significant detail of the finer points which apply to protected entitlements. The explanatory note to the regulations is, in itself, of considerable length but it is reproduced below as it provides a helpful source of reference:

> 'Article 2 provides for the modification of section 161 (meaning of payment). The ambit of section 161(3) is extended to cover payments made or benefits provided, from investments purchased by approved schemes before A day. Paragraph 3 of Article 2 excludes certain annuities bought from insurance companies from this extension. Paragraphs 4 and 5 deal with approved schemes which were wound up prior to A day. The wording of section 161(4) is modified in respect of these schemes so that the payment is deemed to be made by a registered scheme.
>
> Articles 3 to 5 provide for commencement provisions for unsecured pensions. Pensions which are in payment by way of income withdrawal before A day and which become unsecured pensions or dependant's unsecured pension at A day would need to be valued on A day under the existing legislation. These transitional provisions are designed to stagger the date of the valuation exercise to avoid a bottleneck of valuations. Article 3 sets out the pensions which will be covered by these transitional provisions. Article 4 provides for the modification of section 165(1), Pension rule 5. The 120% maximum is reduced to 100% (the pre A day limit) for schemes which have not been re-valued using the new rules. Article 5 makes various modifications to paragraphs 9 and 24 of Schedule 28 to enable pensions referred to in article 3 to be re-valued at any time up to 6th April 2006 (or earlier, if there has been an annuity purchase prior to that date). The modifications provide that the pre A Day valuation will be used as the "basis amount" until the new valuation takes place.
>
> Articles 6 to 8 provide transitional protection for people who have pre A Day rights to life cover lump sums where the rules of the pension scheme included such provision on 10th December 2003. Under the new regime lump sum payments made on or after the member's 75th birthday will be unauthorised. Article 6 sets out the conditions which the member of the registered pension scheme needs to satisfy to qualify for the transitional protection. Article 7 provides for modifications to section 636A of the Income Taxes (Earnings and Pensions) Act 2003 to add life cover lump sums to the list of lump sums exempt from income tax. Article 8 modifies section 168(1) to insert life cover lump sums to the list of lump sum death benefits that a pension scheme is authorised to make under

section 164. Paragraph (3) of article 8 adds a new paragraph 21A to Schedule 29 defining "life cover lump sum".

Articles 9 to 11 provide transitional protection for individuals who qualify for "primary protection" under paragraph 7 to Schedule 36 but whose pre-commencement rights may have been undervalued on 5th April 2006 due to the poor performance of investments held by the scheme. If the scheme receives compensation in respect of the poor performance on or after A day this compensation becomes potentially chargeable to the lifetime allowance charge (section 214). Article 9 sets out the conditions which the individual needs to satisfy to qualify for the transitional protection. Article 10 modifies section 212 (valuation of uncrystallised rights for the purposes of section 210) for the purposes of calculating RR in paragraph 7(3) of Schedule 36. Paragraph (2) deducts the market value of any "relevant compensation" from the amount of RR and paragraph (3) defines "relevant compensation". Paragraph (4) and (5) apply the modifications to hybrid arrangements (section 212(7). Article 11 modifies paragraph 8(5) of Schedule 36 (valuation of the individual's uncrystallised right) to ensure that the modifications made by article 10 apply.

Articles 12 to 14 deal with individuals who qualify for primary protection and a lifetime allowance enhancement factor under section 221 in relation to a period of non-residence. The modifications prevent the individual qualifying for two lifetime allowance enhancement factors in respect of the same increase in benefits. Article 12 contains details of the individuals who will be affected by the modifications. Article 13 contains modifications to the value of OV in section 222(4) and (5)(b) to prevent it being indexed prior to A day. Article 14 contains modifications to section 223 (arrangements that are not money purchase arrangements). The definitions of PB and LSB in sub-section (4) are modified so that the rights referred to are valued at 5th April 2006. Paragraph (3) inserts sub-section (4A) indexing PB and LSB during the active membership period (as defined in section 221(4)).

Articles 15, 16 and 17 provide transitional protection to contributions made by employers where those contributions qualified for corresponding relief under section 76(6A) and (6C) of the Finance Act 1989. Article 15 sets out the contributions that may be treated as if they were relevant migrant member contributions under paragraph 2 of Schedule 33 and the conditions that must be met in respect of those contributions. Paragraph (4) applies the provisions of the Pension Schemes (Information Requirements – Qualifying Overseas Pension Schemes, Qualifying Recognised Overseas Pension Schemes and Corresponding Relief) Regulation 2006 SI 2006/208 to qualifying employees and to exempt employees under article 17. Paragraphs (5) and (6) apply the transitional protection to pension schemes which have received a block transfer from a scheme to which paragraph (2) applies. Article 16 modifies section 245 (restriction of deduction for contributions by employer) for cases which qualify for transitional protection under article 15. Section 245 modifies amends Schedule 24 of the Finance Act 2003 ("the 2003 Act") and the new modification prevents contributions which have been given relief under article 15 being given double relief under Schedule 24 of the 2003 Act. Article 17 provides that the provisions of section 308A of ITEPA 2003 (exemption of contributions to overseas pension scheme) shall apply to employees ("exempt employees") who meet the conditions set out in paragraphs (1) and (2) of the article.

Article 18 switches off paragraph 1(1)(b) of Schedule 29 (requirement that lump sum payable only when lifetime allowance available) in the case of an individual whose pension commencement lump sum is determined by paragraphs 27 and 29 of Schedule 36 (enhanced protection).

Article 19 modifies paragraph 2(6) of Schedule 29 (calculation of the available portion of the member's lump sum allowance) in the case of individuals who fall within paragraph 20(1) of Schedule 36 (individuals who have an actual right to payment of one or more pensions on 5th April 2006). Paragraph 2(6) is modified so that AAC includes any pre-commencement pension rights valued under paragraph 20 of Schedule 36.

Article 20 provides that where a lump sum death benefit is paid in respect of a member who had an actual right to payment of a relevant pension (a pre-commencement pension) immediately before his death, those pre-commencement pension rights will be taken into account when calculating the available amount of lifetime allowance to be set against the lump sum death benefit.

Articles 21 to 23 provide for scheme specific lump sum protection as set out in paragraphs 31 to 34 of Schedule 36 (entitlement to lump sums exceeding 25% of uncrystallised rights) to be lost in respect of rights transferred where there been a partial transfer of those rights (rather than a block transfer) away from a scheme. Article 21 sets out when the modifications in articles 22 and 23 shall apply. Article 22 modifies paragraph 31 of Schedule 36. A new paragraph (2A) is added which provides for the modifications to Schedule 29 made by paragraph 34 (as modified by article 23) to apply to persons where sums and assets representing accrued rights are transferred other than by a block transfer to another scheme. Article 23 modifies paragraph 34 of Schedule 36 so that the amount that has been partially transferred shall be ignored when calculating the "permitted maximum" in paragraph 2 of Schedule 29.

Article 24 disapplies the limit on dependants scheme pensions set out in paragraphs 16A,B and C of Schedule 28 where the member in respect of whom the dependant's scheme pension is being paid was actually entitled to one or more relevant existing pensions (as defined in paragraph 10(2) of Schedule 36) on 5th April 2006.

Article 25 and 26 provides transitional protection for individuals whose benefits will only be payable as a lump sum with no connected pension. Paragraph (2) of article 25 sets out the conditions that the individual must meet to qualify for the protection. Paragraph (3) adds a "stand-alone lump sum to the list of lump sums which are authorised payments in section 166(1). Paragraph (4) inserts a new paragraph 3A into Schedule 29 which provides a definition of a "stand-alone lump sum". Article 26 modifies paragraph 31(3) of Schedule 36 for individuals who meet the conditions set out in paragraph (2) of the article. Paragraph (3) applies the provisions of paragraph 31 of Schedule 36 (entitlement to lump sums exceeding 25% of uncrystallised rights) so that individuals whose benefits are payable as a lump sum only can qualify for the modification of the "permitted maximum" lump sum rules in Schedule 29.

Article 27 deals with contracts which prior to A day, had been approved under section 621(1)(b) of ICTA. Paragraph (3) adds these contracts to the list of pensions in paragraph 1(1) of Schedule 36 which are converted to registered pensions and paragraph (4) adds the contracts to the list of "pre-commencement retirement annuity arrangements" in paragraph 40(3) of Schedule 36.

Article 28 provides that individuals who have become entitled to a tax-free lump sum before A day but deferred their entitlement to the accompanying pension will not become entitled to a second tax-free lump sum under the same arrangement. Paragraph (2) sets out the conditions and paragraph (3)(a) provides that paragraph 1 of Schedule 29 shall be modified so that the tax free lump sum shall be treated as a pension commencement lump sum with a deemed crystallisation on A day. No lifetime allowance charge will arise in respect of the sum however. Paragraph (3)(b) inserts a new paragraph (3A) into paragraph 1 of Schedule 29 which provides that the accompanying pension shall not be a "relevant pension" pursuant to sub-paragraph (3). Any further lump sums paid out in connection with the pension will therefore not be pension commencement lump sums.

Articles 29 modifies paragraphs 8 and 9 of Schedule 28 so that certain types of pension to which the member was entitled immediately before A day shall become unsecured pension funds and accordingly covered by the new regime. Paragraphs (1) and (2) set out the applicable conditions. Paragraph (3) modifies paragraph 8 of Schedule 28 (member's unsecured pension fund) so that the pensions listed will become unsecured pension funds at A day. Sub-paragraph (d) provides that these rights shall form a separate arrangement and that this deemed designation shall not create a benefit crystallisation event. Paragraph (4) contains amendments to paragraph 9 of Schedule 28 (unsecured pension year and basis amount for unsecured pension year). Paragraph (5) modifies section 216 so that benefit crystallisation events 2, 4 and 8 are not triggered when the unsecured pension funds are utilised to provide a scheme pension, lifetime annuity or rights under a qualifying recognised overseas pensions scheme. This paragraph is necessary because the provisions in paragraphs 3 and 4 of Schedule 32 preventing overlap do not apply appropriately to these funds that were in existence before A day.

Article 30 provides similar provisions to article 29 for dependant's pension funds. Paragraphs (1) and (2) set out the conditions which the dependant must meet for the modifications to take effect. Paragraph (3) modifies paragraph 22 of Schedule 28 (dependant's unsecured pension fund) so that the unsecured pensions listed will become dependant's unsecured pension funds at A day. Paragraph (4) contains amendments to paragraph 23 (unsecured pension year and basis amount for unsecured pension year).

Article 31 provides for certain individuals over the age of 75 at A day to be treated as being in alternatively secured pension from A day. Paragraphs (1) and (2) set out the conditions to be met for the modification to apply. Paragraph (3) modifies paragraph 11 of Schedule 28 (member's alternatively secured pension fund) so that the sums and assets that meet the inserted condition C shall become member's alternatively secured pension funds at A day. The effect of paragraphs (4), (5) and (6) is that certain individuals over the age of 75 who were already drawing a pension on 5th April 2006 will have their funds automatically converted to member's alternatively secured pensions funds pursuant to paragraph 11 of Schedule 28. Paragraphs (4) and (5) set out the conditions that must be met for the modifications to apply. Paragraph (6) modifies paragraph 11 of

Schedule 28 so that sums and assets which meet the inserted condition C shall become member's alternatively secured pension funds.

Article 32 contains similar provisions to those in article 31 for dependant's alternatively secured pension funds. Paragraphs (1) and (2) set out the conditions that must be met by the dependant. Paragraph (3) contains modifications to paragraph 25 of Schedule 28 (dependant's alternatively secured pension fund) so that the sums and assets which meet the inserted condition C shall become dependant's alternatively secured pension funds.

Article 33 deals with serious ill-health lump sums, pension protection lump sum death benefits and annuity protection lump sum death benefits. Paragraphs (1) and (2) set out the applicable conditions. Paragraph (3) modifies paragraph 4 of Schedule 29 (serious ill-health sum) to prevent an individual who already had an actual right to payment of a relevant pension at A day being paid a serious ill-health lump sum. This reflects the position in the new regime. Paragraphs (4) and (5) modify paragraphs 14 (pension protection lump sum death benefit) and 16 (annuity protection lump sum death benefit) so payments of pension protection lump sum death benefits and annuity protection lump sum death benefits can be made in respect of individuals who fall within the conditions set out in paragraphs (1) and (2). In the new regime these lump sums must not exceed a protection limit. Individuals who meet the conditions would have a limit of £0 as the limit is defined by reference to "the amount crystallised". The concept of crystallisation is not applicable to pensions before A day so this is changed to the value of the individuals pre-commencement pension rights.

Article 34 provides transitional protection for dependants over the age of 23 who are in full time education or have become incapacitated before that age. The conditions are set out in paragraphs (1) (4), (5) and (6) and paragraph (3) modifies paragraph 15(2) of Schedule 28 (meaning of "dependant").

Article 35 modifies paragraph 12(8) of Schedule 36 ("enhanced protection") so that transfers to insurance companies which are recognised transfers pursuant to section 169(1A) are "permitted transfers". If the transfer was not a permitted transfer, enhanced protection would be lost.

Article 36 protects an individual's right to enhanced protection in the event of a transfer made in connection with a wind-up. Paragraphs (1) and (2) set out the applicable conditions. Paragraph (3) modifies paragraph 15 of Schedule 36 (definition of the "relevant crystallised amount") so that transfers representing crystallised rights which are made in connection with a wind-up shall be valued at £0 for the purposes of calculating the relevant crystallised amount.

Article 37 modifies section 636B ITEPA 2003 (trivial commutation and winding-up lump sums). The section provides for the taxation of trivial commutation lump sums or winding-up lump sums. Paragraph (1) sets out the lump sums that the modification will apply to. Paragraph (2) substitutes a new heading and paragraph (3) adds an "equivalent pension benefits commutation lump sum" to the list in section 636B(1). Paragraph (4) inserts a definition of "equivalent pension benefits commutation lump sum" to the section.

Articles 38 to 41 contain transitional provisions in relation to various lump sums which had become payable under the pre A day regime. Article 38 provides that lump sum payments which meet the conditions set out in paragraph (1) shall be chargeable to income tax in accordance with section 598, 599 or 599A of ICTA even though they were paid after A day. The article applies to lump sums payments which were payable in accordance with the rules of the pension scheme before A day. The article also provides that the reporting requirement shall transfer to the scheme administrator. Article 39 deals with lump sums paid to a member in circumstances of the member's serious ill-health. Paragraph (2) provides that there is no charge to tax under Part 4 if the sum meets the requirements set out in sub-paragraphs (a) to (d) of article 38(1) (i.e that the sum was paid after A day, in accordance with the rules of the scheme as they stood prior to A day). Paragraphs (3) and (4) set out when a lump is paid in circumstances of the member's serious ill-health. Article 40 deals with lump sum death benefits payable in respect of the death of a member who died before A day. Paragraph (1) sets out the circumstances in which the article will apply which are similar to those set out in article 38. Paragraph (2) provides that the lump sum shall not be a relevant lump sum death benefit as defined in paragraph 15 of Schedule 32 (benefit crystallisation event 7: meaning of "relevant lump sum death benefit") and shall be disregarded for the purposes of benefit crystallisation event 7. Paragraph (3) states that the lump sum shall be chargeable under section 648B as if the section was still in force following A day. Paragraph (4) provides that the reporting requirements shall transfer to the scheme administrator. Article 41 provides that paragraphs (3) to (5) of article 40 shall apply to lump sums paid in respect of the death of a dependant of a former member of a pension scheme prior to A day.'

Transfer of UURBS benefits to registered scheme

3.4 During HMRC consultation on the new tax regime it was proposed that benefits within an Unfunded Unapproved Retirement Benefit Scheme (UURBS) might be transferred into a registered pension scheme post A-Day without being subject to the annual allowance. This was carried through into the *Finance Act 2004* and is one of the many transitional provisions contained in *Schedule 36*.

There is a narrow three-month window, from 6 April 2006 to 7 July 2006, when an employer may make a contribution to a registered pension scheme in discharge of any pension or lump sum liability he has incurred in respect of an employee or ex-employee before 6 April 2006. If this is done, then the contribution is deducted from the pension input amount when assessing liability against the individual's annual allowance.

Not everyone who could take advantage of this provision may want to do so. It is likely that an individual in this position could already have benefits in excess of the Lifetime Allowance and so it would make little sense exchanging the 40% tax payable on crystallisation of an UURBS benefit for the 55% lifetime allowance charge on a lifetime allowance excess lump sum.

However, the tax-free growth within a registered pension scheme may be a factor in any calculations done to determine the efficiency of this provision, and if an employee is subject to the *Finance Act 1989* earnings cap yet is well within the lifetime allowance, even after a transfer of UURBS rights, it could look very attractive, certainly from a sponsoring employer's point of view.

There is, unfortunately, a distinct downside to such a course of action from the employee's point of view. Whereas the UURBS benefit could be paid wholly as a lump sum, subject only to the 40% income tax the employee would have to pay in any case, the lump sum payable from a registered pension scheme is generally restricted to only one quarter of the value of benefits vested with the remainder having to provide pension. Take up of this option may therefore be very limited.

Chapter 4

Small Self-Administered schemes, and the EU Pensions Directive

4.1 The HMRC/Treasury report (see 2.8 above) stipulated that the prime objective of the tax simplification changes was to introduce a single tax regime. This regime was to apply to all registered schemes whatever their nature.

With a few exceptions the objective of the report has been carried through into legislation. The main exceptions which have arisen relate to SSASs and SIPPs in relation to their investment activities. This chapter describes the latest position for SSASs, and the pre-A-Day rules. The new single tax regime means that most of the new investment requirements apply equally to SSASs and SIPPs.

Chapter 5 describes the latest position for SIPPs, the pre-A-Day rules which applied and the latest UK investment regulations. Small schemes with influential members are regarded by HMRC as self-directed with regard to their investment activity. This has given some cause for concern in the area of residential property (see 5.4 below) and, most recently, taxable property (see 4.2 below). The full investment changes are contained in Chapter 6 of the 4th edition of Tottel's *Taxation of Pension Benefits*, and the new registered schemes rules are contained in 2.73 to 2.85 above.

The existing exemptions for certain SSASs from many of the provisions of the *Pensions Act 1995* are largely retained. There are also special exemptions for schemes with fewer than 100 members under the EU Pension Directive (see 4.4 below). In view of the special rules which governed SSASs under the pre-A-Day tax legislation and practice (see tables 1 to 9 in 4.9 to 4.26 below) concessions have been granted under the transitional provisions for investments that were held as at that date. In all other cases the single UK tax regime will apply equally to all registered schemes. The transitional provisions for benefits and investments are largely contained in *Sch 36, Finance Act 2004*, and the *Taxation of Pension Schemes (Transitional Provisions) Order 2006* (*SI 2006/572*).

Changes since the last edition of this book

4.2 Some changes which affected SSASs before A-Day, and after the publication of the sixth edition of this book, were included in the supplement to that edition. An extract from the supplement is reproduced in 4.3 below, for completeness.

The new regime means that an employer may have more than one SSAS, although the removal of the earmarking restriction (SSASs were previously essentially common trust funds, but the removal of the trust requirement means that this is no longer a requirement) makes it unlikely that this option will be widely taken up. In addition to these changes, it emerged that the government had developed a major concern over 'self-directed' schemes with regard to the likely impact of the opening up of the investment market to permit investment in residential property after A-Day. This concern gave rise to a welter of statements and changes in practice, and a pre-Budget Report Technical Note, dated 5 December 2005. As the initial government concern was largely focussed on SIPPs, a detailed description of the government's deliberations is given in 5.4 below.

The government's tightening-up on investment activity has since been further extended to a wider category of scheme and their investment activities. A great deal has been published recently on the HMRC website on the matter of indirect investment in 'taxable property'. The new measures also impact on investment in unquoted shares in companies controlled directly or indirectly by a scheme member or someone connected with a scheme member. Major tax charges can be incurred where a company is used as a vehicle for an indirect holding and the scheme and/or its members and persons connected with them control the company in question. If the SSAS holds, say, 10% of the company shares, it will be taxed on 10% of the taxable property of the company. The draft Finance Bill 2006 contains the following provisions, in brief:

- Tax charges will apply where an investment regulated pension scheme holds investments that are taxable property.
- Taxable property consists of residential property and most tangible moveable assets. Residential property can be in the UK or elsewhere and is a building or structure, including associated land, that is used or suitable for use as a dwelling. Tangible moveable property are things that you can touch and move. It includes assets such as art, antiques, jewellery, fine wine, classic cars & yachts.
- An investment regulated pension scheme is one where the member is able (whether directly or indirectly) to direct or influence the manner of investments the scheme makes.
- The provisions apply to taxable property that is held directly and also to indirect holdings of property except through genuinely diverse commercial vehicles.

- If an investment regulated pension scheme directly or indirectly acquires taxable property (residential property or tangible moveable property) this will create an unauthorised payment tax charge on the member whose arrangement acquires the asset. In addition, the scheme administrator will be liable to a scheme sanction charge both on income from the taxable assets and capital gains on their disposal.
- The tax charges will remove the tax advantages on taxable property that may create an opportunity for personal use. So the benefit in kind charge on personal use of registered pension scheme assets will not apply to assets taxed under these measures.
- Income received from taxable property will be charged on the scheme administrator. This will be a charge under the scheme sanction charge and will be taxed at a rate of 40%. If the net income from the property is less than 10% of the value of the property then in place of the actual income the scheme administrator will be taxed on a deemed income. The amount of the deemed income will be 10% of the value of the property.
- Capital gains arising on disposal of taxable property will also be taxed on the scheme administrator as a scheme sanction charge and this will be charged at 40%. The gain will be calculated as if it had been made by a UK resident and domiciled person.
- The legislation on taxable assets will not affect the tax treatment of any income or lump sum paid out of the registered pension scheme. For example, pension benefits, based on taxable property assets, will be taxed in exactly the same way as any other payment from a pension scheme.
- There are special rules to deal with UK tax relieved funds that are put into overseas schemes.
- Certain assets will be protected where they were permitted investments under the pre A-Day regime. The scope of the protection varies depending upon the circumstances concerned.

Although the pre-Budget Report was targeted mainly at residential property and personal chattels, it seems clear that the above references to indirect investment in taxable property extend to the acquisition of unquoted shares in the employer company, or a company directly or indirectly controlled by a member or someone connected with such a person. The net is being cast very wide, and it may be that unintended restrictions are implied in the announcements and draft legislation to date which will be revised on closer inspection.

What is not clear is how the new rules on taxable property as applied to tangible and moveable assets, have effect (if at all) where items such as plant and machinery are concerned. If proper commercial value is paid then such items presumably are not regarded as caught by the new restrictions. As it is often the case that such assets are purchased directly by the sponsoring employer as a business tool and proper rental income is charged, it would seem inappropriate for the new restrictions to apply. Of course, if there is seen to be a clear device to avoid taxation (e g by payment of non-taxable leasing income in the hands of the trustees), there may be a need to report the matter under the tax avoidance rules of the *Finance Act 2004* (see 2.135 to 2.137 above).

The Finance Bill 2006 does not make reference to plant and machinery (or to fixtures and fittings and the like), and the regulations will not be available until some time after the enactment of the Bill. However, there is a tax charge on wasting assets (see 2.85 above), should such items fall within such a category. The availability of assets to members would appear to attract such a charge but, realistically, this must apply to jewellery, paintings, classic cars, etc, rather than plant equipment.

The issue of whether or not a scheme trading, an activity which gives rise to taxable profits (see 2.83 above), depends on the regularity of the activity (see Table 8 below).

Additionally, where alternatively secured pensions are in payment, any left-over funds, once use by the spouse, civil partner or person who is financially dependent (the beneficiary) has come to an end, will be chargeable to inheritance tax on the earlier of the cessation of those benefits and the death of the beneficiary. This is a further restriction, which mainly affects SSASs (and SIPPs), as the remaining funds will be treated as if they were an addition to the original scheme member's estate.

Surcharges and sanctions may be imposed if the provisions are abused and, where high levels of unauthorised payments are made, the registration of the scheme may be withdrawn.

Actions taken before A-Day – supplement to the sixth edition

4.3 Chapter 15 of the supplement to the sixth edition of this book gave an indication of some of the decisions that may need to be considered before A-Day in connection with approved SSASs. The content of that chapter is reproduced in 2.10 below as a guide to trustees, employers, administrators (and others involved in such schemes) when checking the relevant actions which had been taken in respect of their schemes.

The following is an extract from Chapter 15 of the supplement to the sixth edition of this book:

'The main considerations

15.1

The main considerations are whether there may be an advantage in increasing the value of funds beyond the lifetime allowance, or converting the method of benefit accrual, before 6 April 2006 where there is scope to do so. The options must be balanced with the cost of obtaining a current fund value on an actuarial basis before a reasoned decision can be reached. This also applies to Funded Unapproved Retirement Benefit Schemes (FURBS). The deferral of A-Day had allowed more time for schemes and arrangements to reach their conclusions in these matters.

Registering for enhanced protection

15.2

For currently approved schemes, those which [*already*] exceed the lifetime allowance at 6 April 2004 would appear to be able to benefit more under enhanced protection than under primary protection. The *Finance Act 2004* states that a notice of intention to rely on primary and enhanced protection, including pre-commencement pension credit on divorce, must be given no earlier that 6 April 2006 and no later than 5 April 2009. This can also be of importance for funds which are currently below the £1.5 million limit but are already at a significant level.

Alternative benefit provision

15.3

If enhanced protection is sought, an employer may wish to offer different benefits for its employees in the future, such as cash, share schemes or unfunded arrangements. It must be remembered, however, that in order to benefit from enhanced protection, whenever the notice is given, contributions must have ceased from A-Day.

Contributions

15.4

It should be explored whether there is scope to make additional contributions before A-Day. This may be particularly pertinent to gaining advance tax relief on large special contributions.

Investments

15.5

Investments before 6 April 2006, which will not be permitted after that date, will generally be protected under the transitional arrangements following that date. It would seem to be prudent to conduct an investment review before A-Day.

Land development

15.6

In addition to general improvements to land and property, it may be possible to develop land before A-Day with a view to extending its use to residential property post A-Day. The Association of Pensioneer Trustees (APT) [*AMPS*] has issued guidelines to its members advising that proper care must be taken if this action is to be considered. Once the property becomes habitable (a certificate of habitation would be certain evidence), it will be construed as being residential.

Postponing retirement

15.7

It can be attractive to postpone retirement until after 6 April 2006, depending on the circumstances. The relevant changes to consider include:

- a 25% cash option;
- trivial commutation up to 1% of the lifetime allowance;
- income withdrawal whilst in service up to 120% of a flat-rate annuity;
- new alternative secure income payments, and term certain annuities;
- cessation of certification of tax-free cash limits and surplus requirements.

For Primary Protection, under the *Finance Act 2004, Sch 36*, all the actual rights under the employment for the purpose of determining the lifetime allowance will be valued on the basis of the member having reached his expected retirement date on 5 April 2006. A member may take his lump sum from any of his or her chosen arrangements, and the protected value will be the lower of the value of the accrued lump sum, without early retirement factors, and the maximum lump sum allowed under the Inland Revenue's [*HMRC's*] discretionary approval regime on 5 April 2006 (subject to certain assumptions).

Resignation of pensioneer trustee

15.8

The pensioneer trustee should consider signing a formal instrument of resignation from any scheme for which he or she acts, in advance of A-Day, in order to have immediate effect on that date.

Winding up

15.9

The requirements of the Inland Revenue [*HMRC*] or the Department for Work and Pensions must be observed if a scheme is to wind up.'

EU Pensions Directive

4.4 There is no doubt that the changes which have been made to UK pension law have largely been driven by the *EU Pensions Directive (2003/41/EC)* on *IORPs*. The Directive was first published in draft form on 11 October 2000. Thereafter the EC set up occupational pensions regulatory and supervisory committees and the European Parliament set up pensions bodies to consider the application of the draft Pensions Directive. The European Pensions Directive required member states to comply with its terms by 23 September 2005. This date has not been met by all member states, but it is still the effective date that applies. The UK (sometimes under pressure from the EC) has made various changes to its primary statutes and regulations in order to accommodate the main principles of the Directive.

Here is a summary of the main aims of the Directive:

- to establish a framework for IORPs;
- to permit member states to decide on their own investment rules, subject to permitting investment up to 70% in shares and corporate bonds and at least 30% in currencies other than the currency of their future pension liabilities;
- to restrict portfolio self-investment in the sponsoring undertaking to 5% of the portfolio value (under the *Investment Services Directive* this can be disapplied for schemes with fewer than 100 members);
- to achieve a high level of protection for future pensioners and beneficiaries, under prescribed rules of operation;
- to permit freedom to develop effective investment programmes and policy within prudent guidelines (the 'prudent person principle');

- to achieve greater investment security and diversity;
- to improve investment management, and the choice of managers approved by the member state;
- to ensure that schemes have effective liquidity on a needs basis;
- to rationalise tax problems encountered in differing states by pension schemes and arrangements;
- to allow flexibility in scheme design, whether by advance funding or pay-as-you-go schemes;
- to remove obstacles to effective management of pensions schemes across one member state to another (in compliance with the principle of a single integrated financial market, so avoiding an unnecessary multiplicity of managers around the European Union);
- to control administration costs;
- to simplify or remove current restrictions and obstacles to integration;
- to ensure prudent calculation of benefits which are covered by sufficient assets;
- to enable member states to give supervisory powers to relevant authorities to monitor and supervise their IORPs to the required standard;
- to achieve mutual recognition of member states' supervisory regimes to enable cross-border management (the 'home country control' principle);
- to permit a 'host' member state (where the sponsoring employer is located) to be able to request a 'home' member state (where the fund is located) to apply quantative rules to assets held by cross-border schemes, provided that the host member state applies the same, or stricter, rules to its domestic funds – quantative rules concern unlisted assets, assets issued by the sponsoring company and assets held in a different denomination from that in which the scheme liabilities are expressed;
- to permit member states to permit a fund to offer survivor benefits and disability cover, particularly if requested by the employer and employee(s);
- to preserve any existing right to receive a lump sum without restrictions; and
- to give member rights to be informed about transfer rights on a change of employment.

UK investment regulations

4.5 In the UK, the *Occupational Pension Schemes (Investment) Regulations 2005* (*SI 2005/3378*) revoked the *Occupational Pension Schemes (Invest-*

ment) Regulations 1996 (*SI 1996/3127*), and supplement the changes to the *Pensions Act 1995* which were made by the *Pensions Act 2004*. The regulations are described in 5.5 below, and they appear at the end of Chapter 5 by way of an annex.

Exemption regulations

4.6 The *Occupational Pension Schemes* (*Trust and Retirement Benefits Exemption*) *Regulations 2005* (*SI 2005/2360*) prescribe the description of schemes which are exempt from:

- the requirement in *s 252(2), Pensions Act 2004*, that trustees or managers of an occupational pension scheme with its main administration in the UK must not accept funding payments unless the scheme is established under irrevocable trust;
- the requirement in *s 255(1)* of the Act, that an occupational pension scheme with its main administration in the UK must be limited to retirement-benefit activities.

The effect is:

- *s 252(2)* transposes *Article 8* of the *EU Pensions Directive* on the activities and supervision of IORPs (*Article 8* requires legal separation of the assets of an occupational pension scheme and those of a sponsoring employer);
- *s 255(1)* transposes *Article 7* of the *Directive* (*Article 7* requires that occupational pension schemes are limited to retirement-benefit activities).

The rules which applied prior to A-Day

4.7 In view of the introduction of the single tax regime from A-Day, most of the existing rules are now effectively spent. Nevertheless, until SSASs have been operating under the new regime over the next year or so, it will be helpful for the reader to be reminded of the rules which applied. This is of particular importance in the area of investments to which the transitional arrangements apply and in the matter of any outstanding actuarial and accounting procedures.

The book has inevitably expanded considerably in order to cover the new tax regime, and the reader is referred to the sixth edition and supplement thereto for full details of past practice.

The main summaries are contained in Tables 1 to 9 below.

Table 1 Allowances and legislation

Capital Allowances Act 2001

4.8 This Act was the first legislation to emerge from the Tax Law Reform Project, the aim of which was to rewrite existing direct tax legislation to make it clearer and easier to use, but without changing the general effect of it. The Act contains a simplified description of the main provisions of the *Capital Allowances Act 1990*, with few significant changes.

Main contents of the Act

4.9

- *ss 7* and *8* – no double allowances, or relief through pooling (plant and machinery allowances);
- *ss 11* to *14* – plant and machinery allowances;
- *ss 15* to *20* – qualifying allowances, including leasing of plant and machinery;
- *ss 21* to *50* – qualifying expenditure, including plant and machinery;
- *ss 47* to *49* – expenditure of small or medium-sized enterprises;
- *ss 67* to *70* – hire purchase, plant and machinery provided by lessee;
- *ss 213* to *233* – anti-avoidance, including sale and leaseback;
- *ss 272* to *304* – IBA, and qualifying enterprise zones.

The Income Tax (Earnings and Pensions) Act 2003

4.10 'An Act to restate, with minor changes, certain enactments relating to income tax on employment income, pension income and social security income; and for connected purposes'.

Main contents of the Act

4.11

- Part 1 (Overview) sets out what is covered in the Act and where to find abbrevieations and definitions.
- Part 2 (Employment income: charge to tax) introduces the concept of 'the employment income Parts' to cover parts 2 to 7 and sets out the charging provisions for employment income.

- Part 3 (Employment income: earnings and benefits etc. treated as earnings) deals with the general earnings element of employment income, setting out what kinds of income and benefits should be brought into account.
- Part 4 (Employment income: exemptions) gives details of a number of exemptions from various kinds of income that would otherwise be chargeable to tax under the employment income Parts.
- Part 5 (Employment income: deductions allowed from earnings) sets out various deductions that may be allowed from earnings in computing taxable earnings.
- Part 6 (Employment income: income which is not earnings or share-related) covers payments to and benefits from non-approved pension schemes and payments and benefits on termination of employment etc.
- Part 7 (Employment income: share related income and exemptions) contains provisions about share-related remuneration and the various share option schemes and incentive plans.
- Part 8 (Former employees: deductions for liabilities) sets out that certain deductions may be made from a former employee's total income.
- Part 9 (Pension and income) contains the charging provisions for pension income, including any exemptions from those charging provisions.
- Part 10 (Social Security income) contains the charging provisions for taxable social security benefits including any exemptions from those charging provisions.
- Part 11 (Pay As You Earn) sets out the framework for the operation of PAYE and provides for the making of PAYE regulations.
- Part 12 (Payroll giving) sets out the rules for the payroll deduction scheme for charitable donations.
- Part 13 (Supplementary provisions) contains provisions that have effect across the other Parts of the Act.

The Schedules are:

- Schedule 1: Abbreviations and defined expressions
- Schedule 2: Approved share incentive plans
- Schedule 3: Approved SAYE option schemes
- Schedule 4: Approved CSOP option schemes
- Schedule 5: Enterprise management incentives
- Schedule 6: Consequential amendments

- Schedule 7: Transitionals and savings
- Schedule 8: Repeals and revocations.

Table 2 Inland Revenue legislation and guidelines

4.12 SSASs are subject to the following legislation and guidelines:

- *Income and Corporation Taxes Act 1988* and successive Finance Acts;
- Statutory Instruments, in particular the *Retirement Benefit Schemes (Restriction on Discretion to Approve) (Small Self-Administered Schemes) Regulations 1991 (SI 1991/1614)* (Appendix 4) – referred to as the SSAS Regulations;
- Practice Notes (PN) and Updates (formerly Memoranda or Joint Office Memoranda (JOM));
- Changes in Practice such as those published following the Parliamentary Question (PQ) raised in July 1984;
- Pension Schemes Instructions (PSI) – Examiners' Manual and Small Self-Administered Schemes Guidance Notes (SAS GN);
- Consultative Document of September 1987;
- The role of the pensioneer trustee – PSO Update No 69; (see below)*;
- Frequently Asked Questions (FAQs) – i e general enquiries posed to IR SPSS seeking clarification of IR SPSS requirements relating to pension schemes and IR SPSS's responses, which are all posted on the Inland Revenue's website if IR SPSS considers that they will be of general interest and assistance.

* Note – the role of the Pensioneer Trustee will cease from A-Day, but as it was a requirement to have one under pre-A-Day regulations, failure to have appointed one would disqualify a SSAS from becoming a Registered Scheme from 6 April 2006.

Other regulations

4.13

- *Retirement Benefit Schemes (Information Powers) Regulations 1995 (SI 1995/3103)*;
- *Retirement Benefit Schemes (Restriction on Discretion to Approve) (Small Self-administered Schemes) (Amendment) Regulations (SI 1998/728)*;

- *Retirement Benefit Schemes (Restriction on Discretion to Approve) (Excepted Provisions) Regulations (SI 1998/729)*;
- *Retirement Benefit Schemes (Restriction on Discretion to Approve) (Small Self-administered Schemes) (Amendment No 2) Regulations 1998 (SI 1998/1315)*;
- *Personal Pension Schemes (Conversion of Retirement Benefit Schemes) Regulations 2001 (SI 2001/118)*;
- *Personal Pension Schemes (Transfer Payments) Regulations 2001 (SI 2001/119)*; and
- *Retirement Benefits Schemes (Information Powers) (Amendment) Regulations 2002 (SI 2002/3006)*.

Table 3 Documentation and approval

Establishment of a SSAS

4.14 This had to be under irrevocable trusts, by deed, or by company resolution, subject to the company Memorandum and Articles.

Interim deed

4.15 Prior to 6 April 2002 an interim deed may have been used to initiate the Scheme, if so, it had to comply with the following requirements:

- to declare that the trust was irrevocable;
- to set out the main purposes of the Scheme;
- to appoint (among others) the pensioneer trustee;
- to grant powers of investment and administration to the trustees; and
- to set a time limit for production of a definitive deed – normally two years.

After 6 April 2002, all applications to establish a SSAS must be accompanied by a definitive deed and rules – (IR SPSS Update No 103).

Members' announcement letters

4.16 Required to be sent to every member at the inception of the scheme, and whenever any new member joined the scheme, the announcement letter must give written particulars of all essential features of the scheme:

- *Main benefits*
  - At Normal Retirement;
  - On death in service;
  - On death after retirement;
  - On withdrawal from service;
  - On early retirement;
  - On late retirement;
  - Options (e g cash commutation) at retirement.
- *Pension increases*
  - Basis of annual increases and any underpin that applied, e g RPI/3% etc.
- *Members' contributions*
  - Amount;
  - Arrangements for their collection;
  - Effect of temporary absence.
- *Financing details*
  - The basis of the company's contributions.
- *Legal constitution*
  - Documentation;
  - Reference to the legislation under which the scheme was approved.
- *Operational details*
  - The scheme administrator;
  - The trustees;
  - The managing trustees, (if any).
- *Amendments*
  - The powers of amendment and how they may be effected.
- *Actuarial documentation*
  - Supporting actuarial advice or report had to accompany the initial application for approval to IR SPSS (see Sixth edition for details – 9.3 to 9.50).
- *Definitive documentation and scheme abandonment*
  - Definitive documentation could be tailor-made for the particular

scheme, however widespread use of standard 'model' deeds was common. The scheme could, subject to certain criteria, be abandoned with IR SPSS approval if:

- The scheme had not yet received approval.
- If fully insured; the trust provisions allowed for this.
- No member had completed more than two years of qualifying service.
- Policies surrendered and premiums returned to the company and contributions returned to the member(s) and provisional tax relief withdrawn.
- Cancellation of a policy during a 'cooling off' period was not in itself sufficient reason for a scheme to be treated as abandoned.
- Approved schemes could only be abandoned if IR SPSS cancelled the approval, e g on change of status from employed to self-employed after approval had been granted.
- At trustee initiative, e g to make the arrangement paid-up or to wind up the trust in accordance with its own provisions, the trustees being satisfied that their trust rules allowed it.

- *Definitive Deed*

  - Usually two parts, comprising the trust deed with clauses setting out the trustees' powers and discretions, plus provisions for winding up the scheme. Secondly, the rules, normally in schedule form dealing with eligibility, contributions, benefit details and setting out Inland Revenue limits on benefits.

    In addition to the standard clauses and rules for a self-administered scheme set up under irrevocable trust, IR SPSS required the following to be included:

    - Provision for a pensioneer trustee.
    - A rule providing for actuarial valuations, at no longer than triennial intervals.
    - A clause setting out trustees' powers on winding up the scheme, to be allowed only in accordance with the rules, subject to a unanimous decision by all the trustees, including the pensioneer trustee.

    Under SSAS regulations – introduced on 5 August 1991, which then became compulsory from 5 August 1994; inclusion of provisions on:

- borrowings;
- trustee/member transactions;
- certain investments;
- loans;
- the pensioneer trustee;
- reporting requirements.

Model rules were again updated under subsequent regulations, SI 1998/728 and SI 1998/1315 – (see Table 2).

- *Other requirements*
  - Participation by controlling directors in these arrangements meant that additional features were expected to ensure that the specific limitations applicable to them were met. Readers are referred to Chapter 1 of Tolley's *Taxation of Pension Benefits*, 2nd edition, 2001.

    The main additional features were:

    - scheme name, commencement date;
    - interpretation and a recital listing earlier documentation, noting any breach of timescale for completion;
    - powers of appointment and removal of trustees;
    - trustees' own powers, including investment powers, proceedings and scheme administration;
    - powers of appointment and removal of scheme actuary and accountant;
    - provision for actuarial reviews;
    - powers to close, freeze or wind up the scheme;
    - contributions, trustees' costs and indemnification;
    - death benefits, including discretionary distributions and member nominations;
    - power of amendment;
    - eligibility and temporary absence, benefits and limits, transfers and buy-outs.
  - Deeds affecting the scheme would be engrossed by a solicitor.
- *Annuity purchase*

- Flexible provisions, set out in Pension Update No 105, broadly followed the arrangements for personal pensions, subject to the following criteria:
  - any over-funding to be dealt with when benefits commence;
  - the test for buy-out policies was the date when benefits first became payable;
  - in calculating maximum benefits, allocation of benefits under PN 12.5 was not until date of annuity purchase;
  - pension drawdown calculated by use of GAD's 'single life only' tables;
  - drawdown could apply to the whole, or alternatively an annuity could be purchased with one part of it and the remainder applied as drawdown;
  - IR limits applicable to the amount of pension and to the pension equivalent of any lump sum taken;
  - subject to above, a lower and upper range applied, from 35% to 100% of the annuity that could have been purchased at the relevant time;
  - PAYE provisions were applicable;
  - pensions in payment could vary, within the specified range, year on year, but could not cease;
  - if there was a direct relationship between the pension and lump sum, the latter was based on the amount of pension before commutation for cash;
  - reviews were required (at least) triennially after drawdown commenced, where pension had not been secured, employing the GAD tables;
  - after each review, the pension had to be within the 35% to 100% range;
  - restrictions on insured schemes were contained in PN, App XII;
  - members with concurrent membership of more than one scheme could only draw down from one at a time, subject to normal timing requirements;
  - if there was a shortfall on IR maxima at commencement of drawdown, the sponsoring employer was permitted to pay more contributions to secure additional benefits and/or pension increases;

        - on shortfall, where an annuity had already been secured, the additional benefits could be deferred and later applied in drawdown in accordance with these principles;
        - for retained benefit calculation purposes, the maximum level of pension drawdown had to be applied.

- *Spouses and dependants*
    - In addition to the above criteria, spouses' and dependants' benefits were subject to the following:
        - on death of the member during drawdown, he or she was treated as having died in retirement, with special conditions if AVCs had come into payment;
        - any five-year guarantee had to be elected at start of drawdown;
        - the amount above could be calculated as if the member had opted for 100% withdrawal;
        - if an annuity had been purchased in the guarantee period, any attaching guarantee was reduced in proportion to the time that had elapsed since drawdown commenced;
        - any survivors' pension benefits, together with own right pensions were subject to limits applicable at member's death (PN 12.2 and 12.3);
        - the beneficiary was permitted to commence drawdown under the same principles, which would then apply in the same way, on the death of the beneficiary during a period of drawdown.
- *Preservation*
    - The statutory two-year rule applied, but was largely academic, since immediate vesting on leaving was common, regardless of length of service completed.
- *Equal treatment*
    - Rules were subject to the equal treatment requirements, laid down by the European Court.
- *Reporting requirements*
    - The reporting requirements are detailed in the Sixth Edition (3.70), and as amended by the supplement to that edition.
- *Self-assessment requirements*
    - Self assessment applies to the trustees of tax-approved self-administered schemes in the same way that it does to other taxpay-

ers, and the self-assessment legislation covered the power to require pension scheme accounts to be produced (*TMA 1970, s 8A*).

- Scheme administrators did not fall within self-assessment, being covered instead by the reporting requirements.

- *Divorce requirements*
  - Inland Revenue's position on divorce and pension rights was initially set out under Update No 60, and expanded in Updates Nos 62, 76 and 84, which went on to provide specimen rule amendments for adoption by approved schemes. Update No 84 focused on the calculation of pension debits for money purchase schemes.
  - Revised Appendix XIII to PN described how to calculate maximum limits, following reduction by a pension-sharing order.

Table 4 Benefit structure

4.17 IR SPSS approval could be sought under *ss 590 or 591* of *ICTA 1988. Section 590* gave mandatory approval to a range of very restricted benefits, with no enhancement capability, while s 591 gave discretionary approval to higher levels of benefit, so naturally, approval under s 591 was preferred for the great majority of schemes.

Preferably established on a money purchase basis, schemes typically provided for benefits to be provided up to IR limits, to the extent that funding was sufficient.

Normal retirement age could be set at any age between 60 and 75 (PN 6.6). Female members (excluding controlling directors) with pre-1 June 1989 continued rights could retain the option to retire at 55.

Benefit provision could be up to IR maximum, depending on the relevant benefit regime to which the member belonged.

Full 1989 members

4.18 Members of schemes established on or after 14 March 1989 and members of other schemes who joined on or after 1 July 1989 or who have elected to be subject to these limits:

- *Employee contributions*
  - 15% of annual remuneration, subject to the Earnings Cap.

- *Pension at normal retirement age*
  - 2/3 x final remuneration after 20 years' service. If service was less than 20 years, the maximum accrual was 1/30 x final remuneration for each year of service.
- *Lump sum at normal retirement age*
  - 2¼ x the initial annual rate of pension (including any AVC/FSAVC pension under the scheme) before any commutaion or allocation to spouse and/or dependants.
- *Early retirement on grounds of ill-health*
  - Maximum potential amount at normal retirement based on actual final remuneration at date of retirement.
  - A lump sum of 2¼ x the initial annual rate of pension (before commutation or allocation).
- *Normal early retirement benefits*
  - A pension of 1/30 x final remuneration x years of service – maximum 2/3 x final remuneration.
  - A lump sum of 2¼ x the initial annual rate of pension (before commutation or allocation).
- *Leaving service*
  - A deferred pension equal to the ordinary early retirement pension based on final remuneration at the date of leaving service and revalued in deferment;
  - A deferred lump sum of 2¼ x the initial annual rate of pension (before commutation or allocation).
- *Late retirement*
  - A pension of 1/30 x final remuneration x years of service up to a maximum of 20/30;
  - A lump sum of 2¼ x the initial annual rate of pension (before commutation or allocation).
- *Death in service lump sum*
  - 4 x final remuneration plus a refund of employee's contributions with interest.
- *Death in service pension*
  - 2/3 x the maximum potential pension that could have been provided for the member at normal retirement age. With additions for other dependants, the maximum aggregate benefit was equal to the mem-

ber's own maximum pension, as described above. In the absence of a surviving spouse the maximum payable to one dependant was equal to that payable to a surviving spouse.

- *Death after retirement pension*
  - 2/3 x the maximum potential pension that could have been provided for the member at retirement, increased in line with RPI. (No commuted lump sum is available). With additions for other dependants, the maximum aggregate benefit was equal to the member's own maximum pension, as described above. In the absence of a surviving spouse the maximum payable to one dependant was equal to that payable to a surviving spouse.
  - If an unexpired guarantee applied to the member's pension at time of death a tax-free lump sum representing the balance of 5 years' instalments could also be provided. Where the guarantee exceeded 5 years, up to a limit of 10, the remaining instalments would continue for that period, to the dependant(s) at trustee discretion.
- *AVCs*
  - Additional benefits paid in pension form only. Commutation of AVC benefits allowed only if the member had entered into the AVC arrangement prior to 8 April 1987.
  - Surplus AVCs were repayable to the member after deduction of tax.
- *Retained benefits*
  - In most cases pension had to be aggregated with any other retained benefits to assess whether the two thirds pension limit was exceeded.
  - A retained benefits test is not required for the lump sum calculation or dependants' benefits, and no retained benefits need to be taken into account for new entrants on or after 31 August 1991 who earn less than ¼ of the Earnings Cap in their first year of membership.

Pre-1987 members

4.19 (joiners before 17 March 1987)

- *Employee contributions*
  - 15% of remuneration per annum.
- *Pension at normal retirement age (including the pension equivalent of any lump sum)*
  - 2/3 x final remuneration after ten years' service. Where the mem-

ber's service is less than ten years, the fraction of final remuneration is determined from the following uplifted table:

Years of service	60ths
1–5	1 per year
6	8
7	16
8	24
9	32
10	40

- *Lump sum at normal retirement age*
  - 11/2 x final remuneration after 20 years' service. Where the member's service is less than 20 years, the fraction of final remuneration is determined from the following uplifted table:

Years of service	80ths
1–8	3 per year
9	30
10	36
11	42
12	48
13	54
14	63
15	72
16	81
17	90
18	99
19	108
20	120

- *Early retirement on grounds of ill-health*
  - The benefits are:

    (i) the maximum potential pension which could have been provided at normal retirement age;

    (ii) the maximum potential lump sum which could have been provided at normal retirement age;

    both based on actual final remuneration.
- *Normal early retirement benefits*
  - A ratio of completed service to potential service, multiplied by the maxima shown in (i) and (ii) immediately above, is applied. Final remuneration is determined at actual retirement.
- *Leaving service*
  - A deferred pension equal to the ordinary early retirement pension based on final remuneration at date of leaving service and revalued in deferment. This is commutable within normal limits on retirement.
- *Late retirement*
  - Either a pension of:

    (i) 1/60 x final remuneration x years of service (if 40 years have been served by normal retirement age, an additional 1/60 for each later year of service may be accrued up to an overall total of 45/60); or

    (ii) uplifted benefits at normal retirement age, plus interest (see above table) to retirement,

  and either a lump sum of:

    (i) 3/80 x final remuneration x years of service (if 40 years have been served by normal retirement age, an additional 3/80 for each year of later service up to an overall total of 135/80); or

    (ii) uplifted lump sum at normal retirement plus interest (see above table) to retirement.

    For controlling directors there is a restriction on the amount of additional benefits that can be accrued before age 70 (see 4.20).
- *Death in service lump sum*
  - 4 x final remuneration, plus a refund of employee's contributions with interest.
- *Death in service pension*

- 2/3 x the maximum potential pension that could have been provided for the member at normal retirement age. With additions for other dependants, the maximum aggregate benefit was equal to the member's own maximum pension, as described above. In the absence of a surviving spouse the maximum payable to one dependant was equal to that payable to a surviving spouse.

- *Death after retirement pension*
  - 2/3 x the maximum potential pension that could have been provided for the member at retirement, increased in line with RPI. (No commuted lump sum is available). With additions for other dependants, the maximum aggregate benefit was equal to the member's own maximum pension, as described above. In the absence of a surviving spouse the maximum payable to one dependant was equal to that payable to a surviving spouse.
  - A guarantee payment could be provided as for death in retirement for a full 1989 member, described above.
- *AVCs*
  - As for full 1989 Members.
- *Retained benefits*
  - In most cases pensions must be aggregated with any retained benefits to assess whether the 2/3rds limit is exceeded.
  - A retained benefit test was also required for the lump sum calculation.
  - A retained benefit test is not required for dependants' benefits and no retained benefits need to be taken into account for new entrants on or after 31 August 1991, who earn less than ¼ of the Earnings Cap in their first year of membership.

1987 members

4.20 (Members of schemes established before 14 March 1989 who joined between 17 March 1987 and 31 May 1989 inclusive.)

- *Employee contributions*
  - 15% of annual remuneration per annum.
- *Pension at normal retirement age (including the pension equivalent of any lump sum)*
  - 2/3 x final remuneration after 20 years' service. If service was less than 20 years, the maximum accrual was 1/30 x final remuneration for each year of service.

- *Lump sum at normal retirement age*
  - The lump sum may be enhanced above the basic rate of 3/80 accrual (up to 'uplifted 3/80' level) in proportion to a pension enhancement that is above the 1/60 basic rate.
- *Early retirement on grounds of ill-health*
  - The maximum potential pension which could have been provided at normal retirement age;
  - The maximum lump sum which could have been provided at normal retirement age;

  both based on actual final remuneration.
- *Normal early retirement benefits*
  - A ratio of completed service to potential service, multiplied by the maxima shown in (i) and (ii) immediately above, based on final remuneration at actual retirement.
- *Leaving service*
  - A deferred pension equal to the ordinary early retirement pension based on final remuneration at actual retirement.
- *Late retirement*
  - Either a pension of:

    (i) 1/60 x final remuneration x years of service (if 40 years has been served by normal retirement age, an additional 1/60 for each later year of service up to a total of 45/60); or

    (ii) 1/30 x final remuneration x years of service up to a maximum of 20/30 at normal retirement age, plus interest (see above) to retirement:

  and either a lump sum of:

    (i) 3/80 up to maximum of 135/80 as for pre-1987 members; or

    (ii) a higher cash formula enhancement in proportion to the pension.

  For controlling directors there was a restriction on the amount of additional benefits that could be accrued before age 70.
- *Death in service cash sum*
  - 4 x final remuneration, plus a refund of employee's contributions (with interest).
- *Death in service pension*

  - 2/3 x the maximum potential pension that could have been provided for the member at normal retirement age. This benefit could be paid to the surviving spouse. In addition, pensions could be paid to the dependants of the member, subject to an overall limit of 100% of the deceased member's own pension. If no surviving spouse, the maximum payable to one dependant was the same as could be provided to a surviving spouse.
- *Death after retirement pension*
  - 2/3 x the maximum potential pension that could have been provided for the member at retirement, increased in line with RPI (no commuted lump sum was available). This benefit could be paid to the surviving spouse. In addition, pensions could be paid to the dependants of the member, subject to an overall limit of 100% of the deceased member's own pension, as described above. If no surviving spouse, the maximum payable to one dependant was the same as could be provided to a surviving spouse.
  - A guarantee payment could be provided as for death in retirement within a period of up to ten years, as described above.
- *AVCs*
  - As for pre-1987 Members.

1989 members

4.21 (Members of schemes approved before 27 July 1989 who joined on or after 1 June 1989 or who have elected to be subject to the limits which apply to such individuals, or members of schemes established before 14 March 1989 which were not approved before 27 July 1989 and who joined the scheme before 1 June 1989.)

- The benefit regime was the same as for 1987 Members except that the Earnings Cap and the lump sum enhancement of 2¼ x initial rate of actual pension applied by overriding statute.
- The application of the earnings cap affected not only the calculation of the member's pension, lump sum and death benefits under the scheme, but also the maximum remuneration on which the member could make contributions into the scheme in order to augment his or her benefits.

Table 5 Investments – loans

General

4.22 Trust Deeds for SSASs were drafted to give the widest approvable range of investment powers to the trustees, with the aim of enhancing the capability of these arrangements to provide genuine relevant benefits for members. To strengthen that aim, legislative measures introduced in August 2000 enabled pensioneer trustees to take a more prominent role in the ownership of trust assets, as well as an active part in financial transactions, by requiring them to become joint signatories to scheme bank accounts (PSO Update 69).

The main point to be noted in the approach to A Day, is that while regulation of investments and loans will come under a single regime from that date, existing arrangements may have investment features in regard to loans and property, that would no longer be approvable. However, under transitional arrangements, those arrangements will be allowed to stand unless, or until, they are altered post A-Day.

The facility of loans to employers, which was a key feature of these schemes is examined in detail in Chapter 5 of the sixth edition of this book, as summarised below:

- To which employer(s) – any participating company, but with restrictions where controlling directors were involved;
- To members – not allowed, PN 20.52;
- Amount – up to 50% of scheme assets;
- Frequency – the pattern and frequency of loans to employers, compared to the scheme contribution history, dictated whether IR SPSS viewed the arrangements as satisfactory;
- Purpose – for proper business purposes only, investment in luxury items, e g private cars, would jeopardize approval;
- Interest rate – a commercially reasonable one, by general reference to the Clearing Bank Base Rates (CBBR);
- Tax deduction – interest payments allowed gross, from 1 October 2002;
- Capital repayment – preferably built into a series of interest and capital repayment instalments;
- Liquidity – loans could not be approved, that would impede the financial liquidity of the scheme's purpose in paying benefits;
- Security – evidence from a bank that terms and conditions were similar, if loan was made at less than CBBR + 3%.

Table 6 Investment in property and land

4.23 Another attractive feature of the investment facilities with a SSAS was the capability to invest in property and land, in particular to purchase from an employer and then lease it back to them.

Summarised below are the main features which, for detailed description and comment, the reader is referred to Chapter 6 of previous, i.e. 6th edition of this book;

The permitted (or otherwise) categories of sale and purchase transactions were:

- Permitted properties, vendors and purchasers:
  - land or property, freehold or leasehold, comprising:
    - commercial/industrial property;
    - residential property, if held indirectly via unit trust, where no scheme members occupied the property. Other exceptions applied where non-connected persons (e g caretakers) occupied the property;
    - residential property forming an integral part of the business premises, occupied by independent party on commercial terms;
    - agricultural property and land;
    - forestry and woodlands;
    - commercial/industrial property held abroad;
    - permitted vendors/purchasers included the principal company and associated companies – regardless of their participation in the scheme;
    - unconnected third parties;
    - transactions of property owned by the trustees before 15 July 1991 – (see sixth edition).
- Classes of vendor, purchaser and property not permitted:
  - members or their relatives;
  - partnerships involving members;
  - residential property, other than the permitted cases mentioned above;
  - residential property held abroad.

All transactions were reportable within 90 days of completion, whether involving cash sales or not.

Substantial gains in the value of property could in exceptional cases arise where, for example, planning permission became available to change the nature and purpose of the property, giving rise to surpluses within the scheme, long before any subsequent sale or development at a later date. Actuarial advice in such circumstances could lead to refunds having to be made to the employer, incurring a charge of 35%.

Environmental law and health and safety law were further major considerations for the trustees in relation to such investments.

Table 7 Unquoted shares, other investments and borrowings

4.24 Share ownership within participating and associated companies was another feature of SSAS investment that came under scrutiny by IR SPSS. Shareholdings in unconnected unquoted companies were also controlled under the SSAS regulations as transactions of this nature could be misused, to create tax avoidance measures. The regulations specifically prohibited any transactions between the scheme trustees and any of the members or their families.

The Inland Revenue monitored share transactions under powers contained in ICTA 1988, Pt XVII, s 703 *et seq.* Referral to IR technical division was made in connection with a transaction for clearance, if there was any doubt that tax rules might be infringed.

Another aspect of tax avoidance through transactions in shares related to Inheritance Tax. Given the nature of transactions in unquoted companies it was frequently the case that family relationships would exist between vendor and purchaser, so the shares could be transferred at an artificial price, thus reducing or avoiding tax. IR SPSS would therefore refer the details of a transaction to the shares valuation division, for verification of the true value of shares transferred. Clearance from that division enabled ownership of such shareholdings to be accepted as investments under a SSAS.

In order to satisfy liquidity requirements for payment of benefits, share ownership within a SSAS was permissible while there was at least one active member in the scheme, but once the final member retired, measures to discontinue share ownership took effect, with a time limit of five years for their ultimate disposal.

Similarly to transactions in property, share transactions were reportable to IR SPSS within 90 days of execution, under SSAS regulations.

Special provisions relating to holdings in unquoted companies acquired before 5 August 1991 and dealings in shares with members, where the scheme acquired them before 15 July 1991 are detailed in Chapter 7 of the sixth edition of this book. Other aspects covering non-income producing assets, their type and concentration of investment and borrowing against the assets of schemes, up to permissible limits are also discussed in the same chapter.

New borrowings will not be permitted after A-Day, but existing arrangements on 5 April 2006 will be allowed to remain, so long as they are not altered in any way thereafter.

Table 8 Trading and self-assessment

4.25 The range of trustee activity that could be construed as trading was very wide, but the range of such activities that was permissible within a SSAS was limited, generally to ensure that tax avoidance schemes were not involved, but also to ensure that tax on profits from permitted trading was properly assessed and paid. Judgment whether a transaction was taxable was in the hands of the local inspector of taxes.

The intentions of the trustees in their purchases and sales of investments is the key to whether an activity will be classed as trading. IR SPSS's view is that where there is an organised effort to generate profit, this will create taxable income. Carrying out development work for example, on a property with a view to disposal, would constitute such effort.

Investments in the stock market by trustees, although they could involve short-term acquisition and disposals of shares when markets were volatile, did not amount to trading, in IR SPSS's view. This type of activity only attracted their attention if 'bond washing' or 'dividend stripping' could be identified.

Stock lending activities were permissible transactions, common in larger pension schemes. The fees had been taxable up to 2 January 1996, but thereafter became exempt from tax.

From 6 April 1996, self-assessment applied to the trustees of all self-administered pension schemes, which included SSASs. Even if a scheme did not generate any chargeable income under this regime, the requirement to submit a return was nevertheless obligatory, with the imposition of a fine for failure to submit them within the annual deadline of 31 January following the relevant tax-year end.

The scheme administrator was not subject to this regime. The administrator was, however, required under the reporting regulations, to submit details annually, listing chargeable events including refunds of contributions to members on withdrawal in the year and commutation payments on retirement where a taxable element was included, i e on grounds of triviality or serious ill-health.

For further details on the self-assessment regime, readers are referred to Chapter 8 of the sixth edition.

Table 9 Funding and actuarial matters

4.26 In order to satisfy IR SPSS that a scheme had been properly established, on the basis of actuarial recommendations for immediate and long-term funding, the initial application for approval was accompanied by:

- the scheme trust deed and rules;
- an actuarial report or summary; and
- the members' initial announcement/invitation to join the scheme.

The actuarial report was required to be submitted from a qualified actuary. If a full report was not immediately available, this had to follow within a reasonable time.

The actuarial report gave full details of the scheme and its membership which, being small in headcount, enabled detailed analysis of membership salary and service data which could, on occasion, be checked back by IR SPSS with the local inspector for corroboration.

Details of retained benefits and/or personal pensions and retirement annuity contracts were also furnished with the report, in addition to information on pension membership data related to current employment.

Using this and the scheme information from the member's announcement letter, IR SPSS would initially satisfy themselves on two main points:

- That the aim of the arrangement was to provide similar levels of benefits for all members, i.e. ensure that misuse of SSAS regulations was not involved, e g by artificial headcount with an uneven set of benefit levels.
- To ensure that there was a realistic level of funding.

Checking the actuarial assumptions adopted in the initial report enabled IR SPSS to see the basis of long-term funding recommendations; the key points being the 'gap' between the assumed rate of future salary growth, compared with the anticipated rate of investment growth and the latter, compared with assumed future annual pension increases. Statutory requirements on funding, arising under the Pensions Act 1995, had to be applied, by making provision for pensions arising from contributions after April 1997, to increase by 5% or RPI (reduced to 2.5%/RPI from April 2005). Provision for spouses' benefits were relevant only where a marital relationship existed.

A major overhaul of the basis of funding for SSAS arrangements was carried out in the mid-nineties, leading to the introduction of the 'SSAS 1996 Method' of funding. Full details of this development are set out in the sixth edition of this book, along with further discussion on funding, special contributions, surpluses and their remedies etc.

Chapter 5

The UK investment regulations, and the pre-A-Day SIPPs rules

Introduction

5.1 As stated in 4.1 above, the tax simplification changes introduced a single tax regime from A-Day. The few exceptions which have arisen mainly concern SSASs and SIPPs in relation to their investment activities. This chapter describes the new investment regulations which apply to occupational pension schemes, the latest position for SIPPs and the pre A-Day rules by which SIPPs were regulated. The pre-A-Day rules are relevant to the transitional arrangements for the old tax regimes (see tables 1 to 11 below, in 5.6 to 5.19 below).

Chapter 4 describes the latest position for SSASs, and the pre-A-Day rules which applied to those schemes. The full investment changes are contained in Chapter 6 of the 4th edition of Tottel's *Taxation of Pension Benefits* and are summarised in 2.73 to 2.85 above.

The existing SIPPs exemptions from some of the provisions of the *Pensions Act 1995* are largely retained, and there are special provisions for schemes with fewer than 100 members under the European (IORP) Pension Directive. This matter is described in 4.4 above.

Self-investment

5.2 A SIPPs is, by nature, self-invested because of the member's ability to control how the fund is invested. It is a personal pension, and prior to A-Day it was subject to the legislative requirements and HMRC discretionary practice that applied to personal pensions. As stated in 4.1 above, such schemes are now classified by HMRC as 'self-directed'.

Pre-A-Day attraction of SIPPs

5.3 The main attraction of SIPPs has been for the company director, self-employed partner, or sole proprietor to purchase commercial property, such as offices, which can be let on arm's-length terms to the member's business. The purchase could be funded not just from the fund itself, but from borrowings and/or transfer payments brought in from previous pension arrangements. The member could decide on his own investments, subject to HMRC requirements, either as a trustee of his/her own SIPP fund or by instructing the trustee. Such control is not available with an insured personal pension unless it is of the self-managed variety. Many of these attractions remain after A-Day. However, a SIPP was mainly funded by personal contributions by the member (in the absence of an employer's contribution for self-employed taxpayers and the general reluctance of employers to make contributions on behalf of their employees to personal pensions).

The facility to take income withdrawals from a SIPP after retirement and up to age 75, within certain parameters, was undoubtedly a distinct advantage. It was more flexible than either the more common facility under a SSAS to defer the purchase of annuities to age 75, where the level of pension must be maintained, subject to sufficiency of funds, or the less used facility introduced in PSO Update No 54, which was also available to all types of money purchase retirement benefits schemes. The main areas of greater flexibility were those in relation to 'phased' income withdrawals and death benefits. It was also advantageous to director members of retirement benefits schemes who wished to continue in an executive capacity but also draw retirement benefits where this would not be permitted under the rules of the retirement benefits scheme, and to escape the 5% maximum self-investment requirement for occupational schemes.

Pre-A-Day consultation on investment matters (SSASs and SIPPs)

5.4 In a pre-Budget Report (Technical Note dated 5 December 2005), the government published its latest thinking on tax simplification in respect of 'registered pension schemes which are self-directed'. This was a surprise to the SIPPs market, in particular, which had been developing marketing strategies for some time in order to take advantage of the relaxation in the investment rules from A-Day. The government stated that it wished to avoid the potential misuse of schemes for buying second homes.

Whereas the government's statement that such investment is 'a realistic proposition for only those with the largest pension pots' is credible (as diversity of investment is desirable if pension provision is to be reasonably secure), this was a significant change of direction. It places no confidence in the IFA or investment-adviser market. The Report concerned tax avoidance in general, and stated that SIPPs 'will be prohibited from obtaining tax advantages when investing in residential property and certain other assets such as fine wines' from A-Day.

The *Registered Pension Schemes Manual* reflected the growing concern of the government in the area of investment by SIPPs in residential property. RPSM07101060 states:

> 'Using a registered pension scheme to invest in a buy to let residential property or holiday home or any other type of residential property may have the following consequences:
>
> - The property becomes an asset of the pension fund and there is a requirement to put all rental income into the pension fund so it is locked away and cannot be accessed until authorised benefits are paid.
> - If the property is made available to a member of the scheme or members of their family it will give rise to a benefits in kind tax charge if a market rent is not paid (even if they choose not to use it).
> - Any property bought by the pension fund in most cases will need to be sold before the pension can be drawn, to provide a secured income in retirement.
> - Only 25% of the capital in the pension arrangement will be able to be extracted as a lump sum, the remainder will be locked in the pension to be drawn out over the period of retirement.
> - Borrowing to fund a property purchase cannot exceed 50% of the value of the pension arrangement.
> - Although any rental income or capital gains from the disposal of the property will be tax free in the pension fund when the money is paid as a pension it will be taxable at the members' marginal rate of tax. Depending on the rate of tax this may well be higher than the rate that would be paid if the disposal were subject to the CGT [capital gains tax] regime after the property has been held for 7 years.
> - Putting any previously-owned property into the pension scheme will trigger any unrealised chargeable gain on the property, and transaction costs such as stamp duty.
> - Maximum tax relief on contributions made in any year is 100% of UK chargeable earnings, subject to an annual allowance set initially at £215,000. Tax relieved pension savings are also subject to a lifetime allowance initially set at £1.5 million.'

There had been ongoing consultations between government and the pensions industry in late 2005 concerning the effect of the new tax regime on SIPPs. These discussions covered many different areas, in particular investment issues.

The classification of SIPPs and SSASs as 'self-directed schemes' was seen as a withdrawal from the true spirit of simplification. The effect is to prohibit such schemes from certain investments that are available to other schemes.

The consultations also led to reviews of some of the *Finance Act 2004* requirements; the HMRC's Business Income Manual (BIM40000) in relation to the treatment of employer contributions as deductions under *ICTA 1988, s 74*; and the definition of 'market value' (*TCGA 1992, s 272*), particularly in relation to listed stocks and shares and the need to value on the 'plus one-quarter' basis in *TCGA 1992, s 272(3)*.The consultation further highlighted a concern about the effect of ongoing life assurance cover on enhanced protection. For example, the assurance in Simplification Newsletter No 8, that the payment of a lump sum from a *s 226A* policy is a payment from an 'other money purchase arrangement' and therefore does not invalidate enhanced protection, is not borne out by HMRC's own RPSM guidance notes.

There has since been a wider tightening-up on investment activity by registered schemes. This concerns the acquisition of 'taxable property'. Taxable property means residential property and tangible moveable property (see 4.2 above).

The investment regulations in 5.5 below were made following the above-mentioned consultations.

DWP pension investment requirements

The Occupational Pension Schemes (Investment) Regulations 2005

5.5 On 21 March 2005 the DWP issued a consultative document entitled *Pensions: Investment Requirements*. This document related to the draft Occupational Pension Schemes (Investment) Regulations 2005. These regulations have now been made, and are entitled the *Occupational Pension Schemes (Investment) Regulations 2005 (SI 2005/3378)*. They revoke the *Occupational Pension Schemes (Investment) Regulations 1996 (SI 1996/3127)*, and supplement changes made to the *Pensions Act 1995* by the *Pensions Act 2004*.

The purpose of the consultation was to seek views on proposals to implement certain requirements of the EU Directive on the Activities and Supervision of Institutions for Occupational Retirement Provision (IORPs) 2003/41/EC. The main topics were:

- a 'prudent person approach', as the underlying principle for capital investment, in accordance with Article 18 of the IORPs Directive;

- a written statement of investment policy principles, under Article 12 (*s 35, Pensions Act 1995* refers);
- investment restrictions and requirements, including where there is more than one employer.

The regulations contain the relevant provisions, including:

(*a*) Assets must be invested in the best interests of members and beneficiaries; and in the case of a potential conflict of interest, in the sole interest of members and beneficiaries.

(*b*) The powers of investment, or the discretion, must be exercised in a manner calculated to ensure the security, quality, liquidity and profitability of the portfolio as a whole.

(*c*) Assets must consist predominantly of investments admitted to trading on regulated markets, and other investments must be kept to a prudent level. There must also be diversification of assets, and special rules apply to derivatives and collective investment schemes.

(*d*) The requirements of the IORPs Directive are adopted in a proportionate and flexible manner, where appropriate using the 'small scheme exemption' which is contained in Article 5. Schemes with fewer than 100 active and deferred members are exempted from much of the requirements of the regulations, but are still required to have regard to the need for diversification on investment rule.

(*e*) A triennial review of the statement of investment principles is required. The previous requirements on the statement's contents are largely restated.

(*f*) Trustees must consider 'proper advice' on the suitability of a proposed investment, and there are specific requirements in relation to borrowing and a restriction on investment in the 'sponsors' undertaking' to no more than 5% of the portfolio (where a group is concerned, the percentage is no greater than 20%).

The regulations appear as an Annex at the end of this chapter.

The SIPPs rules which applied prior to A-Day

5.6 In view of the introduction of the single tax regime from A-Day, most of the existing rules are now effectively spent. Nevertheless, until SIPPs have been operating under the new regime over the next year or so, it will be helpful for the reader to be reminded of the rules which applied. This is of particular importance in the area of investments to which the transitional arrangements apply and in the matter of any outstanding funding and accounting matters.

5.7 *The UK investment regulations, and the pre-A-Day SIPPs rules*

The main summaries are contained in boxes 1 to 11 below.

1 Legislation and Guidelines
2 Documentation
3 Contributions and benefits
4 Investments
5 Payment of annuities
6 Income withdrawal facility
7 Death benefits
8 VAT aspects
9 Reporting requirements
10 Funding
11 accounts scheme.

1 Legislation and guidelines

5.7 SIPPs are subject to the following:

- *ICTA 1988* and successive Finance Acts
- Statutory Instruments
- Personal Pension Schemes Guidance Notes IR76
- Pensions Updates (formerly PSO Updates and Memoranda)
- Changes in practice announced via the SIPPs Provider Group (SPG).

2 Documentation

5.8 A SIPPs would normally be created and managed under a definitive trust deed and rules, which would include the following provisions:

- to establish the SIPPs under an irrevocable trust;
- to appoint trustees, and give them their powers to act on behalf of the trust and to invest the assets, within their specified powers;
- to appoint the administrator and/or authorised provider – and custodian trustee, if applicable;
- to set appropriate limits on member contributions and provision for repayment if any breach of those limits occurred;

- to prohibit certain investment transactions – e g loans to members, residential property investment etc;
- to require leasing of property in connection with any member to be on a formal commercial basis, determined by independent professional valuation;
- the retirement age for a member could be set between ages 50 and 75, removing the need for early retirement rules;
- benefits on retirement could be taken as pension only, or with ¼ cash and the balance applied as an annuity;
- to specify when the annuity is intended to become payable;
- to specify death benefit provisions if these were to be included, and how they would be secured and paid. Lump sums being distributable at trustee discretion, to ensure that IHT liabilities were not incurred on death;
- provision to make or accept transfer payments to, or from, other schemes;
- to adopt an income withdrawal facility, where this was required;
- that provision was made for compliance with pension sharing orders on divorce;
- that the equal treatment requirements were met by the rules.

3 *Contributions and benefits*

5.9

- To be eligible to contribute, the member had to be under age 75 and be resident or ordinarily resident in the UK (or a Crown Servant or the spouse of a Crown Servant, serving abroad).
- Contribution limits:

Age at start of Tax Year	% of net relevant earnings
Under 36	17.5
36–45	20.0
46–50	25.0
51–55	30.0
56–60	35.0
61–74	40.0

- The table above relates to 'gross' contributions, i e including any basic rate tax to be reclaimed. Personal contributions however, were payable net of basic rate tax.
- Contributions were also restricted by application of the Earnings Cap in each tax year, (2005/2006; £105,600).
- Contributions could in any case be made, up to the 'earnings threshold' for any given tax year regardless of earnings. (2005–2006 £3,600).
- Employer contributions, if any, also counted toward the relevant percentage limit in any year, and were allowable as deductions for corporation tax purposes under *s 640(4)*. Such contributions did not attract liability to tax under Schedule E (earnings, under *ITEPA 2003*) in the hands of members, under *s 643(1)*.

  The benefits payable were not subject to any specific limit, other than the requirement that they should represent the proceeds of investment of contributions that had not in themselves been excessive.

  The range of benefits that could be provided included:

  - an annuity payable to a member;
  - a lump sum payable at the time the annuity commences;
  - an annuity payable on a member's death to the spouse or dependants;
  - a lump sum payable on the member's death before age 75 under a term assurance contract; and
  - if no annuity is payable on the member's death, a lump sum not exceeding the contributions paid by the member and employer.

  The SIPPs could provide for all, or a limited selection, of the above.

4 Investments (*see the Annex to this chapter for regulations in force from 30 December 2005*)

5.10

- Investments that could be held, directly or indirectly for the purposes of a Self-Invested Personal Pension Scheme:
  - Stocks and shares listed or dealt in on a recognised stock exchange.

- Futures and options, relating to stocks and shares, traded on a recognised futures exchange.
- Depository interests.
- Units in authorised unit trust schemes.
- Units in a unit trust scheme which:

  (*a*) is an unauthorised unit trust whose gains are not chargeable gains by virtue *of s 100(2)* of the *Taxation of Chargeable Gains Act 1992*, and

  (*b*) does not hold any freehold or leasehold interest in residential property other than that specified under (i) and (ii) below:

  (i) property which is, or is to be, occupied by an employee, whether or not a member of the self-invested personal pension scheme or connected with a member of the scheme, who is not connected with his employer and is required as a condition of his employment to occupy the property, and

  (ii) property which is, or is to be, occupied by a person who is neither a member of the self-invested personal pension scheme nor connected with a member of the scheme in connection with the occupation by that person of business premises held as an investment by the scheme.

- Eligible shares within the meaning of *s 638(11)* received by the self-invested personal pension scheme as contributions to the scheme.
- Shares in an open-ended investment company.
- Interests (however described) in a collective investment scheme that is either a recognised scheme or a designated scheme within the meaning of *s 86* or *s 87* of the *Financial Services Act 1986*.
- Contracts or policies of insurance linked to insurance company managed funds, unit-linked funds or authorised in accordance with *Article 6* of *Council Directive 79/267* (First Council Directive on Direct Life Assurance).
- Traded endowment policies transacted with a person regulated by the Financial Services Authority.
- Deposits in any currency held in deposit accounts with any deposit-taker.
- A freehold or leasehold interest in commercial property where the interest is acquired from any person other than a member of the

scheme or a person connected with him, or the interest is acquired from a member of the scheme or a person connected with him in circumstances in which regulation 9(3) applies.

- Ground rents, rent charges, feu duties or other annual payments reserved in respect of, or charged on or issuing out of, property, except where the property concerned is occupied by a member of the scheme or a person connected with him.

5 *Payment of annuities*

5.11 Annuities arising under self-invested personal pensions have, since 6 April 1995, been included within the PAYE system, along with all other pensions in payment. The annuity provider took responsibility for this procedure and operated a PAYE code for each annuitant.

Where the proceeds of a SIPPs were insufficient (before payment of any lump sum) to secure an annuity for a scheme member, HMRC SPSS introduced a procedure from 6 April 1996, permitting repayment of the fund to the member. This would not apply if an income withdrawal facility had been adopted, (see next table).

The repayment procedures, set out in PSO Update No 15 and IR76 (2000) applied only to SIPPs that were not contracted-out of S2P (SERPS), and could only be applied, subject to the member:

(a) having attained age 50, or retired early (at any age) on grounds of incapacity;

(b) not being a member of any other personal pension scheme, or in receipt of an annuity under any other such scheme;

(c) having a fund exceeding £2,500;

(d) being aware that part of any repayment was chargeable to tax, consented to the repayment and in consideration waived all rights under the SIPP.

Under PSO Update No 34(12), these procedures were extended to include members with lower normal retirement ages – e g sportsmen.

If the conditions at a) to d) above were met, the repayment could be made without further reference to IR SPSS. The administrator sent an annual summary of all such repayments to IR SPSS and instructed the members to include details of such payments on their own tax returns.

6 *Income withdrawal facility*

5.12 Under the *Finance Act 1995*, members of personal pension schemes were given greater flexibility in the way they could use their funds to provide their retirement income. This development stemmed from the fact that the compulsory purchase of annuities, especially at times when rates available were poor, did not meet the changing needs of members. The Act permitted members to defer the purchase of an annuity beyond their retirement up to age 75, but in the meantime, to allow them to withdraw amounts during the deferment period, broadly equivalent to the level of income that the fund could have secured, if an annuity had been bought at the time of their retirement. This new feature was to be allowed regardless of whether the member had elected to take a tax-free lump sum at retirement. Once the income withdrawal procedure commenced however, no further contributions could be made to the arrangement.

The income taken annually was subject to tax under Schedule E (earnings tax) and withdrawals monitored triennially to ensure that the fund was not being depleted too rapidly. Income and capital gains were nevertheless allowed to accumulate tax free during the period of deferment.

As an upper and lower limit on the annual withdrawal permitted, the maximum was roughly equivalent to the rate of a single life annuity, based initially on the value of the fund after payment of any lump sum. Government Actuary's Department tables were used for the conversion rates. The minimum withdrawal was set at 35% of the maximum rate and tables were obtainable from IR SPSS.

The impact of the decline in world investment markets since 1995 meant that those members who made maximum withdrawals were disadvantaged to a greater extent than others, by depletion of their residual funds in subsequent years. This served to illustrate that income withdrawal was more suited to high net worth members with alternative financial resources to draw upon, other than the SIPP, when such conditions prevailed.

When the first series of triennial reviews was carried out in 1998, it became clear that the requirement to exercise a member's option on the final day could be disadvantageous to the member, so this option period was widened to a 60-day 'window' in which options could be exercised, to give necessary further flexibility in the timing of withdrawals and for forward planning for subsequent triennial periods.

7 *Death benefits*

Death during income withdrawal

5.13 Where a member died during a period of income withdrawal, the remainder of the fund could be paid within two years from the date of death, to the spouse or dependants as a lump sum, subject to a tax charge of 35% on the administrator.

Payment under discretionary powers avoided liability to IHT however, and it was also possible for the spouse and/or dependants to elect instead, to take their own income withdrawal option. For the spouse, this option was conditional upon them deferring the annuity to an age beyond 60. The latest age at which the annuity had to commence being the earlier of the 75th birthday of the spouse or dependant and that of the deceased member.

The upper and lower limits on income withdrawal applied in the same way to the spouse or dependant, based on the value of the fund available for that survivor's annuity at the member's death and a new three-year review period would start on that date.

Cessation of entitlement on remarriage or completion of full-time education did not preclude a spouse/dependant from exercising the withdrawal facility in the interim, but if an annuity was not purchased at the time this entitlement ceased, the remaining fund was forfeit, to be used toward the scheme expenses.

If a surviving spouse or dependant died within two years of commencing their own income withdrawal, the residue was payable as a lump sum, again subject to the 35% tax charge on the administrator, and with the possibility of IHT liability in addition, since the deceased had a 'general power' to dispose of the fund prior to death. Survival beyond two years in income withdrawal meant that the lump sum on death was still subject to the 35% charge, but IHT could again be avoided by payment under discretionary trust.

Death before any benefits taken

5.14 On death of a member where no benefits or deferral had been exercised, the surviving spouse or dependant could defer annuity purchase and commence income withdrawals. Similar rules and restrictions applied, as described above, with the option to take a lump sum, free of the 35% charge.

On death of the surviving spouse or dependant, lump sum benefits payable under the rules could, if paid under discretionary trust, avoid both the IHT liability and the 35% charge on the administrator.

The income withdrawal benefit payable to a beneficiary was subject to the limitation that it could not be greater than the income that could have been paid to the deceased member, as determined at date of death. This restriction could be avoided, however, where the beneficiary elected to take a lump sum.

In cases of serious ill-health, if a member tried to use deferment as a means to maximise benefits payable on death, at the expense of making adequate provision for retirement, this had the potential effect of incurring liability to IHT under the *Inheritance Tax Act 1984, s 3(3)*, where this intention became apparent.

8 VAT aspects

5.15 The various aspects of VAT as they apply to occupational pension schemes are explained in Chapter 8 of this book. Briefly, VAT is divided into two categories:

- Input Tax – VAT incurred on establishment and administration costs, and
- Output Tax – VAT received on income.

HMRC takes the view that the establishment and administration of a pension fund is a business activity of the company and therefore any Input Tax incurred by the company in connection with this activity constitutes recoverable VAT.

Eight categories are identified by HMRC as falling within this description:

- Making of arrangements for setting up a pension fund;
- Management of the scheme, e g collection of contributions and payment of pensions;
- Advice on a review of the scheme, and implementing any change to the scheme;
- Accounting and auditing, insofar as they relate to the management of the scheme, e g preparation of annual accounts;
- Actuarial valuations of the assets of the fund;
- General actuarial advice connected with the fund's administration;
- Providing general statistics in connection with the performance of a fund's investments, properties etc;
- Legal instructions and general legal advice including any drafting of trust deeds insofar as they relate to the management of the scheme.

These provisions also apply in general to all arrangements, including SSASs and SIPPs. However two aspects differ in the case of SIPPs:

- Where a LO or its subsidiary acts as a trustee and administrator to a SIPP, the fees chargeable for such services are not chargeable for VAT (the *Winterthur* case).
- Transfers of property.

9 Reporting requirements

5.16 Until 1 October 2000, *ss 630–655* placed very few reporting requirements on the administrator of a SIPP apart from making applications for approval, tax reclaims and repayments of excess contributions. There was a statutory requirement in SI 1988/1013 for the administrator to keep certain records for inspection by HMRC and to provide certain information when called upon to do so by that Department. Part 17 of IR76 (2000) also required the administrator at the end of each tax year to provide the Inland Revenue with certain information to enable compliance checks to be undertaken. These compliance checks were undertaken by HMRC SPSS (Worthing) (previously undertaken by FICO (Audit & Compliance)) from time to time and have involved checking income tax reclaims in respect of employed member's contributions.

From 6 April 2001, such checks encompassed the self-employed. HMRC SPSS (Worthing) have published a Code of Practice (Code of Practice 4) entitled 'Inspection of Schemes operated by Financial Intermediaries' explaining how HMRC carry out inspections, which is available on request from them (Tel: 01903 509963). Details of the objectives and procedures of an inspection are also contained in Part 16 of IR76 (2000).

Well before the introduction of regulations contained in *SI 2001/117* limiting HMRC discretion in relation to investments by SIPPs, HMRC SPSS had indicated to the SPG that it wished to bring its discretionary requirements for SIPPs transactions and investments and the associated reporting requirements into line with those for SSASs. *Section 651A* provided for regulations to be introduced imposing such reporting requirements and these are now in force.

Like SSASs, there were now statutory requirements for SIPPs to report purchases and sales of investments and scheme borrowings, These were contained in the *Personal Pension Schemes (Information Powers) Regulations 2000* (*SI 2000/2316*) which came into force on 1 October 2000. As for SSASs, the report had to be made on the prescribed form within 90 days of the transaction. However, at the time of writing the 5th edition of this book, forms had not been issued by HMRC SPSS and the SPG was advised that until such forms had been issued, transactions did not need to be reported. HMRC SPSS also advised the SPG that, to start with, only purchases and sales of property and associated borrowings would need to be reported.

In January 2003, HMRC SPSS advised the SPG that in view of the major changes that the proposals in the Treasury report, published in December 2002, would have in relation to audit matters, the implementation of the reporting regime would be delayed further.

HMRC SPSS commenced a compliance audit of SIPPs on a voluntary basis a few years ago. However, *SI 2000/2316* also required the administrator, authorised provider, trustee or anyone who has provided administration services to a personal pension scheme to produce certain information, make it available for inspection and retain certain records. If HMRC served notice, the information, including any supporting documents that must be supplied within 28 days, was virtually identical to that required in respect of a SSAS under *SI 1996/1715*.

The aim of the legislation was to improve the monitoring of personal pension schemes.

10 Funding

5.17 SIPPs, like all other types of approved pension schemes, enjoy tax advantages of various kinds The tax reliefs available to SIPPs are those generally available to other approved pension schemes with some differences.

The 6 April 2001 regime introduced many changes particularly relating to funding and created additional differences not only with other approved pension schemes but also with the situation for personal pensions prior to 6 April 2001. The position before 6 April 2001 is explained in the sixth edition and the position from 6 April 2001 is explained below.

Contributions could only be paid provided the member satisfies the relevant eligibility criteria (see above) and all personal contributions had to be paid net of basic rate tax.

There was no obligation for an employer to contribute to a SIPPs, but where an employer did contribute, the aggregate gross contributions paid by the member and the employer to all personal pensions, retirement annuity contracts and stakeholder schemes, could not exceed either:

(a) the 'earnings threshold' (*s 630(1)(c)*) for the tax year in which the contributions are paid, or where higher level contributions are to be paid;

(b) the relevant percentage (from the table above) of net relevant earnings either for the tax year of payment or for one of the previous five tax years, known as the 'basis year' (*s 646B*), subject to the earnings cap relevant to the year of payment (IR 76 (2000), 4.10).

With regard to (*b*) above, HMRC SPSS originally interpreted the relevant Regulations (*SI 2000/2315*) to apply the earnings cap relevant in the basis year. The change was announced in April 2002 in Pensions Update No 130.

As mentioned earlier, the earnings threshold was set at £3,600 for each tax year but could be amended by Treasury order (*s 630 (1A)*). Anyone who satisfied the eligibility criteria prior to 6 April 2001 could pay contributions up to the earnings threshold whether or not they had relevant earnings (see sixth edition, 14.62 and 14.63).

For contributions exceeding the earnings threshold the net relevant earnings for the basis year could be used not only for the year of payment but also for each of the tax years falling within the five-year period from the end of the basis year. A new basis year could be chosen when required (e g when net relevant earnings have increased), and contributions could be made in respect of net relevant earnings for the new basis year, in that basis year itself, if it was the year of payment, and in each of the five years following the new basis year, subject to production of appropriate evidence of earnings (see sixth edition 14.97 to 14.99).

Section 640(3) was amended by *FA 2000, Sch 13* and limited the proportion of total contributions paid in any tax year that could be taken from those contributions and applied as a premium to secure a lump sum death benefit under a term assurance contract to 10%. Term assurance contracts already in force by 5 April 2001 could continue on the pre-6 April 2001 basis. This included a member's arrangements under a SIPPs which commenced before 6 April 2001 and which included an option to apply for term assurance, even if the option was not exercised until 6 April 2001 or later. In such cases, the SIPP administrator should obtain a declaration that the amount applied to such term assurance contracts will not exceed 5% of net relevant earnings for the year in question.

Before 6 April 2001, it was only possible, under HMRC SPSS's discretionary practice for contributions to a SIPP to be in the form of cash. *FA 2000, Sch 13* made amendments to *s 638* confirming this with effect from 6 April 2001, with the exception of contributions by members in the form of 'eligible shares'. These are shares (whether quoted or unquoted) in respect of which the member has exercised the right to acquire, or which have been appropriated by the member in accordance with the rules of a savings-related share option scheme, approved profit-sharing scheme or share incentive plan (previously called employee share ownership plan). The market value of the shares at the time of transfer to a SIPPs represents a contribution net of basic rate tax (which will be reclaimed by the SIPPs administrator.). However, the gross value must be taken into account when calculating the maximum contributions payable in a tax year. The transfer of the shares must take place no later than 90 days from the date the member exercised the right to acquire or appropriated the shares.

Net relevant earnings

5.18 Mention is made above of the maximum contributions that can be made to a SIPPs in relation to a member's net relevant earnings for any particular year. So, it is important to understand what actually constituted net relevant earnings especially as members could be self-employed or employed.

For self-employed members relevant earnings comprised all earned income assessable to tax under Schedule D, Cases I and II whether as a sole trader or partner. Net earnings are those after deduction of allowable expenses but before personal allowances. These are defined in *ss 644(2)(c)* and *646*.

For employed members net relevant earnings comprised all remuneration assessable to income tax. These are defined in *s 646* and are in line with the definition of pensionable remuneration for occupational schemes, (see sixth edition, 4.21 to 4.27 with the same exceptions). Net relevant earnings are those after allowable expenses but before personal allowances. Remuneration as a controlling director of an investment company (*ss 644(5)* and *644(6)*) does not constitute net relevant earnings. Nor does remuneration as a controlling director of a trading company where the controlling director is in receipt of benefits from either a *Chapter I* scheme of that company or a personal pension which had received a transfer payment from such a *Chapter I* scheme (*s 644(6A)*). Also excluded are earnings from an employment that have already been pensioned in respect of membership of a *Chapter I* scheme (*s 645*), unless the individual qualifies for concurrent membership of both a *Chapter I* scheme and a *Chapter IV* scheme (see sixth edition, 14.69).

Fairly comprehensive lists of the types of income that count as relevant and non-relevant earnings can be found in Appendix 2 and Appendix 3 of IR76 (2000), respectively.

The earnings cap applied to all personal pension schemes and restricted net relevant earnings for both self-employed and employed members of SIPPs for the years 1989/90 onwards. The maximum contributions payable for each age band are limited to the earnings cap for the appropriate year, which can cause some practical problems under the 6 April 2001 regime, particularly for the self-employed (see sixth edition, 14.99).

11 Scheme accounts

5.19 In a money purchase scheme contributions are designated for the purchase of investments for the member on whose behalf the contributions are paid. There is no general pool of assets from which pensions are paid as there is in a final salary scheme. On retirement, the member's investments are applied to buy an annuity for that individual. Thus although the trustees are responsible for the assets, in accounting terms they are already notionally allocated. For this reason, the SORP recommends that the net assets statement shows 'assets allocated to members'. The notes to the accounts normally amplify the rationale for this presentation by referring to the fact that members receive an annual statement confirming the contributions paid on their behalf and the value of their money purchase rights.

The current accounting principles are detailed in Chapter 8.

ANNEX

(SI 2005 No 3378)

Occupational Pension Schemes (Investment) Regulations 2005

1 Citation, commencement and interpretation

5.20

(1) These Regulations may be cited as the Occupational Pension Schemes (Investment) Regulations 2005 and shall come into force on 30th December 2005.

(2) In these Regulations—

'the 1995 Act' means the Pensions Act 1995;

'the 2004 Act' means the Pensions Act 2004;

'the FSM Act' means the Financial Services and Markets Act 2000[2];

'collective investment scheme' has the same meaning as in Part 17 of the FSM Act, but includes arrangements of the type described in paragraphs 4 and 9 of the Schedule to the Financial Services and Markets Act 2000 (Collective Investment Schemes) Order 2001[3] (arrangements not amounting to a collective investment scheme);

'employer-related loan' has for the purposes of regulations 12, 14 and 15 the meaning given in regulation 12(4);

'insurance policy' means a contract of a kind referred to in article 2 of the Life Directive, but excluding a contract of a kind referred to in article 2(c) and (d) of that Directive;

'the Life Directive' means Directive 2002/83EC of the European Parliament and of the Council of 5th November 2002 concerning life assurance[4];

'qualifying insurance policy' means an insurance policy issued by an insurer which is—

(a) a person who has permission under Part 4 of the FSM Act to effect or carry out contracts of long-term insurance; or

(b) an undertaking established in an EEA State (as defined in paragraph 8 of Schedule 3 to the FSM Act) other than the United Kingdom, which is authorised by the competent authorities of that State to carry on the business of direct insurance for the class of assurance as listed in Annex I to the Life Directive in which the insurance policy falls;

'recognised stock exchange' has the same meaning as in section 841 of the Taxes Act;

'scheme undertaking cross-border activities' means a scheme in relation to which the trustees or managers are—

(a) authorised under section 288 of the 2004 Act (general authorisation to accept contributions from European employers); or

(b) approved under section 289 of the 2004 Act in relation to a European employer;

'scheme' (except in the expression 'collective investment scheme') means an occupational pension scheme;

'small scheme' means a scheme with fewer than 12 members, where—

(a) all the members are trustees of the scheme and either—

(i) the provisions of the scheme provide that all decisions which fall to be made by the trustees are made by unanimous agreement by the trustees who are members of the scheme, or

(ii) the scheme has a trustee who is independent in relation to the scheme for the purposes of section 23 of the 1995 Act[5] (power to appoint independent trustees), and is registered in the register maintained by the Authority in accordance with regulations made under subsection (4) of that section; or

(b) all the members are directors of a company which is the sole trustee of the scheme, and either—

(i) the provisions of the scheme provide that any decisions made by the company in its capacity as trustee are made by the unanimous agreement of all the directors who are members of the scheme, or

(ii) one of the directors of the company is independent in relation to the scheme for the purposes of section 23 of the 1995 Act, and is registered in the register maintained by the Authority in accordance with regulations made under subsection (4) of that section;

'specified qualifying insurance policy' means a qualifying insurance policy which is a contract falling within paragraph III of Part II of Schedule 1 to the Financial Services and Markets Act 2000 (Regulated Activities) Order 2001[6];

'Taxes Act' means the Income and Corporation Taxes Act 1988[7].

(3) Regulations 12(4)(b), 13(3) and 15(1) must be read with—

(a) section 22 of the FSM Act (classes of activity and categories of investment);

(b) any relevant order under that section; and

(c) Schedule 2 to that Act (regulated activities).

(4) Subject to paragraph (5), in these Regulations, and for the purposes of section 35 (investment principles) and section 40 (restriction on employer-related investments) of the 1995 Act, 'employer', in relation to a scheme which has no active members, includes every person who was the employer of persons in the description of employment to which the scheme relates immediately before the time at which the scheme ceased to have any active members in relation to it.

(5) In these Regulations, 'employer', in relation to a multi-employer scheme, or a section of a multi-employer scheme, includes—

(a) in the case of a scheme which has no active members, every person who was the employer of persons in the description of employment to which the scheme, or section, relates immediately before the time at which the scheme, or section, ceased to have any active members in relation to it unless after that time—

(i) a debt under section 75 of the 1995 Act[8] (deficiencies in the assets) becomes due from that person to the scheme, or section; and

(ii) either—

(aa) the full amount of the debt has been paid by that person to the trustees or managers of the scheme, or section; or

(bb) in circumstances where a legally enforceable agreement has been entered into between that person and the trustees or managers of the scheme, or section, the effect of which is to reduce the amount which is payable in respect of the debt, the reduced amount of the debt has been paid in full by that person to those trustees or managers; and

(b) in any other case, any person who has ceased to be the employer of persons in the description of employment to which the scheme, or section, relates unless—

(i) at the time when he so ceased, the scheme, or section, was not being wound up and continued to have active members in relation to it; and

(ii) a debt under section 75 of the 1995 Act became due at that time from that person to the scheme, or section, and either—

(aa) the full amount of the debt has been paid by that person to the trustees or managers of the scheme, or section; or

(bb) in circumstances where a legally enforceable agreement has been entered into between that person and the trustees or managers of the scheme, or section, the effect of which is to reduce the amount which is payable in respect of the debt, the reduced amount of the debt has been paid in full by that person to those trustees or managers.

2 Statement of investment principles

5.21

(1) The trustees of a trust scheme must secure that the statement of investment principles prepared for the scheme under section 35 of the 1995 Act is reviewed—

(a) at least every three years; and

(b) without delay after any significant change in investment policy.

(2) Before preparing or revising a statement of investment principles, the trustees of a trust scheme must—

(a) obtain and consider the written advice of a person who is reasonably believed by the trustees to be qualified by his ability in and practical experience of financial matters and to have the appropriate knowledge and experience of the management of the investments of such schemes; and

(b) consult the employer.

(3) A statement of investment principles must be in writing and must cover at least the following matters—

(a) the trustees' policy for securing compliance with the requirements of section 36 of the 1995 Act (choosing investments);

(b) their policies in relation to—

(i) the kinds of investments to be held;

(ii) the balance between different kinds of investments;

(iii) risks, including the ways in which risks are to be measured and managed;

(iv) the expected return on investments;

(v) the realisation of investments; and

(vi) the extent (if at all) to which social, environmental or ethical considerations are taken into account in the selection, retention and realisation of investments; and

(c) their policy (if any) in relation to the exercise of the rights (including voting rights) attaching to the investments.

3 Application of regulation 2 in relation to multi-employer schemes

5.22

(1) In the application of regulation 2 to a scheme in relation to which there is more than one employer, the requirement imposed by paragraph (2)(b) of that regulation—

(a) where a person has been nominated by all the employers to act as their representative for the purposes of that paragraph, is to consult that person;

(b) where no person has been so nominated but the employers have not all notified the trustees that they need to be consulted, is (subject to paragraph (2)) to consult all the employers; and

(c) where no person has been so nominated and the employers have all notified the trustees that they need not be consulted, does not apply.

(2) Where the trustees specify a reasonable period (not being less than 28 days) within which they must

receive representations from the employers, sub-paragraph (1)(b) does not require them to consider any representations received after the end of that period.

4 Investment by trustees

5.23

(1) The trustees of a trust scheme must exercise their powers of investment, and any fund manager to whom any discretion has been delegated under section 34 of the 1995 Act[9] (power of investment and delegation) must exercise the discretion, in accordance with the following provisions of this regulation.

(2) The assets must be invested—

(a) in the best interests of members and beneficiaries; and

(b) in the case of a potential conflict of interest, in the sole interest of members and beneficiaries.

(3) The powers of investment, or the discretion, must be exercised in a manner calculated to ensure the security, quality, liquidity and profitability of the portfolio as a whole.

(4) Assets held to cover the scheme's technical provisions must also be invested in a manner appropriate to the nature and duration of the expected future retirement benefits payable under the scheme.

(5) The assets of the scheme must consist predominantly of investments admitted to trading on regulated markets.

(6) Investment in assets which are not admitted to trading on such markets must in any event be kept to a prudent level.

(7) The assets of the scheme must be properly diversified in such a way as to avoid excessive reliance on any particular asset, issuer or group of undertakings and so as to avoid accumulations of risk in the portfolio as a whole. Investments in assets issued by the same issuer or by issuers belonging to the same group must not expose the scheme to excessive risk concentration.

(8) Investment in derivative instruments may be made only in so far as they—

(a) contribute to a reduction of risks; or

(b) facilitate efficient portfolio management (including the reduction of cost or the generation of additional capital or income with an acceptable level of risk),

and any such investment must be made and managed so as to avoid excessive risk exposure to a single counterparty and to other derivative operations.

(9) For the purposes of paragraph (5)—

(a) an investment in a collective investment scheme shall be treated as an investment on a regulated market to the extent that the investments held by that scheme are themselves so invested; and

(b) a qualifying insurance policy shall be treated as an investment on a regulated market.

(10) To the extent that the assets of a scheme consist of qualifying insurance policies, those policies shall be treated as satisfying the requirement for proper diversification when considering the diversification of assets as a whole in accordance with paragraph (7).

(11) In this regulation—

'beneficiary', in relation to a scheme, means a person, other than a member of the scheme, who is entitled to the payment of benefits under the scheme:

'derivative instrument' includes any of the instruments listed in paragraphs (4) to (10) of Section C of Annex 1 to Directive 2004/39/EC of the European Parliament and of the Council on markets in financial instruments[10];

'regulated market' means—

(a) a regulated market within the terms of Council Directive 93/22/EEC on investment services in the securities field[11];

(b) a regulated market within the terms of Directive 2004/39/EC; or

(c) any other market for financial instruments—

(i) which operates regularly;

(ii) which is recognised by the relevant regulatory authorities;

(iii) in respect of which there are adequate arrangements for unimpeded transmission of income and capital to or to the order of investors; and

(iv) in respect of which adequate custody arrangements can be provided for investments when they are dealt in on that market;

'technical provisions' has the meaning given by section 222(2) of the 2004 Act (the statutory funding objective).

5 Borrowing and guarantees by trustees

5.24

(1) Except as provided in paragraph (2), the trustees of a trust scheme, and a fund manager to whom any discretion has been delegated under section 34 of the 1995 Act, must not borrow money or act as a guarantor in respect of the obligations of another person where the borrowing is liable to be repaid, or liability under a guarantee is liable to be satisfied, out of the assets of the scheme.

(2) Paragraph (1) does not preclude borrowing made only for the purpose of providing liquidity for the scheme and on a temporary basis.

6 Disapplication of section 35 of the 1995 Act and of regulations 2 and 3 in respect of certain schemes

5.25

(1) Section 35 of the 1995 Act and regulations 2 and 3 do not apply to any of the following schemes—

(a) a scheme which has fewer than 100 members; or

(b) a scheme which—

(i) is established by or under an enactment (including a local Act), and

(ii) is guaranteed by a public authority.

(2) In this regulation—

'enactment' includes an enactment comprised in, or in an instrument made under, an Act of the Scottish Parliament;

'local authority' means—

(a) in relation to England, a county council, a district council, a London borough council, the Greater London Authority, the Common Council of the City of London in its capacity as a local authority or the Council of the Isles of Scilly;

(b) in relation to Wales, a county council or county borough council;

(c) in relation to Scotland, a council constituted under section 2 of the Local Government etc. (Scotland) Act 1994[12] (constitution of councils);

(d) an administering authority as defined in Schedule 1 to the Local Government Pension Scheme Regulations 1997[13] (interpretation);

'public authority' means—

(a) a Minister of the Crown (within the meaning of the Ministers of the Crown Act 1975)[14];

(b) a government department (including any body or authority exercising statutory functions on behalf of the Crown);

(c) the Scottish Ministers;

(d) the National Assembly for Wales, or

(e) a local authority.

7 Disapplication of regulations 4 and 5 in respect of schemes with fewer than 100 members

5.26

(1) Regulations 4 and 5 do not apply to a scheme which has fewer than 100 members.

(2) Where regulation 4 does not apply to a scheme by virtue only of paragraph (1), the trustees of the scheme in exercising their powers of investment, and any fund manager to whom any discretion has been delegated under section 34 of the 1995 Act in exercising the discretion, must have regard to the need for diversification of investments, in so far as appropriate to the circumstances of the scheme.

8 Modification of regulation 2 in respect of wholly-insured schemes

5.27

(1) Where, on the preparation or revision of a statement of investment principles under regulation 2, a scheme is a wholly-insured scheme and the trustees do not consider that it should cease to be such a scheme—

(a) sub-paragraphs (b) and (c) of regulation 2(3) shall not apply; and

(b) the statement of investment principles must cover the reasons for the scheme being a wholly-insured scheme.

(2) In this regulation, 'wholly-insured scheme' means a trust scheme, other than a stakeholder pension scheme within the meaning of section 1 of the Welfare Reform and Pensions Act 1999[15] (meaning of 'stakeholder pension scheme'), which has no investments other than specified qualifying insurance policies.

(3) For the purposes of paragraph (2), 'investments' shall not include—

(a) cash held on deposit by the trustees or managers pending payment to the insurer or to members of the scheme;

(b) cash held on deposit by the trustees or managers to meet accrued liabilities or administrative expenses; or

(c) any investments arising from voluntary contributions.

9 Partial disapplication of regulation 4 in respect of schemes being wound up

5.28

(1) The requirements of paragraphs (3) to (7) of regulation 4 shall apply in respect of a scheme which is being wound up except to the extent that—

(a) they conflict with any obligations placed on the trustees arising in consequence of the winding up under or by virtue of the 1995 Act or the 2004 Act, or

(b) it is not reasonably practicable to give effect to them having regard to circumstances in connection with the winding up.

(2) For the purposes of paragraph (1), a scheme shall be taken to be being wound up during the period which—

(a) begins with the day on which the time immediately after the beginning of the winding up of the scheme falls, and

(b) ends when the winding up of the scheme is completed.

10 Connected and associated persons

5.29

(1) Section 249 of the Insolvency Act 1986[16] (connected persons) shall be modified in its application for the purposes of section 40 of the 1995 Act (restriction on employer-related investments) and these Regulations so that a company shall not be connected with another company solely by reason of one or more of its directors being a director of that other company.

(2) Section 74 of the Bankruptcy (Scotland) Act 1985[17] (associated persons) shall be modified in its application for the purposes of section 40 of the 1995 Act and these Regulations to apply as if it contained the same provisions as sections 249 (as modified by paragraph (1)) and 435 (associated persons) of the Insolvency Act 1986.

11 Prescription of investments as employer-related investments

5.30

For the purposes of section 40(2)(e) of the 1995 Act, the following are prescribed as employer-related investments—

(a) the proportion attributable to the scheme's resources (whether directly or through any intervening collective investment scheme) of any investments which—

(i) have been made by the operator of any collective investment scheme, and

(ii) would have been employer-related investments if they had been made by the scheme;

(b) any guarantee of, or security given to secure, obligations of the employer or of any person who is connected with, or an associate of, the employer, and for the purposes of section 40 of the 1995 Act and these Regulations a guarantee or security given by the trustees or managers shall be regarded as an investment of resources of the scheme equal to the amount of the obligations guaranteed or secured;

(c) any loan arrangement entered into with any person whereby the trustees' or managers' right to or expectation of repayment depends on the employer's actions or situation, unless it was not the trustees' or managers' purpose in entering into the arrangement to provide financial assistance to the employer;

(d) where any of a scheme's resources are invested in an insurance policy the terms of which permit—

(i) the premiums or other consideration for the rights acquired under the policy, or

(ii) any monies otherwise credited to or for the benefit of the trustees or managers or the members,

to be invested in a fund created only for the purposes of that policy, the proportion of the scheme's resources invested in that policy which is the same proportion as B is of A where—

A represents all the assets of the insurer held in the fund, and

B represents that part of A which would, if invested by the scheme, be employer-related investments; and

(e) where any of a scheme's resources are invested in an insurance policy (not being resources invested in a fund created only for the purposes of that policy) the terms of which permit the trustees or managers or the employer to direct that—

(i) some or all of the premiums or other consideration for the rights acquired under the policy, or

(ii) any monies otherwise credited to or for the benefit of the trustees or managers or the members,

are invested in employer-related investments, any investments made by the insurer from those premiums or other consideration or monies, which would have been employer-related investments if they had been made by the scheme.

12 Restrictions on employer-related investments

5.31

(1) This regulation applies to trust schemes except small schemes.

(2) Subject to regulations 13 to 16—

(a) not more than five per cent of the current market value of the resources of a scheme may at any time be invested in employer-related investments; and

(b) none of the resources of a scheme may at any time be invested in any employer-related loan.

(3) None of the resources of a scheme may at any time be invested in any employer-related investment the making of which involves the entering by the trustees or managers into a transaction at an undervalue where the agreement to enter into that transaction was made on or after the 6th April 1997.

(4) In this regulation and in regulations 14 and 15 'employer-related loan' means—

(a) a loan mentioned in section 40(2)(d) of the 1995 Act (including, for the purposes of this regulation only, one which falls within section 40(2)(d) by virtue of section 40(3) of that Act);

(b) a security mentioned in section 40(2)(a) of the 1995 Act which is an instrument creating or acknowledging indebtedness, except any such security which is listed on a recognised stock exchange; and

(c) an employer-related investment prescribed as such by regulation 11(b) or (11)(c).

(5) In paragraph (3), 'transaction at an undervalue' has the same meaning in relation to trustees and managers as it has in section 238(4) of the Insolvency Act 1986 (transactions at an undervalue (England and Wales)) in relation to a company to which that section applies.

13 Investments to which restrictions do not apply

5.32

(1) Regulation 12(1) shall not restrict or prohibit investments to which this regulation applies.

(2) This regulation applies to investments prescribed as employer-related investments by regulation 11(e) (but not to investments prescribed as employer-related investments by regulation 11(d)) where the insurance policy—

(a) is a specified qualifying insurance policy; and

(b) is issued by an insurer which is the employer.

(3) This regulation applies to any employer-related investment of resources in an account (including a current, deposit or share account) with—

(a) a person who has permission under Part 4 of the FSM Act (permission to carry on regulated activities) to accept deposits; or

(b) an EEA firm of the kind mentioned in paragraph 5(b) of Schedule 3 to that Act, which has permission under paragraph 15 of that Schedule (as a result of qualifying for authorisation under paragraph 12 of that Schedule) to accept deposits.

(4) This regulation applies to any employer-related investment of resources which derives from a member's voluntary contributions and is invested in employer-related investments with the written agreement of the member who paid those contributions.

(5) This regulation applies to sums due from the employer to the trustees by virtue of a provision in an order under section 7 of the 1995 Act[18] (appointment of trustees) such as is permitted by section 8(1) of that Act[19] (orders appointing trustees may provide that certain sums are to be treated as a debt due from the employer to the trustees).

(6) This regulation applies to sums which fall or fell to be treated as debts due from the employer to the trustees or managers by virtue of—

(a) section 75(2) and (4) of the 1995 Act[20] (deficiencies in the assets);

(b) section 88(2) of the 1995 Act[21] (schedules of payments to money purchase schemes: supplementary – amounts not paid in accordance with the payment schedule); or

(c) section 228(3) of the 2004 Act (failure to make payments),

and to sums which would fall to be so treated by virtue of any of those sections were they not already debts due from the employer to the trustees or managers.

(7) For the purposes of regulation 11(a), the investments made by the operator of any collective investment scheme shall not be taken into account if—

(a) the collective investment scheme in question is operated by a person authorised (within the meaning of section 31 (authorised persons)) of the FSM Act to carry on investment business in the United Kingdom consisting of or including the operation of collective investment schemes;

(b) there are at least 10 participants in a collective investment scheme in question;

(c) not more than 10 per cent. of the assets of the collective investment scheme in question are attributable, whether directly or through any intervening collective investment scheme, to the scheme's resources; and

(d) not more than 10 per cent. of the investments of the collective investment scheme in question are invested in securities falling within paragraph 11 of Schedule 2 to the FSM Act and issued by any one issuer.

(8) All schemes in relation to which the respective employers are within the same group of companies shall be treated as—

(a) a single participant, for the purposes of paragraph (7)(b); and

(b) one scheme, for the purposes of paragraph (7)(c),

and for the purposes of paragraph (7)(d) all issues within a group of companies shall be treated as issued by a single issuer.

(9) For the purposes of paragraph (8), 'group of companies' means a group of companies consisting of a holding company and one or more subsidiaries where 'holding company' and 'subsidiary' have the same meaning as in section 736 of the Companies Act 1985[22] ('subsidiary', 'holding company' and 'wholly owned subsidiary').

(10) Subject to paragraph (11), where the disposal of assets on the winding up of a scheme would otherwise result in a contravention of these Regulations, any employer-related investments held before the commencement of the winding up may be retained while the scheme is being wound up, but there shall be no new investment in employer-related investments while the resources retained under this paragraph exceed five per cent. of the current market value of the resources of the scheme.

(11) Paragraph (10) does not apply to permit the retention of—

(a) employer-related investments which were, prior to the commencement of the winding up, held in contravention of these Regulations or of the Occupational Pension Schemes (Investment) Regulations 1996[23]; or

(b) employer-related loans to which regulation 14(2)(c) applies.

(12) This regulation applies to a loan to the employer or a company associated with the employer, if the scheme has fewer than 100 members, and—

(a) the scheme provides benefits for directors of a company which is the employer, or such directors and others;

(b) there is a qualifying insurance policy taken out under the scheme which is specifically allocated to the provision of benefits under the scheme and the directors' interests under which are used as security for the loan;

(c) Her Majesty's Revenue and Customs' requirements concerning the loan have been satisfied;

(d) the directors agreeing to the interests under the policy concerned being used as security for the loan have so agreed in writing, and

(e) the loan was made and the security given before 9th August 1999.

(13) This regulation applies to any security given over a qualifying insurance policy to secure obligations of the employer, or of any person who is connected with, or an associate of, the employer, where—

(a) the scheme provides benefits for any director of a company which is the employer;

(b) the policy is specifically allocated to the provision of benefits under the scheme for that director;

(c) the obligations secured are to the insurer who issued the policy;

(d) Her Majesty's Revenue and Customs' requirements concerning the loan and the giving of the security have been satisfied; and

(e) the director mentioned in sub-paragraph (b) has agreed in writing to the security being given.

14 Transitional provisions

5.33

(1) Where on the 6th April 1997 the resources of a scheme were invested in—

(a) employer-related loans (including such loans as are mentioned in regulation 5(2)(a) of the Occupational Pension Schemes (Investment of Scheme's Resources) Regulations 1992[24] ('the 1992 Regulations') which were in being on 18th December 1996 and to which regulation 13 does not apply; or

(b) other employer-related investments, to the extent that they exceed five per cent. of the current market value of the resources of the scheme to which regulation 5(2)(d) of the 1992 Regulations applied immediately before 6th April 1997,

those investments may be retained in accordance with paragraph (2).

(2) To the extent that the employer-related investments mentioned in paragraph (1) consist of—

(a) employer-related loans to which regulation 5(2)(a) of the 1992 Regulations applied before 6th April 1997, they may, where by virtue of contractual or other legal obligations repayment cannot be required immediately, be retained until the earliest date on which repayment can be enforced;

(b) securities of the type referred to in regulation 12(4)(b) which, immediately before 6th April 1997, were employer-related investments and—

(i) regulation 5(2)(d) of the 1992 Regulations applied to them; or

(ii) they were investments which did not contravene the 1992 Regulations,

they may be held until the earliest date on which having regard to contractual and other legal obligations, disinvestment may be effected;

(c) an employer-related loan the terms of which have, before 1st January 1996, been specifically approved by a court having jurisdiction in relation to the scheme as being in the interests of the members of the scheme, then, provided that the terms of the loan as so approved are not changed, such part of the loan, repayment of which cannot be required other than on the commencement of the winding up of the scheme, may be retained until the winding up of the scheme commences;

(d) any employer-related loans which do not contravene the 1992 Regulations and to which sub-paragraphs (a) to (c) do not apply, they may be retained until the earliest date on which having regard to the contractual and other legal obligations repayment can be enforced;

(e) other investments mentioned in paragraph (1)(b) (excluding, for the avoidance of doubt, investments in a collective investment scheme), they may be retained.

(3) If any investment referred to in paragraph (2) is listed on a recognised stock exchange, it may be retained for a period of no more than six months beginning with the date on which it was listed.

(4) There shall be no new investment in employer-related investments while the resources of a scheme

retained in employer-related investments (other than investments authorised by regulation 13) exceed five per cent. of the current market value of the resources of the scheme.

(5) In this regulation—

'loans' does not include any sums regarded as loans under section 40(3) of the 1995 Act (restrictions on employer-related investments); and

'retained', in relation to a loan, means left undischarged.

15 Loans that become employer-related

5.34

(1) If either a loan or a security which is an investment creating or acknowledging a debt becomes an employer-related loan on or after 6th April 1997 as a result of a change in the ownership of the employer or the person to whom the loan was made, the loan or security may be retained until whichever is the latest of—

(a) the date falling two years after the date on which it became an employer-related loan; or

(b) where repayment cannot by virtue of contractual or other legal obligations be required or, in the case of securities, disinvestment effected before the date mentioned in sub-paragraph (a), the earliest date on which repayment can be enforced, or disinvestment effected.

(2) In paragraph (1)—

(a) 'loan' does not include any sum regarded as a loan under section 40(3) of the 1995 Act; and

(b) 'retained' means left undischarged.

16 Multi-employer schemes

5.35

(1) Where a scheme in relation to which there is more than one employer is divided into two or more sections and the provisions of the scheme are such that—

(a) different sections of the scheme apply to different employers or groups of employers (whether or not more than one section applies to any particular employer or groups including any particular employer);

(b) contributions payable to the scheme by an employer, or by a member in employment under that employer, are allocated to that employer's section (or, if more than one section applies to the employer, to the section which is appropriate in respect of the employment in question); and

(c) a specified part or proportion of the assets of the scheme is attributable to each section and cannot be used for the purposes of any other section,

then regulations 10 to 15 shall apply as if each section of the scheme were a separate scheme.

(2) Where—

(a) a scheme which has been such a scheme as is mentioned in paragraph (1) is divided into two or more sections some or all of which apply only to members who are not in pensionable service under the section; and

(b) the provisions of the scheme have not been amended so as to prevent the conditions mentioned in paragraph (1)(a) to (c) being satisfied in relation to two or more sections; but

(c) those conditions have ceased to be satisfied in relation to one or more sections (whether before or after 6th April 1997) by reason only of there being no members in pensionable service under the section and no contributions which are to be allocated to it,

then regulations 10 to 15 shall apply as if the section in relation to which those conditions have ceased to be satisfied were a separate scheme.

(3) For the purposes of paragraphs (1) and (2), there shall be disregarded any provisions of the scheme by virtue of which contributions or transfers of assets may be made to make provision for death benefits; and where paragraph (1) or (2) applies and contributions or transfers are so made to a section ('the death benefits section') the assets of which may only be applied for the provision of death benefits, the death benefits section shall also be treated as if it were a separate scheme for the purposes of regulations 10 to 15.

(4) For the purposes of paragraphs (1) to (3), there shall be disregarded any provisions of the scheme by virtue of which on the winding up of the scheme assets attributable to one section may be used for the purposes of another section.

(5) Where there is more than one employer in relation to a scheme (other than a scheme to which paragraph (1) or (2) applies), and at least two of those employers are persons who are neither a company nor a person connected with that company nor associates of each other—

(a) regulation 12(2)(a) shall apply with the substitution for the words 'employer-related investments' of the words 'investments which are employer-related investments in relation to a particular employer, and employer-related investments overall must not exceed a prudent level and in any event must not exceed 20 per cent. of the current market value of the scheme'; and

(b) for regulation 14(4) there shall be substituted—

'(4) There shall be no new investment in employer-related investments while—

(a) the resources of a scheme retained in investments which are employer-related investments in relation to a particular employer (other than investments authorised by regulation 13) exceed five per cent. of the current market value of the resources of the scheme; or

(b) more than 20 per cent. overall of the current market value of the resources of the scheme is retained under this regulation in employer-related investments.'.

17 Scheme undertaking cross-border activities

5.36
The following shall not apply in the case of a scheme undertaking cross-border activities—

(a) regulation 6;

(b) regulation 7;

(c) the words 'except small schemes' in regulation 12(1);

(d) regulation 13(2), (3), (4), (7), (8), (9), (12) and (13);

(e) regulation 14; and

(f) regulation 15.

18 Revocations

5.37
The instruments listed in column 2 of the Schedule to these Regulations are revoked to the extent specified in column 3 of that Schedule.

SCHEDULE

Regulation 18

Revocations

Column 1 *Statutory Instrument Number*	*Column 2* *Statutory Instrument*	*Column 3* *Provisions revoked*
S.I. 1996/3127	The Occupational Pension Schemes (Investment) Regulations 1996	The whole of the Regulations
S.I. 1997/786	The Personal and Occupational Pension Schemes (Miscellaneous Amendments) Regulations 1997	Schedule 1, paragraph 18
S.I. 1997/819	The Occupational Pension Schemes (Reference Scheme and Miscellaneous Amendments) Regulations 1997	Regulation 6
S.I. 1999/1849	The Occupational Pension Schemes (Investment, Assignment, Forfeiture, Bankruptcy etc.) (Amendment) Regulations 1999	Regulation 2
S.I. 2000/1403	The Stakeholder Pension Schemes Regulations 2000	Regulation 31
S.I. 2000/3198	The Occupational Pension Schemes (Republic of Ireland Schemes Exemption) Regulations 2000	Regulation 10
S.I. 2001/3649	The Financial Services and Markets Act 2000 (Consequential Amendments and Repeals) Order 2001	Articles 544 to 548
S.I. 2002/681	The Occupational and Personal Pension Schemes (Contracting-out) (Miscellaneous Amendments) Regulations 2002	Regulation 6
S.I. 2005/678	The Occupational Pension Schemes (Employer Debt) Regulations 2005	Schedule 2, paragraph 3

Chapter 6

Unapproved schemes (Non-registered EFRBS from 6 April 2006)

Introduction

6.1 The popularity of unapproved pension schemes amongst very high earners in recent years has been easily explained by the imposition of the limit on pensionable earnings under occupational pension schemes. Introduced in 1989, the earnings cap gave rise to an increase in various unapproved schemes which, though less tax efficient, were attractive in that the restrictions on benefit provision could be overcome.

Changes introduced by the new tax regime from 6 April 2006, mean that future tax concessions available under these arrangements have largely disappeared. Such schemes (FURBS and UURBS) are be able to register from A-Day (but see 3.4 above for the UURBS timescale), bringing them under the tax regime for registered schemes from the date of registration. If such schemes elect to opt out of the new regime from A-Day, they are allowed a large degree of protection of their existing pre A-day rights under transitional arrangements (see Chapter 3). The new regime is available to everyone who elects to join it, but note the new lifetime allowance will embrace the build up of the post A-Day tax-free fund (the pre-A-Day element being mainly protected).

This chapter will deal with the treatment of various types of non-registered scheme, as set out below:

- Registration refused – see 6.4 below
- Registration withdrawn – see 6.5 below
- Opting out of registration – see 6.11 below
- New schemes post A-Day, not wishing to register – see 6.13 below
- Employer financed retirement benefits schemes – see para 6.14 below

- Registering FURBS and UURBS which exist at 5 April 2006 – see 6.2 below

HMRC has not yet codified how FURBS, UURBS and EFRBS will be treated from A-Day, but it has stated that details will appear on its Trusts, Settlements and Estates Manual. The current guidance under this manual is summarised from 6.17 below.

Employer-financed retirement benefit schemes

6.2 Unapproved schemes will be treated as Employer-Financed Retirement Benefits Schemes from A-Day and they will not receive any privileged tax treatment, except under transitional arrangements. The *Employer-Financed Retirement Benefits Schemes (Provision of Information) Regulations 2005* (*SI 2005/3453*) state that HMRC must be notified within three months of a scheme coming into operation, and by 7 July following the end of the year of assessment in which a benefit is paid.

The main rules are:

- There is an extension to the persons who are responsible for certain actions under the *Taxes Management Act 1970* beyond that of the scheme administrator to 'responsible persons' where assessments are due on certain payments or actions.
- Employers will not receive relief on contributions and administration expenses until benefits come into payment (*ss 245* and *246*, *Finance Act 2004*, respectively).
- An employer's cost of insuring benefits against employer insolvency is chargeable to the member as a benefit-in-kind. The employer can claim the cost as an expense against profits at the time that it is paid.
- For investment gains, capital gains tax is chargeable at the rate applicable to trusts (RAT), which increased from 34% to 40% on 6 April 2004, and amounts held in the fund will not be included in the lifetime allowance.
- The basic rate of tax applies on the first £500 of gains from 6 April 2005, which removes one-third of trusts from the RAT (tax returns are only likely to be issued every five years in such cases, although taxable income should be declared if it arises).
- Elections for the new regime had to be made by 6 April 2006 if they were to apply from 6 April 2004.
- Income tax on the fund for unapproved schemes increased from 22% to 40% from 6 April 2004.

- Lump sum death benefits will be charged to inheritance tax.
- It is thought (subject to formal confirmation) that there will be no NIC charge on any benefits paid out of non-registered schemes provided they are within the limits of benefits that could be paid out of a registered scheme and all employer and connected employer relationship has ceased.

HMRC'S Employment Income Manual

6.3 The RPSM draws attention to HMRC's Employment Income Manual for details of how a trust-based employer-financed retirement benefits scheme is treated for tax purposes. This provides the following additional information:

- only 'relevant benefits' count as employment income under *s 394*, *ITEPA 2003*;
- the charge on lump sums paid out may be reduced where prior employer contributions have been taxed and where the employee has made contributions;
- a pension is charged separately as pension income under *Pt 9*, *ITEPA 2003* (*Pt 9* charges pension income to tax).

In the above:

'relevant benefits' means:

any lump sum, gratuity or other benefit provided:

- on retirement or on death; or
- in anticipation of retirement; or
- after retirement or death in connection with past service; or
- on or in anticipation of or in connection with any change in the nature of the employee's service; or
- by virtue of a pension sharing order or provision.

This includes a non-cash benefit, but not:

- pension income within *Pt 9*, *ITEPA 2003*;
- benefits chargeable under *Sch 34*, *FA 2004*.

Excluded benefits are benefits:

- in respect of ill-health or disablement of an employee during service;
- in respect of death by accident of an employee during service;
- under a 'relevant life policy' (guidance on the meaning of this will be made available in the Policyholder Taxation Manual (IPTM)).

Guidance on how annuities, annual payments and non-cash receipts are dealt with is given in EIM15100.

Registration refused

6.4 HMRC has the power (ss *157* and *158, Finance Act 2004*) to refuse registration of a scheme, where it appears that any of the following situations apply:

(*a*) chargeable payments from the scheme during any period of 12 months exceed the de-registration threshold (of 25% chargeable payments);

(*b*) failure to pay a substantial amount of tax (and/or interest thereon), by the scheme administrator;

(*c*) failure to provide information to HMRC by the scheme administrator, where the information required to be provided is significant;

(*d*) material inaccuracy of any information contained in the application to register the scheme, or otherwise provided to HMRC;

(*e*) false declaration to HMRC of any other material information accompanying the application to register;

(*f*) where there is no scheme administrator.

Appeals against refusal may be made within 30 days of the decision, to the General Commissioners or the Special Commissioners – *s 156, Finance Act 2004*.

Registration withdrawn

6.5 Withdrawal of registration by HMRC from an entire pension scheme would, other than in the most exceptional circumstances, affect all arrangements within that scheme.

Registration threshold

6.6 There is an automatic de-registration threshold, stipulated under *s 158*(*2*) to (*4*), *Finance Act 2004*. This threshold is exceeded if the total of the percentages of the fund used up by each chargeable payment in any 12-month period amounts to 25% or more of the fund. The percentage of the fund used up is determined by the following formula:

$$\frac{\text{Scheme chargeable payment}}{\text{Value of scheme funds}} \times \frac{100}{1}$$

The value of the scheme funds is the market value of the assets held for the purposes of the scheme plus the amount of the sums held for the purposes of the scheme, both taken at the time of the payment.

RPSM example of de-registration

Example

6.7 Two scheme chargeable payments have been made within a 12-month period. The payments were of £14,000 and £10,000. The fund value at the time of the first payment comprised assets with a market value of £80,000 and cash of £20,000 giving a total value of £100,000.

The percentage of the scheme fund used up at the time of the first scheme chargeable payment is:

$$\frac{\pounds 14{,}000}{\pounds 100{,}000} \times \frac{100}{1} = 14\%$$

The fund was valued at £88,000 at the time of the second payment, which was £10,000:

$$\frac{\pounds 10{,}000}{\pounds 88{,}000} \times \frac{100}{1} = 11\%$$

Add together 14% and 11% and the aggregate is 25%. The de-regulation threshold is exceeded. This means there are grounds for HMRC to de-register the scheme.

HMRC actions on de-registration

6.8 Under *s 158*(*2*) to (*4*), *Finance Act 2004*, when HMRC de-registers a scheme it must notify the administrator (or, if there is no administrator, the person(s) who has/have responsibility for the scheme and whom it is reasonably practicable for HMRC to identify) stating the date on and after which the scheme will not be registered. HMRC will also notify the Pensions Regulator that the scheme has been de-registered.

Under *s 242*, a tax charge will be incurred (see 6.5 to 6.7 above) of an amount equal to 40% of the total of:

- the scheme market value, immediately before it ceased to be registered, of the assets held; plus
- the sums held immediately before registration ceased.

The administrator is liable for the charge, regardless of that scheme administrator's residence or domicile status for UK tax purposes. If more than one person is the administrator, each person is jointly and severally liable for the tax due.

Impact on scheme taxation, following de-registration

6.9 The tax reliefs on the scheme are lost and, unless the scheme is wound up, it may continue as a non-registered pension scheme (see 6.2 above). This means that, if it is an occupational pension scheme, it will become subject to the provisions relating to employer-financed retirement benefit schemes (see 6.2 above) and there will be a 40% tax charge of the market value of the pension fund. Any life assurance business will cease to be pension business at the beginning of he company's period of account in which the scheme loses its registration status.

If there is an unauthorised payment, there is a tax charge either on the member or the sponsoring employer, as appropriate. Where the payment relates to a deceased member, the charge is on another person instead of the member. There may also be a tax charge on the scheme administrator.

Appeals against de-registration

6.10 Appeals may be made against a decision to de-register, under *s 159*, *Finance Act 2004* (*s 242* describes the 40% de-registration charge). The appeal must be made by the end of the thirtieth day beginning with the day on which the appellant was notified of the decision. The appeal will usually be made to the General Commissioners, although the appellant may elect for the appeal to be heard instead by the Special Commissioners.

A Commissioner's decision can be appealed by way of case stated.

Opting out of registration

Existing pension schemes at 5 April 2006 which opt out of registration

6.11 Approved schemes became automatically registered with effect from A-Day, unless a written election was made to opt out before that date, (*Sch 36, para 2(1), Finance Act 2004*). There is no special form for notifying HMRC that a scheme is to be treated as having opted out.

After A-Day, the only way for an ongoing scheme to become de-registered is for HMRC to withdraw registration.

Tax position of scheme on opting out

6.12 A tax charge would have been incurred on opting out of registration, (*paras 2(2)* to *2(4)* and *2(6)*, *Sch 36*, *Finance Act 2004*). The charge is 40% of the market value of the pension fund, being assets or other sums held for the purposes of the scheme immediately before A-Day. Any life assurance ceased to be pensions business at the beginning of the company's period of account in which the scheme opted out. The date of opting out for this purpose is A-Day.

The relevant administrator (for the type of scheme or arrangement concerned) was liable for the charge. If more than one person is the administrator, each person was jointly and severally liable for the tax due.

A scheme which is established for the benefit of particular employees will be taxed as an employer-financed retirement benefits scheme (see 6.2 above). As from A-day, employer contributions to unapproved schemes are not taxed on the employees or counted as employment income (*s 247, Finance Act 2004*).

New schemes post A-Day, not wishing to register

6.13 Where a pension scheme, which was set up on or after A-Day, does not wish to be registered HMRC does not need to know about such a scheme. The RPSM states, however, that 'other parts of HMRC may need to be informed of the existence of such a pension scheme' and undertakes to provide more specific details later.

The manual envisages that such a scheme is likely to be an 'employer-financed retirement benefits scheme' for the purposes of the tax legislation.

Registering FURBS and UURBS which existed at 5 April 2006

6.14 Funded Unapproved Retirement Benefit Schemes (FURBS) or Unfunded Unapproved Retirement Benefit Schemes (UURBS) were traditionally set up as 'top-up schemes' for individuals who were subject to the earnings cap from the year 1989. If such a scheme applies for registration, HMRC will register the scheme and it will become subject to the tax regime for registered pension schemes from the date of its registration.

Schemes which lost approval before A-Day

6.15 A scheme which lost approval before A-Day may apply to become a registered pension scheme at any time from that date onwards if its scheme administrator applies for registration for the scheme and satisfies the registration conditions.

Existing FURBS and UURBS

6.16 FURBS and UURBS that do not register from A-Day will be treated as EFRBS under *ss 245–249*, *Finance Act 2004*. However, under transitional arrangements, where the member has been taxed on pre-A-Day contributions to a FURBS, as they were made by the employer, those benefits will be allowed to be paid out, free of tax as before. Unfunded promises made before A-Day under UURBS will also have protection.

Under pre A-Day tax legislation all FURBS benefits could be paid out tax free if a member had been taxed on the employer contributions paid into the scheme. The government does not believe that FURBS and UURBS are essential 'unless the aim is to provide benefits that would not be allowed under a non-registered scheme'. The position for monies which are already held in FURBS as at A-Day, and for promises made under UURBS, is described below:

1 Testing the value of total benefits against the annual allowance or the lifetime allowance will not need to include the value pension promises under UURBS;

2 Security and underwriting costs of setting aside assets or securities in relation to UURBS promises will incur a charge to benefit-in-kind on the member, on and after A-Day;

3 Similarly to 2 above, UURBS promises can be insured against employer default, but the premiums will taxed on the member as a benefit-in-kind;

4 Pre-A-Day UURBS can be consolidated and established as a single entity under the new regime (see 3.4 above), to be counted only towards the lifetime allowance (not the annual allowance) thereafter (*Sch 36*, *Pt 4*, *Finance Act 2004*). If the deadline is missed, both elements will be counted;

5 Contributions to FURBS are allowed after A-Day, (see below), but the tax-free lump sum will be adjusted to take account of the earlier tax-free elements;

6 The existing tax-free lump sum element of a FURBS on A-Day will be protected (see 13 below), with indexation, provided that the related employer contributions, have been taxed on the member or by taxation of all income and gains under the fund;

7 Funds should be valued at A-Day using an 'appropriate fraction', determined from the market value of the assets, on the notional assumption that the scheme had been wound up on that day;

8 Assets built up under a discretionary trust before A-Day in FURBS will retain their normal exemptions under inheritance tax rules. If there are no further contributions after A-Day, the IHT position will remain unchanged. If contributions continue, the relief will be limited to the pre-A-Day funds, with indexation added;

9 From the point made in 8 above, it will become clear that IHT exemptions will not apply to post A-Day assets;

10 Tax-free payments arising from contributions that were already taxed under *s 595*, *ICTA 1988* or *s 386*, *ITEPA 2003*, before A-Day, have that status protected under *Schedule 36*, *paras 52* to *56*, *Finance Act 2004*;

11 FURBS which cease to be funded before A-Day will not incur any additional charges to tax on the lump sum ultimately payable out of the fund;

12 FURBS that become registered on A-Day will be subject to the limit of 25% of the lifetime allowance. Similarly, in the case of UURBS, it would appear that this percentage will also apply, where commutation is exercised to reduce or avoid NIC charges;

13 The *Employer-Financed Retirement Benefits* (*Excluded Benefits for Tax Purposes*) *Regulations 2006* (*SI 2006/210*) prescribe a lump sum benefit as an excluded benefit if it is:

   (*a*) in respect of the non-accidental death of an employee during service; and

   (*b*) already provided for under the rules of a scheme on 6 April 2006.

Trusts, Settlements and Estates Manual

6.17 HMRC's internal Trusts, Settlements and Estates Manual will be revised in respect of unapproved schemes (see 6.1 above).

Until A-Day, new FURBS and UURBS were submitted for consideration to HMRC Trusts, Bootle. If a previously approved scheme lost approval because resident trustees had been replaced by non-resident trustees, the case would be referred to CNR (Non-Resident Trusts) – all other cases are proper to HMRC Trusts, Nottingham.

The existing guidance in the manual is out of date. A summary is given below for general guidance on past tax rules as it is still a primary source of reference. The statutory references applied before A-Day and (in part) the enactment of *ITEPA 2003* and *Finance Act 2004*.

FURBS; resident trustees (EBT2)

6.18 The internal memo contains information, advice and action points for:

- the Trust Office dealing with the FURBS trust;
- the tax office for the company; and
- the employment income tax office.

The main actions are:

- 'Initial action: Issue returns annually to the trustees.
- Information: Income arising from the invested contributions is chargeable at the lower/basic/Sch F rate only. It is not chargeable at the rate applicable to trusts/Schedule F trust rate. This is because the scheme provides for 'Relevant Benefits' (defined in *s 612, ICTA 1988*) only. The exemption is in *s 686(2)(c), ICTA 1988*.

  The exemption does not apply, and the trustees are chargeable at the rate applicable to trusts/Schedule F trust rate, if any of the situations below applies. If you discover such a situation, advise the trustees they are liable at the rate applicable to trusts/Schedule F trust rate. The trustees:

  - are chargeable Case I Schedule D on trading profits;
  - invest the contributions in a way that does not give a commercial return, for example:
    - non-commercial rate loans,
    - investing a significant part of the funds in non-income producing assets.
- Advice: Refer any objection to HMRC Trusts, Bootle.

- Action: If the trustees use the contributions to provide benefits that are not within the definition of Relevant Benefits, for example:
  - non-commercial rate loans to a member;
  - occupation of a trust property either rent free or below the open market rent;
  - free use of a trust asset

  the *s 686* exemption may not apply, or it may be an indication that a member is the settlor, in which case the Settlements legislation may treat the scheme's income as the settlor's. If you become aware that any of the above three points applies, submit the case to HMRC Trusts, Bootle.

The Settlements Legislation

6.19

- Information: The Settlements Legislation in *Part XV*, *ICTA 1988* will not apply if the scheme is operating on normal commercial lines as part of an employment package. But in certain circumstances you may consider whether the Settlements legislation applies to charge the FURBS trust's income and gains on a director.
- Action: Both the Settlements Legislation and the CG equivalent provisions can apply if the trust is apparently not genuinely to provide retirement benefits. Apply the following guidelines when examining trust returns and accounts, and liaise with the tax office for the company and the employment income tax office, or submit to HMRC Trusts, Bootle, as necessary.
  - The Settlements Legislation will not apply where only the employer makes contributions – unless the contributions are:
    - made by a close company which a member controls; or
    - unrealistically large by normal commercial standards.

    For example, if there is only one director who is also the sole shareholder of the employing company, and substantial contributions are made into the FURBS, you may consider whether the Settlements Legislation applies to treat the director/shareholder as the settlor. If you think this may be the case, you must liaise with the tax office for the company. They will consider whether to deny a deduction for the contributions.
  - The Settlements Legislation will not apply if a member makes

contributions and these are reasonable compared with the member's salary. As a rule of thumb contributions not exceeding 15% of remuneration (excluding the payments) are reasonable. If you consider the Settlements Legislation may apply, submit your papers to HMRC Trusts Bootle.

- The Settlements legislation may apply if the relief provided by *s 686(2)(c), ICTA 1988* has been disallowed.

The Tax Office for the company

Contributions

6.20

- Information: Guidance on whether the contributions into the scheme are allowable is at IM8410 onwards. *Section 76, FA 1989* deals with the timing of any deductions due (see IM8412).

  The employer's contributions are allowable only if they are chargeable as employment or pension income on a member or another person. Where due, a deduction is given for the period in which the employer makes the contribution (*s 76 (4)*). This ensures the payer's relief matches the employee's charge as to both time and amount.
- Advice: If you cannot resolve a problem about this, refer the case to Business Tax 1 (Schedule D).
- Action: There may be tax avoidance opportunities if a company is 'close' and a member is a participator with a significant interest in the company. You may want to consider whether amounts put into the scheme by the employer are commensurate with a normal commercial provision for the employee concerned.
- Action: If a schedule D deduction has been successfully denied because the contribution has not been wholly and exclusively expended for the purposes of the employer's trade, submit the file for the employer to HMRC Trusts Bootle so that they can consider whether the Settlements Legislation applies.

The employment Income Tax Office

6.21

- Initial action: Put a sub folder in the 46 file to house relevant correspondence. Ask each participating employer for an annual report on form P11D. The report should state the amount of contributions into the scheme to provide benefits for a member. It is then possible to check if all liability under *s 386, ITEPA 2003* has been met.

Contributions

6.22

- Information: A member is chargeable on the amount of contributions into the scheme as employment income under *s 386, ITEPA 2003*. The charge is for each year of assessment in which there are contributions. Costs of creating or administering the scheme are not chargeable on the member.
- Advice: Refer any problem about the application of *s 386, ITEPA 2003* to Personal Tax (Technical).

Pensions

6.23

- Information: Pensions that the trustees pay are chargeable as pension income by virtue of *s 569, ITEPA 2003* (because of *s 393*(2), *ITEPA 2003*).
- Advice: Refer any problem to Personal Tax (Technical).

Lump sum benefit

6.24

- Information: *s 393, ITEPA 2003* deals with lump sum benefits that trustees pay. A benefit may be chargeable or may be exempt. In particular *s 395(4), ITEPA 2003* exempts from tax lump sums if the contributions are charged under *s 386, ITEPA 2003*.
- Advice: Refer any problem to Personal Tax (Technical).
- Action: Inform IR Capital Taxes, Technical Group, Meldrum House, Drumsheugh Gardens, Edinburgh where a member of a FURBS has died, giving full name and date of death.

National Insurance contributions (NICs) position

6.25 For information about the NICs position on:

- an employer's payments into a FURBS; and
- payments out of a FURBS,

6.26 *Unapproved schemes*

see NIM02155 – NIM02163 and SCS98/03.

For advice, contact your NICs Technical Support Manager.

FURBS: non-resident trustees (NRT40)

6.26 There is also a memo for FURBS where the trustees are non-resident. This is the NRT40. Similar tax requirements apply to those stated above.

Old Code Schemes

6.27 Any remaining *s 608, ICTA 1988* schemes will fall under the new tax regime unless they choose to opt out. As such the Annual Allowance and the Lifetime Allowance will apply from A-Day. If such schemes choose to opt out they will be treated in the same way as non-registered schemes. By way of an alternative, *s 608* schemes (as revised by *ITEPA 2003*) may choose to wind up if their rules so permit, commuting all benefits to a lump sum with a 25% tax free element. This option will only be available for the first year following A-Day.

Foreign pensions

6.28 *Section 573, ITEPA 2003*, applies to any pension paid by or on behalf of a person who is outside the UK to a person who is resident in the UK. *Section 14, ITEPA 2003* (see EIM74001).

Section 574, ITEPA 2003 extends the charge under *s 573* to a pension that is paid voluntarily or is capable of being discontinued if the following conditions are met:

- the pension is paid to a former employee or office holder or to their widow, widower, child, relative or dependant;
- the payment is paid by or on behalf of the person who employed the former employee (or the person under whom the office was held) or by the successors of that person.

Section 575, ITEPA 2003 provides that the taxable amount of a foreign pension is 90% of the actual amount arising in the tax year unless the income is charged on the remittance basis. As foreign pensions are treated as 'relevant foreign income, there is provision for claims to remittance basis, deductions and reliefs and unremittable income.

Extra-statutory concession A10

6.29 This concession is designed to allow exemption on lump sum relevant benefits in like manner to that of exemption or relief for foreign service, under *s 401, ITEPA 2003*, covering lump sums and commutation options received under the rules of such schemes.

If the employee has served abroad in the relevant employment, charges, if any, under *s 394, ITEPA 2003* are reduced or eliminated under this concession.

The wording of the concession is as follows:

- 'Income tax is not charged on lump sum relevant benefits receivable by an employee (or by his personal representatives or any dependant of his) from an Overseas Retirement Benefits Scheme or an Overseas Provident Fund where the employee's overseas service comprises:
  - (*a*) not less than 75 % of his total service in that employment; or
  - (*b*) the whole of the last 10 years of his service in that employment, where total service exceeds 10 years; or
  - (*c*) not less than 50 % of his total service in that employment, including any 10 of the last 20 years, where total service exceeds 20 years.

If the employee's overseas service is less than described above, relief from income tax will be given by reducing the amount of the lump sum which would otherwise be chargeable by the same proportion as the overseas service bears to the employee's total service in that employment.

In addition, income tax is not charged on lump sum relevant benefits receivable by an employee (or by his personal representatives or any dependant of his) from any superannuation fund accepted as being within *s 615, ICTA 1988*.

For the purposes of this concession, the term 'relevant benefits' has the meaning given in *s 612(1), ICTA 1988* and the term 'overseas service' shall be construed in accordance with the definition of 'foreign service' found at *para 10, Sch 11, ICTA 1988*.'

A period of service falling after 5 April 2003 is foreign service if either:

- the earnings from the employment are not general earnings to which *s 15* or *s 21, ITEPA 2003*, apply. This will be the case where:
  - the employee is not resident and ordinarily resident in the UK. So for example if the employee is not resident, neither *s 15* nor *s 21* apply so during that period the employee's service is foreign service; or

- the employee is resident and ordinarily resident in the UK but is not domiciled in the UK, is working for a foreign employer and is carrying out all the duties of the employment outside the UK

or

- the employee is a seafarer eligible for 100% deduction from earnings under *Pt 5, Ch 6, ITEPA 2003*.

If there is a period of service when there are no earnings from the employment, it is possible to apply the above rules in the same way as if there were.

The concession is currently being reviewed in connection with employer-financed retirement benefits schemes. HMRC Newsletter 7 states that the effect of the concession will continue from A-Day. The concession will be interpreted in the following ways in the light of the new simplified tax legislation:

- 'overseas retirement benefits scheme' and 'overseas provident fund' will be interpreted as overseas employer financed retirement benefits schemes, as defined in *s 393A, ITEPA 2003*;
- The concession will continue to apply to lump sums received from schemes within *s 615(6), ICTA 1988*;
- 'relevant benefits' will be defined in accordance with *s 393B, ITEPA 2003*;
- The concession will not apply to any benefits chargeable under *Sch 34, Finance Act 2004*.

Section 249, Finance Act 2004, contains various legislative amendments relating to the taxation of non-pension benefits from funded unapproved schemes.

Schedule 35 contains minor and consequential amendments to various acts and brings in the various changes to FURBS which are described below.

Chapter 7

Overseas considerations

Introduction

7.1 The *Finance Act 2004* and the *Pensions Act 2004* contained provisions which reflected the government's intent to comply with the main principles of the *EU Occupational Pensions Directive* (*2003/41/EC*) on *IORPs*. There have been significant changes and relaxations to the membership, tax and transfer rules which previously applied to overseas matters. These rules are described in this chapter. The HMRC website provides a list of frequently asked questions and answers on UK and overseas matters. This list explains the current thinking of HMRC on various matters.

The regulations

7.2 The main HMRC regulations which apply to overseas matters from A-Day are listed in 7.3 to 7.8 below, together with an explanation of their application in each case. The regulations are reproduced in 7.27 to 7.38 below (and 2.172 to 2.210 above concerning international enhancement). Collectively, the regulations effectively govern the tax reliefs and transferability which apply to overseas matters. There must be strict compliance with their terms if tax charges and penalties are to be avoided (see 7.15 to 7.20 below and 2.109 to 2.137 above concerning general charges).

The Pension Schemes (*Categories of Country and Requirements for Overseas Pension Schemes and Recognised Overseas Pension Schemes*) *Regulations 2006* (*SI 2006/206*)

7.3 These are the main regulations. They prescribe the requirements which must be met by a scheme in order to qualify as an overseas pension scheme under the *Finance Act 2004*. There are two methods of qualifying.

First method

7.4 The first method is that there is, in the country or territory in which the scheme is established, a body which regulates that type of scheme and the scheme itself. The scheme must be recognised for tax purposes in its home state by meeting the primary conditions below and one of Conditions A and B.

Primary condition 1

The scheme is open to persons resident in the country or territory in which it is established.

Primary condition 2

The scheme is established in a country or territory where there is a system of taxation of personal income under which tax relief is available in respect of pensions, and:

1 tax relief (including the grant of an exemption) is not available to the member on contributions made to the scheme by the individual or, if the individual is an employee, by their employer, in respect of earnings to which benefits under the scheme relate; or

2 all or most of the benefits paid by the scheme to members who are not in serious ill-health are subject to taxation.

Condition A

The scheme is approved or recognised by, or registered with, the relevant tax authorities as a pension scheme in the country or territory in which it is established.

Condition B

If no system exists for the approval or recognition by, or registration with, relevant tax authorities of pension schemes in the country or territory in which it is established, it must be resident there; and its rules must provide that:

1 at least 70% of a member's UK tax-relieved scheme funds will be designated by the scheme manager for the purpose of providing the member with an income for life; and

2 the pension benefits payable to the member under the scheme (and any lump sum associated with those benefits) must be payable no earlier than normal pension age under the *Finance Act 2004*.

Second method

7.5 The second method is that there is for a scheme established (outside the UK) by an international organisation for the purpose of providing benefits for, or in respect of, past service as an employee of the organisation which satisfies the requirements below:

- the scheme rules must provide that at least 70% of a member's UK tax-relieved scheme funds will be designated by the scheme manager for the purpose of providing the member with an income for life; and
- the pension benefits payable to the member under the scheme (and any lump sum associated with those benefits) under the scheme must be payable no earlier than normal pension age under the *Finance Act 2004*.

To be a recognised overseas scheme, a scheme must either be established in another EEA State, or in a country or territory with which the UK has a double taxation agreement providing for the exchange of information between the fiscal authorities of the UK and the overseas country or territory and for non-discrimination between UK nationals and nationals of the overseas country or territory. If it is not established in such a country or territory a scheme may nonetheless be recognised if the rules of the scheme must provide that:

- at least 70% of the sums transferred will be designated by the scheme manager for the purpose of providing the member with an income for life;
- the pension benefits (and any lump sum associated with those benefits) payable to the member under the scheme, to the extent that they relate to the transfer, are payable no earlier than normal pension age under the *Finance Act 2004*;
- the scheme is open to persons resident in the country or territory in which it is established.

The Pensions Schemes (Application of UK Provisions to Relevant Non-UK Schemes) Regulations 2006 (SI 2006/207)

7.6 These regulations describe the method of calculation of tax on a payment made by a relevant non-UK scheme (RNUK) in respect of a payment which is referable to a member's UK tax-relieved funds. They also contain provisions for HMRC to mitigate the charge to tax in appropriate circumstances.

The Pension Schemes (Information Requirements – Qualifying Overseas Pension Schemes, Qualifying Recognised Overseas Pension Schemes and Corresponding Relief) Regulations 2006 (SI 2006/208)

7.7 These regulations describe the information which must be sent to HMRC for a qualifying overseas pension scheme and a qualifying recognised overseas pension scheme to be recognised as such. They also describe the information which must be sent to HMRC in respect of an individual's contributions and the 30-day rule which applies to the provision of information following the issue of a notice by HMRC.

The form number for applying for qualifying status is APSS 251, and forms must be submitted by the scheme manager. If all is well HMRC will send the manager a letter of acceptance showing a unique reference number. This will be entered on the HMRC database. HMRC can ask the manager for more evidence before issuing the letter.

The Pension Schemes (Relevant Migrant Members) Regulations 2006 (SI 2006/212)

7.8 These regulations describe the application of migrant member relief for a member of an overseas pension scheme. An individual is a relevant migrant member if he meets the requirements of *Sch 33, Finance Act 2004*.

Migrant member relief

Background

7.9 The corresponding relief provisions which were in place prior to A-Day were restrictive in their application. Individuals could only claim relief when they were not domiciled in the UK and were employed by an overseas employer. This practice did not accord with the *EU Pensions Directive*. The new rules are that corresponding relief is replaced by a tax relief entitlement on contributions made by migrants who come to the UK. It applies when the contributions are made by a relevant migrant member to a qualifying overseas pension scheme.

The rules no longer take the individual's domicile into account and there is no restriction on where the scheme has to be established. However, the individual must be a relevant migrant member and the scheme has to be regulated as a pension scheme in the country where it is established and undertake to provide certain specified information in respect of the member. The changes came about in part following the receipt from the EC of a formal request for the UK to change its original legislation as it considered that the beneficial tax treatment of domestic pension schemes is incompatible with the freedoms mentioned in the EC Treaty.

There is transitional protection for relief on employee and employer contributions where someone entitled to corresponding relief as at A-Day does not qualify for migrant relief. There is no lifetime allowance charge in respect of corresponding relief given for contributions made before A-Day.

Relevant migrant member

7.10 A relevant migrant member is a member of an overseas pension scheme if the individual:

- was not resident in the UK when first a member of the pension scheme;
- was a member of the pension scheme at the beginning of the period of residence in the UK which includes the time when the contributions are paid;
- either was, immediately before the beginning of that period of residence, entitled to tax relief in respect of contributions paid under the pension scheme under the law of the country or territory in which the individual was then resident, or had received tax relief on contributions paid to the pension scheme in the country of residence at any time in the 10 years prior to coming to the UK; and
- has been notified by the scheme manager that information concerning events that are benefit crystallisation events in relation to the individual and the pension scheme will be given to HMRC.

The main provisions are in *Sch 33, Finance Act 2004*.

Member qualification for migrant member relief

7.11 A relevant migrant member of a qualifying overseas pension scheme is entitled to relief on contributions paid by or on behalf of himself in respect of relievable pension contributions paid during a tax year where the individual:

- has relevant UK earnings chargeable to income tax for that year;
- is resident in the UK when the contributions are paid; and
- has notified the scheme manager of an intention to claim relief.

Claimants of migrant member relief, and claimants under double taxation agreements, may elect that a benefit crystallisation event will occur when their claim to relief ceases. A credit may be set off against the member payments charge where foreign tax has been paid on the same payments.

The main provisions are in *s 188, Finance Act 2004*.

Employer relief

7.12 Employers may also receive tax relief on their contributions to a qualifying overseas pension scheme in respect employees who are entitled to migrant member relief. Relief is due in relation to contributions paid by an employer under a registered pension scheme in respect of an individual.

The main provisions are in *ss* (*2*) to (*5*) of *ss 196* and *200, Finance Act 2004*.

Qualifying overseas pension scheme

7.13 For the purpose of receiving an entitlement to relevant migrant member relief, the overseas pension scheme must be a qualifying overseas pension scheme. In order to qualify as such a scheme the scheme manager must:

(*a*) have notified HMRC that the scheme is an overseas pension scheme, and have provided HMRC with any required evidence;

(*b*) undertaken to inform HMRC if the scheme ceases to be an overseas pension scheme;

(*c*) undertaken to HMRC to comply with any prescribed benefit crystallisation information requirements imposed on the scheme manager – these may relate to events that are benefit crystallisation events in relation to members of the pension scheme who have at any time been relevant migrant members of the pension scheme.

Exclusion from being a qualifying overseas pension scheme

7.14 HMRC may exclude an overseas pension scheme from being a qualifying overseas pension scheme if it has decided that:

(*a*) there has been a failure to comply with any prescribed benefit crystallisation information requirements imposed on the scheme manager and the failure is significant; and

(*b*) by reason of the failure it is not appropriate that relief from tax should be given in respect of contributions under the pension scheme.

(*c*) HMRC shall notify the scheme manager, or the person or persons appearing to be the scheme manager, of its decision.

Member payment charges

7.15 *Schedule 34, Finance Act 2004,* contains details of the member payment charges that can apply to payments out of a registered scheme to, or deemed to be to, a RNUK or in respect of transfers of members of such a scheme. The charges arise in respect of RNUK schemes, where UK tax relief has been given on contributions under migrant member relief, or under the terms of a Double Taxation Treaty, or where a transfer has been made from a UK registered scheme to an overseas scheme. They are described in Chapter 5 of the 4th edition of Tottel's *Taxation of Pension Benefits*. They may include:

(*a*) an unauthorised payments charge;

(*b*) an unauthorised payments surcharge;

(*c*) a short service refund lump sum charge;

(*d*) a special lump sum death benefits charge; and

(*e*) charges on trivial commutation, winding-up lump sums and lump sum death benefits.

Transfers which do not meet the criteria above and those in 7.23 below will be deemed to be unauthorised payments, and a tax charge will be levied unless the scheme made the transfer in good faith which was based on false or incorrect information from the member.

Methods of calculation

7.16 The methods of calculation of the charge under *Sch 34* are amplified by the *Pensions Schemes (Application of UK Provisions to Relevant Non-UK Schemes) Regulations 2006 (SI 2006/207)*.

The two methods are:

(*a*) the method of computing the amount of a member's UK tax-relieved fund under a relevant non-UK scheme; and

(*b*) the method of computing the amount of a member's relevant transfer fund under a relevant non-UK scheme.

Incurring the charge

7.17 The charge is incurred if the member was resident in the UK when the transfer was made, or had been so within any of the preceding five years. The rate of tax payable and the person liable to pay the tax in relation to member payment charges are the same as for the relevant payment charge involved.

Mitigating the charge

7.18 The charge may be mitigated in some circumstances, for example some elements of the fund may be discounted, and a discharge or a repayment may be made of any amounts from which tax is incurred overseas from monies emerging from the transfer.

The *Registered Pension Schemes (Discharge of Liabilities under Sections 267 and 268 of the Finance Act 2004) Regulations 2005 (SI 2005/3452)* describe the circumstances when charges may be discharged in connection with the making of applications by scheme administrators of registered pension schemes and other persons for relief from the lifetime allowance charges under *s 267* and the unauthorised payments surcharge, and the scheme sanction charge under *s 268*.

Applications must set out particulars of the ground relied on under the relevant section and be made in writing:

- in the case of a company, not later than six years after the end of the accounting period to which it relates; or
- in the case of any other applicant, no later than five years after the 31 January next following the year of assessment to which it relates.

Provided that:

- if an assessment is made under *s 36, TMA 1970* (assessments for the purpose of making good any loss to the Crown from a loss of income tax, etc.), the *s 267* application or *s 268* application (as the case may be) must be made within two years of the date on which the assessment is issued as stated in the notice of that assessment;
- a *s 267* application or *s 268* application may be made on behalf of an incapacitated person, as defined in *s 118, TMA 1970*, by his trustee, guardian or receiver.

Additionally, the *Pensions Schemes (Application of UK Provisions to Relevant Non-UK Schemes) Regulations 2006 (SI 2006/207)* modify the provisions of *Pt 4, Finance Act 2004*, in its application to RNUK schemes in order to ensure that the new regime for pensions which are subject to UK taxation works in the context of RNUK schemes as defined in *para 1(5), Sch 34* to the Act. *Schedule 34* is revised by inserting a notional *para 19A* to provide HMRC's discretionary power to mitigate, if it appears that any difference in the operation of the

RNUK scheme from that prescribed by the Act is not material and that it is appropriate to mitigate the effect of the strict rules.

Annual allowance charge and lifetime allowance charge

7.19 *Schedule 34, paras 8–12, Finance Act 2004*, explains how the annual allowance charge applies to currently-relieved members of currently-relieved RNUK schemes. Formulae are provided for the purpose of calculating the charge, which take into account the amount of taxable earnings within the meaning of *s 10(2), ITEPA 2003*.

Paragraphs 13–19 of the Act describe how the lifetime allowance charge applies to currently-relieved members of currently-relieved RNUK schemes. The paragraphs apply to benefit crystallisation events. A member may elect to notify HMRC of the applicable date of a benefit crystallisation event in a form specified by HMRC. Transfers will count as benefit crystallisation events unless they form part of a bulk transfer (see 7.25 below).

RNUK schemes

7.20 A scheme is a RNUK scheme if:

- migrant member relief has been given;
- post-5 April 2006 double taxation relief has been given;
- members have been exempted from tax liability under *s 307, ITEPA 2003*, in respect of pension or death benefit provision at any time after 5 April 2006 when the scheme was an overseas scheme; or
- there has been a relevant transfer from a UK scheme after 5 April 2006 when the scheme was a qualifying recognised overseas scheme.

Information requirements on overseas matters, including transfers

7.21 The *Registered Pension Schemes (Provision of Information) Regulations 2006 (SI 2006/567)* contain the main UK information requirements for registered schemes (see 2.91 to 2.101 above). The majority of the reports which are required should be made after 5 April following the year in which any benefit crystallisation event took place in respect of funds which have received, or are receiving, UK tax relief, and before the following 31 January. The lifetime allowance must be checked at the time of any overseas or UK transfer. There are specific requirements for overseas transfers (see 7.27 to 7.32 below and the Annex to Chapter 2).

The main requirements for a qualifying overseas pension scheme are contained in the *Pension Schemes (Information Requirements – Qualifying Overseas Pension Schemes, Qualifying Recognised Overseas Pension Schemes and Corresponding Relief) Regulations 2006* (*SI 2006/208*) – see 7.6 above. These regulations concern:

(*a*) information which must be sent to HMRC for a qualifying overseas pension scheme and a qualifying recognised overseas pension scheme to be recognised as such;

(*b*) information which must be sent to HMRC in respect of an individual's contributions; and

(*c*) the 30-day rule which applies to the provision of information following the issue of a notice by HMRC.

Transfers to a qualified and recognised overseas pension scheme

7.22 Where a registered scheme makes a transfer to a qualified, recognised, overseas pension scheme, the administrator must provide HMRC with the following information:

(*a*) the name;

(*b*) the address;

(*c*) the date of birth; and

(*d*) the National Insurance number;

of the member; and

(*e*) the amount of the sums or assets transferred;

(*f*) the date of the transfer together with the name of the qualified and recognised overseas pensions scheme and the country or territory under the law of which it is established and regulated.

Transfers

General

7.23 The transfer relaxations are summarised in 2.138 above. Registered schemes may transfer to a scheme in another country which is recognised and regulated in that country as a pension scheme. The *Pension Schemes (Categories of Country and Requirements for Overseas Pension Schemes and Recognised Overseas Pension Schemes) Regulations 2006 (SI 2006/206)* explain the main requirements to meet that criterion (see 7.2 above). As transfers may be made freely from registered pension schemes to such overseas pension schemes, and vice versa, this is likely to be of real advantage to any high earner who falls into one or more of the following categories:

- he has overseas employment;
- he is internationally mobile;
- he is non-UK domiciled;
- he is not resident in the UK.

The scheme must undertake to comply with certain information reporting requirements. There will be member payment charges on certain transfers (see 2.107 to 2.133 generally and 7.15 to 7.18 above), which are dependent mainly on the residency status of the member concerned.

Transfers-in

7.24 Transfers from schemes which are described in 7.22 above do not count towards the annual allowance, and only count towards the lifetime allowance to the extent that they include monies which have previously received UK tax relief.

Bulk transfers

7.25 In order to satisfy the meaning of the term 'bulk transfer' the members concerned must not have been members of the receiving scheme prior to the transfer of the sums and assets relating to the transfer. This restriction applies only if a member had been a member of the receiving scheme for one year or longer. There is some transitional protection for transfers in process as at A-Day.

Contracting out

7.26 The requirement for the trustees to satisfy themselves that a member has permanently emigrated before making a transfer payment of contracted-out or safeguarded pension rights to an overseas pension scheme or arrangement was removed with effect from 6 April 2005 by the *Contracting-out, Protected Rights and Safeguarded Rights (Transfer Payment) Amendment Regulations 2005 (SI 2005/555)*.

RPSM overseas guidance

7.27 The following information appears on HMRC's website under the RPSM references shown.

RPSM14102020 – Transfer to a non-registered overseas pension scheme which is not a qualifying recognised overseas pension scheme

7.28

'A transfer from a registered pension scheme to a non-UK pension scheme that is not a qualifying recognised overseas pension scheme is not a recognised transfer. Such a transfer is an unauthorised member payment.

See RPSM14101030 and RPSM14101040 for the conditions for a *recognised overseas pension scheme*.

Tax charges

The *member* incurs a tax charge of 40% on the amount of the payment.

This tax charge, broadly speaking, recoups the tax relief already given in respect of the contributions made by the member or on their behalf, and the income from the investment of those contributions. If the transfer payment and any other unauthorised payments to the member in a 12-month period exceeds 25% of the member's fund, the member is liable to an unauthorised payment surcharge of a further 15% of the payment.

A scheme sanction charge of up to 40% may also apply for which the *scheme administrator* is liable. If the scheme administrator has deducted the member's tax charge from the transfer payment and paid the tax charge to HMRC on the member's behalf, the scheme administrator may reduce the amount of the scheme sanction charge by the lesser of 25% and the amount of member's tax charge deducted as a proportion of the transfer payment.

In addition, if the amounts transferred equate to 25% or more of the scheme fund value, HMRC may withdraw the transferring scheme's registration. This involves a de-registration charge of 40% (see RPSM02105050).

Tax relief

[sections 188(5) & 232]

Tax relief is only given on contributions to *registered pension* schemes. A transfer is not a contribution. The payment is not being made to a registered pension scheme. No UK tax relief is due to the receiving scheme.

Annual allowance

If the transfer is made from a *cash balance arrangement*, or from a *defined benefit arrangement*, the amount transferred is not to be included in the closing value when calculating the member's *pension input amount* for the transferring arrangement (See RPSM06101020 and RPSM0610310). The closing value is not adjusted where the transfer is not a registered pension scheme or a qualifying recognised overseas pension scheme.

In a *money purchase arrangement* that is not a cash balance arrangement, the amount transferred in itself is not included when calculating the member's pension input amount, as only contributions are counted for the pension input amount in such a scheme.

Lifetime Allowance

The transfer is not a *benefit crystallisation event* for the purpose of the member's *lifetime allowance* and is not taken into account for the member's lifetime allowance either on the occasion of the transfer or on any future crystallisation of other benefits the member might take from registered pension schemes.

Reporting requirement

The scheme administrator of the transferring scheme must report the transfer (as an *unauthorised member payment*) to HMRC on the Event Report [RPSM12301010].'

RPSM14103010 – Recognised transfers to registered pension schemes: transfer from another registered pension scheme

7.29

[section 169(1)(a)]

'A transfer of a member's pension rights from a *registered pension scheme* to another registered pension scheme is a *recognised transfer*, (see RPSM14101010).

Although a transfer may be a recognised transfer for tax purposes, if there are contracted-out rights involved, Department for Work and Pensions (DWP) legislation provides that the transfer can only go ahead if the receiving scheme is eligible to hold those rights.'

RPSM14103020 – Recognised transfers to registered pension schemes: transfer from a recognised overseas pension scheme

7.30

[section 188(5) and sections 224–226]

'A transfer to a *registered pension scheme* from a *recognised overseas pension scheme* that is not a registered pension scheme is not a *recognised transfer*. But it is not an unauthorised payment either, because unauthorised payments are payments from registered pension schemes. And the legislation specifically states that an amount received by transfer from another pension scheme is not a contribution, so it does not qualify for tax relief on being received by a registered pension scheme.

Instead, special treatment is given to the *lifetime allowance* of a *member* who transfers-in funds from a recognised overseas pension scheme that is not registered, to a pension scheme that is registered (see RPSM13100010).

No UK tax relief has been received, so it would be unfair if the transferred amount were to use up the member's available lifetime allowance. But, broadly, any part of an amount transferred that relates to UK tax relieved contributions made after 5 April 2006 will count against the member's lifetime allowance.

As explained in RPSM11101050, the member's lifetime allowance is increased, or "enhanced", by an appropriate factor, from the date of the transfer. The member must claim this enhancement no later than five years after 31 January following the tax year in which the transfer is made, and register the amount with HMRC. This process enables HMRC to verify the amount claimed in appropriate cases.

For the member's *annual allowance*, the treatment of the transfer value depends on the type of scheme receiving the transfer. If the receiving scheme is either a *defined benefit* scheme or a *cash balance* scheme, subtract the transfer value from the closing value. If the receiving scheme is any other type of *money purchase* scheme, the transfer is not included, as only contributions are included for the annual allowance.'

RPSM14104010 – Non-recognised transfers to registered pension schemes

7.31

'A registered pension scheme may receive a transfer payment from another scheme that is neither a registered pension scheme nor a recognised overseas pension scheme, for example

- an employer financed retirement benefits scheme, or
- a pension scheme abroad that does not satisfy the requirements to be treated as a recognised overseas pension scheme.

Tax relief

A transfer payment is not a contribution, because section 188(5) specifically excludes transfer payments between pension schemes from being considered as contributions for tax relief purposes (regardless of whether or not the pension schemes concerned are registered or recognised).

No tax relief is due on the transfer payment on receipt. However, any investment income or gain in relation to the funds in the receiving scheme is free of income tax and capital gains tax.

Member's annual allowance

If the rights are being transferred into a defined benefit arrangement or a cash balance arrangement, the value of the transfer payment should be deducted from the closing value of the member's rights.

If the rights are being transferred into any other type of money purchase arrangement, the transfer payment is not included for the annual allowance. This is because, for annual allowance purposes, in a money purchase arrangement only contributions are counted, and a transfer payment is not a contribution.

Member's lifetime allowance

A transfer into a registered pension scheme is not a benefit crystallisation event (BCE) for lifetime allowance purposes. When the member eventually takes benefits, there will be a benefit crystallisation event at that point, and the lifetime allowance test must be carried out.

Where the transfer to a registered pension scheme has come from a scheme abroad, the member's lifetime allowance should only be enhanced if the transferring scheme is a recognised overseas pension scheme. In any other case, the standard lifetime allowance applies on a BCE, unless the member qualifies for an enhancement due to other special circumstances.'

RPSM14107010 – General points for transfers: transfers must be made between pension schemes

7.32

[section 266]

'A *scheme administrator* of a *registered pension scheme* should make sure that the person to whom they are transferring funds is someone with a position of responsibility in the receiving scheme.

A transfer is not a *recognised transfer* unless it is

- between registered pension schemes or
- from a registered pension scheme to a qualifying recognised overseas pension scheme.

Non-recognised transfers incur tax charges.

Where the receiving scheme is an "insured scheme", but the transfer payment is not made directly to the scheme administrator or an insurance company which issues policies under the receiving scheme, the scheme administrator of the transferring registered pension scheme is liable to a maximum penalty of £3,000.

An "insured scheme" is a pension scheme where all the income and other assets are invested in policies of insurance.'

RPSM14107040 – General points for transfers: partial transfers

7.33

'A transfer of part of a member's pension rights in a registered pension scheme leaving the remaining rights in the scheme is a recognised transfer providing

- it is made to either another registered pension scheme or a *qualifying recognised overseas pension scheme*, and
- the pension rights are uncrystallised.'

RPSM14107050 – General points for transfers: reporting transfers to HMRC

'Registered Pension Scheme Return

7.34

The Registered Pension Scheme Return is for a scheme administrator to complete, but this should only be done at HMRC's request. The Return can be submitted through the Pension Schemes Service Online, which can be found on the HMRC website.

- If completing the Registered Pension Scheme Return, the scheme administrator must report the following information concerning transfers to HMRC on it
- the amount transferred to other *pension schemes* that tax year
- the amount received as transfers from other pension schemes that tax year.

The Registered Pension Scheme Return must be received by HMRC by 31 January following the tax year it relates to.

See RPSM12301400 for further guidance on the Registered Pension Scheme Return.

Event Report

A scheme administrator must report to HMRC, using the online Event Report

- a transfer to a qualifying recognised overseas pension scheme

- any transfer which is an unauthorised member payment (for example, a transfer to an employer-financed retirement benefits scheme).

The Event Report must be received by HMRC by 31 January following the end of the tax year in which the transfer took place (but see RPSM12301010 where the scheme is wound up).

Unlike the Registered Pension Scheme Return, the Event Report is to be completed in all cases, without HMRC requesting it.

See RPSM1230 for further guidance on the Event Report.'

RPSM13102510 – International: application of charges to non-UK schemes: lifetime allowance: general

'General

7.35

[Paras 13–19, Schedule 34]

Paragraphs 13 to 19 of schedule 34 modify the *lifetime allowance* provisions so as to apply the *lifetime allowance charge* to members of overseas pension schemes that are not *registered pension schemes* in certain circumstances. The lifetime allowance provisions are explained in detail at RPSM11100000. You should read that section before continuing with the following description of what Schedule 34 does.

Broadly, under the lifetime allowance provisions every individual has a lifetime allowance which is the total capital value of benefits that they can draw from registered pension schemes without triggering a lifetime allowance tax charge. The lifetime allowance also covers transfers to certain *overseas pension schemes*. When an individual's benefits crystallise the capital value of those benefits is tested against their lifetime allowance. Their lifetime allowance is used up or reduced as a consequence, and the capital value of any benefits that crystallise after that will be tested against any remaining allowance.

The lifetime allowance charge is intended to recoup excess UK tax relief that an individual has received. So it has to apply to an individual's benefits from overseas pension schemes that have attracted UK tax relief, as well as to benefits from registered pension schemes.

Schedule 34 applies the lifetime allowance provisions to an individual who is a relieved member (RPSM13102140 refers) of a relieved non-UK pension scheme (RPSM13102520 refers) as if the scheme were a registered pension scheme.

This part explains what relieved non-UK pension schemes are, who relieved members are, and how the lifetime allowance charge provisions apply to them.'

RPSM13100040 – International: enhancement: general principles

'General principles of international enhancement

7.36

[s 221–226]

The *lifetime allowance* is an overall ceiling on the amount of UK tax-relieved pension savings that an individual can draw from *registered pension schemes* and certain overseas pension schemes. If when a *benefit crystallisation event* occurs (see example at rpsm11102040) the total value of an individual's benefits exceeds their unused lifetime allowance then that individual will be subject to a *lifetime allowance charge* (RPSM11103000 refers).

Everyone is entitled to the *standard lifetime allowance*, which is £1.5 million in the 2005/06 tax year and will increase in subsequent years. However, in certain circumstances an individual can notify HMRC that they are entitled to a lifetime allowance that is higher than the standard amount: an "enhanced" lifetime allowance. If so, a lifetime allowance charge would only arise when a benefit crystallisation event occurred if the total value of that individual's benefits exceeded their unused enhanced lifetime allowance.

An individual can notify HMRC of an entitlement to enhance their lifetime allowance in two international situations in which benefits in a registered pension scheme are built up without UK tax relief. These are

1. membership of a registered pension scheme whilst a relevant overseas individual (see RPSM13100100 to RPSM13100310), and
2. transfer to a registered pension scheme from a recognised overseas pension scheme (see RPSM13100410 to RPSM13100570)

Even if an individual is entitled to enhance their lifetime allowance they may not need to do so. A notification will be beneficial where the total value of an individual's UK tax-relieved pension scheme benefits is likely to exceed the standard lifetime allowance.'

RPSM13102020 – International: application of charges to non-UK scheme: basic principles

'Basic principles

7.37

[Sch 34 and related regulations – not yet laid]

Schedule 34 provides for certain charging provisions in Part 4 of the Finance Act 2004 to apply in certain circumstances to members of non-UK pension schemes that are not *registered pension schemes.*

This is necessary because there are circumstances in which an *overseas pension scheme* that is not a registered pension scheme will contain funds that have benefited from UK tax relief. For example, where a migrant individual comes to the UK as a member of an overseas pension scheme, any subsequent contributions to their overseas scheme may benefit from UK tax relief just like contributions to a registered pension scheme. Also, funds in an overseas pension scheme which have built up in a registered pension scheme before being transferred to the overseas pension scheme may equally have benefited from UK tax relief.

The schedule applies three main types of charge to members of non-UK schemes. These are the various charges referred to as the member payment charges (see RPSM13102100), the *annual allowance charge* (see RPSM13102300) and the *lifetime allowance charge* (RPSM13102500).

However, for members of non-UK pension schemes, these charges are targeted only at payments that relate to the part of the member's overseas pension fund that has benefited from UK tax relief.

Schedule 34 modifies the way the charges operate to facilitate their application to these non-UK schemes, and further modifications are contained in The Pension Schemes (Application of UK Provisions to Relevant Non-UK Schemes) Regulations 2005 – not yet laid.

This chapter explains how these charges apply to certain members of non-UK pension schemes as if they were members of registered pension schemes. The Schedule 34 modifications of the charging provisions are described in RPSM13102100 to RPSM13102600. The modifications provided for in the regulations referred to above are described in RPSM13102700 onwards.'

RPSM13103010 – International: overseas membership of a registered pension scheme: eligibility

'Eligibility for membership of a registered pension scheme

7.38

After 5 April 2006 membership of a registered pension scheme is open to anyone regardless of where they are resident or of where their employer (if any) is resident. Nor is there any restriction on the amount that can be contributed by an overseas resident individual or by an employer in respect of them. But relief from UK income tax may not be available, or may be restricted on such contributions in certain circumstances.

Overseas resident members of a registered pension scheme are subject to the annual and lifetime allowances and their associated charges (see RPSM13103040), and to other charges under Part 4, such as the unauthorised payments charge (see RPSM04104500).'

Section 615 schemes

7.39 *Section 615, ICTA 1988,* schemes are now covered by *ss 647 to 654, ITEPA 2003*. They are schemes which were generally for non-residents who are in overseas employment. Under the new regime, if such schemes cease, assets can be transferred into registered schemes. Although they were deemed by government to be unnecessary under the new regime, *Ch 6, ss 245*(*5*) and *249*(*3*)*, Finance Act 2004,* indicate that such schemes may continue.

Countering cross-border tax evasion

7.40 HMRC publishes guidance notes on its website concerning overseas savings and the moves to prevent tax loss on chargeable savings. The guidance is based on the *EU Savings Directive* (*Council Directive 2003/48/EC*) dated 3 June 2003. This is of particular interest to high networth individuals who invest monies, or wish to invest monies, overseas. The tax advantage of being a member of a recognised overseas scheme on a bona fide basis (rather than investing independently in an overseas financial institution) is clear.

The objective of the Directive is to collect and exchange information (Tax Information Exchange Agreements – TIEAs) about foreign resident individuals receiving savings income outside their resident state (the relevant territory). This mainly affects banks, registrars, custodians and other financial institutions that make interest payments to individuals in prescribed territories. TIEAs are bilateral agreements under which territories agree to co-operate in tax matters through exchange of information.

The Directive came into effect on 1 July 2005 and the first savings income reports cover the period 1 July 2005 to 5 April 2006. They must be submitted to HMRC by 30 June 2006.

The website publishes agreements when they have completed the necessary parliamentary procedures in both countries. The agreements take the form of statutory instruments. Effectively, a withholding tax is held by the relevant territory unless the individual fully declares the interest in his own territory. To date, the initial rate of tax is normally 15%, rising to 20% (by an agreed date, often 2008) and to 35% thereafter.

Conclusion

7.41 The changes to the overseas rules as at A-Day are far-reaching. They open up many opportunities for international pension provision on a tax-efficient basis for the future, and less restriction on pension transfers. The rules are still complex, as the UK legislation seeks to claw back tax on monies which have previously built up tax free in the UK. However, there are significant exemptions, and high earners (particularly those who are internationally mobile, or who have non-UK domicility), are likely to benefit from seeking professional tax advice on their future pension savings.

Chapter 8

VAT, IPT and accounting and auditing requirements

VAT

Introduction

8.1 The Value Added Tax (VAT) implications for a SSAS or a SIPPs can often be overlooked as pension schemes are generally not liable for direct tax or a SSAS/SIPP's turnover is relatively small. However, VAT can have an impact on the income of a SSAS or SIPPs, particularly in respect of rental income or charges for financial services. It may therefore be possible to offset VAT incurred by a SSAS or SIPPs on its administration costs against the VAT received on rent from property it leases or to take advantage of the VAT exemption on financial services or to adopt the VAT flat-rate scheme. These aspects and others, including whether a SSAS or SIPPs should register for VAT purposes, are covered in this chapter, together with the Insurance Premium Tax (IPT) and the accounting and auditing principles that apply.

Administration costs

8.2 The question of whether the company/business or trustees pay the administration costs of a SSAS or of a SIPPs, if applicable, is most relevant. It may be that the company pays the administration costs of its SSAS in order to claim relief from corporation tax on such expenditure and also to recover VAT incurred (Input Tax) from VAT it receives on its income (Output Tax), unless it is partially or fully exempt. Partial exemption entails making some supplies which carry the right to recovery of Input Tax and some which do not. Full exemption applies to the sale of securities or to a solicitor's fee for the lease of a property where no option to tax has been exercised (see 8.7). Sales of securities to a purchaser outside the EU are zero-rated. This is acceptable if the expenses incurred are legitimately those of the company and it has Output Tax available for such a set off.

HMRC takes the view that the establishment and administration of a pension fund is a business activity of the company/business and therefore any Input Tax incurred by the company/business in connection with this activity is recoverable. In HMRC's VAT Leaflet 700/17/02, 'Value Added Tax Funded Pension Schemes', those services rendered to the trustees of a pension scheme by the company/business which constitute the Input Tax of the company/business are given as:

(*a*) making of arrangements for setting up a pension fund;

(*b*) management of the scheme, e g collection of contributions and payment of pensions;

(*c*) advice on a review of the scheme, and implementing any change to the scheme;

(*d*) accounting and auditing, insofar as they relate to the management of the scheme, e g preparation of annual accounts;

(*e*) actuarial valuations of the assets of the fund;

(*f*) general actuarial advice connected with the fund's administration;

(*g*) providing general statistics in connection with the performance of a fund's investments, properties etc;

(*h*) legal instructions and general legal advice including drafting of trust deeds insofar as they relate to the management of the scheme.

If the company/business pays any of the above costs on behalf of the trustees of a SSAS or SIPPs it will be able to claim Input Tax in respect of the VAT incurred provided it holds a tax invoice made out in the company/business's name unless it is partially or fully exempt. Strangely, this is at odds with the *Pensions Act 1995, s 47,* where the trustees are required to appoint the scheme auditor and actuary, and have obligations regarding other professional advisers such as legal advisers, as it could have been expected that Input Tax incurred on their fees would have been the Input Tax of the trustees. The VAT leaflet makes no comment on this. If the company/business recharges any of these costs to the trustees, the recharge is not subject to VAT. This follows from *National Coal Board v Commissioners of Customs and Excise [1982] STC 863*, where it was decided that there was no consideration for any supplies to the trustees by the employer so therefore there could be no supply of services.

The VAT leaflet goes on to explain that the trustees are responsible for investing and dealing in the assets of the fund and in HMRC's view these aspects are business activities of the pension fund and not of the company/business. Thus, any VAT incurred on costs related to the trustees' investment activities in respect of a SSAS/SIPPs are not recoverable by the company/business. It may, however, be recovered by the trustees as Input Tax if the SSAS/SIPPs is registered for VAT, unless it is partially exempt. The following are examples of costs related to investment activity:

(*a*) advice in connection with making investments;

(*b*) brokerage charges;

(*c*) rent and service charge collection for property holdings;

(*d*) producing records and accounts in connection with property purchases, lettings and disposals, investments etc;

(*e*) trustees services, ie services of a professional trustee in managing the assets of the fund;

(*f*) legal fees on behalf of representative beneficiaries in connection with changes in pension fund arrangements;

(*g*) custodian charges.

In the case of the *Wellcome Trust Ltd v Commissioners of Customs and Excise [1986] PLR 419* heard before the European Court of Justice (ECJ) the question was considered whether brokerage, agents' charges and all other services relating to the acquisition of assets are a business activity or not of a non-taxable body. The former HM Customs and Excise contended that the shares and other securities held by the Wellcome Trust were held for charitable purposes and the disposals thereof had not been made in the course or furtherance of any business carried on by the trust, but in pursuance of the normal management of investments in order to fund charitable activities. So the VAT charged on the provision of the professional services of which the trust had availed itself in connection with sales of shares did not constitute Input Tax that was recoverable. The trust appealed to the VAT Tribunal which deferred to the ECJ for a ruling. That body concluded that irrespective of whether the activities in question are similar to those of an investment trust or pension fund, the Wellcome Trust must be regarded as confining its activities to managing an investment portfolio in the same way as a private investor. It ruled that the business carried on by the Wellcome Trust was not within the VAT concept of economic activities. The purchase and sale of shares and other securities by a trustee in the course of management of the assets of a charitable trust was not within the common system of VAT and therefore Input Tax incurred on fees paid in these circumstances was not recoverable.

The ruling in the *Wellcome Trust* case had clear implications for self-administered pension schemes. It was widely feared that the former HM Customs and Excise would use this ruling to restrict the recovery of Input Tax payable on brokers' fees on share sales and possibly on solicitors' and valuers' fees on property sales. In the event this did not happen as the Department made it clear that it did not feel this judgment applied to pension schemes and that pension schemes' investment activities should be treated in the same way as any other taxable person for VAT purposes. However, if the company/business pays such fees, the Input Tax is not recoverable (see below). Also if a management or administration company charges these fees to the trustees, then the Input Tax attributable would not be recoverable (see 8.3 and 8.5).

If the company/business pays any of the costs in 8.4 on behalf of the trustees, it cannot reclaim the Input Tax paid thereon. This was one of the points at issue in *Ultimate Advisory Services Ltd v Commissioners of Customs and Excise [1993] PLR 273*, where the company had a SSAS. The case concerned *inter alia* whether certain payments made to legal advisers were of such a nature that the company was entitled to treat its payment of the VAT thereon as Input Tax. The payments were made by the company as the scheme trust deed provided for all costs, charges and expenses of the administration and management of the SSAS to be paid by the company. The payments were, however, in respect of solicitors' fees for legal services supplied to the trustees, not to the company. Despite the trust deed providing for such costs to be met by the company it was held that this did not mean such expenses are necessarily incurred for the company's business. The VAT Tribunal concluded that events which affect the scheme as a total entity can properly be regarded as being within the business activities of the company, whereas the deployment of the fund within the SSAS is the responsibility of the trustees. The company's claim to recover Input Tax therefore failed because the VAT was not its liability. The findings on this case are most important when considering whether the trustees of a SSAS or SIPPs should register for VAT if they wish to recover Input Tax.

A similar decision was reached by the VAT Tribunal in *Plessey v Commissioners of Customs and Excise [1996] PLR 89* where the VAT on the legal costs incurred by the company on behalf of the beneficiaries of its pension schemes was at issue. The company wanted to wind up three pension schemes, but the trustees insisted on court approval. This could not be effected without the court being advised of the position of the beneficiaries. The beneficiaries in turn were not prepared to join the proceedings unless their costs were met and the trustees were advised that the court was most likely to award costs against the pension schemes' funds. The Input Tax on the costs was disallowed because the advice was given to the beneficiaries, who were the clients, not to the trustees, let alone the company, which sought the reclaim. The invoices were addressed to the beneficiaries. Even though satisfied that the trustees had to meet the costs and that the services could be said to have been used for the purposes of the company's business, the VAT Tribunal found the costs had not been supplied to the company, but to the beneficiaries.

Financial services

8.3 There are certain VAT exemptions available to banks, LOs and other financial services providers for services bought in. They may be involved to some extent with SSASs, but are more likely to be involved with SIPPs. In addition both administration and investment-related services may be supplied by a professional trustee or administration company (see 8.5) to the principal company and trustees of a SSAS. In the latter case the overall charges include VAT for services provided to the company in the general administration of the scheme and for investment services provided to the trustees. This situation is similar to some degree with SIPPs, but with the overall charges including VAT provided to the member in general administration of the SIPP and for investment services provided to the trustees and to the member if he appoints an investment manager. However, some of the administration and investment services are provided by LOs who are exempt from VAT in relation to some of the costs involved, e g provision of insurance or dealing with money.

The question as to whether these charges were exempt from VAT or standard-rated was decided before a VAT Tribunal in 1997 in relation to two SIPPs, the *Winterthur Life Self-administered Personal Pension Scheme* and the *Personal Pension Management Scheme,* in the case of *Winterthur Life UK Ltd (formerly Provident Life Association Ltd)* (*LON/1787*) (*14935*) – the *Winterthur* case. The provider of both SIPPs was Winterthur Life (UK) Ltd and two of its wholly-owned subsidiaries provided services by or through their agency to both SIPPs, Winterthur Life (UK) Ltd being the representative member of a VAT group which included the two subsidiaries. Both SIPPs authorised members to control the management and investment of the funds, and the subsidiaries were entitled to recover administrative expenses from the fund for investment costs, remuneration of investment managers and advisers, and other professional fees and disbursements. The former HM Customs and Excise claimed that the charges were standard-rated as trust administration. The Tribunal held however that the two SIPPs embodied contracts of insurance between the provider, a LO, and the members even if this was operated through the agency of subsidiaries. This meant the administration services incidental to the implementation of those contracts were part of the provision of insurance by a permitted insurer and exempt from VAT under *VAT Act 1994, Sch 9.*

The ruling in the *Winterthur* case means that where a LO or its subsidiary acts as trustee and administrator to a SIPP, VAT is not chargeable on administration fees. This exemption also applies to non-insured SIPP business where a LO brands a SIPP through, say, a stockbroker. The question of the exemption from VAT for administration fees charged by a LO in respect of a SIPP arose again in 2002 (see below).

The *Value Added Tax* (*Finance*) *Order 1999* (*SI 1999/594*) further clarified the VAT exemptions for financial services by providing an exemption for intermediary services supplied in respect of an exempt financial transaction. This replaced the former exemption for the making of arrangements. The *Order* defined intermediary arrangements as bringing together persons wishing to buy financial services with persons providing such services, e g banks, financial institutions, together with the work preparatory to the conclusion of a contract for the provision of financial services. This brought SSASs within the scope of the exemption when the service is being supplied to a bank, LO or financial institution administering the SSAS portfolio. Intermediary services in relation to a transaction in securities remained exempt also. This had obvious benefits for SSASs and SIPPs and included the service of introducing clients wishing to buy or sell securities to a person effecting transactions in securities.

The question of exemption from VAT arose again in a VAT Tribunal case also involving Winterthur, *Winterthur Life* (*UK*) *Ltd* (*LON/98/1339*) (*17572*), where a subsidiary of Winterthur Life (UK) Ltd, Personal Pension Management Ltd (PPML), provided SIPP administration services in respect of the self-invested element of a SIPPs provided by the LO, Scottish Equitable. Relying on the decision in the earlier *Winterthur* case (see 8.7), PPML deducted its charges for these services from the members' funds, but charged no VAT because in its view the services were exempt as agency services in connection with the supply of insurance and PPML was a member of the VAT group (see 8.24) of a LO, i e its parent company, Winterthur. Somewhat surprisingly, in view of the decision in the earlier *Winterthur* case, the former HM Customs and Excise advised PPML that these supplies to Scottish Equitable were not exempt either under *VAT Act 1994, Sch 9, Group 2* or *Group 5* and VAT should be charged. Winterthur appealed and the VAT Tribunal again decided in their favour, with reference to the terms of *Article 13B*(*a*) *of the Sixth Directive* (which, broadly, provides an exemption for the provision by an insurance broker or agent of services relating to the provision of insurance) and the decision in the case of *Century Life plc v Commissioners of Customs and Excise [2000] STC 276*, (in which pensions were held to be insurance transactions), on the basis that the Scottish Equitable SIPP, i e both the insured and self-invested elements, was providing related services as an insurance agent, thus satisfying the criteria for exemption under *Article 13B*(*a*) and *VAT Act 1994, Sch 9, Group 2*.

A more detailed analysis of this VAT Tribunal case can be found in an article by John Hayward in the 30 September 2002 issue of *The Tax Journal*.

The question of the VAT exemption for insurance-related services also arose as a result of the decision of the ECJ in the Netherlands case of *Arthur Andersen & Co Accountants* (*C-472/03*), the *Andersen* case, in March 2005. This concerned the VAT liability of certain back office services provided by the accountants to a life insurance company. The services included the issuing, management and cancellation of policies, the management of claims, making amendments to contracts and modifying premiums, receiving premiums, setting and paying commissions to the insurer's agents and dealing with third parties on behalf of the insurer. The ECJ was asked to consider whether these activities carried out for an insurance company were exempt from VAT under *Article 13B*(*a*) *of the Sixth Directive* as related services performed by insurance brokers and insurance agents. To be exempt the accountants had to qualify as either insurance brokers or agents. The ECJ held that the essential characteristic of insurance brokers was that they had complete freedom as to choice of insurer for their clients and that, although insurance agents were tied to a particular insurer, their essential characteristic was that they introduced prospective customers to that insurer. The accountants did not qualify on either count, so their services were taxable at the standard rate. This suggested a restrictive scope to the exemption, in that unless the agent is actively involved in the sales process, it would not fall within the VAT exemption.

As a result of the *Andersen* case, HMRC took the view that the UK VAT exemption for insurance-related services in *VAT Act 1994, Sch 9, Group 2* was drawn too widely and it would need to be amended to bring it into line with the ECJ judgment. This clearly had implications for outsourcing some of the services relating to the provision of SIPPs in particular. Back office/policy administration, run off administration, claims handling, pensions/endowment reviews and in-bound call centre operations could all be caught by any tightening up by HMRC. In July 2005 HMRC published a Consultation Document, *Consultation on Changes to the VAT Exemption for Insurance-Related Services*, containing its proposals to bring the UK legislation into line with the ECJ decision in the *Andersen* case with effect from 1 January 2006. As part of the Pre-Budget Report of 5 December 2005, HMRC announced that having considered the responses to the Consultation Document on VAT and insurance-related services, it would await a review of the VAT treatment of financial services to be carried out by the European Commission in 2006. It is understood that HMRC will review the position again in September 2006 with a view to implementation of the *Andersen* decision unless the EU review starts to make useful progress in defining the scope of the VAT exemption in the insurance sector.

Management charges

8.4 In 8.2 it was mentioned that the company/business or the trustees could pay the running costs of the pension scheme. If the trustees pay these costs they can recover them by making a management charge to the company/business for those costs. The company/business would obtain corporation /income tax relief on payment of the management charge and the trustees, by charging Output Tax, would then be able to set off any Input Tax against it, unless they are partially exempt. Some care is needed, however, as only Input Tax attributable to the taxable outputs covered in the management charge may be set off. For instance, if the management charge includes any of the costs for which the trustees are responsible (see 8.2) VAT thereon cannot be set off by the trustees.

If more than one company participates in the pension scheme it may be preferable for the trustees to make a management charge on each company, particularly if the companies concerned wish to obtain relief for corporation tax purposes on the management charge. It may, however, be difficult to establish which part of the scheme's administration is attributable to a particular company. The reverse situation is acceptable, whereby each company, instead of the trustees, pays its share of the administration costs, including the VAT thereon.

The VAT treatment of pension fund management was considered by the former HM Customs and Excise in 2002 when it issued a Consultation Document, *VAT Treatment of Pension Fund Management*. This sought views on the differences in treatment between pension schemes provided through LOs and non-LOs with a view to removing undesirable distortions between different types of funds and creating a level playing field between different types of fund managers. The Consultation Document contained three options on charging VAT in future:

(*a*) making all pension fund management exempt from VAT;

(*b*) applying VAT to all pension fund management;

(*c*) extending the VAT borderline to exempt charges from the appointment of an investment manager, for handling income drawdown payments and to annual administration charges.

A wide range of conflicting responses was received to this Consultation Document, so the former HM Customs and Excise announced in March 2004 that there would be no immediate changes in the current VAT treatment of fund management services, but it would keep the matter under review.

The VAT leaflet sets out in detail the services provided in relation to the investment activities of a pension scheme (see 8.2). It provides advice on whether each activity should be regarded as an 'investment' or 'management' function and concludes that where it is not possible to segregate the services in this way HMRC will be prepared to allow an apportionment of 30% to the company ('management') and 70% to the trustees ('investment'). This is commonly known as the '30/70 split', but some pension schemes may have special arrangements agreed with the former HM Customs and Excise prior to 2002 when the VAT leaflet was issued.

HMRC announced in *Business Brief 15/05* of 9 August 2005 that it had increasing concerns that businesses were applying the 30/70 split more generously than intended and recovering Input Tax to which they were not entitled. It proposed new arrangements from 1 October 2005. So third parties providing investment and administration services, who are able to determine the actual values of each, must provide separate invoices to trustees and companies/businesses showing the actual value of services provided. If the third party is unable to determine separate values for investment and administration services, HMRC will continue to accept use of the 30/70 split, but only where the third party is administering the pension scheme fully or providing the bulk of the administration element of the scheme.

In all other cases companies/businesses must agree a fair and reasonable apportionment with HMRC that is robust, transparent and able to be tested. If a company/business considers that the administration work undertaken amounts to more than 30% of the total services provided, they will have to agree an apportionment with HMRC.

HMRC's proposals were met with substantial representations from the pensions and asset management industries to allow managers time to amend their systems in order to comply with the new rules. As a result implementation was deferred. The pensions and asset management industries are consulting their members with a view to determining a more relevant split in the light of changes to the management of funded pension schemes. HMRC has since withdrawn its proposals until a further announcement is made. Companies/businesses may continue with their current VAT recovery arrangements, but they should note that any moves by HMRC meanwhile to terminate any special arrangements should be resisted if HMRC is not using its powers to secure a fair and reasonable attribution if the decision to terminate results in the use of a method which is less fair and reasonable (see *Merchant Navy Officers Pension Fund Trustees Ltd; Merchant Navy Ratings Pension Fund Trustees Ltd LON/95/2944 (24262)*).

Administration companies

8.5 It is not uncommon for both administration and investment-related services to be supplied by a professional trustee or administration company, sometimes with a SSAS/SIPPs appointing the professional trustee itself, or a company associated with the professional trustee or the LO concerned supplying the services. Their overall charge will include VAT for both services provided to the company/business in the general administration of the scheme and for the investment services provided to the trustees. The company/business is not, however, entitled to claim Input Tax in respect of investment services provided to the trustees (see 8.2) even if they are invoiced together with general administration services.

If the company/business hold one VAT invoice for both types of supplies in its own name, it can make a deduction for Input Tax provided the invoice shows the details separately relating to the services for which it is entitled to make a claim. It is preferable though for the professional trustee or administration company to separate the charges so that one invoice is made out to the company/business for administration costs and another is made out to the trustees for investment-related costs. If they prefer, the trustees may pay the professional trustee or administration company for administration-related services and the company/business itself will still be able to recover Input Tax thereon, provided the invoice is made out to the company/business.

Professional trustee liability for VAT

8.6 Some years ago the former HM Customs and Excise had been pursuing some pensioneer trustees for VAT liabilities relating to SSAS of which they were a trustee. The Department's claim was apparently based on an extension of the rules applicable to group registrations for VAT. Under such registrations (by a corporate trustee and the principal company) the parties to the registration are jointly and severally liable for VAT due from the representative member and in the event of that member failing to meet the VAT debt of the registered group, the Department holds each member of the group registration liable for the amount of the debt. The former HM Customs and Excise advised that this liability extends to all assets of the group members including the assets of any pension scheme whose trustee is, or was, within the group registration. Thus the Department was seeking to recover VAT liabilities from the assets of a SSAS of which a pensioneer trustee was a trustee in respect of the VAT debts due by another SSAS of which the pensioneer trustee was also a trustee.

This inequitable claim was successfully challenged by the former APT as group registrations did not apply to pensioneer trustees. How could the assets of a pension scheme that is totally unassociated with another pension scheme be at risk from a claim for VAT liabilities in respect of another pension scheme simply because one of the trustees of both schemes is the same? Fortunately, the Department accepted it had no right of recourse against another pension scheme of which the pensioneer trustee (or any other trustee for that matter) is a trustee. This is of particular relevance to individual professional and corporate trustees under the new pensions regime. It should also be noted that, at paragraph 15 of the VAT leaflet, HMRC has given an assurance that a representative member will not be held liable for the debts of other members of the group.

As between the trustee and the pension scheme the trustee is entitled to have VAT borne by the pension scheme, but if the funds are insufficient for any reason the trustee would have to pay HMRC from his own pocket. So where an individual professional or corporate trustee is asked to consent to a SSAS or SIPPs being registered for VAT, (see 8.13) it is worth considering obtaining indemnities from co-trustees at the same time.

Since 1999 HMRC has had the power to remove from groups companies that are no longer eligible to be grouped or whose membership of a group poses a threat to the revenue. The intention was to make the grouping provisions more flexible for business whilst at the same time tidying up on the prevention of abuse. However, many corporate trustees of SSASs and SIPPs act not just as trustees, but also as scheme administrators. Most of them are subsidiaries of a parent company which provides a range of financial services, one of which is pensions administration. Some are simply trustees who do not trade at all. Corporate trustees are however registered as part of an employer's group for VAT purposes, so they set off VAT more easily.

It was not totally clear from the Budget notice 56/99 whether such companies would no longer be eligible to be grouped or posed a threat to the revenue, although there do not appear to have been any adverse moves subsequently in this direction by HMRC. It is clear though that HMRC will use its powers to remove a company from a group if it is not established in the UK where VAT avoidance is suspected.

Property

8.7 Under the former discretionary tax approval regime the trustees of a SSAS and SIPP have been unable to own residential property, with two exceptions, and in one instance commercial property would also be involved anyway. In addition the Chancellor's Pre-Budget Report proposals of 5 December 2005 (see 5.4) virtually ensure, because of the prohibitive tax implications, that SSASs and SIPPs will not invest in residential property. So paragraphs 8.7 to 8.8 are concerned solely with VAT chargeable on the acquisition or sale of commercial property and the rent payable to the trustees therefrom.

Dealing in property may be exempt, zero-rated or standard-rated in respect of property situated in the UK. Zero-rating applies to the grant of a major interest, meaning the freehold or a lease etc, exceeding 21 years, in a qualifying building by the person constructing. Zero-rating is also available for a qualifying building which is Grade 1 or Grade 2 listed (or the equivalent in Scotland and Northern Ireland) if it has been a substantial reconstruction by the trustees. The trustees must grant a major interest following the substantial reconstruction. A 'substantial reconstruction' is either, that at least 60% of the costs undertaken relate to approved alterations or, the reconstructed building incorporates no more of the original building than the external walls and any external features of architectural or historic interest. The definition of approved alterations can cause difficulties and, in applying this part of the rules, professional advice is recommended. This is also recommended when the trustees undertake the construction of a building on their land as the developer's self-supply charge must be taken into account (see below) and trader registration may be desirable.

The grant of a short lease is exempt from VAT. However, the landlord has the option to waive this exemption and charge the tenant VAT on the rent on a short lease. If the trustees decide to exercise their option and charge VAT on the rent, they must notify their local VAT office in writing. The sale of a long lease from 21 July 1994 of a new dwelling is also exempt from VAT provided it was created by the conversion of non-residential buildings. It is understood in this connection that a public house with living accommodation or a shop with a flat would not be exempt from VAT on conversion. If the trustees own more than one property and decide to charge VAT on the rent on them all, they must elect to tax each property. They cannot be covered by a general election for all properties.

Where the trustees are the landlord of a property and they intend to carry out building work on that property, if the rent they receive has previously been exempt from VAT, they must obtain permission from HMRC if they intend to recover future Input Tax on the building works and day-to-day overheads.

Since 1 April 1989 all new commercial properties have been subject to VAT at the standard rate. So if the trustees sell the freehold of their commercial property they have to account for the Output Tax they receive. If they buy freehold commercial property they are likely to incur Input Tax which will not be recoverable unless they receive Output Tax against which it may be set off. From a practical point of view, the solicitor acting for the trustees should ask at the pre-contract stage if the vendor will be charging VAT. If VAT is not to be charged the contract for sale should include a clause whereby the vendor agrees not to exercise the option to charge VAT in the period between contract date and completion. The trustees have also to account for the Output Tax on any rents received where they have elected to charge VAT. It can therefore be seen that the trustees have an important decision to take as to whether or not to register for VAT purposes so they can recover any Input Tax against Output Tax. That decision will depend on whether the annual rents on which they can charge VAT exceed the VAT registration threshold (see 8.13) or they sell a property worth more than the threshold. Unfortunately, this decision was further complicated by legislation from 26 November 1996 (see below).

Trustees may develop their property or land from scheme funds and they are warned in this connection (see above) that if they construct a building on their land the developer's self-supply charge must be taken into account. In the case of *C & E Commissioners v R & R Pension Fund Trustees LON/95/2274A* (*13733*) the trustees constructed a commercial building and recovered Input Tax incurred during the course of the work. They then granted a lease of the building from 1 August 1993 for 15 years, which triggered the self-supply charge of the building itself. To recover VAT on that supply the trustees sought to elect to waive exemption on the supply of the building under the lease, thus making taxable all subsequent rental payments. However, the date the election was to take effect (1 August 1993 when the lease commenced) required the prior written consent of the former HM Customs and Excise. This was refused and the trustees appealed. They were successful before the VAT Tribunal, but the Department appealed and the case was heard in the High Court. There it was held that the Department should only give permission for an election where there could be a fair and reasonable attribution of the Input Tax concerned, as was the case here, otherwise it would lead to the trustees being subject to assessment for VAT under the self-supply charge with no means of recovering Input Tax as there would be no taxable outward supply of the property. The trustees' appeal was therefore upheld and their election to waive exemption granted. Subsequently the Department published *Business Brief 17/96* clarifying the position of the recovery of Input Tax following an election to waive exemption.

Fortunately, the self-supply charge is being gradually abolished. Any development where construction commenced after 1 March 1995 will not be liable to a taxable self-supply charge. It is no longer the case that a taxable supply will always be made of commercial property. It will only be so if the developer intends to make a taxable sale of the freehold of a new property or has opted to tax the property and intends to let it. This change means it is essential for HMRC to establish the developer's intentions at an early stage. Trustees are therefore recommended to seek good accountancy advice in these areas so that the written consent of HMRC will be given.

SSASs and SIPPs are allowed to lease commercial property to the company, to scheme members or to partnerships of which the partners are scheme members on arm's-length terms. Whilst these lessees and the trustees are all connected persons, there is no longer any need to consider the provisions of the *Value Added Tax (Buildings and Land) Order 1994* (*SI 1994/3013*) of 30 November 1994, which disapplied the option to charge VAT on leases between connected persons, when considering the option to charge VAT on the rent of a property. This legislation and the ensuing extra-statutory concessions that were afforded to SSASs and SIPPs were repealed by *FA 1997, s 37* and from 19 March 1997 both SSASs and SIPPs have retained the option to charge tax on the rent payable to them (see above), subject to certain provisions in *FA 1997, s 37* (see below).

The former HM Customs and Excise was concerned in 1996 at the position of banks and insurance companies, which were substantially exempt from VAT and which were exploiting the option to tax through the use of associated leasing companies so as to increase their Input Tax recovery significantly. The provisions of the *Value Added Tax* (*Buildings and Land*) *Order 1994* (see above) were apparently ineffective to counter this. So *FA 1997, s 37* replaced the *VAT Buildings and Land Order* by more comprehensive anti-avoidance provisions from 19 March 1997 which do not apply to transactions between unconnected persons.

From 19 March 1997 the option to tax land and buildings by the trustees of a SSAS or SIPPs or a developer or someone who finances a development or a person connected with any of them, is not available for supplies made to persons who do not use the property wholly or mainly for taxable purposes. This applies to the rent or sale of property to an exempt person. This prevents SSASs/SIPPs from electing to charge VAT on a commercial property lease or sale to a tenant or purchaser whose business is VAT exempt. The trustees are also unable to recover Input Tax attributable to such a property.

VAT exempt businesses include banks, building societies, insurance companies and brokers, providers of private education (schools) and private health. Fortunately, certain types of premises are excluded from the type of commercial property being leased or sold, e g shops, public houses, hotels, small workshops, markets and exhibition centres. SSASs and SIPPs do lease high street premises to banks, building societies, insurance companies and brokers, and are subject to these measures, but they only apply if the property is potentially within the capital goods scheme (see 8.10) and costs more than £250,000 or major alterations to the building cost more than that amount. Moreover, if the parties entered into an agreement for the lease before 26 November 1996, the lease will be excepted from the requirements provided the actual lease was granted before 30 November 1999 (*FA 1997, s 37*(*5*)). A further restriction has been imposed by the *Value Added Tax* (*Buildings and Land*) *Order 1999* (*SI 1999/593*) with effect from 10 March 1999. This is where, at the time of the grant of the lease, the development was not a capital item within the capital goods scheme, but it was nonetheless the intention that it would become so either for the business or anyone to whom the property is sold or transferred.

The legislation in *FA 1997, s 37* raises a number of problems with significant financial implications for the trustees of SSASs and SIPPs as the landlords of property. The trustees cannot charge VAT on the rent receivable nor can they set off Input Tax they incur attributable to the property. The Input Tax could be irrecoverable if it relates to legal or agents' costs in setting up the lease although it may be possible to invoice the lessee for irrecoverable VAT as part of any service charge. The trustees may be reluctant to lease a property in these circumstances except at an increased rent or with a covenant from the lessee to compensate for the VAT drawbacks. The increased rent would also have to be justified to HMRC with an independent valuation because the lease would be connected. Some trustees may decide it is not worth proceeding with VAT exempt tenants and seek a letting to a VATable business instead.

Another point to watch is that land is not being developed by the trustees and the member's business or company, i e connected persons, or buildings are not being refurbished even on arm's-length terms via a contract, which may have to be the case anyway to satisfy HMRC. It should be noted that in HMRC's view an employer company and its pension scheme(s) are not connected parties if one or more of the trustees of the schemes is an independent party. The trustees of the SSASs/SIPPs involved and the company would be well advised to obtain a ruling from HMRC on this point. If land is being developed by the trustees and the member's business or company, and the ultimate letting is to a VAT exempt business, e g a bank, insurance company, building society etc, the provisions of *FA 1997, s 37* are likely to apply, the trustees of the SSAS/SIPPs and the member should seek specific VAT advice from their accountancy advisers.

There has in fact been a SIPPs case where the provisions of *FA 1997, s 37* apply – *Winterthur Life* (*UK*) *Ltd* (*No* 2) *LON/98/127* (*15785*). Once again a company in the Winterthur group, Personal Pension Management Ltd (PPML), was the trustee of a number of SIPPs and a member of a VAT group. It purchased a long leasehold interest in a newly built property for £270,000 plus VAT as the vendor had elected to waive the exemption. PPML then granted a lease of the property to three SIPP members whose personal contributions had been used to fund the property acquisition together with a bank mortgage. The three SIPP members occupied the property for an exempt insurance business. PPML needed to opt to tax the rent receivable to recover the Input Tax incurred on the lease premium, so it elected to waive the exemption to charge Input Tax on the rent. The former HM Customs and Excise ruled that the election by PPML was ineffective and that the lease to the three SIPP members remained exempt. The representative member of PPML's VAT group appealed to the VAT Tribunal on the grounds that the legislation in *VAT Act 1994*, *Sch 10*, *para 2(3AA)* introduced by *FA 1997*, *s 37* was intended to counter tax avoidance whereas the transaction at issue was a legitimate commercial transaction.

The VAT Tribunal dismissed the appeal and upheld the ruling of the Department. The SIPP members had provided the finance for the acquisition of the property even though this was done indirectly through the pension scheme. Thus a person who had financed the development was connected with the tenant and at the same time the tenant was using the building other than for a taxable purpose, i e an exempt insurance business. The conditions of *VAT Act 1994*, *Sch 10*, *para 2(3AA)* were satisfied and the election to waive the exemption to charge Input Tax on the rent was ineffective. The facts that the transactions were not for the avoidance of tax and the terms of the lease were fully commercial were not conclusive. There was no ambiguity in the legislation to permit a different decision. The anti-avoidance rules were designed to prevent businesses which make exempt supplies from planning to recover VAT on the full cost of standard-rated property at the cost of paying much smaller amounts of rent.

It was foreseen in the 1997 legislation that trustees would need to protect themselves in some areas, for instance if the tenant at a later stage uses the premises wholly or mainly for taxable purposes (see above) or assigns the lease to an exempt tenant. *FA 1997*, *s 37* requires tenants to notify landlords of any relevant change in their use of the property. It may also be worthwhile ensuring that the tenant indemnifies the trustees against any adverse Input Tax consequences.

Sales

8.8 The sale of a freehold commercial property less than three years old is standard-rated for VAT purposes. The sale of other freehold commercial property by a SSAS/SIPP to a VAT exempt business is however caught by the provisions of *FA 1997*, *s 37* as are assignments or surrenders of leases. The trustees as vendors will need to ascertain at the outset the VAT status of the prospective purchaser and the extent of the use of the property before they can decide whether or not to charge VAT on the sale price. The criteria for the purchaser's status and for the extent of the use of the property are as set out in 8.7.

Where the trustees sell property to a VAT exempt business which will not use the property wholly or mainly for taxable purposes, they will not be able to charge VAT on the sale and will have to consider the financial implications of not being able to recover Input Tax attributable to the property. They may as a result decide not to sell to this type of purchaser and look elsewhere for a buyer. They could increase the sale price to compensate themselves for Input Tax drawbacks. It is important to note that if the purchaser claims to be an exempt purchaser and therefore that the sale is exempt, it is incumbent on the trustees to require proof of the same. If the purchaser misleads the trustees and they do not in consequence collect any VAT on completion, the trustees as the vendor remain liable for Output Tax to HMRC.

'Going concern' principles

8.9 Where a property is owned by a third party and purchased by the trustees of a SSAS/SIPP with vacant possession, 'going concern' does not apply. However, where the third party owned the property and continued as the tenant after the property was purchased by the trustees, 'going concern' provisions may apply. The vendor and subsequent tenant may often be the sponsoring company of a SSAS or the business of a SIPP member.

These arrangements would mean that the purchasing trustees, who would have opted to tax in respect of the rent, although registered for VAT, would not be able to reclaim VAT if it has already been paid. This could result in potential action against the vendor – embarrassing if it is the company/business – who should not have charged VAT. Both parties should be registered for VAT for the 'going concern' provisions to apply. The VAT leaflet 700/9/94 is available from local VAT offices to assist trustees in this connection.

It should be noted that where a SSAS/SIPP acquires property that has been opted to tax, in respect of a transfer *in specie* (see 2.138), and at the time of transfer the property is either vacant or there is to be a change of tenant following the transfer, 'going concern' does not apply. Therefore, VAT would be charged on the value of the property. The receiving SSAS/SIPP, having registered and opted to tax in respect of any rent, would have to pay the VAT and reclaim it later. If there are not sufficient liquid assets in the SSAS/SIPP to pay the VAT, both may borrow (see 2.75) within the current limits in order to meet this short-term liability.

Capital goods scheme

8.10 The legislation for the operation of the capital goods scheme may be found in the *Value Added Tax (General) Regulations 1995 (SI 1995/2518)*. The scheme operates to ensure that the correct amount of VAT is reclaimed on higher value business purchases of land and property and computer equipment by requiring the tax reclaimed to be adjusted over a period of years if the use to which the asset is put changes. The scheme also covers refurbishment and fitting out costs for existing properties, including civil engineering works carried out by the owner, subject to a minimum value and an adjustment period of up to ten years. Rent will also be included in the scheme if it is paid, due or invoiced more than 12 months in advance. It will be included in the value of the taxable interest supplied to the owner when determining whether it exceeds the minimum value. There are also capital goods scheme adjustments to compare the later use of the assets with the initial deduction of Input Tax. Because of the amount involved large self-administered schemes are more likely to be within the capital goods scheme than SSASs or SIPPs.

A more detailed analysis of how the capital goods scheme operates can be found in articles by Peter Hewitt in the 9 and 16 January 2006 issues of *The Tax Journal*.

Nominee ownership

8.11 Finally, regarding property, the former HM Customs and Excise issued a Statement of Practice on 1 June 1996 covering the situation where the legal title in land is held by a nominee for a named beneficial owner, which is often the case where the legal title is held on trust for a pension scheme. The named beneficial owner of the land, and not the nominee, will be considered as the transferee for the purpose of establishing the transfer of a property letting business as a 'going concern' (see 8.9) provided both parties agree to such treatment. Persons transferring an interest in land to a person who is a nominee for a named beneficial owner are expected to check the VAT registration and, where necessary, the elections made by the beneficial owner.

Disclosure

8.12 Just as there are provisions for disclosing direct tax avoidance schemes involving pension schemes to HMRC (see 2.135), so there are similar provisions for disclosing VAT avoidance schemes involving pension schemes to HMRC. The legislation is contained in *VAT Act 1994, Sch 11A*, the provisions of which came into effect on 1 August 2004. This is supported by secondary legislation, the most important of which are the *Value Added Tax (Disclosure of Avoidance Schemes) Regulations 2004 (SI 2004/1929)*, and the *Value Added Tax (Disclosure of Avoidance Schemes) (Designations) Order 2004 (SI 2004/1933)*, the '*Designations Order'*, as amended by the *Value Added Tax (Disclosure of Avoidance Schemes) (Designations) (Amendment) Regulations 2005 (SI*

2005/1724). Further guidance may be found in HMRC's VAT Notice 700/8/04. There are some important differences in the timing and criteria for disclosure of VAT avoidance schemes which are covered below.

The use by a taxable person of a scheme by which he seeks to obtain a tax advantage has to be disclosed to HMRC. The obtaining of a tax advantage is defined as enabling someone to reduce the amount of VAT for which he is required to account or to obtain a VAT credit or a larger or earlier credit than he would otherwise be entitled to. The definition also includes cases where someone's non-deductible tax is reduced as a result of using an avoidance scheme.

HM Treasury has the power to designate a scheme which it believes someone might enter into to obtain a tax advantage and it is unlikely that they would enter into such a scheme unless the main purpose thereof was to obtain a tax advantage. The following schemes have been designated under the *Designations Order*:

1 First grant of a major interest in a building;

2 Payment handling service;

3 Value shifting;

4 Leaseback agreement;

5 Extended approval period;

6 Groups: third party suppliers;

7 Exempt education or vocational training by a non-profit making body;

8 Taxable education or vocational training by a non-eligible body;

9 Exploitation of the differences between another Member State's treatment of vouchers and that applied in the UK;

10 The surrender of the occupier of a building which is subject to the option to tax, where the occupier is the lessor or owner of it or is connected with him, so that VAT is avoided on rental receipts from the building.

HM Treasury also has the power to designate a provision, i e any agreement, transaction, act or course of conduct, which it believes may be associated with, or included in, a VAT avoidance scheme. These are known as 'hallmarks' and are set out in the *Designations Order*:

1 Confidentiality condition;

2 The sharing of a tax advantage with another party to the scheme or with the promoter;

3 Fee payable to a promoter which is in whole or in part contingent on tax savings from the scheme;

4 Prepayment between connected parties;

5 Funding by loan, share subscription or subscription in securities;

6 Offshore loops;

7 Property transactions between connected persons;

8 The issue of certain face-value vouchers whose level of redemption is expected to be very low (less than 25%).

A 'promoter' at 2 and 3 above is someone who, in the course of a trade, profession or business which involves the provision to other persons of services relating to taxation, if:

(*a*) they are to any extent responsible for the design of the proposed arrangements; or

(*b*) they invite someone to enter into contracts for the implementation of the proposed arrangements.

It should be noted that this definition of promoter is not subject to the qualifications applied to a promoter under the direct tax disclosure provisions (see 2.135).

A scheme is notifiable to HMRC by a taxable person, i e the pension scheme itself for a SSAS or SIPPs, if either:

(*a*) it is a designated scheme (see above) and its annual turnover of taxable and exempt supplies is at least £600,000; or

(*b*) it includes, or is associated with, a designated provision, 'hallmark scheme', (see above) and its annual turnover of taxable and exempt supplies is at least £10m.

These monetary limits should ensure that most SSASs and SIPPs do not have to disclose. Nonetheless, the £10m limit may apply if the VAT avoidance scheme is spread across several pension schemes. If however, either event does apply, the pension scheme must notify HMRC within 30 days of the due date of the VAT return concerned. If a designated scheme is involved the appropriate number above must be quoted. A taxable person may also voluntarily disclose an avoidance scheme which has not already been designated.

Failure to report the use of a designated scheme renders the pension scheme liable to a penalty of 15% of the tax 'saved'. Failure to report the use of a non-designated scheme attracts a fixed penalty of £5,000. It should be noted that there are provisions to prevent the artificial separation of business activities to circumvent the turnover limits.

The likely reaction of HMRC to a pension scheme involved in disclosure of VAT avoidance is at present unknown, but the Department could take counter action via new legislation if the VAT avoidance is widespread and substantial.

Registration

8.13 It is most advisable that the trustees of SSASs and SIPPs seek their accountant's advice on whether or not they should register for VAT purposes with HMRC. So far as a SSAS is concerned the decision to register will very much depend on the scheme's property transactions and the rents the trustees receive on which they can charge VAT. For SIPPs, the manner in which they are administered is particularly important as the structure and ease of administration must also be considered.

It is possible for the whole of the SIPP to be registered for VAT purposes, usually by the administration or trustee company operating the SIPP. That may give rise to administration difficulties in allocating Input Tax recovered to the correct member's fund within the SIPP. On the other hand, if a SIPP is established under a master trust, it is possible to register each individual part of the SIPP whether or not the member is a trustee in respect of that part. This obviously means multiple registrations, but the allocation of recovered Input Tax is greatly simplified. If a property is not registered for VAT, for instance the tenants do not wish to pay VAT on the rent, the member's fund will have to pay the VAT.

Generally, a person is required to register for VAT if the value of the taxable supplies in a 12-month period has exceeded the registration threshold (see below). If they are making taxable supplies, but the value of such supplies has not exceeded the threshold, they are still entitled to register if they wish to, but they are not required to do so. One sale only of a property worth over the threshold will put a SSAS/SIPP above the threshold, so that the question of registration should be considered whenever a property is sold. On the other hand, the level of the trustees' Input Tax must be considered and who pays it – the trustees or the company/business – as only the Input Tax attributable to the trustees can be recovered against their Output Tax (see 8.2).

The trustees may apply for voluntary registration if their taxable turnover does not exceed the threshold. They can then claim Input Tax provided they are making taxable supplies, i e their supplies are zero-rated at least for VAT purposes. Input Tax cannot otherwise be reclaimed. Should the trustees' Input Tax exceed their Output Tax they may claim a repayment.

Registration must be in the name of the trustees of the pension scheme. The registration of a pension scheme that has been set up under trust is continuous and does not take account of changes in trustees as the trust has a continuing legal entity. A separate registration is required for each funded pension scheme as the trustees as individuals or corporate bodies may be registered for VAT in their own right or as trustees of other schemes. A professional trustee may be a corporate body anyway and then the problems in 8.6 will be avoided. So the SSAS/SIPP is treated as a separate business carried on by the trustees and they will account for VAT to HMRC monthly or quarterly under the usual arrangements.

The decision to register for the trustees of a pension scheme is further complicated where they jointly own property and let it to one tenant. At present all joint owners must register separately for VAT if Output Tax is to be charged on the rent receivable. This cannot be done if only one joint owner registers for VAT. Each joint owner cannot opt individually to tax their own share of the rent. This situation can create confusion where one of a number of owners wishes to opt to tax and the other co-owners do not. Difficulties may also arise where some of the owners are registered and some are not.

It is possible that, by unanimous decision, co-owners, including the trustees of a pension scheme, will choose to register for VAT and be jointly and severally liable for the VAT consequences. However, this will not effectively deal with the position of professional trustees. This is because the co-owners will be treated as the same taxable person for the supply in question and any other supplies. So where there are professional trustees who will act for a number of schemes, they would appear to be treated the same as the taxable person for all supplies of land and buildings owned by any of these schemes.

The registration threshold for VAT from 1 April 2006 is £61,000 (£60,000 for the year prior to 1 April 2005). The standard rate remains at 17.5%.

Flat-rate scheme

8.14 A flat-rate scheme was introduced on 24 April 2002 by *FA 2002, s 23*. This inserted *s 26B* into the *VAT Act 1994*. It enables a small business (with an annual taxable turnover of not more than £100,000 and total turnover including exemptions of not more than £150,000) to elect to use the scheme to account for VAT. The thresholds were increased to £150,000 and £187,500 respectively with effect from 10 April 2003.

It should be noted that:

(*a*) businesses that are currently registered for VAT are required to account for Output Tax on a quarterly basis to HMRC, which can be costly in both time and administration;

(*b*) the flat-rate scheme requires annual accounting at a reduced rate, depending on the nature of the business (the rates are contained in the *Value*

Added Tax (Amendment) (No 2) Regulations 2002 (*SI 2002/1142*) and the *Value Added Tax (Amendment) (No 2) Regulations 2003* (*SI 2003/1069*));

(*c*) there is no specific category for pension schemes; the rate depends on the nature of the business itself;

(*d*) some SSAS and SIPPs only register for VAT purposes in respect of their property, and the scheme could apply where property values and rents are liable to VAT;

(*e*) it is most likely that the nature of the business under (*d*) will either be 'property management' (11.5% rate) or 'business services not elsewhere listed' (12.5% rate).

If a VAT-registered SSAS/SIPP is within the £187,500 threshold, in respect of its properties/rents, the relevant percentage in (*e*) can be applied to its turnover. This means that the VAT payable on (say) a rent of £20,000 at 17.5%, payable quarterly, is reduced on application from £3,500 to an amount of £2,300, payable annually. Administrative costs are also greatly reduced, and there will be no need to identify specific Input and Output Tax. The trustees can add VAT at 17.5% to their rents, but only account to HMRC for 11.5% (see simplified example below). However, as SIPPs may need to reclaim VAT in a timely manner in certain circumstances, the flat-rate scheme is unlikely to be appropriate for most SIPPs.

Example

The trustees of ABC Ltd Directors Pension Scheme opt for the flat-rate scheme. They are receiving annual rent of £50,000. Their annual statement would have shown:

Output Tax	£8,750
Less Input Tax	£1,600
(VAT on repairs renewals etc)	
Net VAT due	£7,150
The annual statement will now show:	
Flat-rate VAT scheme	£50,000 @ 11.5%
Net VAT due	£5,750 (a saving of
Net increase in the fund during the year	£1,400)

The flat-rate scheme is quite detailed, and proper accounting advice on its use is recommended. Further advice can be found in the former HM Customs and Excise's Notice No 733.

Insurance Premium Tax

8.15 IPT was introduced from 1 October 1994 by *FA 1994, s 48*. Insurance companies pay IPT at the current rate of 5% (previously 4% to 30 June 1999) on most general insurance to HMRC. Insurance companies are required to register and make quarterly returns to the Department. The tax does not apply to long-term insurance including pensions. Long-term insurance is defined in the *Insurance Companies Act 1982, Sch 1* and this includes life and pensions.

So far as SSASs/SIPPs are concerned, premiums paid by the company/business to a LO operating a SSAS/SIPP invested in policies will be exempt from IPT, as are premiums paid by the trustees towards a policy investment of a SSAS/SIPP. Term assurance is, however, not within the *Insurance Companies Act 1982, Sch 1*, but it is understood that premiums paid by the trustees or the company/business to provide death-in-service cover for a member should not attract IPT, whether to a SSAS or a SIPP. Exemption should be confirmed by reference to the actual wording of the insurance contract.

If the trustees of a SSAS/SIPP own a property or any other fixed asset and insure it, they will pay IPT on the relevant insurance premium.

Accounting and auditing requirements

Introduction

8.16 There are a number of accounting and auditing requirements relating to pension schemes. Firstly, in the circumstances outlined below, trustees must obtain audited annual accounts. Secondly, sponsoring employers are required to account for the cost of pensions in their own accounts in accordance with Financial Reporting Standard 17 (FRS 17), 'Retirement Benefits, which replaces Statement of Standard Accounting Practice No 24 (SSAP 24), 'Accounting for Pension Costs'. Finally, there are *Companies Act 1985* (*CA 1985*) requirements specifying matters to be disclosed relating to directors' pensions in corporate accounts and additional Stock Exchange requirements for listed companies. This chapter examines each of these in turn.

Scheme accounts

8.17 The need for SSAS trustees to produce scheme accounts and the related statutory requirements depend on the nature of the SSAS and its trust deed and rules. The statutory requirements are discussed in 8.16 below as they are directly related to audits under the *Pensions Act 1995*. Some SSASs have a requirement to produce annual accounts in the deed and rules but this is by no means invariable. However, it is clearly advisable to produce scheme accounts on a timely basis at least once a year so that the trustees can monitor contributions and investments. With the introduction of self-assessment, schemes have to submit scheme accounts with their tax returns. If accounts have not been prepared, HMRC asks for a statement of assets and liabilities at the beginning and end of the tax year, i e as at 6 April 2005 and 5 April 2006 for the 2005/06 return.

HMRC must give at least 30 days' notice where it asks for scheme accounts (*s 252, Finance Act 2004*). However, it has indicated that it will generally give schemes the later of 30 days from the date of notice and 7 months from the end of the previous scheme year. The seven months is designed to tie in with the DWP's Disclosure Regulations which require scheme accounts to be completed within seven months of the scheme year end. In addition, actuaries generally ask for scheme accounts at the time of any scheme valuation.

As from A-Day schemes will only need to send in the new registered scheme tax return (see 2.101 above) if they have declarable income or if a notice is served on the trustees by HMRC for a return to be completed.

The form and content of scheme accounts intended to provide a 'true and fair view' are set out in the Statement of Recommended Practice (SORP) 'Financial Reports of Pension Schemes' issued by the Pensions Research Accountants Group in September 1996. The SORP was updated in 2002 to reflect new accounting standards. The revised SORP is effective for accounting periods beginning on or after 1 January 2003 and the notes below reflect the 2002 version.

The accounts comprise two statements, a fund account and a net assets statement, and the format as set out in the SORP for money purchase schemes (as SSASs are almost invariably of this type) is given below.

Defined contribution scheme fund account

	2003 *£,000s*	**2002** *£,000s*
Contributions and benefits		
Contributions receivable	276	302
Transfers in	33	34
Other income	11	180
	320	516
Benefits payable	–	177

	2003 £,000s	2002 £,000s
Leavers	63	55
Other payments	47	44
Administrative expenses	18	22
	128	298
Net additions from dealings with members	192	218
Returns on investments		
Investment income	13	10
Change in market value of investments	805	(210)
Investment management expenses	(7)	(5)
Net returns on investments	811	(205)
Net increase in the fund during the year	1,003	13
Net assets of the scheme		
At 1 January 2003	4,461	4,448
At 31 December 2003	5,464	4,461

Defined contribution scheme Net Assets Statement

	2003 £,000s	2002 £,000s
Assets designated to members		
Investments		
Managed funds	5,205	4,240
Debtors and prepayments	19	18
	5,224	4,258
Assets not designated to members		
Investments		
Managed funds	239	204
Current assets and liabilities		
Bank balances	5	4
Debtors and prepayments	2	3
Creditors and accruals	(6)	(8)
	240	203
Net assets of the scheme at 31 December 2003	5,464	4,461

8.19 There are a number of disclosures required by the SORP which generally closely match those required by the *Occupational Pension Schemes*

(*Requirement to Obtain Audited Accounts and a Statement from the Auditor*) *Regulations 1996* (*SI 1996/1975*), the 'Audited Accounts Regulations' issued under the *Pensions Act 1995* which prescribe the content of scheme accounts where these are required by legislation. The significant disclosures relating to analysis of investments are as follows:

(*a*) insurance policies;

(*b*) public sector fixed interest investments;

(*c*) other fixed interest investments;

(*d*) index-linked securities;

(*e*) equities (including convertible shares);

(*f*) property (freehold and leasehold land and buildings);

(*g*) unit trusts invested in property;

(*h*) other unit trusts;

(*i*) managed funds invested in property;

(*j*) other managed funds.

The 2003 SORP suggests that all unitised funds be referred to under the heading of pooled investment vehicles, irrespective of whether they are held under a contract of insurance or as managed funds or unit trusts. Explanation as to their particular legal form should be given in the notes to the scheme accounts to comply with the legal requirements of the Audited Accounts Regulations, as well as to give the members a breakdown of the types of pooled funds in which scheme monies are being invested.

Accounting issues

Money purchase arrangements

8.20 In a money purchase scheme contributions are designated for the purchase of investments for the member on whose behalf the contributions are paid. There is no general pool of assets from which pensions are paid as there is in a final salary scheme. On retirement, the member's investments are applied to buy an annuity for that individual. Thus although the trustees are responsible for the assets, in accounting terms they are already notionally allocated. For this reason, the SORP recommends that the net assets statement shows 'assets allocated to members'. The notes to the accounts normally amplify the rationale for this presentation by referring to the fact that members receive an annual statement confirming the contributions paid on their behalf and the value of their money purchase rights.

Insurance policies

8.21 The Audited Accounts Regulations state that, where the assets include insurance policies:

> 'which are specifically allocated for the provision of benefits for, and which provide all the benefits payable under the scheme to, particular members or other persons in respect of particular members or both, those policies must be included in the [net assets] statement and there must be a note of the existence of such policies, but that entry need not include their market value or an estimate'.

This means that annuities purchased at retirement are excluded from the net assets of the scheme, and as a corollary, the associated pension payments are also excluded.

This statutory requirement may be interpreted as extending to money purchase insurance policies which provide all scheme benefits. This may lead to the apparently anomalous situation where a member's designated assets which are spread across different types of investments, including insurance policies, are included in the net assets statement, and another member's assets which comprise only such policies are omitted. Since there should be consistency of treatment of similar assets in scheme accounts, trustees should discuss problems of this nature with their accountants and auditors.

Valuation of assets

8.22 All investments of a pension scheme should be included in the net assets statement at market value, with the exception of certain insurance policies (see 8.21). The SORP recommends the following bases be adopted:

(*a*) quoted securities should be included at closing prices; these may be the last trade prices or mid-market prices, depending on the convention of the stock exchange or other market on which they are quoted;

(*b*) unquoted securities should be included at the market value estimated by the trustees, based on the advice of the investment managers or other appropriate professional adviser;

(*c*) unitised securities, referred to as pooled investment vehicles, should be included at the average of the bid and offer prices, or if single priced, at the closing single price;

(*d*) properties should be included at open market value or other appropriate basis of valuation determined in accordance with the Royal Institution of Chartered Surveyors' Appraisal and Valuation Manual and the Practice

Statements contained therein. The SORP notes that detailed guidance on valuation of assets owned by pension schemes is contained in Practice Statement UKPS 2.5. It also states:

> 'The valuation of properties may involve additional expense in professional fees and the frequency of valuation is therefore a matter of judgement for the trustees, subject to any specific requirements in the scheme documentation. Where property comprises a significant proportion of total investments, it is recommended that property valuations should be carried out by independent valuers at least at the same frequency as actuarial valuations of the fund, but in any case not less frequently than triennially.'

As actuarial valuations have in the past generally been carried out every three years for a SSAS, a professional valuation of property holdings is often undertaken at that time. As from A-Day actuarial input will only be needed where the trustees need to seek the advice of an actuary, and many schemes are expected to dispense with any requirement under the rules for triennial reports. Valuations underpinned or defined benefits arrangements will need to call for valuations to check funding levels under the provisions of the *Pensions Act 1995*.

Insurance policies should also be valued at market value. This is a difficult area; the SORP points out that there is no single generally accepted method of valuation and the usual methods are surrender value, premium value, modified premium value and actuarial value.

The SORP emphasises that the choice of method depends on the circumstances and is a matter of judgement; the trustee's objective should be to select an appropriate method that produces a reasonable estimate of fair value, without incurring undue expense, on a consistent basis from year to year.

Self-investment disclosure

8.23 Most SSASs are exempt from the *Pensions Act 1995* requirements restricting self-investment to 5% of scheme assets, and the new regulations described in 5.10 above. However, the SORP requires disclosure of all self-investment at any time during the period as well as at the scheme year end. The Audited Accounts Regulations also require disclosure of the percentage of self-investment.

Investment income

8.24 Interest and rents receivable should be accounted for on an accruals basis. Rents may be shown gross or net of property outgoings, but the basis should be made clear in the notes to the accounts and consistently applied.

Income from shares should be accounted for on an 'ex-div' basis. Some unitised funds do not distinguish investment income from capital growth/decreases in value, such income being reflected in the value of the units. In such cases, changes in value will appear as change in the market value of investments, and there will be no investment income shown in the accounts.

Actuarial position

8.25 The vast majority of SSASs are money purchase arrangements. Under the *Occupational Pension Schemes (Disclosure of Information) Regulations 1996 (SI 1996/1655)* (the 'Disclosure Regulations'), there is no need for an actuarial statement in such a scheme's annual report and thus there need be no reference to such a statement in the scheme's accounts (see 8.17).

However, it is important to indicate that the accounts do not include liabilities to pay future benefits, and the first two sentences in the example wording below may be used to convey this. Where a scheme provides final salary benefits the Disclosure Regulations require an actuarial statement in the scheme's annual report. In these circumstances, the SORP states that the accounts should refer to the actuary's statement by way of a note.

> 'The financial statements summarise the transactions and net assets of the scheme. They do not take account of obligations to pay pensions and benefits which fall due after the end of the scheme year. The actuarial position of the fund, which does take account of such obligations, is dealt with in the statement(s) by the actuary on pages 00 to 00 of the annual report and these accounts should be read in conjunction with it (them).'

If the actuary's report is not recent and the actuary's statement has not been updated by an interim or supplementary statement, the above wording may need to be amended. The requirement for an actuary's statement is removed once the scheme has a funding valuation under the *Pensions Act 2004*, per the *Occupational Pension Schemes (Scheme Funding) Regulations 2005 (SI 2005/3377)*.

The legal requirements for the audit of a SSAS

8.26 The statutory audit requirement was introduced in the *Occupational Pension Schemes (Disclosure of Information) Regulations 1986 (SI 1986/1046)* and it included SSASs with more than one member. The *Occupational Pension Schemes (Scheme Administration) Regulations 1996 (SI 1996/1715)*, (the 'Scheme Administration Regulations'), which apply for accounting periods ending on or after 6 April 1997, contain a number of exemptions, including certain SSASs. Single member SSASs are exempt from the requirement to appoint an auditor like all other schemes with only one member. Certain other SSASs are exempt from the requirement to appoint a scheme auditor under the *Pensions Act 1995* if:

(*a*) they fall within the definition of a SSAS as set out in *regulation 2*(*1*) of the SSAS Regulations;

(*b*) they are money purchase schemes (as SSASs are almost invariably); and

(*c*) all members are trustees; and

(*d*) all decisions are made only by the trustees who are members (excluding the pensioneer trustee) by unanimous agreement.

For accounting periods beginning on or after 22 September 2005, the rules are changed by the *Occupational Pension Schemes* (*Administration and Audited Accounts*) (*Amendment*) *Regulations 2005* (*SI 2005/2426*). The definition of small self-administered scheme is revoked by Regulation 4. This inserts a new exemption (h) in Regulation 3 of the Scheme Administration Regulations which is as follows:

'a scheme—

(i) with fewer than 12 members where all the members are trustees of the scheme and either—

  (aa) the provisions of the scheme provide that all decisions which fall to be made by the trustees are made by unanimous agreement by the trustees who are members of the scheme; or

  (bb) the scheme has a trustee who is independent in relation to the scheme for the purposes of *s 23* of the 1995 Act (power to appoint independent trustees), and is registered in the register maintained by the Authority in accordance with regulations made under subsection (4) of that section; or

(ii) with fewer than 12 members where all the members are directors of a company which is the sole trustee of the scheme, and either—

  (aa) the provisions of the scheme provide that any decisions made by the company in its capacity as trustee are made by the unanimous agreement of all the directors who are members of the scheme; or

  (bb) one of the directors of the company is independent in relation to the scheme for the purposes of *s 23* of the 1995 Act, and is registered in the register maintained by the Authority in accordance with regulations made under subsection (4) of that section'.

The exemption from the need to appoint an auditor brings with it the exemption from a statutory audit under the *Pensions Act 1995*. This means that audited accounts are not required to be prepared within the seven-month deadline for their completion imposed by the Audited Accounts Regulations. If these conditions are not met and sometimes, for example, decisions may not be made unanimously, then the scheme must appoint a statutory scheme auditor and the trustees must obtain audited accounts within seven months of the scheme year end.

Unapproved/non-registered schemes

8.27 Funded unapproved retirement benefit schemes (FURBS) are exempt from the requirement to appoint an auditor and thus from the requirement to obtain audited accounts. The wording of the exemption has been changed from unapproved schemes to 'occupational pension schemes which provide relevant benefits and which on or after 6 April 2006 is not a registered scheme' (the *Occupational Pension Schemes (Scheme Administration) Regulations 1996 (SI 1996/1715) Regulation 3,* as amended by the *Occupational Pension Schemes (Administration and Audited Accounts) (Amendment) Regulations 2005 (SI 2005/2426)*.

Appointment, resignation and removal of auditor

8.28 The Scheme Administration Regulations require trustees to provide the auditor with a written notice of appointment specifying:

(*a*) the date the appointment is to take effect; and

(*b*) from whom the auditor is to take instructions.

The auditor is required to acknowledge the appointment within one month and to confirm in writing that he will notify the trustees immediately he becomes aware of any conflict of interest. Model statutory appointment and acceptance letters are included at Appendices 36 and 37.

Professional standards require scheme auditors to issue a formal letter of engagement to the trustees (or other appointing body) which sets out the responsibilities of the trustees and the auditor. The letter covers such matters as:

(*a*) the responsibility for producing accounts;

(*b*) the statutory and professional duties of the auditor;

(*c*) the trustees' statutory duties in relation to the audit (where applicable);

(*d*) the trustees' responsibilities for the maintenance of records and safeguarding assets; and

(*e*) other services, staffing, timetable and fees.

An auditor must resign in writing or may be removed by written notice from the trustees. In each case, the auditor must provide:

(*a*) either a statement which specifies any circumstances connected with his resignation or removal which in his opinion significantly affect the interest of the members, prospective members or beneficiaries; or

(*b*) a declaration that he knows of no such circumstances.

A statement must be included in the statutory annual report where one is prepared.

Appointment of an auditor in the capacity of professional adviser

8.29 Where the conditions for exemption are met, but the SSAS's deed and rules require an audit, or the trustees decide to have one, then the auditor should be appointed not as statutory scheme auditor but as a professional adviser. This means undertaking the formal appointment procedures under *PA 1995*, *s 47*(*3*). (These statutory appointment procedures do not apply to a FURBS). However, because the scheme accounts are not statutory accounts, the seven-month deadline for the completion of audited accounts does not apply. Some SSASs only obtain audited accounts for the triennial actuarial valuation, which is required by IR SPSS. Provided that the scheme is exempt from the statutory audit requirements, this is not a regulatory problem.

Duty to provide the auditor with information

8.30 If an auditor is appointed, whether in the capacity of statutory auditor or professional adviser, the Scheme Administration Regulations impose a duty on the employer and employer's auditor to disclose on request to the trustees such information as is reasonably required for the audit. The trustees have a similar duty towards the scheme's auditor, and have to make available to the auditor any books and records.

Eligibility to act as auditor

8.31 The scheme auditor must be independent of any trustee and may not be:

(*a*) a scheme member;

(*b*) employed by the trustees or managers;

(*c*) a participating employer;

(*d*) ineligible to audit the accounts of a scheme employer under *CA 1985, s 27*.

There is no requirement for a scheme auditor to be a different person or firm from the auditor of the sponsoring employer.

Pension scheme audit reports

8.32 Where the Audited Accounts Regulations apply, they require the auditor to report on three matters:

(*a*) firstly, whether the accounts contain the information required to be disclosed by the regulations;

(*b*) secondly, whether the accounts show a true and fair view of the transactions of the scheme during the year and of the disposition of the assets at the year end; and

(*c*) thirdly, whether the contributions to the scheme during the year have been paid in accordance with the schedule of contributions (defined benefit scheme) or payment schedule (money purchase scheme).

Auditors' reports are drafted in accordance with International Standard on Auditing (ISA) (UK and Ireland) 700, and explain the respective responsibilities of trustees and auditors as well as providing the opinion required by the Disclosure Regulations. In many cases, SSASs have a non-statutory audit report because their audit is not subject to the legislation.

ISA 700 expects the trustees to include with the audited accounts a statement of trustees' responsibilities in relation to the accounts. Otherwise, the auditors will refer to these responsibilities in their reports. The wording will depend on whether the accounts are statutory or non-statutory and scheme auditors usually provide their trustee clients with appropriate wording.

Pension costs in the accounts of the employer

8.33 The procedure for dealing with pension costs in the accounts of sponsoring employers has been in a period of transition from that set out in Statement of Standard Accounting Practice 24 (SSAP 24) 'Accounting for Pension Costs' to that in Financial Reporting Standard 17, 'Retirement Benefits'. The latter should be regarded as standard for accounting periods beginning on or after 1 January 2005.

Defined contribution schemes

8.34 For a defined contribution scheme, the charge against profits is the contributions payable to the scheme for the accounting period. The cost is recognised in the operating profit in the profit and loss account (FRS 17 para 7):

(*a*) the nature of the scheme (i e defined contribution);

(*b*) the pension cost charge for the period; and

(*c*) any outstanding or prepaid contributions at the balance sheet date (FRS 17 para 75).

Nearly all SSASs fall into this category, and the accounting disclosures required are thus straightforward.

However, it should be noted that only contributions actually paid in the accounting period are allowed as a charge against profits for corporation tax (*s 592(4)*). This may also have deferred tax consequences in the company's accounts to allow for the timing differences between the contributions being paid and the tax allowances being given.

Defined benefit schemes

8.35 In 2005, FRS 17 replaced SSAP 24 and the Urgent Issues Task Force (UITF) Abstract 6 'Accounting for post-retirement benefits other than pensions'. It addresses all retirement benefits which an employer is committed to providing, whether the commitment is statutory, contractual or implicit in the employer's actions. The standard is not limited to benefits arising in the UK – benefits arising overseas also fall within its scope – and it requires a liability to be recognised as benefits are earned, not when they are due to be paid, thus capturing funded and unfunded amounts.

The standard was issued in November 2000, but its full implementation has been delayed from 2003 to accounting periods beginning on or after 1 January 2005, though early implementation was encouraged.

FRS 17 introduces new complexities into the calculation of pensions costs for defined benefit schemes. The Accounting Standards Board (ASB) sets out the main requirements of FRS 17 for defined benefit schemes as follows:

- Pension scheme assets are measured using market values.
- Pension scheme liabilities are measured using a projected unit method and discounted at an AA bond rate.
- The pension scheme surplus (to the extent it can be recovered) or deficit is recognised in full on the balance sheet.

- The movement in the scheme surplus or deficit is analysed into the current service cost and any past service costs, these being recognised in operating profit; the interest cost and expected return on assets, which are recognised as other finance costs; and actuarial gains and losses which are recognised in the statement of total recognised gains and losses.

International Accounting Standard 19 Employee Benefits (IAS 19)

8.36 All listed companies in the EU must adopt International Accounting Standards in their consolidated financial statement for accounting periods beginning on or after 1 January 2005. Such companies must therefore apply IAS 19 rather than FRS 17 at group level.

Statutory disclosure of pension costs in company accounts

8.37 Disclosure requirements for a particular company will depend upon its listing status and, if not listed, whether it qualifies as a small company. Companies whose equity share capital is quoted on the London Stock Exchange Official List, the official list in another European Economic Area state, the New York Stock Exchange or Nasdaq are defined as 'quoted'. All other companies, including those listed on AIM or Ofex are referred to as 'unquoted'. Directors should consult their auditors for specific advice on their particular circumstances.

Unquoted companies

Aggregate emoluments

8.38 *Paragraph 1, Pt 1, Sch 6* to the *Companies Act 1985* requires the disclosure in company accounts of details of emoluments and other remuneration receivable by directors. These disclosure requirements, which include those relating to directors' pensions, were changed in 1997 by the *Company Accounts (Disclosure of Directors' Emoluments) Regulations 1997* (*SI 1997/570*), which came into effect on 31 March 1997 for companies' financial years ending on or after that date. As a result of the changes *SI 1997/570* made to *Sch 6*, the term 'emoluments' now does not include pension scheme contributions paid or treated as paid in respect of a director, nor pension benefits to which he or she is entitled. Instead, there is a requirement to show the aggregate value of any 'company contributions' paid or treated as paid to a money purchase pension scheme in respect of directors' qualifying services. There is also a requirement to disclose the number of directors to whom retirement benefits are accruing in respect of service under both money purchase and final salary pension schemes.

Disclosure of highest paid director's remuneration and other particulars

8.39 Where the total of the aggregate amounts disclosed under directors' emoluments amounts to £200,000 or more, the accounts must disclose:

(*a*) the amount of that total which is attributable to the 'highest paid director'; and

(*b*) the amount of company contributions to a money purchase pension scheme which is attributable to the 'highest paid director'.

Where the scheme is a defined benefit scheme, the accounts must show for that director:

1 the amount of his accrued pension at the end of the financial year; and

2 the amount at the end of the financial year of his 'accrued lump sum';

accrued pension and accrued lump sum being the amount of the annual pension and the amount of the lump sum which would be payable when he attained normal pension age if:

(i) he had left the company's service at the end of the financial year;

(ii) there were no increases in the general level of prices in the UK during the period beginning with the end of that year ending with his attaining normal retirement age;

(iii) no question arose of any commutation of the pension or inverse commutation of the lump sum; and

(v) director's additional voluntary contributions and any money purchase benefits which would be payable under the scheme were disregarded.

Excess retirement benefits

8.40 There is also a requirement for disclosure of increases during the financial year in retirement benefits paid to or receivable by directors and past directors that are in excess of the retirement benefits to which they were entitled on the date on which the benefits first became payable or 31 March 1997, whichever is the later. The exception to this requirement is where the increase was (or could have been) paid without recourse to additional contributions *and* the increase was given to all pensioner members of the scheme on the same basis.

Quoted companies

8.41 There are two sets of regulations that apply to quoted companies; the *Directors' Remuneration Report Regulations 2002* (*SI 2002/1986*) and the Listing Rules of the Financial Services Authority. Both sets of regulations include requirements to disclose information regarding pension arrangements which, while similar, are subtly different and lead to duplication of disclosure. These are discussed further below.

Part 1 of *Schedule 6* to the *Companies Act 1985* does not apply to quoted companies, with the exception of paragraph 1 'Aggregate emoluments', which is described above.

The Directors' Remuneration Report Regulations 2002

8.42 These regulations (*SI 2002/1986*) came into force on 1 August 2002 and affect companies' financial years ending on or after 31 December 2002. Companies falling within their scope (that is, 'quoted companies', as defined above) are required to prepare a statutory remuneration report that adheres to prescribed contents as set out in *Sch 7A* to the *Companies Act 1985*. Broadly speaking, numerical disclosures are subject to audit, narrative disclosures concerning policy are not.

The disclosure requirements relevant to pension entitlements, and subject to audit, are as follows.

(*a*) Defined benefit schemes

Where a director has rights under a defined benefit pension scheme and any of those rights relates to qualifying services, the following should be provided on an individual director basis:

- details of any changes during the year in the director's accrued benefit;
- the accrued benefits as at the year end;
- the transfer value of the director's accrued benefits at the start of the year, calculated in a manner consistent with *Retirement Benefit Schemes – Transfer Values* (GN 11);
- the transfer value of the director's accrued benefits at the end of the year, also calculated in a manner consistent with GN 11; and

- the amount obtained by subtracting the transfer value at the start of the year from the transfer value at the end of the year, and then deducting any contributions made by the director.

Note that unlike similar disclosures required by the Listing Rules (see 8.43), no adjustment is made for inflation. It is also noteworthy that the disclosures refer to the start and end of the year irrespective of whether a director was appointed or resigned during the year.

Schedule 6, paragraph 1 requires disclosure of the number of directors that were members of defined benefit schemes. Normally this will be self-evident from the number of directors listed in the above disclosure.

(*b*) Defined contribution schemes

Where a director has rights under a defined contribution or money purchase scheme, the remuneration report should contain details of any contribution to the scheme in respect of the director individually.

Paragraph 1 of *Pt 1* of *Sch 6* to the *Companies Act 1985* requires aggregate contributions to money purchase schemes to be disclosed and the number of directors in such schemes, although, as above, the latter requirement will normally be self-evident. A comparative figure for aggregate contributions is also required.

Additionally, audited numerical disclosure must be made by individual directors of any excess retirement benefits of directors and past directors. This requirement is the same as that described above for an unquoted company, except that the disclosures must be made on an individual basis.

Furthermore, a section describing remuneration policy should contain details of the company's policy with respect to the provision of pension benefits to directors, and explain whether any element of pension contributions is subject to performance conditions. Narrative disclosure of policy is not subject to audit.

Listing Rules of the Financial Services Authority requirements

8.43 In May 1997, the Listing Rules introduced a requirement for most listed companies to disclose particulars concerning the pension benefits of each director. For money purchase schemes, disclosure of the contribution or allowance made by the company in respect of each director during the period under review is required. This requirement is the same as that required by the *Directors' Remuneration Report Regulations 2002* (*SI 2002/1986*) as described at 8.42 above.

For final salary schemes, disclosure is required of the amount of the increase in the period under review (excluding inflation) and the accumulated total amount at the end of the period, in respect of the accrued benefit to which each director would be entitled on leaving service or is entitled having left service during the period, and:

(*a*) either the transfer value (less the director's contributions) of the relevant increase in accrued benefit as at the end of the period; or

(*b*) as much of a list of prescribed information as is necessary to make a reasonable assessment of the transfer value in respect of each director.

The above disclosures differ from those set out in the *Directors' Remuneration Report Regulations 2002* in that they *exclude* inflation. By contrast, those required by the DRRR *include* inflation. Accordingly, duplication of disclosure will exist until such time as the Listing Rules are amended.

Note that the scope of the auditor's report on the financial statements is required to cover these disclosures.

Small companies

8.44 If an unquoted company meets the size and eligibility criteria for a small company, there are exemptions which allow the company to produce modified accounts. In such cases, instead of showing separately the aggregate amounts of directors' emoluments, long-term incentive schemes and company contributions to a money purchase scheme, the modified accounts may disclose only the aggregate of these three amounts. Details of the highest paid director's emoluments and of any excess retirement benefits need also not be given.

Other considerations

Pension 'top-ups' instead of a bonus (or other emoluments foregone)

8.45 A director may make a bonus sacrifice, or forgo some other benefit, and have an equivalent amount paid into the pension scheme. The issue then arises of whether this is a company pension contribution or is part of directors' emoluments or long-term incentive payments. In practice, the matter should be established by determining whether the director is choosing to have as a top-up an amount which would otherwise be paid to him or her as salary or long-term incentive payments, and if this is the case, the payment should be included within directors' emoluments or long-term incentive payments.

Where payments are made in connection with a director ceasing to hold office, there will be a similar need to exercise judgement as to whether a particular amount falls to be included as compensation for loss of office or as a company contribution to a pension scheme. For benefits receivable under a final salary scheme, this compensation amount would generally be the actuarial value of the pension enhancement.

FURBS

8.46 Contributions payable to a money purchase FURBS are disclosable as contributions paid to a money purchase pension scheme. If the company or group operates more than one money purchase scheme, there is no requirement to sub-analyse the contributions made to the different schemes. Remuneration reports of the board usually disclose the existence of any directors' FURBS, the nature of those FURBS and the amounts paid to them in respect of each director during the year. It is common for any payments made to directors that provide compensation for the tax suffered on the contribution to be treated as additional salary.

The European Communities (Definition of Treaties) (Cooperation Agreement between the European Community and its Member States and the Swiss Confederation to Combat Fraud) Order 2006

8.47 The European Communities (Definition of Treaties) (Cooperation Agreement between the European Community and its Member States and the Swiss Confederation to Combat Fraud) Order 2006 came into effect on 14 February 2006. The explanatory note states:

> 'This Order declares the Cooperation Agreement between the European Community and its Member States, of the one part, and the Swiss Confederation, of the other part, to combat fraud and any other illegal activity to the detriment of their financial interests to be a Community Treaty as defined in section 1(2) of the European Communities Act 1972.
>
> The object of the Agreement is to extend administrative and judicial assistance in order to combat illegal activities in customs; agricultural legislation; value added tax, special taxes on consumption, and excise duties; the charging and retention of funds from the budgets of the parties to the Agreement or from budgets managed by them or on their behalf; and procedures for the award of contracts by them.

The principal effect of declaring this Agreement to be a Community Treaty is that the provisions of section 2 of the European Communities Act 1972 (which provide for the general implementation of Community Treaties) apply to it.'

Termination of UK's reciprocal agreements on transfers of pension rights

8.48 HMRC has terminated its existing reciprocal agreements with the Republic of Ireland, Jersey, Guernsey and the Isle of Man for the transfer of pension rights with effect from A-Day. This reflects the removal of HMRC's discretionary powers from that date and the easements in pension schemes transfers under the new regime. No longer will individuals have to meet any conditions as is the case under the current tax rules and the reciprocal agreements. HMRC have announced that the new rules will make it easier to make transfers than the existing bilateral arrangements and all parties to the agreements have therefore agreed that they should be terminated.

Regulations

The Occupational and Personal Pension Schemes (Consultation by Employers and Miscellaneous Amendment) Regulations 2006 (SI 2006/349)

8.49 The *Finance Act 2004* and the *Pensions Act 2004* contained provisions which reflected the government's intent to comply with the main principles of the *EU Occupational Pensions Directive* (*2003/41/EC*) on *IORPs*. There have been significant changes and relaxations to the membership, tax and transfer rules which previously applied to overseas matters. These rules are described in this chapter.

The Occupational Pension Schemes (Investment) Regulations 2005 (SI 2005/3378)

8.50 These regulations revoked the *Occupational Pension Schemes* (*Investment*) *Regulations 1996* (*SI 1996/3127*). Their effect is described in 4.5.

The Occupational Pension Schemes (Trust and Retirement Benefits Exemption) Regulations 2005 (SI 2005/2360)

8.51 These regulations are described in 4.6. They prescribe the description of schemes which are exempt from:

- the requirement in *s 252(2) of the Pensions Act 2004*, that trustees or managers of an occupational pension scheme with its main administration in the UK must not accept funding payments unless the scheme is established under irrevocable trust;
- the requirement in *s 255(1)* of the Act, that an occupational pension scheme with its main administration in the UK must be limited to retirement-benefit activities.

Countering cross-border tax evasion

8.52 HMRC publishes guidance notes on its website concerning overseas savings and the moves to prevent tax loss on chargeable savings. The guidance is based on the *EU Savings Directive* (*Council Directive 2003/48/EC*) dated 3 June 2003. This is of particular interest to high networth individuals who invest monies, or wish to invest monies, overseas. The tax advantage of being a member of a recognised overseas scheme on a bona fide basis (rather than investing independently in an overseas financial institution) is clear.

The objective of the Directive is to collect and exchange information (Tax Information Exchange Agreements – TIEAs) about foreign resident individuals receiving savings income outside their resident state (the relevant territory). This mainly affects banks, registrars, custodians and other financial institutions that make interest payments to individuals in prescribed territories. TIEAs are bilateral agreements under which territories agree to co-operate in tax matters through exchange of information.

The Directive came into effect on 1 July 2005 and the first savings income reports cover the period 1 July 2005 to 5 April 2006. They must be submitted to HMRC by 30 June 2006.

The website publishes agreements when they have completed the necessary parliamentary procedures in both countries. The agreements take the form of statutory instruments. Effectively, a withholding tax is held by the relevant territory unless the individual fully declares the interest in his own territory. To date, the initial rate of tax is normally 15%, rising to 20% (by an agreed date, often 2008) and to 35% thereafter.

Conclusion

8.53 The changes to the overseas rules as at A-Day are far-reaching. They open up many opportunities for international pension provision on a tax-efficient basis for the future, and less restriction on pension transfers. The rules are still complex, as the UK legislation seeks to claw back tax on monies which have previously built up tax free in the UK. However, there are significant exemptions, and high earners (particularly those who are internationally mobile, or who have non-UK domicility), are likely to benefit from seeking professional tax advice on their future pension savings.

Transfers overseas to a qualifying recognised overseas pension scheme will be tested against the lifetime allowance and any amounts transferred above the individual's lifetime allowance will be subject to a tax charge of 25%. Transfers below the lifetime allowance will not attract a tax charge. The individual will not have to emigrate to transfer out. After the transfer, other charges may also be applicable, because certain payments made out of overseas schemes containing funds which have benefited from UK tax reliefs may be liable to UK tax charges such as the annual allowance, lifetime allowance and unauthorised payment charges. The latter will apply if the payment could not have been paid out of a registered UK scheme.

Transfers to an overseas pension scheme that is not a qualifying recognised overseas pension scheme are treated as unauthorised payments and will be subject to tax charges.

The new rules provide details of certain tax charges that arise in respect of 'relevant non-UK schemes', where UK tax relief has been given on contributions under migrant member relief, or under the terms of a Double Taxation Treaty, or where a transfer has been made from a UK registered scheme to an overseas scheme.

Pensions Regulator's planned regulatory approach to cross-border pension schemes

8.54 UK pension schemes that wish to operate cross border have to obtain authorisation and approval from the Pensions Regulator. This requirement came in during January 2006. The Pensions Regulator is responsible for regulating such schemes. Schemes that may already be operating as cross border will need to get authorisation and approval, and should contact the Regulator as soon as possible. The Regulator has stated that it has positive feedback on its regulatory approach which will go ahead as planned.

Appendix 1

HMRC Regulations and Orders

Employer-Financed Retirement Benefits (Excluded Benefits for Tax Purposes) Regulations 2006 (SI 2006/210)

Employer-Financed Retirement Benefits Schemes (Provision of Information) Regulations 2005 (SI 2005/3453)

Establishment of Schemes Regulations 2006

Finance Act 2004, Part 4 (Pension Schemes – Transitional and Transitory Provisions and Savings: Pipeline Lump Sums) Order 2006

Finance (No 2) Act 2005, Section 45 (Appointed Day) Order 2005 (SI 2005/3337)

Pension Benefits (Insurance Company Liable as Scheme Administrator) Regulations 2006 (SI 2006/136)

Pension Protection Fund (Tax) (2005–06) Regulations 2005 (SI 2005/1907)

Pension Protection Fund (Tax) Regulations 2006

Pensions Schemes (Application of UK Provisions to Relevant Non-UK Schemes) Regulations 2006 (SI 2006/207)

Pension Schemes (Categories of Country and Requirements for Overseas Pension Schemes and Recognised Overseas Pension Schemes) Regulations 2006 (SI 2006/206)

Pension Schemes (Information Requirements – Qualifying Overseas Pension Schemes, Qualifying Recognised Overseas Pension Schemes and Corresponding Relief) Regulations 2006 (SI 2006/208)

Pension Schemes (Part 4 of the Finance Act 2004 Transitional and Transitory Provisions) Order 2005

Pension Schemes (Reduction in Pension Rates) Regulations 2006 (SI 2006/138)

Pension Schemes (Relevant Migrant Members) Regulations 2006 (SI 2006/212)

Registered Pension Schemes (Accounting and Assessment) Regulations 2005 (SI 2005/3454)

Registered Pension Schemes and Employer-Financed Retirement Benefits Schemes (Information) (Prescribed Descriptions of Persons) Regulations 2005 (SI 2005/3455)

Registered Pension Schemes and Overseas Pension Schemes (Electronic Communication of Returns and Information) Regulations 2005

Registered Pension Schemes (Authorised Member Payments) Regulations 2006 (SI 2006/137) for demutualisation of insurance companies and members of qualifying pension schemes

Registered Pension Schemes (Authorised Payments) Regulations 2006 (SI 2006/209)

Registered Pension Schemes (Authorised Payments) (Transfers to the Pension Protection Fund) Regulations 2006 (SI 2006/134)

Registered Pension Schemes (Audited Accounts) (Specified Persons) Regulations 2005 (SI 2005/3456)

Registered Pension Schemes (Block Transfers) (Permitted Membership Period) Regulations 2006 (SI 2006/498)

Registered Pension Schemes (Co-ownership of Living Accommodation) Regulations 2006 (SI 2006/133)

Registered Pension Schemes (Defined Benefits Arrangements and Money Purchase Arrangements – Uprating) Regulations 2005

Registered Pension Schemes (Discharge of Liabilities under Sections 267 and 268 of the Finance Act 2004 Regulations 2005 (SI 2005/3542)

Registered Pension Schemes (Enhanced Lifetime Allowance) Regulations 2006 (SI 2006/131)

Registered Pension Schemes (Meaning of Pension Commencement Lump Sum) Regulations 2006 (SI 2006/135)

Registered Pension Schemes (Minimum Contributions) Regulations 2005 (SI 2005/3450)

Registered Pension Schemes (Modification of the Rules of Existing Schemes) Regulations 2006 (SI 2006/364)

Registered Pension Schemes (Prescribed Interest Rates for Authorised Employer Loans) Regulations 2005 (SI 2005/3449)

Registered Pension Schemes (Prescribed Schemes and Occupations) Regulations 2005 (SI 2005/3541)

Registered Pension Schemes (Provision of Information) Regulations 2005

Registered Pension Schemes (Relevant Annuities) Regulations 2006 (SI 2006/129)

Registered Pension Schemes (Relief at Source) Regulations 2005 (SI 2005/3448)

Registered Pension Schemes (Restriction of Employer's Relief) Regulations 2005 (SI 2005/3548)

Registered Pensions (Splitting of Schemes) Regulations 2006

Registered Pension Schemes (Surrender of Relevant Excess) Regulations 2006 (SI 2006/211)

Registered Pension Schemes (Unauthorised Payments by Existing Schemes) Regulations 2006 (SI 2006/365)

Registered Pension Schemes (Uprating Percentages for Defined Benefits Arrangements and Enhanced Protection Limits) 2006 (SI 2006/130)

Registered Pensions (Splitting of Schemes) Regulations 2006

Taxes Management Act (Modifications to Schedule 3 for Pension Scheme Appeals) Order 2005 (SI 2005/3457)

Transitional Provision Order: Pre A-Day Assets 2005

Transitional Provision Order: Protection of Large Lump Sums under Enhanced Protection 2005

Transitional Provision Order: Scheme Specific Lump Sums 2005

Transitional Provision Order: Transfer of Crystallised Rights With Enhanced Protection 2005

Transitional Provision Order: Transfers and Wind-ups Secured by Individual Contracts of Insurance 2005

Transitional Provision Order: Transitional Protection for Lump Sum Only Schemes 2005

Transitional Provision Order: Lump Sum Death Benefit 2005

Transitional Provision Order: Lump Sum Only Contracts Becoming Registered Pension Schemes 2005.

Appendix 2

Registered Pension Schemes (Enhanced Lifetime Allowance) Regulations 2006

No 131

Preliminary

1 Citation and commencement

These Regulations may be cited as the Registered Pension Schemes (Enhanced Lifetime Allowance) Regulations 2006 and shall come into force on 6th April 2006.

2 Interpretation

(1) In these Regulations–

'the closing date' is to be read in accordance with regulation 3(4), 4(4), 5(4), 6(4), 7(4) or 8(4) as the case may require;

'notification' is to be read in accordance with regulation 3(3), 4(3), 5(3), 6(3), 7(3) or 8(3) as the case may require;

'the Revenue and Customs' means Her Majesty's Revenue and Customs.

(2) In these Regulations references to sections, without more, are references to sections of the Finance Act 2004, and references to provisions of Schedule 36 are references to provisions of Schedule 36 to that Act.

(3) The expressions defined or otherwise explained in the list in section 280(2) have the same definitions or explanations in these Regulations as in Part 4 of the Finance Act 2004.

Reliance on Provisions of the Finance Act 2004

3 Reliance on paragraph 7 of Schedule 36 (lifetime allowance enhancement: 'primary protection')

(1) This regulation applies if the amount of the relevant pre-commencement pension rights of an individual (determined in accordance with paragraph 7(5) of Schedule 36) exceeds £ 1,500,000.

(2) The individual may give notice of intention to rely on paragraph 7 of Schedule 36 ('paragraph 7').

(3) If the individual intends to rely on paragraph 7, the individual must give a notification to the Revenue and Customs on or before the closing date.

(4) For the purposes of this regulation the closing date is 5th April 2009.

(5) Paragraph (6) applies if–

(a) the individual gives the notification to the Revenue and Customs, and

(b) the Revenue and Customs issue a certificate to the individual in response to the giving of the notification.

(6) The individual may rely on paragraph 7 during the period beginning on 6th April 2006 and ending on the day on which the Revenue and Customs–

(a) revoke the certificate, or

(b) issue an amended certificate to the individual.

(7) Paragraph (8) applies if the Revenue and Customs–

(a) issue a certificate to which paragraph (6) applies to the individual, and

(b) later issue an amended certificate ('the subsequent certificate') to the individual.

(8) The individual may rely on paragraph 7 during the period beginning on the day specified on the subsequent certificate and ending on the day on which the Revenue and Customs–

(a) revoke the subsequent certificate, or

(b) issue an amended certificate to the individual.

(9) The day so specified must not be earlier than 6th April 2006.

4 Reliance on paragraph 12 of Schedule 36 (lifetime allowances: 'enhanced protection')

(1) This regulation applies in the case of an individual to whom paragraph 12(1) of Schedule 36 has applied at all times on and after 6th April 2006.

(2) The individual may give notice of intention to rely on paragraph 12 of Schedule 36 ('paragraph 12').

(3) If the individual intends to rely on paragraph 12, the individual must give a notification to the Revenue and Customs on or before the closing date.

(4) For the purposes of this regulation the closing date is 5th April 2009.

(5) Paragraph (6) applies if–

(a) the individual gives the notification to the Revenue and Customs, and

(b) the Revenue and Customs issue a certificate to the individual in response to the giving of the notification.

(6) The individual may rely on paragraph 12 during the period beginning on 6th April 2006 and ending on the day on which the Revenue and Customs–

(a) revoke the certificate,

(b) issue an amended certificate to the individual, or

(c) receive notice, given by the individual, that the individual no longer wishes to rely on paragraph 12.

(7) Paragraph (8) applies if the Revenue and Customs–

(a) issue a certificate to which paragraph (6) applies to the individual, and

(b) later issue an amended certificate ('the subsequent certificate') to the individual.

(8) The individual may rely on paragraph 12 during the period beginning on the day specified on the subsequent certificate and ending on the day on which the Revenue and Customs–

(a) revoke the subsequent certificate,

(b) issue an amended certificate to the individual, or

(c) receive notice, given by the individual, that the individual no longer wishes to rely on paragraph 12.

(9) The day so specified must not be earlier than 6th April 2006.

5 Reliance on paragraph 18 of Schedule 36 (lifetime allowance enhancement: pre-commencement pension credits)

(1) This regulation applies if a benefit crystallisation event occurs in relation to an individual in the circumstances specified in paragraph 18(1) of Schedule 36.

(2) The individual may give notice of intention to rely on paragraph 18 of Schedule 36 ('paragraph 18').

(3) If the individual intends to rely on paragraph 18, the individual must give a notification to the Revenue and Customs on or before the closing date.

(4) For the purposes of this regulation the closing date is 5th April 2009.

(5) Paragraph (6) applies if–

(a) the individual gives the notification to the Revenue and Customs, and

(b) the Revenue and Customs issue a certificate to the individual in response to the giving of the notification.

(6) The individual may rely on paragraph 18 during the period beginning on 6th April 2006 and ending on the day on which the Revenue and Customs–

(a) revoke the certificate, or

(b) issue an amended certificate to the individual.

(7) Paragraph (8) applies if the Revenue and Customs–

(a) issue a certificate to which paragraph (6) applies to the individual, and

(b) later issue an amended certificate ('the subsequent certificate') to the individual.

(8) The individual may rely on paragraph 18 during the period beginning on the day specified on the subsequent certificate and ending on the day on which the Revenue and Customs–

(a) revoke the subsequent certificate, or

(b) issue an amended certificate to the individual.

(9) The day so specified must not be earlier than 6th April 2006.

6 Reliance on section 220 (lifetime allowance enhancement: registration of pension credits)

(1) This regulation applies if an individual acquires rights under a registered pension scheme in the circumstances specified in section 220(1).

(2) The individual may give notice of intention to rely on section 220.

(3) If the individual intends to rely on section 220, the individual must give a notification to the Revenue and Customs on or before the closing date.

(4) For the purposes of this regulation use the rules in this paragraph to find the closing date.

First rule: Find the 31st January following the tax year in which the pension sharing order or provision takes effect.

Second rule: Find the 31st January five years after that.

The date so found is the closing date.

(5) Paragraph (6) applies if–

(a) the individual gives the notification to the Revenue and Customs, and

(b) the Revenue and Customs issue a certificate to the individual in response to the giving of the notification.

(6) The individual may rely on section 220 during the period beginning on the day on which the pension sharing order or provision takes effect and ending on the day on which the Revenue and Customs–

(a) revoke the certificate, or

(b) issue an amended certificate to the individual.

(7) Paragraph (8) applies if the Revenue and Customs–

(a) issue a certificate to which paragraph (6) applies to the individual, and

(b) later issue an amended certificate ('the subsequent certificate') to the individual.

(8) The individual may rely on section 220 during the period beginning on the day specified on the subsequent certificate and ending on the day on which the Revenue and Customs–

(a) revoke the subsequent certificate, or

(b) issue an amended certificate to the individual.

7 Reliance on section 221 (lifetime allowance enhancement: relevant overseas individuals)

(1) This regulation applies if, at any time on or after 6th April 2006, an individual is a relevant overseas individual during any part of a period that is the active membership period in relation to an arrangement relating to the individual.

(2) The individual may give notice of intention to rely on section 221.

(3) If the individual intends to rely on section 221, the individual must give a notification to the Revenue and Customs on or before the closing date.

(4) For the purposes of this regulation use the rules in this paragraph to find the closing date.

First rule: Find the 31st January following the tax year in which the accrual period ends (see paragraph (10)).

Second rule: Find the 31st January five years after that.

The date so found is the closing date.

(5) Paragraph (6) applies if–

(a) the individual gives the notification to the Revenue and Customs, and

(b) the Revenue and Customs issue a certificate to the individual in response to the giving of the notification.

(6) The individual may rely on section 221 during the period beginning on the accrual day (see paragraph (10)) and ending on the day on which the Revenue and Customs–

(a) revoke the certificate, or

(b) issue an amended certificate to the individual.

(7) Paragraph (8) applies if the Revenue and Customs–

(a) issue a certificate to which paragraph (6) applies to the individual, and

(b) later issue an amended certificate ('the subsequent certificate') to the individual.

(8) The individual may rely on section 221 during the period beginning on the day specified on the subsequent certificate and ending on the day on which the Revenue and Customs–

(a) revoke the subsequent certificate, or

(b) issue an amended certificate to the individual.

(9) The day so specified must not be earlier than the accrual day.

(10) For the purposes of this regulation–

(a) the accrual period ends–

(i) when the individual ceases to be a relevant overseas individual,

(ii) immediately before a benefit crystallisation event occurring in relation to the arrangement relating to the individual, or

(iii) when benefits cease to accrue to or in respect of the individual under the arrangement,

whichever is the earliest; and

(b) 'the accrual day' is the day on which the accrual period ends.

8 Reliance on section 224 (lifetime allowance enhancement: transfer from recognised overseas pension scheme)

(1) This regulation applies if, in relation to an individual, there is a recognised overseas scheme transfer in the circumstances specified in section 224(1).

(2) The individual may give notice of intention to rely on section 224.

(3) If the individual intends to rely on section 224, the individual must give a notification to the Revenue and Customs on or before the closing date.

(4) For the purposes of this regulation use the rules in this paragraph to find the closing date.

First rule: Find the 31st January following the tax year in which the recognised overseas scheme transfer takes place.

Second rule: Find the 31st January five years after that.

The date so found is the closing date.

(5) Paragraph (6) applies if–

(a) the individual gives the notification to the Revenue and Customs, and

(b) the Revenue and Customs issue a certificate to the individual in response to the giving of the notification.

(6) The individual may rely on section 224 during the period beginning on the day on which the recognised overseas scheme transfer takes place and ending on the day on which the Revenue and Customs–

(a) revoke the certificate, or

(b) issue an amended certificate to the individual.

(7) Paragraph (8) applies if the Revenue and Customs–

(a) issue a certificate to which paragraph (6) applies to the individual, and

(b) later issue an amended certificate ('the subsequent certificate') to the individual.

(8) The individual may rely on section 224 during the period beginning on the day specified on the subsequent certificate and ending on the day on which the Revenue and Customs–

(a) revoke the subsequent certificate, or

(b) issue an amended certificate to the individual.

Loss of Enhanced Protection

9 Loss of enhanced protection

(1) This regulation applies if conditions A to F are met.

(2) Condition A is that an individual has one or more relevant existing arrangements (within the meaning given by paragraph 12(4) of Schedule 36).

(3) Condition B is that the lump sum condition specified in paragraph 24(2) of Schedule 36 is met in relation to the individual.

(4) Condition C is that the first notice requirement condition specified in paragraph 24(5) of Schedule 36 is not met in relation to the individual.

(5) Condition D is that the second notice requirement condition specified in paragraph 24(6) of Schedule 36 is met in relation to the individual.

(6) Condition E is that the individual has a certificate issued under regulation 4 on which the individual may rely.

(7) Condition F is that paragraph 12 of Schedule 36 has ceased to apply to the individual.

(8) Paragraph 31 of Schedule 36 applies in relation to the individual and to a registered pension scheme which is a protected pension scheme.

(9) In paragraph (8) 'protected pension scheme' has the meaning given by paragraph 31 of Schedule 36.

Notifications

10 Form of notification

(1) A notification must be in a form prescribed by the Commissioners for Her Majesty's Revenue and Customs.

(2) The individual must sign and date the notification.

11 Preservation of documents

(1) This regulation applies if–

(a) an individual gives a notification to the Revenue and Customs, and

(b) the Revenue and Customs issue a certificate to the individual in response to the giving of the notification.

(2) The individual must preserve all documents relating to the information given in the notification for a period of six years beginning with the day on which the individual gives the notification to the Revenue and Customs.

12 Late submission of notification

(1) This regulation applies if an individual–

(a) gives a notification to the Revenue and Customs after the closing date,

(b) had a reasonable excuse for not giving the notification on or before the closing date, and

(c) gives the notification without unreasonable delay after the reasonable excuse ceased.

(2) If the Revenue and Customs are satisfied that paragraph (1) applies, they must consider the information provided in the notification.

(3) If there is a dispute as to whether paragraph (1) applies, the individual may require the Revenue and Customs to give notice of their decision to refuse to consider the information provided in the notification.

(4) If the Revenue and Customs gives notice of their decision to refuse to consider the information provided in the notification, the individual may appeal to the Commissioners.

(5) The appeal is to the General Commissioners, except that the individual may elect (in accordance with section 46(1) of the Taxes Management Act 1970) to bring the appeal before the Special Commissioners instead of the General Commissioners.

(6) The notice of appeal must be given to the Revenue and Customs within 30 days after the day on which notice of their decision is given to the individual.

(7) On an appeal, the Commissioners shall determine whether the individual gave the notification to the Revenue and Customs in the circumstances specified in paragraph (1).

(8) If the Commissioners allow the appeal, they shall direct the Revenue and Customs to consider the information provided in the notification.

Procedure on Giving of Notifications

13 Procedure on giving of notification to the Revenue and Customs

(1) If an individual gives a notification to the Revenue and Customs, and there are no obvious errors or omissions in the notification (whether errors of principle, arithmetical mistakes or otherwise), the Revenue and Customs must issue a certificate to the individual.

(2) If an individual gives a notification to the Revenue and Customs, and there are obvious errors or omissions in the notification (whether errors of principle, arithmetical mistakes or otherwise), the Revenue and Customs must return the notification to the individual.

14 Appeal against refusal to issue certificate

(1) This regulation applies if there is a dispute as to whether the Revenue and Customs are entitled to take the view that there are obvious errors or omissions in the notification (whether errors of principle, arithmetical mistakes or otherwise).

(2) The individual may require the Revenue and Customs to give notice of their decision to refuse to issue a certificate.

(3) If the Revenue and Customs give notice of their decision to refuse to issue a certificate, the individual may appeal to the Commissioners.

(4) The appeal is to the General Commissioners, except that the individual may elect (in accordance with section 46(1) of the Taxes Management Act 1970) to bring the appeal before the Special Commissioners instead of the General Commissioners.

(5) The notice of appeal must be given to the Revenue and Customs within 30 days after the day on which notice of their decision is given to the individual.

(6) On an appeal, the Commissioners shall determine whether the Revenue and Customs were entitled to take the view that there were obvious errors or omissions in the notification (whether errors of principle, arithmetical mistakes or otherwise).

(7) If the Commissioners allow the appeal, they may direct the Revenue and Customs to issue a certificate to the individual with effect from a date specified by the Commissioners.

Certificates

15 General

(1) A certificate must be in a form prescribed by the Commissioners for Her Majesty's Revenue and Customs.

(2) A certificate must have a unique reference number.

(3) An individual to whom a certificate is issued must preserve the certificate until no further benefit crystallisation event can occur.

16 Aggregate certificates

(1) This regulation applies if–

(a) an individual is a relevant overseas individual during any part of a period that is the active membership period in relation to an arrangement relating to an individual, and

(b) condition A, B or C is met.

(2) Condition A is that–

(a) the individual has given a notification under regulation 7 to the Revenue and Customs in relation to a part of the active membership period, and

(b) the individual gives a further notification under regulation 7 to the Revenue and Customs in relation to a further part of the same active membership period.

(3) Condition B is that–

(a) the Revenue and Customs have issued a certificate to an individual in response to a notification under regulation 7 given by the individual in relation to a part of the active membership period, and

(b) the individual gives a further notification under regulation 7 to the Revenue and Customs in relation to a further part of the same active membership period.

(4) Condition C is that–

(a) the Revenue and Customs have issued a certificate to an individual in response to a notification under regulation 7 given by the individual in relation to a part of the active membership period, and

(b) the Revenue and Customs issue a further certificate to the individual in response to a further notification under regulation 7 given by the individual in relation to a further part of the same active membership period.

(5) The individual may require the Revenue and Customs to issue a single certificate (an 'aggregate certificate') to the individual.

(6) An aggregate certificate supersedes the certificates mentioned in paragraphs (3)(a) and (4).

(7) If the Revenue and Customs issue an aggregate certificate to an individual, paragraphs (6) to (10) of regulation 7 apply as if the aggregate certificate were the certificate referred to in paragraph (5)(b) of that regulation.

(8) Any notification mentioned in this regulation must be given on or before the closing date; and regulation 7 applies to find the closing date for a notification mentioned in this regulation in the same way as it applies to find the closing date for a notification given under that regulation.

17 Incorrect information given in connection with notification

(1) This regulation applies if–

(a) after the giving of a notification, the Revenue and Customs have issued a certificate ('the first certificate') to an individual, and

(b) either condition A or condition B is met.

(2) Condition A is that the individual informs the Revenue and Customs that information given in the notification was incorrect or has become incorrect.

(3) Condition B is that the individual informs the Revenue and Customs that information given in connection with the notification was incorrect or has become incorrect.

(4) The Revenue and Customs may revoke the first certificate and issue an amended certificate to the individual.

(5) The amended certificate supersedes the first certificate.

(6) If an individual realises that any information given in the notification, or given in connection with the notification, was incorrect or has become incorrect, the individual must inform the Revenue and Customs without undue delay.

(7) If condition A is met, the individual must inform the Revenue and Customs in a form prescribed by the Commissioners for Her Majesty's Revenue and Customs.

18 Incorrect information given in certificate

(1) This regulation applies if–

(a) the Revenue and Customs have issued a certificate ('the first certificate') to an individual, and

(b) the individual informs the Revenue and Customs that information given in the certificate was incorrect or has become incorrect.

(2) The Revenue and Customs may–

(a) revoke the first certificate,

(b) revoke the first certificate and issue an amended certificate to the individual, or

(c) issue an additional certificate to the individual.

(3) The amended certificate supersedes the first certificate.

(4) This regulation is subject to regulation 16.

(5) If an individual realises that any information given in the certificate was incorrect or has become incorrect, the individual must inform the Revenue and Customs without undue delay.

19 Further supply of information given in certificate

(1) This regulation applies if, after the Revenue and Customs have issued a certificate to an individual, the individual no longer possesses information given in the certificate.

(2) The individual may require the Revenue and Customs to give the information to the individual.

Compliance

20 Review of notification after certificate issued

(1) This regulation applies if–

(a) an individual has given a notification to the Revenue and Customs, and

(b) the Revenue and Customs have issued a certificate to the individual in response to the giving of the notification.

(2) The Revenue and Customs may review any information given–

(a) in the notification, or

(b) in connection with the notification.

(3) The Revenue and Customs may begin a review under this regulation at any time within a period of twelve months beginning with the day on which the notification was given to them.

(4) The procedure to be followed on the review is set out in regulation 22.

21 Review of notification after receipt of further information

(1) This regulation applies if–

(a) an individual has given a notification to the Revenue and Customs,

(b) the Revenue and Customs have issued a certificate to the individual in response to the giving of the notification, and

(c) after the certificate has been issued, the Revenue and Customs have reason to believe that information given in the notification, given in connection with the notification, or given in the certificate, either was incorrect or has become incorrect.

(2) The Revenue and Customs may review any information given in the notification, in connection with the notification, or in the certificate.

(3) The Revenue and Customs may begin a review under this regulation at any time.

(4) The procedure to be followed on the review is set out in regulation 22.

22 Reviews of notifications: procedure to be followed

(1) This regulation applies if the Revenue and Customs decide to begin a review under regulation 20 or 21.

(2) The Revenue and Customs must give notice to the individual requiring the individual to provide any information, particulars and documents specified in the notice which the Revenue and Customs may reasonably require.

(3) A notice under this regulation must specify the period within which it is to be complied with; and that period may not end earlier than the period of 30 days beginning with the day on which the notice is given.

(4) An individual may comply with a notice under this regulation requiring the production of a document by producing a copy of the document.

(5) But where an individual produces a copy of a document in compliance with a notice under this regulation, the Revenue and Customs may by notice require the production of the original for inspection within a period specified in the notice; and that period may not end earlier than the period of 30 days beginning with the day on which the notice is given.

(6) The Revenue and Customs may take copies of, or make extracts from, any document produced in compliance with a notice under this section.

(7) A notice under this section does not require an individual–

(a) to produce or make available for inspection any document, or

(b) to provide any particulars,

relating to any pending appeal by the individual relating to tax.

23 Appeals against notices under regulation 22

Section 253 (appeal against notices) applies to a notice under regulation 22 as it applies to a notice under section 252(1).

24 Revocation or amendment of certificate

(1) The Revenue and Customs may revoke or amend a certificate at any time if–

(a) after the certificate has been issued, the Revenue and Customs have reason to believe that any information given in the notification, given in connection with the notification, or given in the certificate, either was incorrect or has become incorrect, or

(b) after notice has been given to an individual under regulation 22, the individual does not reply to the notice within the time specified in the notice.

(2) If the Revenue and Customs revoke or amend a certificate, they must give notice to the individual of the revocation or amendment.

(3) The individual may appeal to the Commissioners against the revocation or amendment of the certificate.

(4) The appeal is to the General Commissioners, except that the individual may elect (in accordance with section 46(1) of the Taxes Management Act 1970) to bring the appeal before the Special Commissioners instead of the General Commissioners.

(5) The notice of appeal must be given to the Revenue and Customs within 30 days after the day on which notice of the revocation or amendment is given to the individual.

(6) On an appeal, the Commissioners shall determine whether the Revenue and Customs revoked or amended the certificate in the circumstances specified in paragraph (1).

(7) If the Commissioners allow the appeal, they may direct the Revenue and Customs to issue a certificate to the individual with effect from a date specified by the Commissioners.

(8) If the Revenue and Customs revoke a certificate and, on appeal, the Commissioners determine that the certificate should have been amended, the Commissioners shall order that the certificate shall be amended in such terms as the Commissioners may specify.

(9) If the Revenue and Customs amend a certificate and, on appeal, the Commissioners determine that the certificate should have been amended in other terms, the Commissioners shall order that the certificate shall be amended in such terms as the Commissioners may specify.

Supplementary

25 Special classes of individuals

(1) If an individual is a person who is incapable, by reason of mental disorder, of managing and administering his property and affairs, anything under these Regulations which could have been done by the individual may be done–

(a) in England and Wales or Northern Ireland, by the individual's attorney or receiver, or the person managing and administering the individual's property and affairs,

(b) in Scotland, by the individual's guardian within the meaning of the Adults with Incapacity (Scotland) Act 2000, and

(c) in a country or territory outside the United Kingdom, by a person authorised by a Court having jurisdiction, in that country or territory, to regulate the property and affairs of an individual to whom this paragraph applies.

(2) If an individual is a person who is suffering from a physical disability, by reason of which that person has difficulty executing documents in respect of the management and administration of his property and affairs, anything under these Regulations which could have been done by the individual may be done–

(a) in the United Kingdom, by a person having a power of attorney in relation to the individual's property and affairs, and

(b) in a country or territory outside the United Kingdom, by a person authorised, under the laws of that country or territory, to execute documents in relation to the individual's property and affairs.

26 Personal representatives

If an individual dies, anything under these Regulations which could have been done by the individual may be done by the individual's personal representatives.

Appendix 3

Registered Pension Schemes (Meaning of Pension Commencement Lump Sum) Regulations 2006

No 135

Citationand commencement

1

These Regulations may be cited as the Registered Pension Schemes (Meaning of Pension Commencement Lump Sum) Regulations 2006, and shall come into force on 6th April 2006.

Application of these Regulations: general

2

These Regulations apply for the purposes of paragraph 1(6) of Schedule 29 to the Finance Act 2004 (regulations relating to meaning of ′pension commencement lump sum′).

Circumstances in which these Regulations apply

3

The circumstances in which incorrect income tax has been paid by the scheme administrator in relation to the member by way of the lifetime allowance charge are circumstances in which–

(a) the scheme administrator has made an overpayment by way of the lifetime allowance charge in relation to the member, and

(b) Her Majesty's Revenue and Customs refund the overpayment to the scheme administrator.

4

The circumstances in which a lump sum subsequently paid to the member is to be treated as a pension commencement lump sum even though either or both of the conditions in paragraphs (c) and (e) of paragraph 1(1) of Schedule 29 to the Finance Act 2004 are not met are circumstances in which–

(a) Her Majesty's Revenue and Customs refund an overpayment by way of the lifetime allowance charge in relation to the member to the scheme administrator, and

(b) the scheme administrator pays part or all of the overpayment to the member within the period of three months beginning with the day on which the scheme administrator receives the overpayment from Her Majesty's Revenue and Customs.

Appendix 4

Registered Pension Schemes (Modification of the Rules of Existing Schemes) Regulations 2006

No 364

1 Citation, commencement and interpretation

(1) These Regulations may be cited as the Registered Pension Schemes (Modification of the Rules of Existing Schemes) Regulations 2006 and shall come into force on 6th April 2006.

(2) In these Regulations–

'the Act' means the Finance Act 2004 and a reference (without more) to a numbered provision is a reference to the provision of the Act bearing that number;

'the commencement day' means 6th April 2006;

'existing scheme' means a pension scheme to which paragraph 1(1) of Schedule 36 applies;

'the permitted maximum'–

(a) in relation to times before the commencement day, has the meaning which it has by virtue of section 590C of the Income and Corporation Taxes Act 1988; and

(b) in relation to times during the transitional period has the meaning which it would have had if–

(i) section 590C of the Income and Corporation Taxes Act 1988 (permitted maximum) had continued in force, and

(ii) the Treasury had made the orders required by that section, as it had effect immediately before its repeal, in respect of each tax year during that period;

'rules', in relation to an existing scheme, means the rules (whether contained in the governing instruments or otherwise) of an existing scheme;

'the transitional period', in relation to an existing scheme, means the period beginning with the commencement day and ending with the date on which, by virtue of paragraph 3(2) of Schedule 36, the modifications in these Regulations cease to have effect.

(3) In the application of these Regulations to an annuity contract falling within paragraph 1(1)(d) of Schedule 36, references to the trustees or managers of a scheme are to be read as references to the insurance company with whom that contract is made.

(4) For the purposes of these Regulations whether something would have prejudiced the approval of an existing scheme by the Inland Revenue or by Her Majesty's Revenue and Customs is to be determined–

(a) in the case of an occupational pension scheme, in accordance with the publication IR 12(2001) (known as the Occupational Pension Scheme Practice Notes) published by the former Inland Revenue Pension Scheme Office on 23rd March 2001 , and

(b) in the case of a personal pension scheme, in accordance with the publication IR 76(2000) published by the former Inland Revenue Pension Scheme Office on 20th November 2000,

as each of those publications stood immediately before the making of these Regulations.

2 Existing schemes to which these Regulations apply

Each of the following provisions of these Regulations apply to existing schemes, unless–

(a) before the commencement day amendments have been adopted, to have effect on and after that day, which have a corresponding effect to the modification contained in that provision; or

(b) the rules of the scheme are framed in a way which means that no such amendment is necessary.

3 Schemes rules not to require the making of unauthorised payments

(1) Any provision (however framed) in the rules of an existing scheme as they stood immediately before the commencement day, which would require the trustees or managers of the scheme–

(a) to make a payment which, by virtue of section 160 would be an unauthorised payment, or

(b) to make such a payment if the consent of the sponsoring employer or any other person was given for their doing so,

shall be construed, in respect of the transitional period, as conferring a discretion upon the trustees or managers to make that payment.

This is subject to the following qualification.

(2) If, immediately before the commencement day, the consent of a sponsoring employer, or any other person, was required before the trustees or managers of a pension scheme could make any other discretionary payment under the scheme, then the discretion conferred by paragraph (1) may only be exercised with the consent of that person.

4 References to the permitted maximum

(1) If the rules of an existing scheme, as they stood immediately before the commencement day, imposed a limit on a person's entitlement to any benefit, or liability to make any contribution, by reference to the permitted maximum (whether expressly or by necessary implication), paragraph (2) applies.

(2) If this paragraph applies, the permitted maximum shall continue to apply in respect of the transitional period.

5 Limits on amounts of remuneration to be taken into account

(1) This paragraph applies in the case of the rules of an existing scheme which becomes a registered pension scheme by virtue of paragraph 1(1)(a), (c) or (d) of Schedule 36–

(a) where the existing scheme came into existence before 14th March 1989, as regards an employee who became a member of that scheme on or after 1st June 1989;

(b) where the existing scheme came into existence on or after 14th March 1989, as regards any employee who is a member of that scheme (whenever he became a member).

This paragraph is subject to the following qualifications.

(2) Paragraph (1) does not apply to the rules of an existing scheme in their application to an employee to whom paragraph 20 of Schedule 6 to the Finance Act 1989 did not apply, immediately before its repeal, by virtue of regulation 3(2), (3), (4), (6) or (8) or 3A(2) of the Continuation of Rights Regulations.

(3) If, and to the extent that, paragraph (1) applies, paragraphs (4) to (7) have effect–

(a) in respect of the transitional period and

(b) regardless of anything contained in the rules of the existing scheme to the contrary.

(4) In arriving at the employee's relevant annual remuneration for the purposes of calculating benefits, any excess of what would be the employee's relevant annual remuneration (apart from this paragraph) over the permitted maximum for the year of assessment in which his participation in the scheme ceases shall be disregarded.

(5) In arriving at the employee's remuneration for the year 2006–07 or any subsequent year of assessment for the purposes of any restriction on the aggregate amount of contributions payable under the scheme by the employee and the employer, there shall be disregarded any excess of what would be his remuneration for the year (apart from this paragraph) over the permitted maximum for the year.

(6) If–

(a) a transfer payment having been accepted by the existing scheme under its rules, the payment has been treated as entitling the employee to be regarded as having additional years of service ('inserted years'), and

(b) by virtue of the modification of paragraph 20 of Schedule 6 to the Finance Act 1989 contained in regulation 5 of the Continuation of Rights Regulations that paragraph did not apply to the inserted years, but did apply to the member's actual years of service,

paragraph (5) applies only to the computation of pension benefits so far as they are referable to the member's actual years of service.

(7) The amount of contributions payable under the scheme by an employee in the year 2006–07 or any subsequent year of assessment shall be limited to 15 per cent of the employee's remuneration for the year in respect of the employment.

(8) In this regulation 'the Continuation of Rights Regulations' means the Retirement Benefits Schemes (Continuation of Rights of Members of Approved Schemes) Regulations 1990.

6 Payments not prejudicing HM Revenue and Customs approval

(1) If the rules of an existing scheme–

(a) provide for an absolute entitlement to the making of a transfer or the payment of a specified sum or rate of pension; and

(b) refer (in whatever terms) to the possibility of making a transfer or a payment in any greater amount which would not prejudice approval of the scheme by–

(i) the Inland Revenue, or

(ii) Her Majesty's Revenue and Customs,

the following provisions of this regulation apply.

(2) The scheme's rules shall be construed, in respect of the transitional period, as–

(a) authorising the trustees or managers of the scheme to make transfers or payments falling within paragraph (1)(b) only to the extent that the payments would have been authorised by the rules immediately before the coming into force of these Regulations; and

(b) to prohibit the making of transfers or payments which would not have been so authorised.

This is subject to the following qualification.

(3) If, immediately before the commencement day, the consent of a sponsoring employer, or any other person except Her Majesty's Revenue and Customs, was required before the trustees or managers of a pension scheme could make a payment of the kind referred to in paragraph (1)(b), then the power conferred by paragraph (2)(a) may only be exercised with the consent of that person.

7 Limits on payments in amounts 'which would not prejudice Revenue approval'

(1) If the rules of an existing scheme provide for an absolute entitlement to–

(a) the making of a transfer, or

(b) the payment of a specified sum or rate of pension,

in an amount which would not prejudice approval of the scheme by the Inland Revenue or Her Majesty's Revenue and Customs, paragraph (2) applies.

(2) If this paragraph applies the rules of the existing scheme shall be construed, in respect of the transitional period, as prohibiting the trustees or managers of the scheme from making payments to the extent that they would not have been authorised by the rules immediately before the commencement day.

8 Recovery of tax in respect of lifetime allowance charge

(1) The rules of an existing scheme shall be modified, during the transitional period, so as to provide for the recovery, from present or future benefits or entitlement under the scheme in respect of a member, of an amount reflecting any liability of the scheme administrator in respect of the lifetime allowance charge under section 215 in respect of that member.

But this does not authorise the reduction of entitlement to a benefit which has not crystallised, except that in relation to which the lifetime allowance charge arises.

(2) The methods of recovery authorised by virtue of paragraph (1) include reduction of benefits or entitlement determined in accordance with normal actuarial practice.

This paragraph does not limit the generality of paragraph (1).

Appendix 5

Registered Pension Schemes (Uprating Percentages for Defined Benefits Arrangements and Enhanced Protection Limits) Regulations 2006

No 130

1 Citation, commencement and interpretation

(1) These Regulations may be cited as the Registered Pension Schemes (Uprating Percentages for Defined Benefits Arrangements and Enhanced Protection Limits) Regulations 2006 and shall come into force on 6th April 2006.

(2) In these Regulations a reference to a numbered section or Schedule (without more) is a reference to the section of, or Schedule to, the Finance Act 2004 which bears that number.

(3) In the application of these Regulations to Northern Ireland, a reference to an enactment applying only in Great Britain shall be construed as including a reference to any enactment having corresponding effect in Northern Ireland.

2 Percentage referred to for the purposes of section 235(3)(c)

(1) For the purpose of section 235(3)(c) (defined benefits arrangements: uprating of opening value) the percentage to which these Regulations refer is the percentage found as follows.

(2) In this regulation 'the relevant percentage' is any of–

(a) the percentage by which the individual's guaranteed minimum pension rights falls to be adjusted by virtue of one or more orders under section 148 of the Social Security Administration Act 1992;

(b) the percentage by which the individual's earnings factors in respect of contracted-out employment by reference to the scheme shall be taken to be increased in accordance with section 16 of the Pension Schemes Act 1993 (revaluation of earnings factors);

(c) the percentage by which the individual's occupational pension falls to be adjusted by virtue of the application of subsections (1) and (2) of section 84 of the Pension Schemes Act 1993 (which provide that the method of revaluation is to be the final salary method except where the trustees or managers otherwise provide); or

(d) the percentage by which a pension, payment of which has been deferred until after normal pension age in accordance with the rules of the pension scheme in question, falls to be increased so that the scheme's trustees or managers can be reasonably satisfied that, when the member's benefit becomes payable, the total value of the benefits provided under regulation 8 of the Occupational Pension Schemes (Preservation of Benefit) Regulations 1991(early retirement or deferred retirement) is at least equal to the amount prescribed in regulation 11 of those Regulations (value of alternatives to short service benefit).

(3) The percentage in a particular case is found as follows.

Step 1

Determine whether any of the relevant percentages applies to the defined benefit arrangement.

Step 2

If any of the relevant percentages applies to the arrangement, determine whether that percentage applies to the whole of the arrangement.

Step 3

If one relevant percentage applies to the whole of the arrangement, that is the percentage to which these Regulations refer.

Step 4

If different percentages apply to different parts of the arrangement, the percentage to which these Regulations refer is that found by the formula–

$$(RP1 \times (P1 / W)) + (RP2 \times (P2 / W)) + (RP3 \times (P3 / W)) + (RP4 \times (P4 / W)) + (SP \times (1 - (PT / W)))$$

Here–

RP is the relevant percentage;

P is the amount of that part of the individual's rights under the arrangement to which the relevant percentage applies;

W is the whole amount of the individual's rights under the arrangement; and

SP is the greater of–

(a) 5%, or

(b) the percentage (if any) by which the retail prices index for the month in which the pension input period ends is higher than it was for the month in which it began;

PT is the sum of the amounts of *P1, P2, P3* and *P4*;

(c) expressions with the suffix 1 refer to the percentage described in paragraph (2)(a);

(d) expressions with the suffix 2 refer to the percentage described in paragraph (2)(b);

(e) expressions with the suffix 3 refer to the percentage described in paragraph (2)(c);

(f) expressions with the suffix 4 refer to the percentage described in paragraph (2)(d).

This step is subject to paragraph (4).

(4) If–

(a) any relevant percentage is a value less than the greater of–

(i) 5%, or

(ii) the percentage (if any) by which the retail prices index for the month in which the pension input period ends is higher than it was for the month in which it began;

the value shall instead be taken to be whichever is the greater of the two values given in this sub-paragraph;

(b) two or more relevant percentages apply to the same part of the arrangement, the value of P1, P2, P3 or P4 (as the case may be) is found by determining which of those relevant percentages produces the greatest increase in the opening value in the pension input period in question.

3 Percentage increases in enhanced protection limits

(1) For the purposes of paragraph 15(5)(b) of Schedule 36 (relevant indexation percentage for the purposes of the appropriate limit in relation to a relevant event), the annual percentage rate referred to in these Regulations is found by the formula–

$$((RP1 \times (P1 / W)) + (RP2 \times (P2 / W)) + (RP3 \times (P3 / W)) + (RP4 \times (P4 / W)) + (PP \times (1 - (PT / W)))) / (MRE / 12)$$

(2) In paragraph (1)–

terms defined in regulation 2(3) bear the same meaning as they do there;

MRE is the number of complete tax months which have elapsed since 6th April 2006 at the time when the relevant event occurs; and

PP is the greater of–

(a) an annual rate of 5% for the period beginning on 6th April 2006 and ending with the last day of the tax month in which the relevant event occurs, or

(b) the percentage (if any) by which the retail prices index for the month in which the relevant event occurs is higher than it was for April 2006;

(3) For the purposes of paragraphs 16(5A)(b) and 17(6)(b) of Schedule 36 (relevant indexation percentages for the purposes of limit on post-commencement earnings) the annual percentage rate referred to in these Regulations is that which would be found by the formula in paragraph (1) if–

(a) for MRE there were substituted MBE, where MBE is the number of complete tax months between the date on which the appropriate three year period ends and the date of the first relevant event; and

(b) in the definition of PP–

(i) in paragraph (a) for '6th April 2006' there were substituted 'the first day of the tax month in which the appropriate period ends'; and

(ii) in paragraph (b) for 'April 2006' there were substituted 'the month in which the appropriate period ends'.

(4) In this regulation 'tax month' means the period beginning on the 6th day of a calendar month and ending on the 5th day of the following calendar month.

Appendix 6

Taxation of Pension Schemes (Transitional Provisions) Order 2006

No 572

38 Lump sum payments–general

(1) This paragraph applies to a lump sum payment–

(a) the entirety of which is made in accordance with the rules of the existing scheme as they stood immediately before the 6th April 2006;

(b) which is made on or after the 6th April 2006 but before 6th July 2006;

(c) to which the member became entitled before the 6th April 2006;

(d) which would not have given the Commissioners grounds for withdrawing approval of the scheme had it been made before the 6th April 2006; and

(e) which is not a lump sum paid in circumstances of the member's serious ill-health.

(2) In this article and articles 39, 40 and 41–

'the 1995 Regulations' means the Retirement Benefits Schemes (Information Powers) Regulations 1995;

'the Commissioners' means the Commissioners for Her Majesty's Revenue and Customs and, in relation to times before 18th April 2005, includes the Commissioners of Inland Revenue;

'existing scheme' means a scheme which becomes a registered pension scheme by virtue of paragraph 1(1) of Schedule 36 (pension schemes etc: transitional provisions and savings –deemed registration of existing schemes);

'lump sum paid in circumstances of the member's serious ill-health' has the meaning given in article 39(3);

'member' means a member of an existing scheme;

(3) A payment to which paragraph (1) applies shall be chargeable to income tax in accordance with section 598, 599 or 599A of ICTA (which deal respectively with charges to tax on repayment of employee's contributions, on the commutation of the entire pension in special circumstances and on payments out of surplus funds), or Chapter 13 of Part 9 of ITEPA 2003 (return of employee's additional voluntary contributions) (as the case requires)–

(a) to the same extent as it would have been if the provision in question had not been repealed; and

(b) as if the references in section 598(2), 599(3) and section 599A(2)(b) of ICTA to the administrator of the scheme were instead references to the scheme administrator (within the meaning of section 270) of the registered pension scheme which is treated as coming into being by virtue of paragraph 1(1) of Schedule 36.

(4) For the purposes of a lump sum payment to which paragraph (1) applies, regulations 10 and 11 of the 1995 Regulations (reporting of chargeable events) shall continue to have effect, subject to the following modifications–

(a) in paragraph (1) for the words preceding sub-paragraph (a) substitute–

'The scheme administrator of the registered pension scheme which, immediately before the coming into force of Part 4 of the Finance Act 2004, was both a retirement benefits scheme and–';

(b) in paragraph (3) omit sub-paragraph (d); and

(c) omit paragraph (4).

(5) In section 98(5) of the Taxes Management Act 1970 the entry in Table 1 relating to regulations under section 605(1A) of ICTA shall continue to have effect so far as it relates to regulations 10 and 11 of the 1995 Regulations as saved, with modifications, by paragraph (4).

39 Lump sums–serious ill-health

(1) This article applies to a lump sum–

(a) paid to a member in circumstances of the member's serious ill-health; and

(b) which satisfies the requirements set out in sub-paragraphs (a) to (d) of article 38(1).

(2) There is no charge to tax under Part 4 on a lump sum to which paragraph (1) applies.

(3) A lump sum is paid in circumstances of the member's serious ill-health if–

(a) before it is paid the scheme administrator, or the administrator of the scheme which became a registered pension scheme on the 6th April 2006, received evidence from a registered medical practitioner that the member is expected to live for less than one year; and

(b) all of the member's uncrystallised rights under the scheme making the payment, other than those which are–

(i) required to be maintained in order to meet contracted-out rights or safeguarded rights, or

(ii) retained by the scheme in accordance with its rules as they stood immediately before the 6th April 2006 to provide benefits for the member's dependants,

are paid out as a lump sum.

(4) In paragraph (3)(b)(i)–

'contracted-out rights' means–

(a) entitlement to payment of, or accrued rights to–

(i) guaranteed minimum pensions within the meaning of section 8(2) of the Pension Schemes Act 1993; and

(ii) a pension in respect of protected rights within the meaning of section 10 of that Act;

(b) section 9(2B) rights within the meaning of regulation 1(2) of the Occupational Pension Schemes (Contracting-Out) Regulations 1996, or

(c) any of the rights in sub-paragraphs (a), (b) or (c) which themselves derive from any of those rights which have been the subject of a transfer payment; and

'safeguarded rights' have the same meaning as in section 68A of the Pension Schemes Act 1993.

(5) In the application of this article to Northern Ireland, a reference to a provision applying only in Great Britain shall be construed as a reference to any provision having corresponding effect in Northern Ireland.

40 Lump sum death benefits–death of member

(1) This paragraph applies to a lump sum paid–

(a) in respect of the death, occurring before the 6th April 2006, of a member of a pension scheme;

(b) within two years of the member's death;

(c) by a scheme which is treated as becoming a registered pension scheme on the 6th April 2006 by virtue of paragraph 1(1) of Schedule 36;

(d) in accordance with the rules of that scheme as they stood–

(i) immediately before the death; or

(ii) immediately before the 6th April 2006; and

(e) in circumstances which would not have given the Commissioners grounds for withdrawing the approval of the scheme.

(2) A lump sum to which paragraph (1) applies is not a relevant lump sum death benefit as defined in paragraph 16 of Schedule 32, and the payment of such a death benefit is to be disregarded for the purposes of benefit crystallisation event 7.

(3) A lump sum to which paragraph (1) applies shall be chargeable to income tax in accordance with section 648B of ICTA as if–

(a) that section had not been repealed;

(b) references in that section to the administrator of the scheme were references to the scheme administrator of the registered pension scheme which is treated as coming into being by virtue of paragraph 1(1)(g) of Schedule 36;

(c) subsection (3) were omitted; and

(d) the reference in subsection (4) to the rules of the scheme were a reference to the rules of the personal pension scheme as they stood immediately before the 6th April 2006.

(4) For the purposes of a lump sum payment to which paragraph (1) applies, regulation 5 of the Personal Pension Schemes (Information Powers) Regulations 2000 ('the 2000 Regulations') shall continue to have effect, subject to the following modifications–

(a) references to the scheme administrator of the personal pension scheme are to be read as references to the scheme administrator of the registered pension scheme which is treated as coming into being by virtue of paragraph 1(1)(g) of Schedule 36; and

(b) in paragraph (2) of that regulation for 'an approved personal pension scheme' substitute 'the registered pension scheme'.

(5) In section 98(5) of the Taxes Management Act 1970 the entry in Table 1 relating to regulations under section 651A(1)(b) to (d) of ICTA shall continue to have effect, so far as it relates to regulation 5 of the 2000 Regulations as saved, with modifications, by paragraph (4).

41 Lump sum death benefits–death of a dependant

(1) This paragraph applies to a lump sum paid–

(a) in respect of the death, occurring before the 6th April 2006, of a dependant of a former member of a pension scheme;

(b) by a scheme which is treated as becoming a registered pension scheme on the 6th April 2006 by virtue of paragraph 1(1)(g) of Schedule 36 (personal pension schemes);

(c) within two years of the dependant's death;

(d) in accordance with the rules of that scheme as they stood–

(i) immediately before the dependant's death; or

(ii) immediately before the 6th April 2006; and

(e) in circumstances which would not have given the Commissioners grounds for withdrawing the approval of the scheme.

(2) Paragraphs (3) to (5) of article 40 apply for the purposes of paragraph (1) as they apply for the purposes of paragraph (1) of that article.

Appendix 7

Retirement Benefits Schemes (Information Powers) Regulations 1995

No 3103

Part I
Introductory

Citation and commencement

1

These Regulations may be cited as the Retirement Benefits Schemes (Information Powers) Regulations 1995 and shall come into force on 1st January 1996.

Interpretation

2

[(1)] In these Regulations unless the context otherwise requires–

'actuary' means–

(a) a Fellow of the Institute of Actuaries, or

(b) a Fellow of the Faculty of Actuaries, or

(c) person with other actuarial qualifications who has been approved as being a proper person to act for the purposes of regulation 8 of the Occupational Pension Schemes (Disclosure of Information) Regulations 1986 in connection with the scheme;

'approved', in relation to a retirement benefits scheme, means–

(a) approved by the Board for the purposes of Chapter I, or

(b) before the Board in order for them to decide whether to give approval for the purposes of that Chapter;

'the Board' means the Commissioners of Inland Revenue;

'Chapter I' means Chapter I of Part XIV of the Taxes Act;

'company' means any body corporate or unincorporated association, but does not include a partnership;

['controlling director' in relation to a company means a person who is, or was within the ten years immediately preceding the event in question–

(a) a director as defined in section 612(1) of the Taxes Act (interpretation for the purposes of Chapter 1 of Part 14), and

(b) within paragraph (b) of section 417(5) of the Taxes Act (meaning of director for the purposes of provisions about close companies);]

['electronic communications' includes any communications conveyed by means of an electronic communications network;]

'exempt approved scheme' means an approved scheme which is for the time being within paragraph (a) or (b) of section 592(1) of the Taxes Act;

'friendly society' has the meaning given by section 116 of the Friendly Societies Act 1992;

['governing instrument' in relation to a retirement benefits scheme means a trust deed, or other document by which the scheme is established, and any other document (except an enactment) which contains provisions by which the administration of the scheme is governed;]

'insurance company' has the meaning given by section 659B of the Taxes Act;

'insured scheme' means an approved scheme, the contributions to which, apart from voluntary contributions made by members, are invested wholly by way of insurance premiums, and the policies in respect of which do not provide that levels of contributions require to take account of surpluses, but does not include a scheme–

(a) the policies in respect of which provide only for lump sum benefits for members on death before the normal retirement date, or

(b) which is a simplified defined contribution scheme;

'large self-administered scheme' means a self-administered scheme which is not a small self-administered scheme and is not a simplified defined contribution scheme;

'member', in relation to a retirement benefits scheme, means a member of the scheme to whom benefit is currently accruing as a result of service as an employee;

'normal retirement date' means the date specified in the rules of a retirement benefits scheme as the date at which an employee will normally retire;

'permitted maximum' has the meaning given by section 590C of the Taxes Act;

'relevant statutory scheme' has the meaning given by section 611A of the Taxes Act;

'retirement benefits scheme' has the meaning given by section 611(1) of the Taxes Act;

'scheme year' means–

(a) a year specified for the purposes of the scheme in any document comprising the scheme or, if no year is specified, a period of 12 months commencing on 1st April or on such other date as the trustees select; or

(b) such other period (if any) exceeding 6 months but not exceeding 18 months as is selected by the trustees–

(i) in respect of the scheme year in which the scheme commences or terminates, or

(ii) in connection with a variation of the date on which the scheme year is to commence;

'self-administered scheme' means an approved scheme some or all of the income and other assets of which are invested otherwise than in insurance policies;

'shares' includes stock;

['signed' in relation to a document includes the incorporation in it, or the logical association with it, of an electronic signature, as defined in section 7(2) of the Electronic Communications Act 2000;]

'simplified defined contribution scheme' means a retirement benefits scheme approved by the Board by reference to limitations on–

(a) the aggregate amount of the contributions which may be paid by a member and his employer,

(b) the maximum lump sum which may be provided under the scheme, and

(c) the benefits payable on death which may be provided under the scheme;

['small self-administered scheme' means an approved scheme which is a small self-administered scheme within the meaning given by regulation 2(1) of the 1991 Regulations;]

'special contribution' means any contribution paid to a retirement benefits scheme by an employer which is neither a fixed amount paid annually, whether in instalments or otherwise nor an annual amount, that is payable over a period of three years or more and is calculated on a consistent basis in accordance with actuarial principles by reference to the earnings, contributions or number of members of the scheme;

'Taxes Act' means the Income and Corporation Taxes Act 1988;

…

'1991 Regulations' means the Retirement Benefits Schemes (Restriction on Discretion to Approve) (Small Self-administered Schemes) Regulations 1991.

[(2) In these Regulations, a reference to a notice or other document (other than a consent under paragraph (3) below) includes a notice or other document in such form and delivered by such means of electronic communications as the Board may approve by directions.

(3) The Board or an officer of theirs shall only deliver a notice or other document under these Regulations to a person by means of electronic communications if that person–

(a) has given his consent in writing to the delivery of documents by the Board by that means; and

(b) has not notified the Board that that consent has been withdrawn.]

Part II
Information Required Without Notice

Prescribed person

3

For the purposes of this Part of these Regulations, 'the prescribed person' in relation to a retirement benefits scheme means–

(a) the person who is, or the persons who are, for the time being the administrator in relation to the scheme by virtue of section 611AA of the Taxes Act; or

(b) where section 606(1) of the Taxes Act applies at any time in relation to the scheme, the person who is, or the persons who are, by virtue of that section responsible at that time for the discharge of all duties imposed on the administrator under Chapter I (whenever arising) and liable for any tax due from the administrator in the administrator's capacity as such (whenever falling due); or

(c) where section 599(7) of the Taxes Act applies in relation to an insurance company, that insurance company.

Actuarial valuation reports–self-administered schemes and insured schemes

4

(1) The prescribed person in relation to a self-administered scheme or an insured scheme shall furnish to the Board, at the time prescribed by paragraph (2) below, any valuation report of the scheme's assets in relation to its liabilities having an effective date that falls on or after the date of coming into force of these Regulations, where the report–

(a) was commissioned for the purposes of the scheme, and

(b) consists of an actuarial valuation determined and dated and signed by an actuary.

(2) The time prescribed–

(a) where the valuation report relates to a large self-administered scheme or an insured scheme, is any time not later than two years after the date stated to be the effective date in the valuation;

(b) where the valuation report relates to a small self-administered scheme, is any time not later than one year after the date stated to be the effective date in the valuation.

Investment and borrowing transactions of small self-administered schemes

5

(1) The prescribed person in relation to a small self-administered scheme shall furnish to the Board, at the time prescribed by paragraph (2) below, such information (including copies of any relevant books, documents or other records) as–

(a) is specified on the relevant form supplied by [or in the relevant document delivered by] the Board, and

(b) relates to any transaction that is–

(i) of a kind specified in paragraph (3) below, and

(ii) entered into by or on behalf of the trustees or the administrator of the scheme on or after the date of coming into force of these Regulations.

(2) The time prescribed is any time not later than 90 days after the date of the transaction in question.

(3) The transactions specified in this paragraph are–

(a) the acquisition or disposal of land;

(b) the lending of money to an employer in relation to the scheme or any company associated with him;

(c) the acquisition or disposal of shares in an employer in relation to the scheme or any company associated with him;

(d) the acquisition or disposal of shares in an unlisted company;

(e) the borrowing of money;

(f) the purchase, sale or lease from or to an employer in relation to the scheme, or any company associated with him, of any asset other than one specified in sub-paragraph (a), (c) or (d).

[(4) In paragraph (3) above–

(a) 'unlisted company' means a company which is not listed on a recognised stock exchange within the meaning of section 841(1) of the Taxes Act (recognised stock exchanges and recognised investment exchanges), but does not include an open-ended investment company within the meaning of section 236 of the Financial Services and Markets Act 2000 (meaning of open-ended investment company for the purposes of Part 17 of that Act); and

(b) references to a company associated with an employer shall be construed in accordance with regulation 2(9) of the 1991 Regulations.]

Participation of employers in a scheme

6

(1) The prescribed person in relation to an approved scheme shall furnish to the Board, at the time prescribed by paragraph (2) below, such information (including copies of any relevant books, documents or other records) relating to an event specified in paragraph (3) below and occurring on or after the date of coming into force of these Regulations as is specified on the relevant form supplied by [or in the relevant document delivered by] the Board.

(2) The time prescribed is any time not later than 180 days after the end of the scheme year in which the event in question occurs.

(3) The events specified in this paragraph are–

(a) the admission of a new employer as a participant in the scheme;

(b) in relation to any employer who is a participant in the scheme–

(i) a change in his name or address;

(ii) the occasion of his ceasing to carry on a trade or business;

(iii) a change in his association with any other employer who is a participant in the scheme.

(4) For the purposes of paragraph (3)(b)(iii) above, an employer is associated with another employer if–

(a) the association falls within the meaning given by subsection (3) of section 590A of the Taxes Act, read with subsection (4) of that section, or

(b) there exists some other basis of association between the employers which, for the purpose of granting or maintaining approval of the scheme, the Board have accepted as being sufficient to establish a permanent community of interest between the employers, whether by reason of the association falling within any of the situations specified in paragraph (5) below or otherwise.

(5) The situations specified are where–

(a) all the employees of the employers are the same individuals;

(b) the operations of the employers are interdependent;

(c) in the case of employers who are companies, the same individuals comprise the majority of the directors of, or hold the majority of the ordinary share capital in, each of the companies.

Special contributions by employers

7

(1) The prescribed person in relation to an exempt approved scheme shall furnish to the Board, at the time prescribed by paragraph (2) below, such information (including copies of any relevant books, documents or other records) relating to the special contribution specified in paragraph (3) below as is specified on the relevant form supplied by [or in the relevant document delivered by] the Board.

(2) The time prescribed is any time not later than 180 days after the end of the scheme year[, in which there falls the end of the chargeable period, in the course of] which the special contribution was paid to the scheme by the employer.

(3) The special contribution specified in this paragraph is any special contribution paid to the scheme by an employer on or after the date of coming into force of these Regulations, other than a contribution which–

(a) has been certified by an actuary as made solely to finance cost of living increases for existing pensioners under the scheme; or

(b) when aggregated with other special contributions paid by that employer to the scheme in the same chargeable period other than a contribution falling within sub-paragraph (a) above, does not result in an amount which exceeds–

(i) one half of the permitted maximum as at the end of the scheme year referred to in paragraph (2) above, or

(ii) the total contributions, other than special contributions, made by the employer to the scheme in the same chargeable period,

whichever is the greater.

Controlling directors as members of schemes

8

(1) The prescribed person in relation to an approved scheme shall furnish to the Board, at the time prescribed by paragraph (2) below, such information (including copies of any relevant books, documents or other records) relating to an event specified in paragraph (3) below and occurring on or after the date of coming into force of these Regulations as is specified on the relevant form supplied by [or in the relevant document delivered by] the Board.

(2) The time prescribed is any time not later than 180 days after the end of the scheme year in which the event in question occurs.

(3) The events specified in this paragraph are–

[(a) the admission of any person to membership of the scheme who is a controlling director of a company which is an employer in relation to the scheme; or]

(b) the occasion of an existing member of the scheme becoming a controlling director of a company which is an employer in relation to the scheme.

Controlling directors–benefits on retirement due to incapacity or serious ill-health

9

(1) The prescribed person in relation to an approved scheme shall furnish to the Board, at the time prescribed by paragraph (2) below–

(a) notification of any proposal such as is specified in paragraph (3) below and is made on or after the date of coming into force of these Regulations, and

(b) the information specified in paragraph (4) below.

(2) The time prescribed–

(a) in the case of the proposal specified in paragraph (3)(a) below, is any time not less than 28 days prior to the proposed payment of the benefits;

(b) in the case of the proposal specified in paragraph (3)(b) below, is any time not less than 14 days prior to the proposed payment of the benefits.

(3) The proposals specified in this paragraph are–

(a) any proposal for the scheme to pay benefits to a person who is a controlling director of a company which is an employer in relation to the scheme in circumstances where that person is to retire on grounds of incapacity prior to the normal retirement date;

(b) any proposal for the scheme to pay benefits commuted wholly to lump sum form to a person who is a controlling director of a company which is an employer in relation to the scheme in circumstances where that person is to be retired on grounds of serious ill-health.

(4) The information to be furnished shall be in the form of copies of documents relating to the decision of the administrator of the scheme to permit retirement on grounds of incapacity prior to the normal retirement date or, as the case may be, full commutation of benefits to lump sum form on retirement on grounds of serious ill-health, including copies of medical reports and other documents in the possession or under the control of the prescribed person containing details of the medical evidence which formed the basis of that decision.

(5) In this regulation–

'incapacity' means physical or mental deterioration which is sufficiently serious to prevent a person from following his normal employment or which seriously impairs his earning capacity;

'serious ill-health' means ill-health which is such as to give rise to a life expectancy of less than one year.

Reporting of chargeable events

10

(1) A person who is a prescribed person within regulation 3(a) or (b) in relation to a retirement benefits scheme which is–

(a) an approved scheme, or

(b) a relevant statutory scheme established under a public general Act,

shall furnish to the Board, at the time prescribed by paragraph (2) below, such information (including copies of any relevant books, documents or other records) relating to an event specified in paragraph (3) below as is specified on the relevant form supplied by[, or in the relevant document delivered by] the Board.

(2) The time prescribed is any time not later than 30 days after the end of the year of assessment in which the event in question occurs.

(3) The events specified in this paragraph are–

(a) any repayment under the scheme to which section 598 of the Taxes Act applies (repayment of employee's contributions);

(b) any commutation of an employee's pension under the scheme to which section 599 of the Taxes Act applies;

(c) any payment under the scheme to which section 599A of the Taxes Act applies (payment to or for the benefit of an employee or his personal representatives out of surplus funds);

(d) any payment to an employer to which section 601 of the Taxes Act applies (charge to tax on payments to employer out of funds of an exempt approved scheme).

[(4) In this regulation and regulation 11 references to an approved scheme include a scheme which has at any time been approved.]

11

(1) An insurance company which is a prescribed person by virtue of regulation 3(c) in relation to a retirement benefits scheme which is–

(a) an approved scheme, or

(b) a relevant statutory scheme established under a public general Act,

shall furnish to the Board, at the time prescribed by paragraph (2) below, such information (including copies of any relevant books, documents or other records) relating to an event specified in paragraph (3) below as is specified on the relevant form supplied by [or in the relevant document delivered by] the Board.

(2) The time prescribed is any time not later than 180 days after the end of the chargeable period of the insurance company in which the event in question occurs.

(3) The events specified in this paragraph are–

(a) any repayment under the scheme to which section 598 of the Taxes Act applies;

(b) any commutation of an employee's pension under the scheme to which section 599 of the Taxes Act applies;

(c) any payment to an employer to which section 601 of the Taxes Act applies.

[11A

[(1) The prescribed person within regulation 3(a), (b) or (c) in relation to–

(a) an approved retirement benefits scheme,

(b) a relevant statutory scheme, or

(c) an annuity contract referred to in section 605(1B)(c) of the Taxes Act other than a contract which provides for the immediate payment of benefits,

shall furnish to the Board, at the time prescribed by paragraph (2) below, such information (including copies of any relevant books, documents or other records) relating to an event specified in paragraph (3) below, as is specified by the Board.

(2) The time prescribed is any time not later than 28 days after the event in question.

(3) The event specified in this paragraph is one satisfying all the following conditions.

First condition

A transfer payment ('the payment') is made from–

(a) an approved retirement benefits scheme,

(b) a relevant statutory scheme, or

(c) a fund held subject to an annuity contract falling within paragraph (1)(c),

('the paying scheme').

Second condition

The market value of the payment–

(a) equals or exceeds £ 250,000; or

(b) when aggregated with the market value of any other payments relating to the same person, made from the paying scheme within any period of 365 days, beginning with the first of those payments and including the date of the payment in question, equals or exceeds £ 250,000.

Third condition

The payment is not made to a relevant statutory scheme, an approved statutory scheme or an annuity contract which provides for the immediate payment of benefits.]

[11B

[(1) The prescribed person within regulation 3(a), (b) or (c) in relation to–

(a) a retirement benefits scheme for the time being approved by the Board, other than a statutory scheme, or

(b) an annuity contract referred to in section 605(1B)(c) of the Taxes Act, other than a contract which provides for the immediate payment of benefits,

shall furnish to the Board, at the time prescribed by paragraph (2) below, such information (including copies of any relevant books, documents or other records) relating to an event specified in paragraph (3) below, as is specified by the Board.

This is subject to the qualification in paragraph (5).

(2) The time prescribed is any time not later than 28 days after the event in question.

(3) The event is one satisfying both of the following conditions.

First condition

A transfer payment ('the payment') is received by–

(a) a retirement benefits scheme which is for the time being approved by the Board, or

(b) a fund held subject to an annuity contract falling within paragraph (1)(b)

('the receiving scheme').

Second condition

The market value of the payment, when aggregated with the market value of any other transfer payments relating to the same person, made to the receiving scheme within a period of 365 days, beginning with the first such payment and including the date of the payment in question, equals or exceeds £ 250,000.

(4) If a payment has fallen within the second condition in paragraph (3), all subsequent transfer payments made to the receiving scheme within the period referred to in that condition, so far as they relate to the same person, shall be notified individually to the Board by the prescribed person in relation to the receiving scheme.

This is subject to the following qualification.

(5) The prescribed person in relation to the receiving scheme shall not be under an obligation to furnish information under this regulation if the prescribed person in respect of the paying scheme is under an obligation to furnish information in respect of the same transaction under regulation 11A.]

[11C

[(1) In regulations 11A and 11B–

'market value' has the meaning given in section 272 of the Taxation of Chargeable Gains Act 1992 (valuation: general provisions for the purposes of that Act); and

'transfer payment' includes a payment under paragraph 1(3) of Schedule 5 to the Welfare Reform and Pensions Act 1999 or paragraph 1(3) of Schedule 5 to the Welfare Reform and Pensions (Northern Ireland) Order 1999.

(2) In relation to an annuity contract mentioned in section 605(1B)(c) of the Taxes Act, references to a prescribed person within regulation 3 include a reference to the insurance company with which the contract is made.]

Part III
Notices Requiring Particulars and Documents

Approved schemes and relevant statutory schemes

12

(1) The Board may by notice require any of the persons prescribed by paragraph (2) below, within the time prescribed by paragraph (3) below, to furnish to the Board such particulars, and to produce to the Board such documents, as they may reasonably require relating to–

(a) any monies received or receivable by an approved scheme or a relevant statutory scheme, or

(b) any investments or other assets held by that scheme, or

(c) any monies paid or payable out of funds held under that scheme.

(2) The persons prescribed are–

(a) the person who is, or the persons who are, for the time being by virtue of section 611AA of the Taxes Act the administrator of the scheme which is the subject of the notice;

(b) any person who was, or any persons who were, at any time prior to the relevant date by virtue of section 611AA of the Taxes Act the administrator of that scheme, other than an excluded person;

(c) the trustee or trustees of that scheme, or any person who was, or any persons who were, at any time prior to the relevant date the trustee or trustees of that scheme, other than an excluded person;

(d) any person who is, or has been at any time prior to the relevant date, an employer in relation to that scheme, other than an excluded person;

(e) any person who is, or has been at any time prior to the relevant date, a scheme sponsor in relation to that scheme, other than an excluded person;

(f) any person who provides, or has at any time prior to the relevant date provided, administrative services to that scheme, other than an excluded person.

(3) The time prescribed is such time (not being less than 28 days) as may be provided by the notice.

(4) A notice under paragraph (1) above may require particulars to be furnished, and documents to be produced, relating to more than one scheme.

[(4A) In paragraph (1) above 'approved' has the same meaning as in regulation 10.]

(5) In paragraph (2) above–

(a) 'excluded person' means a person who, on ceasing to act in relation to the scheme or, as the case may be, provide administrative services to the scheme, transferred all documents in his possession or under his control relating to the scheme to another person who succeeded him in acting in relation to the scheme or providing administrative services to the scheme;

(b) 'the relevant date' means the date on which the time prescribed by regulation 15(3)(f) ends.

Annuity contracts

13

(1) The Board may by notice require any of the persons prescribed by paragraph (2) below, within the time prescribed by paragraph (3) below, to furnish to the Board such particulars, and to produce to the Board such documents, as they may reasonably require relating to any annuity contract issued by that person by means of which benefits provided under an approved scheme or a relevant statutory scheme have been secured.

(2) The persons prescribed are–

(a) the insurance company which issued the annuity contract, where that company is a body corporate;

(b) the chief executive and the manager, within the meaning of [sections 417(1) and 423 of the Financial Services and Markets Act 2000 respectively], of the insurance company which issued the annuity contract;

(c) the friendly society which issued the annuity contract, where that friendly society is a society incorporated under the Friendly Societies Act 1992;

(d) the chief executive and the secretary, or any assistant or deputy chief executive, or assistant or deputy secretary, of the friendly society which issued the annuity contract.

(3) The time prescribed is such time (not being less than 28 days) as may be provided by the notice.

(4) A notice under paragraph (1) above may require particulars and documents relating to more than one annuity contract.

Part IV
Inspection and Retention of Records

Inspection of records

14

(1) The Board may by notice require any of the persons prescribed by paragraph (2) below to make

available for inspection by an officer of the Board authorised for that purpose, within the time prescribed by paragraph (3) below, all books, documents and other records in his possession or under his control relating to–

(a) any monies received or receivable by an approved scheme or a relevant statutory scheme, or

(b) any investments or other assets held by that scheme, or

(c) any monies paid or payable out of funds held under that scheme, or

(d) any annuity contract by means of which benefits provided under that scheme have been secured.

(2) The persons prescribed are–

(a) the person who is, or the persons who are, for the time being by virtue of section 611AA of the Taxes Act the administrator of [a scheme];

(b) any person who was, or any persons who were, at any time prior to the relevant date, by virtue of section 611AA of the Taxes Act the administrator of [a] scheme, other than an excluded person;

(c) the trustee or trustees of [a] scheme, or any person who was, or any persons who were, at any time prior to the relevant date the trustee or trustees of [a] scheme, other than an excluded person;

(d) any person who is, or has been at any time prior to the relevant date, an employer in relation to [a] scheme, other than an excluded person;

(e) any person who is, or has been at any time prior to the relevant date, a scheme sponsor in relation to [a] scheme, other than an excluded person;

(f) any person who provides, or has at any time prior to the relevant date provided, administrative services to [a] scheme, other than an excluded person.

(3) The time prescribed is such time (not being less than 28 days) as may be provided by the notice.

(4) A notice under paragraph (1) above may require books, documents and other records relating to more than one scheme to be made available for inspection [and may specify matters falling within paragraph (1)(a) to (d) by reference to schemes generally, or those of a limited description, without naming individually each scheme which is the subject of the notice].

(5) Where records are maintained by computer the person required to make them available for inspection shall provide the officer making the inspection with all the facilities necessary for obtaining information from them.

(6) The authorised officer may take copies of, or make extracts from, any books, documents or other records made available for inspection in accordance with paragraph (1) above.

(7) In paragraph (2) above 'excluded person' and 'the relevant date' have the meanings given by regulation 12(5).

Retention of records

15

(1) Each of the persons prescribed by paragraph (2) below shall preserve, for the time prescribed by paragraph (3) below, all books, documents and other records in his possession or under his control relating to–

(a) any monies received or receivable by an approved scheme or a relevant statutory scheme, or

(b) any investments or other assets held by that scheme, or

(c) any monies paid or payable out of funds held under that scheme, or

(d) any annuity contract by means of which benefits provided under that scheme have been secured, or

(e) any person who is, or has been, a controlling director of a company which is an employer in relation to the scheme.

(2) The persons prescribed are–

(a) the person who is, or the persons who are, for the time being by virtue of section 611AA of the Taxes Act the administrator of the scheme;

(b) any person who was, or any persons who were, at any time prior to the relevant date, by virtue of section 611AA of the Taxes Act the administrator of that scheme, other than an excluded person;

(c) the trustee or trustees of that scheme, or any person who was or any persons who were, at any time prior to the relevant date the trustee or trustees of that scheme, other than an excluded person;

(d) any person who is, or has been at any time prior to the relevant date, an employer in relation to that scheme, other than an excluded person;

(e) any person who is, or has been at any time prior to the relevant date, a scheme sponsor in relation to that scheme, other than an excluded person;

(f) any person who provides, or has at any time prior to the relevant date provided, administrative services to that scheme, other than an excluded person.

(3) The time prescribed–

(a) in the case of accounts and actuarial valuation reports relating to the scheme, including books, documents and other records on which such accounts or reports are based, is 6 years from the end of the scheme year in which falls the date on which the accounts were signed or, as the case may be, the report was signed;

(b) in the case of books, documents or other records containing information which is required to be furnished pursuant to regulation 5, is 6 years from the end of the scheme year in which the transaction in question occurred;

(c) in the case of books, documents or other records containing information which is required to be furnished pursuant to regulation 6, 8, [10, 11, 11A or 11B], is 6 years from the end of the scheme year in which the event to which the information relates occurred;

(d) in the case of books, documents or other records containing information which is required to be furnished pursuant to regulation 7, is 6 years from the end of the scheme year in which the special contribution to which the information relates was paid to the scheme;

(e) in the case of books, documents or other records containing information which is required to be furnished pursuant to regulation 9, is 6 years from the end of the scheme year in which the benefits to which the information relates began to be paid;

(f) in the case of books, documents or other records relating to an event specified in paragraph (4) below, is 6 years from the end of the scheme year in which the event occurred.

(4) The events specified are–

(a) the provision by the scheme of any benefit to an employee, or to the widow, widower, [surviving civil partner,] children, dependants, or personal representatives, of an employee;

(b) the refund of contributions to a person who left service as an employee without entitlement to benefits under the scheme;

(c) the payment of contributions to the scheme by an employer or employee;

(d) the making of payments by the scheme to any employer participating in the scheme;

(e) the payment of transfer values or the purchase of annuities under the scheme;

(f) the acquisition or disposal of any asset by the scheme;

(g) the undertaking of any transaction for the purposes of the scheme;

(h) the receipt by the scheme of any income resulting from–

(i) the investment of assets held by the scheme, or

(ii) any trading activity carried on by the scheme.

(5) The duty under paragraph (1) above to preserve books, documents and other records may be discharged by the preservation of the information contained in them.

(6) In paragraph (2) above 'excluded person' and 'the relevant date' have the meanings given by regulation 12(5).

Appendix 8

Registered Pension Schemes (Provision of Information) Regulations 2006

No 567

1 Citation, commencement and effect

These Regulations may be cited as the Registered Pension Schemes (Provision of Information) Regulations 2006, shall come into force on 6th April 2006, and have effect in relation to any reportable event which takes place on or after 6th April 2006.

2 Interpretation

(1) In these Regulations–

'the Act' means the Finance Act 2004 and a reference, without more, to a numbered section or Schedule is a reference to the section of, or Schedule to the Act bearing that number;

'associated company' has the meaning given by section 416 of ICTA;

'the Commissioners' means the Commissioners for Her Majesty's Revenue and Customs;

'director' has the meaning given by section 417 of ICTA;

'event report' means the report required by regulation 3(1);

'relevant lump sum death benefit' means a defined benefits lump sum death benefit or an uncrystallised funds lump sum death benefit;

'reportable event' means an event in relation to which information is required to be provided by virtue of these Regulations;

'reporting year' means the tax year to which an event report relates.

(2) Section 839 of ICTA applies for the purpose of determining whether a person is connected with another for the purposes of these Regulations.

(3) Expressions defined, or otherwise explained, in section 280, have the same meaning in these Regulations as they have in Part 4 of the Act.

3 Provision of information by scheme administrator to the Commissioners

(1) The scheme administrator of a registered pension scheme shall provide to the Commissioners an event report in respect of all of the reportable events specified in column (1) of the Table below which have occurred in respect of the scheme during the reporting year, containing the information specified in column (2).

Table

Reportable event	*Information*
1 Unauthorised payments	
The scheme makes an unauthorised member payment or an unauthorised employer payment.	The name, date of birth (if applicable), address and national insurance or company registration number of the person to whom the payment was made, together with the nature, amount and date of the payment.

Table

2 Payments exceeding 50% of standard lifetime allowance	
The scheme makes a lump sum death benefit payment to a person in respect of the death of a member, and that payment, either alone or when aggregated with other such payments from that scheme, amounts to more than 50% of the standard lifetime allowance applicable at the time of the member's death.	The name, date of birth, last known address and national insurance number of the deceased member, together with the name and address of the person to whom the payment was made, and the amount and date of the payment.
3 Early provision of benefits	
The scheme provides benefits to a member of the scheme who is under the normal minimum pension age and before the benefits were provided the member was, either in the year in which they were provided or any of the preceding six years– (a) in relation to the sponsoring employer, or an associated company of that employer, a director or a person connected with a director; (b) whether alone or with others, the sponsoring employer; or (c) a person connected with the sponsoring employer.	The name, address, date of birth and national insurance number of the member, the nature, date and amount of the benefits provided, and reasons for those benefits having been provided under normal minimum pension age.
4 Serious ill-health lump sum	
A scheme pays a member of the scheme a serious ill-health lump sum and before the payment was made the member was, either in the year in which they were provided or any of the preceding six years– (a) in relation to the sponsoring employer, or an associated company of that employer, a director or a person connected with a director; or (b) whether alone or with others, the sponsoring employer; or (c) a person connected with the sponsoring employer.	The name, address, date of birth and national insurance number of the member, and the date and amount of the payment.
5 Suspension of ill-health pension	
An ill-health pension which has been paid, pursuant to pension rule 1 in section 165(1), is not now paid because the ill-health condition is no longer met.	The name, address, date of birth and national insurance number of the member to whom the pension had been paid, the date on which the period of non-payment began and the annual rate of the pension, to which the member was entitled, immediately before that period began.
6 Benefit crystallisation events and enhanced lifetime allowance or enhanced protection	
A benefit crystallisation event occurs in relation to a member in respect of the scheme and– (a) the amount crystallised by the event– (i) exceeds the standard lifetime allowance, or (ii) together with amounts crystallised by other events in relation to that member, exceeds the standard lifetime allowance, for the year in which the event occurs; and (b) the member relies on entitlement to either an enhanced lifetime allowance or enhanced protection in order to reduce or eliminate liability to the lifetime allowance charge.	The name, address, date of birth and national insurance number of the member, the amount crystallised by the event, the date of the event and the reference number given by the Commissioners under the Registered Pension Schemes (Enhanced Lifetime Allowance) Regulations 2006.

Table

7 Pension commencement lump sum

The scheme makes a pension commencement lump sum payment to a member which– (a) when added to the amount crystallised, by reason of the member becoming entitled to the pension with which the lump sum payment is associated, exceeds 25% of the total so found; and (b) is more than 7.5%, but less than 25%, of the standard lifetime allowance for the tax year in which the sum is paid.	The name, address, date of birth and national insurance number of the member, together with– (a) the amount and date of payment of the lump sum; and (b) the amount crystallised on the member becoming entitled to the pension, with which the lump sum is associated.

8 Pension commencement lump sum: primary and enhanced protection provisions of Schedule 36

The scheme makes a pension commencement lump sum payment to a member and the amount of the payment is an authorised payment by reason only of the application of paragraphs 24 to 30 of Schedule 36.	The name, address, date of birth and national insurance number of the member, the amount and date of the payment, and the reference number given to the member by the Commissioners under the Registered Pension Schemes (Enhanced Lifetime Allowance) Regulations 2006.

9 Transfers to qualifying recognised overseas pension schemes

The scheme makes a recognised transfer to a qualifying recognised overseas pension scheme which is not a registered pension scheme.	The name, address, date of birth and national insurance number of the member, the amount of the sums or assets transferred, the date of the transfer together with the name of the qualifying recognised overseas pension scheme and the country or territory under the law of which it is established and regulated.

10 Member able to control scheme assets

A member of the scheme, whether alone or with others, gains or loses the ability to control the way in which scheme assets are used to provide pension benefits.	The dates on which– (a) at least one member becomes able to exercise control where none had been able to do so immediately before; and (b) no member is able to exercise control, where at least one had been able to do so immediately before.

11 Changes in scheme rules

The scheme changes its rules to– (a) entitle any person to require the making of unauthorised payments; or (b) permit investment other than in policies of insurance.	The fact of the change and the date on which the change takes effect.

12 Changes to rules of pre-commencement scheme treated as more than one scheme

The scheme, being one which immediately before 6th April 2006 was treated in accordance with section 611 of ICTA as two or more separate schemes, changes its rules in any way.	The fact of the change and the date on which the change takes effect.

Table

13 Change in legal structure of scheme	
The legal structure of the scheme changes from one of the following categories to another. The categories are– (a) a single trust under which all of the assets are held for the benefit of all members of the scheme; (b) an overall trust within which there are individual trusts applying for the benefit of each member; (c) an overall trust within which specific assets are held as, or within, sub-funds for each member; (d) an annuity contract; (e) a body corporate; and (f) other.	The date on which the change took effect, together with– (a) the new category listed in column 1 which applies to the scheme; and (b) in the case of a change falling within category (f), a brief description of the nature of the new category of legal structure of the scheme.
14 Change in number of members	
The number of scheme members falls in a different band at the end of a tax year from that in which it fell at the end of the previous tax year. The bands are– (a) 0 members; (b) 1 to 10 members; (c) 11 to 50 members; (d) 51 to 10,000 members; and (e) more than 10,000 members.	The new band applicable to the number of scheme members.
15 Alternatively secured pension	
Sums or assets in respect of at least one member of the scheme meets Condition A or Condition B in paragraph 11 of Schedule 28 for the first time during the reporting year.	The number of members who, having met Condition A or Condition B in paragraph 11 of Schedule 28 for the first time during the reporting year, fall within each of the following bands in respect of the funds or assets held. The bands are– (a) £ 1–50,000; (b) £ 50,001-£ 100,000; (c) £ 100,001-£ 250,000; (d) £ 250,001-£ 500,000; and (e) more than £ 500,000.
16 Transfer lump sum death benefit	
At least one transfer lump sum death benefit is paid during the reporting year	The number of transfer lump sum death benefits paid during the reporting year, the value of which falls in each of the following bands. The bands are– (a) £ 1–50,000; (b) £ 50,001-£ 100,000; (c) £ 100,001-£ 250,000; (d) £ 250,001-£ 500,000; and (e) more than £ 500,000.
17 Lump sum payment after the death of a member aged 75 or over	
A lump sum payment is made in respect of a member after the member has died after reaching the age of 75.	The name, date of birth, last known address and national insurance number of the deceased member, together with the name and address of the person to whom the lump sum payment was made, and the amount, nature and date of the payment.

(2) No obligation to report a national insurance number arises by virtue of paragraph (1) unless that number is known to the scheme administrator.

(3) For the purposes of reportable event 3 'benefits' does not include a payment–

(a) which is reportable as reportable event 1 or reportable event 4; or

(b) which falls within paragraph 10 of Schedule 29.

(4) No event report is required by virtue of reportable event 10 in respect of arrangements–

(a) where all the assets held by the scheme comprise contracts or policies of insurance, units in unit trust schemes or shares in open-ended investment companies and in managing those investments, the scheme administrator does not consult with any member of the scheme except to the extent necessary by virtue of the investment offering choices that are available to any person; and

(b) under which all contributions paid are, after deduction of expenses, invested in deposits with deposit takers and the payment of interest on those deposits comprises the only income of the scheme from its investments.

(5) No event report is required by virtue of reportable event 17–

(a) if the same event constitutes reportable event 1; or

(b) in respect of the payment of a life cover lump sum.

Here 'life cover lump sum' has the same meaning as it has in the paragraph 21A treated as inserted into Part 2 of Schedule 29 by article 8(3) of the Taxation of Pension Schemes (Transitional Provisions) Order 2006.

(6) The event report shall–

(a) be in a form specified by the Commissioners, and

(b) be delivered (subject to the qualification in regulation 4(3)) at any time which falls–

(i) after the end of the end of the tax year to which the report relates, but

(ii) no later than the 31st January following the tax year to which the report relates.

Other information requirements

4 Provision of information in respect of a pension scheme which has been wound-up

(1) The person who, immediately before the winding-up of a registered pension scheme, was the scheme administrator shall give notice to the Commissioners of the fact that the scheme has been wound up and the date on which the winding up was concluded.

(2) No notice is required by virtue of paragraph (1) in respect of–

(a) an annuity contract or a trust scheme which is treated as a registered pension scheme by virtue of paragraph 1(1)(d), or (f) of Schedule 36, or article 27 of the Taxation of Pension Schemes (Transitional Provisions) Order 2006 (contracts approved under section 620 or 621 of the Income and Corporation Taxes Act 1988); or

(b) a former approved superannuation fund within the meaning of paragraph 1(3) of Schedule 36.

(3) Where a pension scheme is wound up, the time prescribed in respect of any information required to be delivered under these Regulations (whether in the event report or otherwise) is any time on or before–

(a) the last day of the period of 3 months beginning with the day on which the winding up is completed, or

(b) the last day otherwise prescribed by these Regulations for the provision of that information,

whichever is the earlier.

5 Provision of information by employer company to the Commissioners

(1) Where a registered pension scheme makes an unauthorised employer payment to a company, the company shall provide the information specified in paragraph (2).

(2) The information required is–

(a) details of the scheme that made the payment;

(b) the nature of the payment;

(c) the amount of the payment; and

(d) the date on which the payment was made.

(3) This information shall be provided to the Commissioners no later than the 31st January following the tax year in which the payment is made.

6 Scheme administration

The person who has been, but has ceased to be, the scheme administrator must notify the Commissioners of the termination of his appointment, together with the date on which the termination took effect, within 30 days.

7 Percentage of standard lifetime allowance expended on the happening of a benefit crystallisation event

(1) The percentage of standard lifetime allowance expended on the happening of each relevant benefit crystallisation event for the purposes of the provisions listed in paragraph (3) is found by the application of the formula–

(AE / RSLA) x (100 / 1)

Here–

AE is the amount of lifetime allowance expended on the happening of the benefit crystallisation event; and

RSLA is the relevant standard lifetime allowance at the time of that event.

(2) The amount of lifetime allowance expended on the happening of a benefit crystallisation event is the sum of AC and SFTP.

Here–

AC is the amount crystallised by the benefit crystallisation event; and

SFTP is the amount covered by a scheme-funded tax payment (within the meaning of section 215) in relation to that benefit crystallisation event.

(3) The provisions to which this paragraph applies are–

(a) regulation 8(2) and (3);

(b) regulation 9(2);

(c) regulation 14(3);

(d) regulation 15(2);

(e) regulation 16(2) and (3);

(f) regulation 17(2), (3) (5) and (7).

(4) The total percentage of standard lifetime allowance expended in relation to a member is the sum of the percentages found in accordance with paragraph (1) in respect of benefit crystallisation events in respect of the member.

8 Death: provision of information by scheme administrator to personal representatives

(1) The scheme administrator of a registered pension scheme shall provide to the personal representatives (within the meaning of section 279) of a deceased member of that scheme, the information specified in paragraphs (2) and (3).

(2) The information is the percentage of standard lifetime allowance expended by, and the amount and the date of payment of, a relevant lump sum death benefit by the scheme in relation to the member.

The information shall be provided no later than the last day of the period of 3 months beginning with the day on which the final such payment is made.

(3) The information is the total percentage of standard lifetime allowance expended, at the date of the statement, by–

(a) any benefit crystallisation event in respect of the deceased member's rights under the scheme to the extent that–

(i) the sums or assets subject to any such event; and

(ii) any sums or assets subsequently representing those sums or assets;

have not been transferred to another registered pension scheme, and

(b) where sums or assets have been transferred to the scheme from another registered pension scheme (whether directly or indirectly) in respect of the deceased member any benefit crystallisation event in connection with–

(i) those sums or assets; and

(ii) any other sums or assets held prior to the transfer which the sums and assets mentioned in sub-paragraph (i) represented,

but excluding from that percentage any amount in respect of any relevant lump sum death benefit payment in respect of the deceased member.

The information shall be provided no later than the last day of the period of 2 months beginning with the day on which a request for it is received from the member's personal representatives.

9 Death: provision of information by insurance company to personal representatives

(1) Where–

(a) an insurance company has paid a lifetime annuity or a scheme pension to an individual who has been a member of a registered pension scheme purchased with sums or assets held for the purposes of that scheme, and

(b) the member to whom that annuity or pension was payable has died,

the insurance company shall, on request by the member's personal representatives, provide them with the information specified in paragraph (2).

(2) The information is the total percentage of standard lifetime allowance expended, at the date of the statement, by–

(a) any benefit crystallisation event in respect of the deceased member under the registered pension scheme to the extent that–

(i) the sums and assets subject to that event, or

(ii) sums and assets subsequently representing those sums and assets,

have not been transferred to another such scheme, and

(b) where sums or assets have been transferred to the scheme from another registered pension scheme (whether directly or indirectly) in respect of the deceased member's rights, any benefit crystallisation event in connection with–

(i) those sums or assets; and

(ii) any other sums or assets held prior to the transfer which the sums or assets mentioned in sub-paragraph (i) represented.

(3) The information shall be provided no later than the last day of the period of 2 months beginning with the day on which the request was received.

10 Death: provision of information by personal representatives to the Commissioners

(1) Where–

(a) a relevant lump sum death benefit is paid in respect of a deceased member of a registered pension scheme, and

(b) that payment, of itself or together with any other relevant lump sum death benefit, results in a lifetime allowance charge,

the personal representatives of the member shall provide to the Commissioners the information specified in paragraph (2).

(2) The information required is–

(a) the name of the pension scheme from which, and the name and address of the scheme administrator by whom, the benefits were paid;

(b) the name of the deceased member in respect of whom the benefits were paid;

(c) the amount and date of payment of the benefits; and

(d) the chargeable amount in respect of which a lifetime allowance charge is payable by virtue of the payments.

(3) The information required shall be provided on or before the later of–

(a) the end of the period of 13 months beginning with the death of the member; or

(b) the end of the period of 30 days beginning with the date on which the personal representatives (or any of them) became aware that paragraph (1) applied to the deceased member.

(4) Where a requirement to provide information under this regulation arises after the period specified in paragraph (3) has expired, the information shall be provided no later than the last day of the period of 30 months beginning with the death of the member.

(5) If the personal representatives discover after the latest date for providing information under paragraph (4) any information required to be provided under paragraph (1), that information shall be provided no later than the last day of the period of 3 months beginning with the discovery of that information.

11 Information provided by member to scheme administrator: enhanced lifetime allowance

If the member of a registered pension scheme intends to rely on entitlement to an enhanced lifetime allowance, or to enhanced protection, by virtue of any of the provisions listed in section 256(1), he must give to the scheme administrator the reference number issued by the Commissioners under the Registered Pension Schemes (Enhanced Lifetime Allowance) Regulations 2006 in respect of that entitlement.

12 Information about scheme administrator's liability for a lifetime allowance charge

If the scheme administrator of a registered pension scheme has made or intends to make a payment, on account of his liability to account for tax in respect of a lifetime allowance charge on a benefit crystallisation event, the scheme administrator shall within 3 months after the benefit crystallisation event provide the member with a notice stating–

(a) the chargeable amount in respect of the benefit crystallisation event;

(b) how that chargeable amount has been calculated;

(c) the amount of the resulting charge to tax; and

(d) whether the scheme administrator has accounted for the tax or intends to do so.

13 Provision of information about unauthorised payments

(1) Where a registered pension scheme has made to a member of the scheme an unauthorised payment under section 173(1) (provision of benefits), the scheme administrator shall provide to the member before 7th July following the tax year in which the payment is made the information specified in paragraph (2).

(2) The information is–

(a) the nature of the benefit provided;

(b) the amount of the unauthorised payment which is treated as being made by the provision of the benefit; and

(c) the date on which the benefit was provided.

14 Information provided to members by scheme administrators about benefit crystallisation events

(1) The scheme administrator shall provide a statement containing the information in paragraph (3) to each member of the scheme–

(a) who has an actual (as opposed to prospective) entitlement to be paid a pension, at least once in each tax year, or

(b) in respect of whom a benefit crystallisation event has occurred, within 3 months of that event.

This paragraph is subject to the following qualification.

(2) No obligation to provide a statement arises–

(a) under paragraph (1) if a statement is required to be provided under regulation 16 or 17 containing the same information as is required by paragraph (3);

(b) under paragraph (1)(a) in relation to a relevant existing pension (within the meaning of paragraph 10(2) of Schedule 36) to which an individual has an actual (as opposed to prospective) entitlement to be paid a pension on 5th April 2006;

(c) under paragraph (1)(b) if a statement is required to be provided under paragraph (1)(a) or under regulation 8(2).

(3) The information is the percentage of standard lifetime allowance expended by–

(a) benefit crystallisation events in respect of the scheme, to the extent that the sums or assets subject to any such event have not been transferred to another registered pension scheme, and

(b) where the first-mentioned scheme has received (whether directly or indirectly) a transfer in respect of the member, any benefit crystallisation event, prior to the transfer, in connection with–

(i) the sums or assets represented by the transfer;

(ii) sums and assets replaced by the sums or assets mentioned in paragraph (i).

15 Information between scheme administrators

(1) This regulation applies if, and to the extent that, a member's crystallised rights under one registered pension scheme ('Scheme A'), are transferred to another such scheme ('Scheme B').

(2) The scheme administrator of Scheme A shall provide to the administrator of Scheme B, within 3 months of the transfer, a statement of the total percentage of the standard lifetime allowance expended, at the date of the statement, by–

(a) benefit crystallisation events in respect of Scheme A in connection with the sums and assets represented by the transfer; and

(b) where Scheme A has received (whether directly or indirectly) a transfer in respect of the member, any benefit crystallisation event prior to the occurrence of the transfer in connection with–

(i) the sums or assets represented by the transfer; and

(ii) sums and assets replaced by the sums and assets mentioned in paragraph (i).

16 Pensions and annuities in payment: information provided to and by insurance companies

(1) This regulation applies if a registered pension scheme has provided an insurance company with funds, otherwise than from an unsecured pension fund, to secure the payment of–

(a) a scheme pension, or

(b) a lifetime annuity.

(2) The scheme administrator shall provide the insurance company, within 3 months of the date on which the recipient becomes entitled to the pension or annuity, with a statement of the total percentage of standard lifetime allowance expended, at the date of the statement by benefit crystallisation events in respect of that pension or annuity, and any pension commencement lump sum connected with that pension or annuity.

(3) The insurance company shall provide to each pensioner or annuitant, at least once in each tax year, a statement of the percentage of the standard lifetime allowance expended at the date of the statement, by benefit crystallisation events in respect of that pension or annuity and any pension commencement lump sum paid in connection with that pension or annuity.

17 Payments to insurance companies from unsecured pension funds

(1) This regulation applies if a registered pension scheme has provided an insurance company with sums or assets from an unsecured pension fund, to secure the payment of–

(a) a scheme pension, or

(b) a lifetime annuity.

(2) If the sums or assets provided comprise part of the member's unsecured pension fund, the scheme administrator shall provide the insurance company, within 3 months of the purchase of the pension or annuity, with a statement of the percentage of standard lifetime allowance expended by the member becoming entitled to the scheme pension or the lifetime annuity.

(3) The insurance company shall provide to each pensioner or annuitant, at least once in each tax year, a statement of the percentage of the standard lifetime allowance expended at the date of the statement, in respect of that pension or annuity.

But no statement is required if the percentage expended is nil.

(4) If the sums or assets provided comprise the whole of the member's unsecured pension fund, the scheme administrator shall provide the insurance company, within 3 months of the purchase of the pension or annuity, with a statement containing the information in paragraph (5).

(5) The information is–

(a) the sum of the percentages of standard lifetime allowance expended by–

(i) benefit crystallisation events in respect of the scheme referred to in paragraph (4) ('A'), to the extent that the sums and assets subject to those events have not been the subject of a transfer to another registered scheme; and

(ii) where A has received (whether directly or indirectly) a transfer in respect of that member, any benefit crystallisation event prior to the transfer in connection with the sums and assets represented by the transfer and sums and assets which were replaced by the sums and assets mentioned in paragraph (i), less

(b) the sum of the percentages of standard lifetime allowance expended by benefit crystallisation events–

(i) which have been the subject of a statement under paragraph (2),

(ii) which have been the subject of a statement under regulation 16(2), or

(iii) which are referable to sums or assets which continue to be held by A.

(6) The insurance company shall provide to the pensioner or annuitant, once in each tax year, a statement containing the information in paragraph (7).

(7) The information is–

(a) the sum of the percentages of standard lifetime allowance expended by–

(i) benefit crystallisation events in respect of the scheme referred to in paragraph (4) ('A'), to the extent that the sums and assets subject to those events have not been the subject of a transfer to another registered scheme;

(ii) benefit crystallisation events in respect of a scheme pension after the pensioner first became entitled to it; and

(iii) where A has received (whether directly or indirectly) a transfer in respect of that member, any benefit crystallisation event prior to the transfer in connection with the sums and assets represented by the transfer and sums and assets which were replaced by the sums and assets mentioned in paragraph (i), less

(b) the sum of the percentages of standard lifetime allowance expended by benefit crystallisation events–

(i) which have been the subject of a statement under paragraph (2),

(ii) which have been the subject of a statement under regulation 16(3), or

(iii) which are referable to sums or assets which continue to be held by A.

Record-keeping

18 Retention of records

(1) The persons prescribed by paragraph (2) shall preserve any documents in their possession or under their control in relation to a registered pension scheme and relating to–

(a) any monies received by or owing to the scheme;

(b) any investments or assets held by the scheme;

(c) any payments made by the scheme;

(d) any contracts to purchase a lifetime annuity in respect of a member of the scheme; and

(e) the administration of the scheme.

(2) In relation to a registered pension scheme the persons prescribed are–

(a) any person who is or has been the scheme administrator;

(b) any person who is or has been a trustee of the scheme;

(c) any person who provides or has provided administrative services to the scheme; and

(d) if the scheme is an occupational pension scheme, any person who is or has been a sponsoring employer or a director of an employer company.

This is subject to the following qualification.

(3) Any person who has ceased to act in relation to the scheme or ceased to provide administrative services to the scheme shall not be required to preserve documents where he has transferred all the documents to another person who has succeeded him in acting in relation to the scheme or providing administrative services to the scheme.

(4) Documents must be preserved for the tax year to which they relate and for a period of 6 years following that year.

Appendix 9

Employer-Financed Retirement Benefits Schemes (Provision of Information) Regulations 2005

No 3453

1 Citation and commencement

These Regulations may be cited as the Employer-Financed Retirement Benefits Schemes (Provision of Information) Regulations 2005 and shall come into force on 6th April 2006.

2 Interpretation

(1) In these Regulations–

'the Act' means the Finance Act 2004; and

'ITEPA 2003' means the Income Tax (Earnings and Pensions) Act 2003.

(2) In these Regulations–

'employer-financed retirement benefits scheme' has the same meaning as in section 393A of ITEPA 2003;

'relevant benefits' has the same meaning as in section 393B of ITEPA 2003;

'responsible person' has the same meaning as in section 399A of ITEPA 2003;

'year of assessment' means a year beginning with 6th April in any year and ending with 5th April in the following year.

3 Prescribed person

The responsible person in relation to an employer-financed retirement benefits scheme is the person prescribed for the purposes of these Regulations.

4 Provision of information in relation to the coming into operation of schemes

(1) The responsible person shall supply to the Board the particulars prescribed in paragraph (3) on or before 31st January next following the end of the year of assessment during which the scheme first came into operation.

(2) For the purposes of this regulation a scheme 'comes into operation' on whichever is the first date, on or after that on which these Regulations come into force, on which–

(a) an employer makes a contribution to that scheme; or

(b) relevant benefits are provided.

(3) The prescribed information for the purposes of this paragraph is–

(a) the name of the scheme;

(b) the address of the responsible person; and

(c) the date the scheme came into operation.

5 Provision of information in relation to relevant benefits

(1) The responsible person shall supply to the Board the particulars prescribed in paragraph (3) in respect of all relevant benefits provided during the year of assessment at the time prescribed by paragraph (4).

This is subject to the following qualification.

(2) Information is not required to be supplied under this regulation in respect of pensions which are chargeable to tax under Chapter 2 of Part 9 of ITEPA 2003.

(3) The prescribed information is–

(a) the name, address and national insurance number of the recipient of the relevant benefit;

(b) the nature of the relevant benefit provided; and

(c) the amount of the relevant benefit calculated in accordance with section 398(2) of ITEPA 2003.

(4) The prescribed time is not later than 7th July following the end of the year of assessment in which the relevant benefit was provided.

Appendix 10

Employer-Financed Retirement Benefits (Excluded Benefits for Tax Purposes) Regulations 2006

No 210

1 Citation and commencement

These Regulations may be cited as the Employer-Financed Retirement Benefits (Excluded Benefits for Tax Purposes) Regulations 2006 and come into force on 6th April 2006.

2 Excluded benefit

(1) For the purposes of section 393B(3)(d) of the Income Tax (Earnings and Pensions) Act 2003 (prescribed benefits to be excluded benefits for the purpose of Chapter 2 of Part 6 of that Act) a lump sum benefit which is–

(a) in respect of the non-accidental death of an employee during service, and

(b) already provided for under the rules of a scheme on 6th April 2006,

is prescribed.

(2) In paragraph (1) 'scheme' means any scheme which, on 6th April 2006–

(a) will be an employer-financed retirement benefits scheme, or

(b) would be such a scheme but for the fact that it provides for a benefit which is an excluded benefit by virtue of this regulation.

(3) In paragraph (2) 'employer-financed retirement benefits scheme' has the meaning given in section 393A of the Income Tax (Earnings and Pensions) Act 2003.

Appendix 11

Registered Pension Schemes and Employer-Financed Retirement Benefits Schemes (Information) (Prescribed Descriptions of Persons) Regulations 2005

No 3455

1 **Citation, commencement and interpretation**

(1) These Regulations may be cited as the Registered Pension Schemes and Employer-Financed Retirement Benefits Schemes (Information) (Prescribed Descriptions of Persons) Regulations 2005 and shall come into force on 6th April 2006.

(2) In these Regulations any reference, without more, to a numbered section, is a reference to the section of the Finance Act 2004 which is so numbered.

2 **Prescribed descriptions of persons for the purposes of section 252of the Finance Act 2004**

(1) For the purposes of section 252 (notices requiring documents or particulars about registered pension schemes and employer-financed retirement benefit schemes) the prescribed descriptions of persons are those prescribed in the following paragraphs.

For the purposes of this regulation 'the relevant period' means the period which–

(a) begins with the time at which occurred the event in relation to which information is required by the notice under section 252, and

(b) ends with the end of the sixth tax year following that in which that event occurred.

(2) In relation to a pension scheme referred to in subsection (3)(a), (b) or (c) of section 252 the prescribed descriptions of person are–

(a) any person who is, or at any time during the relevant period has been, the scheme administrator,

(b) any person who is, or at any time during the relevant period has been, a trustee of the scheme,

(c) any person who is, or at any time during the relevant period has been, a sponsoring employer in relation to the scheme, and

(d) any person who is, or at any time within the relevant period has been, a member of the scheme,

in respect of which the notice is given.

(3) In relation to an annuity purchased with sums or assets held for the purposes of a registered pension scheme, the prescribed description of person is the insurance company or other person from whom the annuity has been purchased.

(4) In relation to an employer-financed retirement benefits scheme, the prescribed description of person–

(a) for the purposes of section 252(3)(e), is the responsible person at the time the scheme comes into operation; and

(b) for the purposes of section 252(3)(f) is the responsible person at the time that the notice under that section is issued.

(5) For the purposes of paragraph (4)–

(a) a scheme 'comes into operation' on whichever is the first date, on or after that on which these Regulations come into force on which–

(i) an employer makes a contribution to that scheme; or

(ii) relevant benefits are provided; and

(b) 'responsible person' has the meaning given in section 399A of the Income Tax Earnings and Pensions Act 2003.

Appendix 12

Registered Pension Schemes and Overseas Pension Schemes (Electronic Communication of Returns and Information) Regulations 2006

No 570

Part 1
Introduction

1 Citation and commencement

These Regulations may be cited as the Registered Pension Schemes and Overseas Pension Schemes (Electronic Communication of Returns and Information) Regulations 2006 and shall come into force on such days or days as may be appointed by the Commissioners and specified in a notice in the London, Edinburgh and Belfast Gazettes.

2 Interpretation

(1) In these Regulations–

(a) 'the Act' means the Finance Act 2004;

(b) 'Part 4' means Part 4 of the Act; and

(c) any reference to a numbered section or Schedule (without more) is a reference to the section or Schedule bearing that number in the Act.

(2) In these Regulations, except where the context otherwise requires–

'approved method of electronic communications', in relation to the delivery of information in accordance with a provision of these Regulations, means a method of electronic communications which has been approved, by specific or general directions issued by the Commissioners, for the delivery of information of that kind under that provision;

'the Commissioners' means the Commissioners for Her Majesty's Revenue and Customs;

'the ELA Regulations' means the Pension Schemes (Enhanced Lifetime Allowance) Regulations 2006;

'electronic communications' has the meaning given in section 132(10) of the Finance Act 1999;

'official computer system' means a computer system maintained by or on behalf of the Commissioners or on behalf of an officer of Revenue and Customs;

'relevant information' means information which is required or authorised by virtue of these Regulations to be delivered to Revenue and Customs by an approved method of electronic communications;

'Revenue and Customs' means Her Majesty's Revenue and Customs; and

'the tax appeal Commissioners' means, as the case requires, the General Commissioners or the Special Commissioners.

3 Introduction

(1) Part 2 of these Regulations makes provision about returns and information which must be delivered to Revenue and Customs by an approved method of electronic communications.

(2) Part 3 of these Regulations makes provision about returns and information which may be delivered to Revenue and Customs by an approved method of electronic communications.

Part 2
Information which Must be Delivered by Electronic Communications

4 Information which must be delivered by electronic communications

(1) The information specified in Schedule 1 to these Regulations must be delivered to Revenue and Customs–

(a) in a form approved for that purpose; and

(b) by a method of electronic communications approved for that purpose.

(2) The Commissioners may make a general or specific direction requiring a scheme administrator to deliver specified information to Revenue and Customs by a particular method of electronic communications.

(3) Information specified in Schedule 1 which is delivered to Revenue and Customs in a form, or by a method, otherwise than that required by virtue of this regulation must be treated as not having been delivered.

Part 3
Information which May be Delivered by Electronic Communications

5 Information which may be delivered by electronic communications

(1) Information specified in Schedule 2 to these Regulations may be delivered to Revenue and Customs, if–

(a) it is in a form approved for that purpose;

(b) it is sent by a method of electronic communications approved for that purpose; and

(c) the sender is authorised by Revenue and Customs to use electronic communications for that purpose.

(2) Information specified in Schedule 2 may be supplied by Revenue and Customs if–

(a) the proposed recipient has consented to the use of electronic communications for the delivery of information by Revenue and Customs; and

(b) that consent has not been withdrawn.

Part 4
Evidential Provisions

6 Whether relevant information has been delivered electronically

(1) For the purposes of these Regulations, relevant information is to be taken to have been delivered to an official computer system by an approved method of electronic communications only if it is accepted by that official computer system.

This is subject to the following qualification.

(2) Relevant information which is delivered to an official computer system must meet the standards of accuracy and completeness set by specific or general directions given by the Commissioners.

(3) Relevant information which fails to meet those standards must be treated as not having been delivered.

7 Proof of content of electronic delivery

(1) A document certified by Revenue and Customs to be a printed-out version of information delivered by an approved method of electronic communications is evidence, unless the contrary is proved, that the information–

(a) was delivered by an approved method of electronic communications on that occasion; and

(b) constitutes everything which was delivered on that occasion.

(2) A document which purports to be a certificate given in accordance with paragraph (1) is presumed to be such a certificate unless the contrary is proved.

8 Proof of identity of person sending or receiving electronic delivery

The identity of–

(a) the person sending any information delivered by an approved method of electronic communications to Revenue and Customs, or

(b) the person receiving any information delivered by an approved method of electronic communications by Revenue and Customs,

is presumed, unless the contrary is proved, to be the person recorded as such on an official computer system.

9 Information sent electronically on behalf of a person

(1) Any information delivered by an approved method of electronic communications–

(a) to Revenue and Customs, or

(b) to an official computer system,

on behalf of a person, is taken to have been delivered by that person.

(2) But this does not apply if the person proves that the information was delivered without the person's knowledge or connivance.

10 Proof of information sent electronically

(1) The use of an approved method of electronic communications is presumed, unless the contrary is proved, to have resulted in the delivery of information–

(a) to Revenue and Customs, if the delivery of the information has been recorded on an official computer system;

(b) by Revenue and Customs, if the despatch of the information has been recorded on an official computer system.

(2) The use of an approved method of electronic communications is presumed, unless the contrary is proved, not to have resulted in the delivery of relevant information–

(a) to Revenue and Customs, if the delivery of the information has not been recorded on an official computer system;

(b) by Revenue and Customs, if the despatch of the information has not been recorded on an official computer system.

(3) The time of receipt or despatch of any relevant information delivered by an approved method of electronic communications is presumed, unless the contrary is proved, to be the time recorded on an official computer system.

This is subject to the following qualification.

(4) The Commissioners may by a general or specific direction provide for information to be treated as delivered upon a different date (whether earlier or later) than that given by paragraph (3).

(5) Information shall not be taken to have been delivered to an official computer system by means of electronic communications unless it is accepted by the system to which it is delivered.

11 Authentication of information in document otherwise required to be signed

If–

(a) information specified in Schedule 2 to these Regulations is delivered to Revenue and Customs by a method of electronic communications; and

(b) the information is required to be signed by or on behalf of the person delivering it,

the requirement for a signature shall be treated as satisfied if the information is authenticated by or on behalf of the sender in such manner as may be approved by the Commissioners.

12 Use of unauthorised method of electronic communications

(1) This regulation applies to information–

(a) which is required to be delivered to Revenue and Customs under a provision of Part 2 of these Regulations; or

(b) which is permitted to be delivered to Revenue and Customs under a provision of Part 3 of these Regulations.

(2) The use of a method of electronic communications for the purpose of delivering such information is conclusively presumed not to have resulted in the delivery of that information, unless that method of electronic communications is for the time being approved for the delivery of information of that kind under that provision.

SCHEDULE 1
INFORMATION WHICH MUST BE SUPPLIED TO REVENUE AND CUSTOMS BY AN APPROVED METHOD OF ELECTRONIC COMMUNICATIONS

Regulation 4

A form of application for the registration of a pension scheme under section 153 (registration of pension schemes).

A return under section 250(2) (registered pension scheme return) in response to a notice under section 250(1).

A return under section 254 (accounting for tax by scheme administrators), and any amendment of that return.

A declaration under section 270 (scheme administrator's obligations).

An event report under regulation 3 of the Registered Pension Schemes (Provision of Information) Regulations 2006 (provision of information by scheme administrator to Revenue and Customs).

Information furnished under regulation 4 of the Registered Pension Schemes (Provision of Information) Regulations 2006 (information about a pension scheme which has been wound up).

A notice under regulation 6 of the Registered Pension Schemes (Provision of Information) Regulations 2006 (termination of scheme administrator's appointment).

SCHEDULE 2
INFORMATION WHICH MAY BE SUPPLIED EITHER TO OR BY REVENUE AND CUSTOMS BY AN APPROVED METHOD OF ELECTRONIC COMMUNICATIONS

Regulation 5

A notification by Revenue and Customs under section 153(6) of a decision on an application to register a pension scheme under section 153(4).

A notification by Revenue and Customs under section 157(2) (withdrawal of registration) of withdrawal of the registration of a pension scheme under section 157(1).

A notification under section 169(2)(a) (recognised transfers) by a scheme manager (within the meaning of section 169(3)) that a scheme is a recognised overseas pension scheme.

An undertaking by the scheme manager under section 169(2)(b) that he will inform Revenue and Customs if the scheme ceases to be a recognised overseas pension scheme.

An undertaking by the scheme manager under section 169(2)(c) that he will comply with any prescribed information requirements.

A notification by Revenue and Customs of a decision under section 169(5), the effect of which is to exclude a recognised overseas pension scheme from being a qualifying recognised overseas pension scheme.

A notification by Revenue and Customs of a decision under section 169(7) that a recognised overseas pension scheme is to cease to be excluded from being a qualifying recognised overseas pension scheme.

A notice under section 250 requiring the scheme administrator of a registered pension scheme to deliver a return under that section.

A notice under section 252 (notices requiring documents or particulars about registered pensions schemes, etc) to a person of a description prescribed by the Registered Pension Schemes and Employer-Financed Retirement Benefits Schemes (Information) (Prescribed Descriptions of Persons) Regulations 2005 to produce or provide documents or particulars.

An assessment made by Revenue and Customs under section 254 or 255 (assessments on scheme administrators and others under Part 4).

A notice issued by Revenue and Customs in respect of a penalty imposed under any of sections 257 to 266 (penalties for non-compliance with requirements to provide information or furnish returns).

An application–

(a) under section 267 for the discharge of the scheme administrator's liability to the lifetime allowance charge;

(b) under section 268 for the discharge of the scheme administrator's liability to the scheme sanction charge; or

(c) under that section for the discharge of a person's liability to the unauthorised payments surcharge

and a notification by Revenue and Customs of their decision upon that application.

An application by a former scheme administrator under section 271(5) (release of former scheme administrator) to be released from the liability as scheme administrator, and a notification by Revenue and Customs of their decision on that application.

A notification under paragraph 10(3) of Schedule 29 (winding up lump sum: employer's undertaking).

A notification, information or an undertaking provided by a scheme manager under paragraph 5(1) of Schedule 33 given for the purpose of securing that a pension scheme is a qualifying overseas pension scheme.

A notification by Revenue and Customs of their decision under paragraph 5(3) of Schedule 33 (exclusion of overseas pension scheme from being a qualifying overseas pension scheme).

A notification by Revenue and Customs of their decision under paragraph 5(5) of Schedule 33 (overseas pension scheme ceasing to be excluded from being a qualifying overseas pension scheme).

A notification by an individual under regulation 3, 4, 5, 6, 7 or 8 of the ELA Regulations .

A requirement by an individual under regulation 12 of the ELA Regulations that Revenue and Customs give notice of their decision to refuse to consider the information in a notification by the individual; the notice given of that decision; and a notice of appeal to the tax appeal Commissioners against that decision.

A requirement by an individual under regulation 14 of the ELA Regulations that Revenue and Customs give notice of their refusal to issue a certificate under those Regulations; the notice given of that refusal; and a notice of appeal to the tax appeal Commissioners against that refusal.

A requirement by an individual under regulation 16 of the ELA Regulations that Revenue and Customs issue an aggregate certificate.

A notice given by an individual under regulation 17 of the ELA Regulations that any information given in a notification, or in connection with a notification under those Regulations, was incorrect or has become incorrect.

A notice given by an individual under regulation 18 of the ELA Regulations that information given in a certificate issued by Revenue and Customs under those Regulations was incorrect or has become incorrect.

A notice by Revenue and Customs under regulation 22 of the ELA Regulations requiring an individual to provide information, particulars or documents; and a notice of appeal to the tax appeal Commissioners against such a notice.

A notice by Revenue and Customs under regulation 24 of the ELA Regulations of the revocation or amendment of a certificate under those Regulations; and a notice of appeal to the tax appeal Commissioners against such a notice.

A certificate by Revenue and Customs under the ELA Regulations, and an amendment, under those Regulations, of such a certificate.

Information furnished by a company about an unauthorised employer payment under regulation 5 of the Registered Pension Schemes (Provision of Information) Regulations 2006.

Information furnished by personal representatives under regulation 10 of the Registered Pension Schemes (Provision of Information) Regulations 2006.

A notice of appeal against a decision by Revenue and Customs under section 153(6), 157(2), 169(5), 267, 268 or 271(6) or paragraph 5(3) of Schedule 33.

A notice of appeal against a notice requiring the production of documents or the furnishing of particulars under section 252.

A notice of appeal against an assessment under regulation 4 of the Registered Pension Schemes (Accounting and Assessment) Regulations 2005 (assessment in respect of supplementary charges under Part 4).

Information required from qualifying overseas pension schemes and qualifying recognised overseas pension schemes under regulations 2 and 3 of the Pension Schemes (Information Requirements–Qualifying Overseas Pension Schemes, Qualifying Recognised Overseas Pensions Schemes and Corresponding Relief) Regulations 2006.

A notice of appeal against the imposition of a penalty under–

(a) section 98 of TMA 1970 by virtue of section 258 (penalties for failure to provide information required by regulations under section 251(1)(a) or (4) of the Finance Act 2004);

(b) section 257 (scheme administrator failing to make a registered pension scheme return or negligently or fraudulently making an incorrect return or delivering incorrect documents);

(c) section 259 (failure to deliver documents or particulars required by notice);

(d) section 260 (failure to deliver accounting return);

(e) section 261 (enhanced lifetime allowance regulations: documents and information);

(f) section 262 (enhanced lifetime allowance regulations: failures to comply);

(g) section 263 (lifetime allowance enhanced protection: benefit accrual);

(h) section 264 (fraudulent or negligent misstatements, etc);

(i) section 265 (winding up wholly or mainly to facilitate payment of lump sums); or

(j) section 266(2) (transfer of sums representing accrued rights to a registered pension scheme which is an insured scheme otherwise than to scheme administrator of the transferee scheme or an insurance company).

Appendix 13

Pension Schemes (Information Requirements–Qualifying Overseas Pension Schemes, Qualifying Recognised Overseas Pensions Schemes and Corresponding Relief) Regulations 2006

No 208

1 Citation, commencement and interpretation

(1) These Regulations may be cited as the Pension Schemes (Information Requirements for Qualifying Overseas Pension Schemes, Qualifying Recognised Overseas Pension Schemes and Corresponding Relief) Regulations 2006 and shall come into force on 6th April 2006.

(2) In these Regulations–

'the Act' means the Finance Act 2004 and a reference to a numbered section or Schedule, without more, is a reference to the section of; or Schedule to, the Act bearing that number; and

'tax year' means a period beginning on 6th April of one year and ending on 5th April of the immediately following year.

2 Information–benefit crystallisation events in relation to relevant migrant members and individuals entitled to corresponding relief

(1) For the purposes of paragraph 5(2) of Schedule 33 and paragraph 51(4) of Schedule 36 (information about benefit crystallisation events in cases of relevant migrant members and individuals entitled to corresponding relief) the prescribed benefit crystallisation information is–

(a) the name and address of the relevant migrant member or individual (as the case may be) in respect of whom there has been a benefit crystallisation event in the tax year; and

(b) the date, amount and nature of the benefit crystallisation event.

(2) The information must be provided by 31st January next following the end of the tax year in which the benefit crystallisation event occurs.

3 Information–qualifying recognised overseas pension schemes

(1) For the purposes of section 169(4) (meaning of qualifying recognised overseas pension scheme), a qualifying recognised overseas pension scheme must provide to an officer of Revenue and Customs–

(a) the name of the country or territory in which it is established;

(b) in the case of a scheme falling within regulation 3(4) of the Pension Schemes (Categories of Country and Requirements for Overseas Pension Schemes and Recognised Overseas Pension Schemes) Regulations 2006, evidence demonstrating that it fulfils the requirement set out in that paragraph; and

(c) any other evidence required in writing by the officer.

(2) When a qualifying recognised overseas pension scheme makes, or is treated under the relevant provisions as making, a payment in respect of a relevant member, it must provide to an officer of Revenue and Customs–

(a) the name and address of the relevant member; and

(b) the date, amount and nature of that payment.

Here 'the relevant provisions' means sections 172 to 174 and paragraph 2A of Schedule 28.

This paragraph is subject to the qualifications in paragraphs (3) and (4).

(3) No obligation arises under paragraph (2) if the relevant member to whom the payment is made or treated as made is a person to whom the member payment provisions do not apply (see paragraph 2 of Schedule 34).

(4) In the case of a payment by way of a pension the obligation under paragraph (2) applies only to the first such payment.

(5) The information required by paragraph (2) must be provided by 31st January next following the tax year in which the payment is made or is treated as made.

This paragraph is subject to regulation 4.

(6) For the purposes of this regulation–

'payment' has the meaning given in section 161(2); and

'relevant member' means a member of a scheme in respect of whom there is a relevant transfer fund within the meaning of the Pension Schemes (Application of UK Provisions to Relevant Non-UK Schemes) Regulations 2006.

4 Notice in cases of serious prejudice to proper assessment or collection of tax

(1) If an officer of Revenue and Customs has reasonable grounds for believing that the pension scheme in question–

(a) has failed or may fail to comply with any of the requirements imposed upon it under or by virtue of these Regulations, and

(b) such failure is likely to have led or to lead to serious prejudice to the proper assessment or collection of tax,

paragraph (2) applies.

(2) If this paragraph applies, the officer may notify the pension scheme that he requires such information to be provided within 30 days of the issue of that notice, notwithstanding the provisions set out in regulations 2 and 3.

Appendix 14

The new HMRC forms

The HMRC website (http://www.hmrc.gov.uk/pensionschemes/tax-simp-forms.htm) provides links to the latest versions of the new forms that were first published in April 2005. HMRC does not anticipate there being any major changes to these forms. Any amendments to these forms will appear on the 'What's New' page of the HMRC website.

The forms available are as follows:

APSS100	Pension scheme tax registration
APSS100A	Pension scheme registration for relief at source
APSS101	Election to contract out
APSS102	Election for industry-wide money purchase schemes
APSS103	Relief at source details
APSS105	Relief at source interim claim
APSS108	Declaration as a scheme administrator of a deferred annuity contract scheme
APSS109	Notification of succession to a 'split' scheme
APSS110	Notification of succession to a sub-scheme
APSS150	Authorising and de-authorising a practitioner
APSS151	Add scheme administrator
APSS152	Add scheme details
APSS153	Change of scheme administrator/practitioner
APSS154	Associate scheme administrator to scheme
APSS155	Election to vary a contracting-out or appropriate scheme certificate
APSS160	Cessation of scheme administrator
APSS161	Pre-register as sheme administrator/practitioner
APSS200	Protection of existing Rrghts
APSS201	Enhanced lifetime allowance (pension credit rights)
APSS202	Enhanced lifetime allowance (international)

APSS203	Authorisation of scheme administrator(s) to view lifetime allowance certificate(s)
APSS209	Request by scheme administrator for lifetime allowance certificate details
APSS250	Qualifying overseas pension schemes
APSS251	Qualifying recognised overseas pension schemes
APSS254	Election for a deemed benefit crystallisation event
APSS300	Event report

The following forms are available in draft on http://www.hmrc.gov.uk/pensionschemes/tax-simp-draft-forms.htm

APSS252	QROPS – Benefit crystallisation events in relation to relevant migrant members
APSS253	QROPS – Payments in respect of relevant members
APSS301	Registered pension scheme return
APSS302	Accounting for tax by scheme administrator
APSS413	Notice of appeal and application to postpone payment

Appendix 15

Pensions Schemes (Application of UK Provisions to Relevant Non-UK Schemes) Regulations 2006

No 207

Part 1
Introduction

1 Citation, commencement and interpretation

(1) These Regulations may be cited as the Pensions Schemes (Application of UK Provisions to Relevant Non-UK Schemes) Regulations 2006 and shall come into force on 6th April 2006.

(2) In these Regulations–

'the Act' means the Finance Act 2004 any reference (without more) to a numbered section or Schedule is a reference, as the case requires, to the section of, or Schedule to, the Act which bears that number;

'benefit crystallisation event 8' means the event which constitutes benefit crystallisation event 8 in section 216;

'recognised overseas pension scheme' has the meaning given by section 150(8); and

'relevant non-UK scheme' has the same meaning given by paragraph 1(5) of Schedule 34.

Part 2
Application and Computation of UK Tax Charges

2 Computation of a member's UK tax-relieved fund under a relevant non-UK scheme

The amount of a member's UK tax-relieved fund under a relevant non-UK scheme is the aggregate of–

(a) the amounts which, for each tax year before that in which the computation falls to be made, would have been arrived at in relation to arrangements under the relevant non-UK scheme relating to the individual as pension input amounts under sections 230 to 238 of the Act (annual allowance) as they apply by virtue of paragraph 8 of Schedule 34 to the Act, and

(b) the amount which would be so arrived at if the period beginning with 6th April of the tax year in which the computation falls to be made; and ending immediately before the making of the computation, were a tax year,

assuming that section 229(3) did not apply.

3 Computation of a member's relevant transfer fund

The amount of a member's relevant transfer fund under a relevant non-UK scheme (that scheme being referred to here as 'the RNUKS') is the sum of–

(a) the amount crystallised by virtue of benefit crystallisation event 8 on the transfer from a UK registered scheme to the RNUKS; and

(b) so much of the member's UK tax-relieved fund under any other relevant non-UK scheme as has been transferred to the RNUKS but has not been subject to the unauthorised payments charge; and

(c) so much of the member's relevant transfer fund under any other relevant non-UK scheme as has been transferred to the RNUKS–

(i) without being subject to the unauthorised payments charge; and

(ii) at a time when the other relevant non-UK scheme is a recognised overseas pension scheme.

4 Attributing payments to particular funds under a relevant non-UK scheme

(1) This regulation applies to determine to which part of a relevant non-UK scheme a payment to, or in respect of, a member is referable.

(2) It shall be assumed that–

(a) payments made by the scheme to or in respect of the member are made out of the member's UK tax-relieved fund in priority to any other fund under that scheme; and

(b) the amount of the member's UK tax-relieved fund is reduced by the amount paid out of the scheme.

(3) If the member's UK tax-relieved fund is nil, or has been reduced to nil, it shall be assumed that–

(a) payments made by the scheme to or in respect of the member are made out of the relevant transfer fund in priority to any other fund under that scheme; and

(b) the amount of the relevant transfer fund is reduced by the amount paid out of the scheme.

Part 3

5 Modifications to Part 4 of the Finance Act 2004 in respect of relevant non-UK schemes

Part 4 of the Finance Act 2004 shall be modified in respect of relevant non-UK schemes, within the meaning of paragraph 1(5) of Schedule 34, in accordance with the following provisions of these Regulations.

6 Modification of pension rules

In section 165, in pension rules 4 and 6 omit from 'but a scheme pension' to the end.

7 Modification of pension death benefit rules

In section 167 in pension death benefit rules 3 and 5 omit from 'but a dependants' scheme pension' to the end.

8 Modification of section 227

In section 227(3)(b) for 'scheme administrator' substitute 'scheme manager'.

9 Modification of section 231

In section 231–

(a) in subsection (3)–

(i) in paragraph (b) for 'the retail prices index' substitute 'a relevant index';

(ii) omit paragraph (c); and

(b) at the end add–

'(4) In this section 'relevant index' means–

(a) an index of the movement of retail prices maintained, or officially recognised, by the government of the country or territory in which the recognised overseas scheme is established; or

(b) if there is no such index as is mentioned in paragraph (a) of this definition, the retail prices index.'.

10 Modification of section 235

In section 235–

(a) in subsection (3)–

(i) in paragraph (b) for 'the retail prices index' substitute 'a relevant index';

(ii) omit paragraph (c); and

(b) at the end of the section add–

'(4) In this section 'relevant index' means–

(a) an index of the movement of retail prices maintained, or officially recognised, by the government of the country or territory in which the recognised overseas scheme is established; or

(b) if there is no such index as is mentioned in paragraph (a) of this definition, the retail prices index.'.

11 Modification of section 275

(1) In the heading of section 275 at the end add 'and Non-EEA annuity provider'.

(2) At the end of the section add–

'(3) In this Part 'non-EEA annuity provider' means a person resident in a country or territory outside the European Economic Area–

(a) whose normal business includes the provision of annuities; and

(b) who is regulated in the conduct of that business–

(i) by the government of that country or territory; or

(ii) a body established under the law of that country or territory for the purpose of regulating such business.'.

12 Modification of section 276

In section 276(2) for 'scheme administrator' substitute 'scheme manager'.

13 Modification of section 279

(1) Section 279(1) shall be modified as follows.

(2) At the appropriate points in the alphabetical list insert–

''applicable pension scheme', in relation to a pension sharing order in respect of a member's spouse or ex-spouse, means a scheme which is–

(a) a recognised overseas pension scheme within the meaning of this Part; or

(b) a scheme which is recognised for tax purposes under the law of either the country or territory in which it is situate or that of the country or territory in which the pension sharing order is made;'; and "ex-spouse', in relation to a member, means the other party to a marriage with the member that has been dissolved or annulled;';

(3) For the definitions of 'pension credit' and 'pension debit' substitute–

"pension credit' and 'pension debit' mean respectively the amount by which–

(a) the entitlement of a member's spouse or ex-spouse under an applicable pension scheme, is increased; and

(b) the entitlement of a member under a qualifying recognised overseas pension scheme is decreased,

pursuant to a pension sharing order;'.

(4) For the definition of 'pension sharing order or provision' substitute–

"pension sharing order' means an order of a court, by virtue of which amounts are transferred from a recognised overseas pension scheme of a member to an applicable pension scheme of that member's spouse or ex-spouse, in or in connection with proceedings relating to the dissolution or annulment of the marriage of the parties;'.

14 Modification of Schedule 28

(1) Schedule 28 is modified as follows.

(2) In paragraph 1–

(a) in sub-paragraph (a) after 'registered medical practitioner' insert 'or a recognised medical practitioner';

(b) at the end of the paragraph add–

'In this paragraph 'recognised medical practitioner' means a medical practitioner practising outside the United Kingdom who is authorised, licensed or registered to practise medicine in the country or territory, outside the United Kingdom, in which either the scheme or the member is resident.'.

(3) In the following provisions for 'scheme administrator' substitute 'scheme manager'.

The provisions are–

(a) paragraph 1(a);

(b) paragraph 2 (in each place where the expression occurs);

(c) paragraph 10(3)(b);

(d) paragraph 13(3);

(e) paragraph 16(1) and (2);

(f) paragraph 24(3)(b); and

(g) paragraph 27(3).

(4) Omit paragraphs 3(1)(b), 6(1)(c), 17(1)(b) and 20(1)(c).

(5) In paragraph 15(2)(b) and (3) omit ', in the opinion of the scheme administrator'.

(6) At the end of the Schedule add–

'Part 3
Relevant Non-UK Schemes–Interpretation

Construction of references to insurance companies

28

(1) In this Schedule, in its application to a scheme established in a country or territory outside the European Economic Area, any reference to an insurance company includes a non-EEA annuity provider.

(2) Section 275(3) defines 'non-EEA annuity provider'.'.

15 Modification of Schedule 29

(1) Schedule 29 is modified as follows.

(2) In paragraph 1 after sub-paragraph (4) insert–

'(4A) In determining whether all or part of the member's lifetime allowance is available–

(a) an amount treated as crystallising by virtue of benefit crystallisation event 8 shall be disregarded; and

(b) the amount of the allowance available shall be reduced by the aggregate of–

(i) the amount of any previous pension commencement lump sum paid to or in respect of the member by a recognised overseas pension scheme, to the extent that the lump sum is referable to the member's relevant transfer fund, and

(ii) the amount which would have crystallised by virtue of the member becoming entitled to a pension, had the scheme paying it been a registered pension scheme, to the extent that it is so referable.

(4B) For the purposes of sub-paragraph (4A) 'the member's relevant transfer fund' has the meaning given in paragraph 4(2) of Schedule 34.'.

(3) In paragraph 2–

(a) in sub-paragraph (6) for the definition of AAC substitute–

'AAC is the aggregate of–

(a) the amounts crystallised by each benefit crystallisation event (other than benefit crystallisation event 8) which has occurred in relation to the member before the member becomes entitled to the lump sum (or treated as crystallised) on each occasion on which entitlement to a pension arises; and

(b) the amount which would have crystallised, had the scheme paying it been a registered pension scheme–

(i) on entitlement arising to any pension commencement lump sum, to the extent that the lump sum is referable to the member's relevant transfer fund, or

(ii) on entitlement arising to a pension, to the extent that it is so referable.';

(b) after sub-paragraph (6) insert–

'(6A) The member's becoming entitled to a pension commencement lump sum, or to a pension, as mentioned in paragraph (b) of the definition of AAC in paragraph (6) shall be treated as a benefit crystallisation event for the purposes of sub-paragraph (7).'.

(4) In paragraph 4–

(a) in sub-paragraph (1)(a) after 'registered medical practitioner' insert 'or a recognised medical practitioner';

(b) at the end of the paragraph add–

'(3) In sub-paragraph (1) 'recognised medical practitioner' means a medical practitioner practising outside the United Kingdom who is authorised, licensed or registered to practise medicine in the country or territory, outside the United Kingdom, in which either the scheme or the member is resident.

(4) In determining whether all or part of the member's lifetime allowance is available–

(a) an amount crystallising by virtue of benefit crystallisation event 8 shall be disregarded; and

(b) the amount of the allowance available shall be reduced by the aggregate of–

(i) the amount of any previous pension commencement lump sum which has been paid to or in respect of the member by a recognised overseas pension scheme, to the extent that it is referable to the member's relevant transfer fund and

(ii) the amount which would have crystallised on the member becoming entitled to a pension, had the scheme paying it been a registered pension scheme, to the extent that it is so referable.'.

(5) In paragraph 5(1)(c) after 'benefit crystallisation event' insert–

', other than an event which constitutes benefit crystallisation event 8'.

(6) At the end of paragraph 7 add–

'(6) In determining whether all or part of the member's lifetime allowance is available–

(a) an amount crystallising by virtue of benefit crystallisation event 8 shall be disregarded; and

(b) the amount of the allowance available shall be reduced by the aggregate of–

(i) the amount of any previous pension commencement lump sum which has been paid to or in respect of the member by a recognised overseas pension scheme, to the extent that it is referable to the member's relevant transfer fund and

(ii) the amount which would have crystallised on the member becoming entitled to a pension, had the scheme paying it been a registered pension scheme, to the extent that it is so referable.'.

(7) At the end of paragraph 10 add–

'(4) In determining whether all or part of the member's lifetime allowance is available–

(a) an amount crystallising by virtue of benefit crystallisation event 8 shall be disregarded; and

(b) the amount of the allowance available shall be reduced by the aggregate of–

(i) the amount of any previous pension commencement lump sum which has been paid to or in respect of the member by a recognised overseas pension scheme, to the extent that the lump sum is referable to the member's relevant transfer fund, and

(ii) the amount which would have crystallised on the member becoming entitled to a pension, had the scheme paying it been a registered pension scheme, to the extent that it is so referable.'.

(8) In paragraph 11 after sub-paragraph (b) insert–

'(bb) it is not paid from the relevant transfer fund of a qualifying recognised overseas pension scheme,'.

(9) In paragraph 4(1)(a), and paragraph 19(1)(d) and (2)(e) for 'scheme administrator' substitute 'scheme manager'.

16 Modification of Schedule 32

In paragraph 11(6) of Schedule 32–

(a) for 'the retail prices index' (in both places) substitute 'a relevant index'; and

(b) at the end add–

'Here 'relevant index' means–

(a) an index of the movement of retail prices maintained, or officially recognised, by the government of the country or territory in which the recognised overseas scheme is established; or

(b) if there is no such index as is mentioned in paragraph (a) of this definition, the retail prices index.'.

17 Modification of Schedule 34

In Schedule 34 after paragraph 19 add–

'Revenue and Customs discretion

19A

(1) Sub-paragraph (2) applies to–

(a) the member payment provisions to a payment made (or treated by this Part as made) to or in respect of–

(i) a relieved member of a relevant non-UK scheme, or

(ii) a transfer member of such a scheme;

(b) the annual allowance provisions in relation to an individual who is a currently-relieved member of a currently-relieved non-UK scheme; and

(c) the lifetime allowance provision charge in relation to an individual who is a relieved member of a relieved non-UK pension scheme.

(2) If it appears to an officer of Revenue and Customs that, by reason of some non-compliance with the requirements set out in this Part, which in the officer's view does not materially affect the nature of a payment, the payment, or the member in respect of whom it is payable, would be treated less favourably by the strict application of the provisions mentioned in paragraph (1) than in the officer's view is appropriate, sub-paragraph (3) applies.

(3) If this sub-paragraph applies, an officer of Revenue and Customs–

(a) may decide, and

(b) if requested to do so by a member falling within any of the descriptions in paragraphs (a) to (c) of sub-paragraph (1), shall decide,

whether, notwithstanding the non-compliance referred to in sub-paragraph (2), the treatment which, but for that non-compliance, would have applied under this Part should apply to the payment or the member (as the case may be).

This is subject to the qualification in sub-paragraph (4).

(4) An officer of Revenue and Customs shall not make a decision under sub-paragraph (3) that, notwithstanding the difference referred to in sub-paragraph (2), the provisions of this Part shall apply to the payment or the member unless–

(a) it appears to the officer that the effect of the decision would be to reduce the total cumulative tax liability in respect of the charges mentioned in subparagraph (1) of the member whose tax liability would be affected by it, taking one year with another;

(b) the officer has first given at least 28 days' notice of his intention to make the decision to the member whose tax liability would by affected by it; and

(c) the member has–

(i) consented to the making of the decision; or

(ii) failed to respond to the notice within the period specified in paragraph (b).

(5) If an officer of Revenue and Customs decides under sub-paragraph (3) that–

(a) the conditions for the exercise of his discretion under that paragraph are not met; or

(b) the conditions for its exercise are met, but that it is otherwise inappropriate for him to exercise it in favour of the member,

the member may appeal against the decision.

(6) Subsections (3) to (5) of section 170 apply for the purposes of a decision by an officer of Revenue and Customs under sub-paragraph (3) as they apply to a decision under section 169(5).

(7) The Commissioners before whom an appeal under paragraph (5) is brought must consider–

(a) whether the conditions for the exercise of the discretion of an officer of Revenue and Customs have been met; and

(b) if they are satisfied that those conditions have been met, whether the discretion ought to have been exercised in favour of the member.

(8) If they decide that the conditions for the exercise of that discretion have not been met, they must dismiss the appeal.

(9) If they decide that the conditions for the exercise of that discretion have been met, they must decide whether the discretion ought to have been exercised in favour of the member.

(10) If they decide that although the conditions are met, the discretion ought not to have been exercised in favour of the member, they must dismiss the appeal.

(11) If they decide that the discretion ought to have been exercised in favour of the member they may so decide and the provisions of this Part shall apply accordingly to the member or the payment in question (as the case may be).

(12) A decision under sub-paragraph (8) or (10) is final but subject to any further appeal or any determination on, or in consequence of, a case stated.'.

Appendix 16

Pension Schemes (Categories of Country and Requirements for Overseas Pension Schemes and Recognised Overseas Pension Schemes) Regulations 2006

No 206

1 Citation, commencement and interpretation

(1) These Regulations may be cited as the Pension Schemes (Categories of Country and Requirements for Overseas Pension Schemes and Recognised Overseas Pension Schemes) Regulations 2006 and shall come into force on 6th April 2006.

(2) In these Regulations a reference, without more, to a numbered section or Schedule is a reference to the section of, or Schedule to, the Finance Act 2004 which is so numbered.

2 Requirements of an overseas pension scheme

(1) For the purposes of section 150(7) (meaning of overseas pension scheme) an overseas pension scheme must–

(a) satisfy the requirements in paragraphs (2) and (3); or

(b) be established (outside the United Kingdom) by an international organisation for the purpose of providing benefits for, or in respect of, past service as an employee of the organisation and satisfy the requirements in paragraph (4).

(2) This paragraph is satisfied if–

(a) the scheme is an occupational pension scheme and there is, in the country or territory in which it is established, a body–

(i) which regulates occupational pension schemes; and

(ii) which regulates the scheme in question;

(b) the scheme is not an occupational pension scheme and there is in the country or territory in which it is established, a body–

(i) which regulates pension schemes other than occupational pension schemes; and

(ii) which regulates the scheme in question; or

(c) neither sub-paragraph (a) or (b) is satisfied by reason only that no such regulatory body exists in the country or territory and–

(i) the scheme is established in another member State, Norway, Iceland or Liechtenstein; or

(ii) the scheme's rules provide that at least 70% of a member's UK tax-relieved scheme funds will be designated by the scheme manager for the purpose of providing that individual with an income for life, and the pension benefits payable to the member under the scheme (and any lump sum associated with those benefits) are payable no earlier than they would be if pension rule 1 in section 165 applied.

(3) This paragraph is satisfied if the scheme is recognised for tax purposes.

A scheme is 'recognised for tax purposes' under the tax legislation of a country or territory in which it is established if it meets the primary conditions and also meets one of Conditions A and B.

Primary condition 1

The scheme is open to persons resident in the country or territory in which it is established.

Primary condition 2

The scheme is established in a country or territory where there is a system of taxation of personal income under which tax relief is available in respect of pensions and–

(a) tax relief is not available to the member on contributions made to the scheme by the individual or, if the individual is an employee, by their employer, in respect of earnings to which benefits under the scheme relate; or

(b) all or most of the benefits paid by the scheme to members who are not in serious ill-health are subject to taxation.

For the purposes of this condition 'tax relief' includes the grant of an exemption from tax.

Condition A

The scheme is approved or recognised by, or registered with, the relevant tax authorities as a pension scheme in the country or territory in which it is established.

Condition B

If no system exists for the approval or recognition by, or registration with, relevant tax authorities of pension schemes in the country or territory in which it is established–

(a) it must be resident there; and

(b) its rules must provide that–

(i) at least 70% of a member's UK tax-relieved scheme funds will be designated by the scheme manager for the purpose of providing the member with an income for life, and

(ii) the pension benefits payable to the member under the scheme (and any lump sum associated with those benefits) must be payable no earlier than they would be if pension rule 1 in section 165 applied.

(4) In the case of an overseas pension scheme falling within paragraph (1)(b) the requirements are that–

(a) the scheme rules must provide that at least 70% of a member's UK tax-relieved scheme funds will be designated by the scheme manager for the purpose of providing the member with an income for life, and

(b) the pension benefits payable to the member under the scheme (and any lump sum associated with those benefits) under the scheme must be payable no earlier than they would be if pension rule 1 in section 165 applied.

(5) In this regulation–

'international organisation' means an organisation to which section 1 of the International Organisations Act 1968 applies by virtue of an Order in Council under subsection (1) of that section;

occupational pension scheme' has the meaning given by section 150(5); and

'UK tax-relieved scheme funds' means, in relation to a member, the sum of the member's UK tax-relieved fund and his relevant transfer fund, as defined respectively by regulations 2 and 3 of the Pension Schemes (Application of UK Provisions to Relevant Non-UK Schemes) Regulations 2006.

3 Recognised overseas pension schemes: prescribed countries or territories and prescribed conditions

(1) For the purposes of section 150(8) (recognised overseas pension schemes), in addition to satisfying the requirements set out in regulation 2 above, the pension scheme must–

(a) be established in a country or territory mentioned in paragraph (2); or

(b) satisfy the requirement in paragraph (4).

(2) The countries and territories referred to in paragraph (1)(a) are–

(a) the member States of the European Communities, other than the United Kingdom;

(b) Iceland, Liechtenstein and Norway; and

(c) any country or territory in respect of which there is in force an Order in Council under section 788 of the Income and Corporation Taxes Act 1988 giving effect in the United Kingdom to an agreement which contains provision about–

(i) the exchange of information between the parties, and

(ii) non-discrimination.

(3) For the purposes of paragraph (2)(c)(ii) an agreement 'contains provision about non-discrimination' if it provides that the nationals of a Contracting State shall not be subjected in the territory of the other Contracting State to any taxation, or any requirement connected to such taxation, which is other than, or more burdensome than, the taxation and connected requirements to which the nationals of the other State are or may be subjected in the same circumstances.

(4) The requirement is that, at the time of a transfer of sums or assets which would, subject to these Regulations, constitute a recognised transfer, the rules of the scheme must provide that–

(a) at least 70% of the sums transferred will be designated by the scheme manager for the purpose of providing the member with an income for life;

(b) the pension benefits (and any lump sum associated with those benefits) payable to the member under the scheme, to the extent that they relate to the transfer, are payable no earlier than they would be if pension rule 1 in section 165 applied; and

(c) the scheme is open to persons resident in the country or territory in which it is established.

Appendix 17

Pension Schemes (Relevant Migrant Members) Regulations 2006

No 212

1 Citation and commencement

These Regulations may be cited as the Pension Schemes (Relevant Migrant Members) Regulations 2006 and shall come into force on 6th April 2006.

2 Alternative condition for relevant migrant member relief

(1) For the purposes of paragraph 4(c) of Schedule 33 to the Finance Act 2004 (meaning of 'relevant migrant member'), the prescribed condition, in relation to the individual is set out in paragraph (2).

(2) The individual was at any time in the 10 years before the beginning of that period of residence, whether before or after the coming into force of these Regulations, entitled to tax relief in respect of contributions paid under the pension scheme under the law of the country or territory in which the individual was then resident.

Appendix 18

Registered Pension Schemes (Accounting and Assessment) Regulations 2005

No 3454

Citation and commencement

1

These Regulations may be cited as the Registered Pension Schemes (Accounting and Assessment) Regulations 2005 and shall come into force on 6th April 2006.

Interpretation

2

(1) In these Regulations–

'the Act' means the Finance Act 2004;

'ITEPA' means the Income Tax (Earnings and Pensions) Act 2003;

'TMA' means the Taxes Management Act 1970.

(2) In these Regulations a reference to a numbered case is a reference to the case bearing that number in Table 2.

The particulars required to be included in returns under section 254

3

If the scheme administrator is liable to income tax in respect of a charge listed in column 1 of Table 1, the return under section 254 of the Act must include the particulars in respect of that liability specified in column 2.

Table 1

Column 1: charge	*Column 2: specified particulars*
Charge under section 207 of the Act (authorised surplus payments charge).	1 The number of employers to whom an authorised surplus payment was made. 2 The name, registered address and, if appropriate, company registration number of each employer to whom an authorised surplus payment was made. 3 The date the authorised surplus payment was made. 4 The amount of tax due and payable in respect of each authorised surplus payment.
Charge under section 214 of the Act (lifetime allowance charge).	1 The number of individuals liable to a lifetime allowance charge. 2 The name, date of birth, address and national insurance number of each individual liable to a lifetime allowance charge. 3 The date of the benefit crystallisation event in relation to the lifetime allowance charge. 4 The amount of tax due in respect of each chargeable amount as constitutes a lump-sum amount and each chargeable amount as constitutes a retained amount.
Charge under section 242 of the Act (de-registration charge).	The date the registration of the registered pension scheme was withdrawn.

The making of assessments

4

(1) In the cases listed in column 1 of Table 2 an officer of Revenue and Customs must issue an assessment to tax to the assessable person specified in column 2.

Table 2

Column 1	*Column 2: assessable person*
Case 1: a charge to tax arises under section 208 of the Act (unauthorised payments charge) and the person liable to the charge is a company.	The person liable to the charge under section 208(2) of the Act.
Case 2: a charge to tax arises under section 209 of the Act (unauthorised payments surcharge) and the person liable to the charge is a company.	The person liable to the charge under section 209(3) of the Act.
Case 3: a charge to tax arises under section 217(2) of the Act (lifetime allowance charge on receipt of a lump sum death benefit).	The person liable under section 217(2) of the Act.
Case 4: a charge to tax arises under section 239 of the Act (scheme sanction charge).	The scheme administrator, or the person or persons liable to the scheme sanction charge under section 239(3) of the Act.
Case 5: the correct tax due under section 254 of the Act has not been paid on or before the due date.	The scheme administrator.

(2) Subject to paragraph (3), tax assessed under this regulation is payable within 30 days after the issue of the notice of assessment.

(3) Tax assessed under cases 1 and 2 is payable on the day following the expiry of nine months from the end of the accounting period in which the unauthorised payment was made or, if later, within 30 days after the issue of the notice of assessment.

(4) An assessment under case 3 may be made at any time not later than six years after an officer of Revenue and Customs is notified of the relevant lump sum death benefit, but cannot be made later than 20 years after 31st January following the end of the tax year in which the relevant lump sum death benefit was paid.

(5) Any tax assessable under one or more cases of Table 1 may be included in one assessment if the tax so included is all due on the same date.

Interest on tax due under section 254 or assessed under regulation 4

5

(1) Tax which–

(a) becomes due and payable in accordance with section 254(5) of the Act, or

(b) is assessed under regulation 4,

carries interest at the prescribed rate from the reckonable date until payment ('the interest period').

(2) The 'prescribed rate' means the rate applicable under section 178 of the Finance Act 1989 for the purposes of section 86 of TMA.

(3) In relation to each of the cases listed in column 1 of Table 3, the 'reckonable date' is specified in column 2.

Table 3

Column 1	*Column 2: reckonable date*
Tax due under section 254 of the Act.	The due date under section 254(5) of the Act.
Tax assessed under case 1 or 2.	The day following the expiry of nine months from the end of the accounting period in which the unauthorised payment was made.
Tax assessed under case 3.	31st January following the end of the tax year in which the relevant lump sum death benefit was paid.
Tax assessed under case 4.	31st January following the end of the tax year in which the scheme sanction charge arose.
Tax assessed under case 5.	The due date under section 254(5) of the Act.
Tax assessed under case 6 or 7.	The date the tax was due before sections 272 or 273 of the Act applied in relation to the pension scheme.
Tax assessed under case 8.	31st January following the end of the tax year in which the benefit within section 393 of ITEPA is received.

(4) Paragraph (1) applies even if the reckonable date is a non-business day as defined by section 92 of the Bills of Exchange Act 1882.

(5) Any change made to the prescribed rate during the interest period applies to the unpaid amount from the date of the change.

The making of amended returns

6

If the scheme administrator becomes aware–

(a) that anything which ought to have been included in a return made under section 254 of the Act for any period has not been so included,

(b) that anything which ought not to have been included in a return made under section 254 of the Act for any period has been so included, or

(c) that any other error has occurred in a return made under section 254 of the Act for any period,

the scheme administrator must immediately make an amended return to an officer of Revenue and Customs for that period.

Adjustments, repayments and interest on tax overpaid

7

(1) If the correct tax due under section 254 of the Act has not been paid on or before the due date or if an amended return is made under regulation 6, an officer of Revenue and Customs may make such adjustments or repayments as may be required for securing that the resulting liabilities to tax (including interest on unpaid or overpaid tax) whether of the scheme administrator or of any other person are the same as they would have been if the correct tax had been paid or if a correct return had been made.

(2) Tax overpaid which is repaid to the scheme administrator or any other person carries interest at the prescribed rate from the later of the due date and the date on which the tax was paid until the date of repayment ('the interest period').

(3) The 'prescribed rate' means the rate applicable under section 178 of the Finance Act 1989 for the purposes of section 824 of the Income and Corporation Taxes Act 1988.

(4) Any change made to the prescribed rate during the interest period applies to the overpaid amount from the date of the change.

Modifications and application of TMA

8

(1) Section 9(1A) of TMA (tax not to be assessed by a self-assessment) applies with the following modifications in relation to an assessment to tax under case 3, 6 or 7.

(2) At the end of paragraph (a) delete 'or'.

(3) After paragraph (b) insert–

'(c) is chargeable on a person under section 217(2) of the Finance Act 2004 (liability to lifetime allowance charge by reason of the payment of a relevant lump sum death benefit),

(d) is chargeable on a person or persons under section 272 of the Finance Act 2004 (trustees etc liable as scheme administrator), or

(e) is chargeable on a person or persons under section 273 of the Finance Act 2004 (members liable as scheme administrator).'.

9

(1) Section 29(1)(a) of TMA (assessment where loss of tax discovered) applies with the following modification in relation to an assessment to tax under case 1, 2 or 3.

(2) After 'any income' insert–

', unauthorised payments under section 208 of the Finance Act 2004 or surchargeable unauthorised payments under section 209 of that Act or relevant lump sum death benefit under section 217(2) of that Act'.

10

(1) Section 34(1) of TMA (ordinary time limit of six years) applies with the following modifications in relation to an assessment to tax under case 8.

(2) For 'income tax or' substitute 'income tax,'.

(3) After 'capital gains tax' insert–

'or to tax chargeable under section 394(2) of the Income Tax (Earnings and Pensions) Act 2003'.

11

(1) Section 36(1) of TMA (fraudulent or negligent conduct) applies with the following modifications in relation to an assessment to tax under case 8.

(2) For 'income tax or' substitute 'income tax,'.

(3) After 'capital gains tax' insert 'or to tax chargeable under section 394(2) of the Income Tax (Earnings and Pensions) Act 2003'.

12

In relation to any assessment under case 5–

(a) section 34 of TMA applies notwithstanding that the assessment may relate to a quarter or other period which is not a year of assessment, and

(b) for the purposes of section 36 of TMA any such assessment relates to the year of assessment in which the quarter or other period ends.

Modification of Schedule 18 to the Finance Act 1998

13

(1) Schedule 18 to the Finance Act 1998 (company tax returns, assessments and related matters) applies with the following modification in relation to an assessment to tax under case 8.

(2) In paragraph 1 after 'as if it was corporation tax' insert–

'but does not include any tax which is chargeable on the person who is (or persons who are) the responsible person in relation to an employer-financed retirement benefits scheme under section 394(2) of the Income Tax (Earnings and Pensions) Act 2003'.

Appendix 19

Registered Pension Schemes (Audited Accounts) (Specified Persons) Regulations 2005

No 3456

1 Citation and commencement

These Regulations may be cited as the Registered Pension Schemes (Audited Accounts) (Specified Persons) Regulations 2005 and shall come into force on 6th April 2006.

2 Specified descriptions of persons in relation to the audit of registered pension scheme accounts

In relation to the audit of the accounts of a registered pension scheme, the following descriptions of person are specified namely–

(a) a person specified in section 25 of the Companies Act 1989 or Article 28 of the Companies (Northern Ireland) Order 1990 (eligibility as a scheme auditor); and

(b) a person eligible for appointment as a scheme auditor under section 47(1) of the Pensions Act 1995 or Article 47(1) of the Pensions (Northern Ireland) Order 1995 (professional advisers).

This is subject to regulation 3.

3 Circumstances in which a person specified under regulation 2 is not to audit scheme accounts

Notwithstanding regulation 2, a person shall not be a registered pension scheme's auditor if he is–

(a) a member of the scheme;

(b) employed under a contract of service by the scheme administrator;

(c) an employer in relation to the scheme; or

(d) ineligible, by virtue of section 27 of the Companies Act 1989, to audit the accounts of a company which is an employer in relation to the scheme.

Appendix 20

Retirement Benefits Schemes (Restriction on Discretion to Approve) (Small Self-administered Schemes) Regulations 1991

No 1614

Citation and commencement

1

These Regulations may be cited as the Retirement Benefits Schemes (Restriction on Discretion to Approve) (Small Self-administered Schemes) Regulations 1991 and shall come into force on 5th August 1991.

Interpretation

2

(1) In these Regulations unless the context otherwise requires–

'Act' means the Income and Corporation Taxes Act 1988;

'actuary' means–

(a) a Fellow of the Institute of Actuaries,

(b) a Fellow of the Faculty of Actuaries, or

(c) a person with other actuarial qualifications who has been approved as a proper person to act for the purposes of regulation 8 of the Occupational Pension Schemes (Disclosure of Information) Regulations 1986 in connection with the scheme;

...

'the Board' means the Commissioners of Inland Revenue;

'business' includes a trade or profession and includes any activity carried on by a body of persons, whether corporate or unincorporate, except the activity of making or managing investments where those investments do not consist of shares in 51 per cent subsidiaries of the body of persons which do not themselves carry on the activity of making or managing investments;

'close company' has the meaning given by sections 414 and 415 of the Act;

'company' means any body corporate or unincorporated association, but does not include a partnership;

'control', in relation to a body corporate or partnership, shall, subject to paragraph (2), be construed in accordance with section 840 of the Act; and the like construction of 'control' applies (with the necessary modifications) in relation to an unincorporated association as it applies in relation to a body corporate;

'controlling director' means a director to whom subsection (5)(b) of section 417 of the Act (read with subsections (3), (4) and (6) of that section) applies;

'director' means a director within the meaning of section 612(1) of the Act;

'employer' in relation to a scheme means an employer who, by virtue of the governing instrument, is entitled to pay contributions to the scheme;

['ex-spouse' has the meaning given by section 659D(1) of the Act;]

['former civil partner' has the meaning given by section 659D(1A) of the Act;]

'governing instrument' in relation to a scheme means a trust deed, or other document by which the scheme is established, and any other document which contains provisions by which the administration of the scheme is governed;

'pensioneer trustee' means a trustee of a scheme who–

(a) is approved by the Board to act as such, and

(b) is not connected with–

(i) a scheme member,

(ii) any other trustee of the scheme, or

(iii) a person who is an employer in relation to the scheme.

['pension sharing order or provision' means any such order or provision as is mentioned in section 28(1) of the Welfare Reform and Pensions Act 1999 or Article 25(1) of the Welfare Reform and Pensions (Northern Ireland) Order 1999;]

'relative' means brother, sister, ancestor or lineal descendant;

'residential property' means property normally used, or adapted for use, as one or more dwellings;

'scheme' means a retirement benefits scheme as defined in section 611(1) of the Act;

['small self-administered scheme' means a retirement benefits scheme where–

(a) some or all of the income and other assets are invested otherwise than in insurance policies;

(b) a scheme member is connected with–

(i) another scheme member, or

(ii) a trustee of the scheme, or

(iii) a person who is an employer in relation to the scheme; and

(c) there are fewer than 12 scheme members [to whom benefits are currently accruing as a result of service as employees];]

['scheme member' in relation to a scheme means–

(a) a member of the scheme to whom benefit is currently accruing as a result of service as an employee, or

(b) a person who is an ex-spouse [or former civil partner] of a member of the scheme and whose rights under the scheme derive from a pension sharing order or provision;]

'shares' includes stock;

'the trustees' in relation to a scheme includes any person having the management of the scheme;

'unlisted company' means a company which is not officially listed on a recognised stock exchange within the meaning of section 841 of the Act;

'51 per cent subsidiary' has the meaning given by section 838 of the Act.

(2) The interpretation of 'control' in paragraph (1) does not apply in relation to a body corporate which is a close company and in relation to such a body corporate 'control' shall be construed in accordance with section 416 of the Act.

(3) For the purposes of these Regulations any question whether a person is connected with another shall be determined in accordance with paragraphs (4) to (8) (any provision that one person is connected with another being taken to mean that they are connected with one another).

(4) A person is connected with an individual if that person is the individual's [spouse or civil partner], or is a relative, or the [spouse or civil partner] of a relative, of the individual or of the individual's [spouse or civil partner].

(5) Without prejudice to paragraph (4) a person, in his capacity as a scheme member, is connected with an employer in relation to a scheme if–

(a) where the employer is a partnership, he is connected with a partner in the partnership, or

(b) where the employer is a company, he or a person connected with him is, or at any time during the preceding 10 years has been, a controlling director of the company.

(6) A company is connected with another company–

(a) if the same person has control of both, or a person has control of one and persons connected with him, or he and persons connected with him, have control of the other, or

(b) if a group of two or more persons has control of each company, and the groups either consist of the same persons or could be regarded as consisting of the same persons by treating (in one or more cases) a member of either group as replaced by a person with whom he is connected.

(7) A company is connected with another person if that person has control of it or if that person and persons connected with him together have control of it.

(8) Any two or more persons acting together to secure or exercise control of a company shall be treated in relation to that company as connected one with another and with any person acting on the directions of any of them to secure or exercise control of the company.

(9) For the purposes of these Regulations a company is associated with an employer if (directly or indirectly) the employer controls that company or that company controls the employer or if both are controlled by a third person.

Restrictions on the Board's discretion

3

The Board shall not exercise their discretion to approve a scheme by virtue of section 591 of the Act in circumstances where the scheme is a small self-administered scheme and–

(a) the Board have previously approved such a scheme–

(i) of which an employee of any employer in relation to the scheme has at any time been a scheme member, and

(ii) to which any such employer was entitled to pay contributions, and

(iii) which has not been wound up; or

(b) subject to regulation 11, the governing instrument of the scheme does not contain provisions of a description specified in regulations 4 to 10.

Provisions as to borrowing

4

(1) The description of provision specified in this regulation is a provision to the effect that at the time of any borrowing the trustees of the scheme in their capacity as such shall not have borrowed an aggregate amount, including the amount of that borrowing but excluding any amount which has been repaid before that time, in excess of the total of–

(a) three times the ordinary annual contribution paid by employers;

(b) three times the annual amount of contributions paid by scheme members as a condition of membership in the year of assessment ending immediately before that time;

[(c) the amount found by the formula–

((A – B) x 45)/100

where–

A is the market value of the assets of the scheme at that time, other than assets franking any pension in payment under the rules of the scheme where the purchase of an annuity has been deferred (including any pension that would be payable to a widow or widower [or surviving civil partner] of a member of the scheme following the member's death in a case where the rules of the scheme limit such pension to the person to whom the member was married [or with whom the member had formed a civil partnership] at retirement), and

B is the aggregate of any sums borrowed to purchase those assets [which are outstanding at that time], and any other liabilities incurred by the trustees which are outstanding at that time, other than liabilities to pay benefits under the scheme.]

(2) In this regulation 'ordinary annual contribution' means the amount which is the smaller of–

[(a) the amount found–

(i) where the scheme has been established for three years or more at the time of any borrowing, by dividing the amount of the contributions paid by employers in the period of three years which ended at the end of the previous accounting period of the scheme by three, or

(ii) where the scheme has been established for less than three years at the time of any borrowing, by dividing the amount of the contributions paid by employers in the period since the scheme was established ending at the time of that borrowing by the number of years falling within that period (a part of a year being counted as one year), and]

(b) the amount of the annual contributions which, within the period of three years immediately before the date of any borrowing, an actuary has advised in writing would have to be paid in order to secure the benefits provided under the scheme.

Provisions as to investments

5

(1) The description of provision specified in this regulation is a provision to the effect that the trustees of the scheme in their capacity as such shall not directly or indirectly hold as an investment–

(a) personal chattels other than choses in action (or, in Scotland, movable property other than incorporeal movable property);

(b) residential property other than that specified in paragraph (2);

(c) shares in an unlisted company which–

(i) carry more than 30 per cent of the voting power in the company, or

(ii) entitle the holder of them to more than 30 per cent of any dividends declared by the company [in respect of shares of the class held].

(2) The residential property specified in this paragraph is–

(a) property which is, or is to be, occupied by an employee who is not connected with his employer and who is required as a condition of his employment to occupy the property; and

(b) property which is, or is to be, occupied by a person who is neither a scheme member nor connected with a scheme member in connection with the occupation by that person of business premises held by the trustees of the scheme in their capacity as such.

(3) For the purposes of paragraph (1), trustees shall not be regarded as indirectly holding as an investment residential property other than that specified in paragraph (2) where they hold as an investment units in a unit trust scheme–

(a) which is an authorised unit trust within the meaning of section 468(6) of the Act, or

(b) where all the unit holders would be wholly exempt from capital gains tax or corporation tax (otherwise than by reason of residence) if they disposed of their units,

and the trustees of the scheme hold such property as an investment subject to the trusts of the scheme.

[(4) For the purposes of paragraph (1), trustees shall not be regarded as indirectly holding as an investment residential property other than that specified in paragraph (2) where–

(a) they hold as an investment subject to the trusts of the scheme a right which confers entitlement to receive payment of any rentcharge, ground annual, feu duty or other annual payment reserved in respect of, or charged on or issuing out of, that property, and

(b) the property is not occupied by a scheme member or a person connected with him.]

Provisions as to lending and the acquisition of shares

6

(1) The description of provision specified in this regulation is a provision to the effect that the trustees of the scheme in their capacity as such shall not directly or indirectly lend money–

(a) to a member of the scheme or a person connected with him, other than an employer in relation to the scheme or any company associated with that employer, or

(b) to an employer in relation to the scheme, or any company associated with that employer, unless the lending is within the exception contained in paragraph (2).

(2) Lending is within the exception contained in this paragraph–

(a) only if the amount lent is utilised for the purposes of the borrower's business, and

(b) if it is–

(i) for a fixed term,

(ii) at a commercial rate of interest, and

(iii) evidenced by an agreement in writing which contains the provisions specified in paragraph (3) and all the conditions on which it is made.

(3) The provisions specified in this paragraph are provisions to the effect that the amount lent shall be immediately repayable–

(a) if the borrower–

(i) is in breach of the conditions of the agreement,

(ii) ceases to carry on business, or

(iii) becomes insolvent; or

(b) if it is required to enable the trustees to pay benefits which have already become due under the scheme.

(4) Subject to paragraphs (5) and (6), for the purposes of this regulation a borrower shall be taken to have become insolvent if–

(a) he has been adjudged bankrupt or has made a composition or arrangement with his creditors;

(b) he has died and his estate falls to be administered in accordance with an order under section 421 of the Insolvency Act 1986 or Article 365 of the Insolvency (Northern Ireland) Order 1989;

(c) where the borrower is a company, a winding-up order … has been made with respect to it, [or it has entered administration,] or a resolution for voluntary winding-up has been passed with respect to it, or a receiver or manager of its undertaking has been duly appointed, or possession has been taken, by or on behalf of the holders of any debentures secured by a floating charge, of any property of the company comprised in or subject to the charge, or a voluntary arrangement is approved under Part I of the Insolvency Act 1986 or Part II of the Insolvency (Northern Ireland) Order 1989.

(5) Until the coming into operation of Article 365 of the Insolvency (Northern Ireland) Order 1989, paragraph (4) above shall have effect in its application to Northern Ireland subject to the following modifications–

(a) in sub-paragraph (b) of that paragraph for the reference to that Article there shall be substituted a reference to section 30(1) of, and Part I of Schedule 1 to, the Administration of Estates Act (Northern Ireland) 1955; and

(b) in sub-paragraph (c) of that paragraph the words from 'or an administration order' to 'to it' (where those words first occur) and the words from 'or a voluntary arrangement' onwards shall be omitted.

(6) In the application of this regulation to Scotland, for sub-paragraphs (a), (b) and (c) of paragraph (4) above there shall be substituted the following sub-paragraphs–

(a) an award of sequestration has been made on his estate, or he has executed a trust deed for his creditors or has entered into a composition contract;

(b) he has died and a judicial factor appointed under section 11A of the Judicial Factors (Scotland) Act 1889 is required by the provisions of that section to divide his insolvent estate among his creditors; or

(c) where the borrower is a company, a winding up order … has been made, or a resolution for voluntary winding-up is passed with respect to it, [or it has entered administration,] or a receiver of its undertaking is duly appointed, or a voluntary arrangement for the purposes of Part I of the Insolvency Act 1986 is approved under that part.

(7) For the purposes of this regulation and of regulation 8 a member of a scheme includes–

(a) a scheme member;

(b) a person who is in receipt of a pension from the scheme;

(c) a person who has left the service of the employer but was a scheme member during that service;

(d) a person who is in the service of the employer but is no longer a scheme member.

7

(1) The description of provision specified in this regulation is a provision to the effect that at the time that any money is lent, or any shares in an employer or any company associated with that employer are acquired, the aggregate of–

(a) the total amount outstanding of money lent to an employer and any company associated with him in accordance with regulation 6(2) and (3), and

(b) the market value of shares in an employer and any company associated with him held by the trustees in their capacity as such,

shall not, where that time is during the period of two years from the date on which the scheme was established, exceed the figure specified in paragraph (2) or, where that time is after the end of that period, exceed the figure specified in paragraph (3).

[(2) The figure specified in this paragraph is the amount found by the formula–

((C – D) x 25)/100

where–

C is the market value at the time in question of the assets of the scheme which are derived from contributions made by an employer and by employees since the scheme was established, other than assets franking any pension in payment under the rules of the scheme where the purchase of an annuity has been deferred (including any pension that would be payable to a widow or widower [or surviving civil partner] of a member of the scheme following the member's death in a case where the rules of the scheme limit such pension to the person to whom the member was married [or with whom the member had formed a civil partnership] at retirement), and

D is the aggregate of any sums borrowed to purchase those assets [which are outstanding at that time], and any other liabilities incurred by the trustees which are outstanding at that time, other than liabilities to pay benefits under the scheme.

(3) The figure specified in this paragraph is the amount found by the formula–

((E – F) x 50)/100

where–

E is the market value at the time in question of all the assets of the scheme, other than assets franking any pension in payment under the rules of the scheme where the purchase of an annuity has been deferred (including any pension that would be payable to a widow or widower [or surviving civil partner] of a member of the scheme following the member's death in a case where the rules of the scheme limit such pension to the person to whom the member was married [or with whom the member had formed a civil partnership] at retirement), and

F is the aggregate of any sums borrowed to purchase those assets [which are outstanding at that time], and any other liabilities incurred by the trustees which are outstanding at that time, other than liabilities to pay benefits under the scheme.]

Provisions as to transactions with scheme members and others

8

(1) The description of provision specified in this regulation is a provision to the effect that the trustees of the scheme in their capacity as such shall not directly or indirectly purchase, sell or lease any asset–

(a) from or to a member of the scheme or a person connected with him, other than an employer in relation to the scheme or any company associated with that employer, or

(b) from or to an employer, or any company associated with that employer, except in accordance with paragraph (2).

(2) A purchase, sale or lease is in accordance with this paragraph only when it is made–

(a) after the trustees have obtained independent professional advice in writing, and

(b) in accordance with that advice.

(3) For the purpose of this regulation–

(a) a purchase by the trustees shall not be regarded as a purchase indirectly from a member of the scheme, or a person connected with him, if the purchase by the trustees took place three years or more after the sale by the member or person connected with him; and

(b) a sale by the trustees shall not be regarded as a sale indirectly to a member of the scheme, or a person connected with him, if the purchase by the member or person connected with him took place three years or more after the sale by the trustees.

[Provisions as to pensioneer trustees]

[9

[(1) The description of provision specified in this regulation is a provision to the effect that–

(a) one of the trustees of the scheme shall be a pensioneer trustee,

(b) the appointment of that trustee as a pensioneer trustee, and his obligation and entitlement to act as such, shall be incapable of termination at any time except–

(i) by the death of the trustee,

(ii) by an order of the court,

[(iia) by virtue of section 3, 4 or 29 of the Pensions Act 1995 or Article 3, 4 or 29 of the Pensions (Northern Ireland) Order 1995 (prohibition, suspension or disqualification),]

(iii) by withdrawal by the Board of their approval of the trustee to act as a pensioneer trustee, or

(iv) in the circumstances specified in paragraph (2), and

(c) where termination occurs by virtue of any of the events specified in paragraph (1)(b)(i) to (iii) or in the circumstances specified in paragraph (2)(b), the appointment of a successor to the former pensioneer trustee of the scheme is made no more than 30 days after the termination.

(2) The circumstances specified in this paragraph are where–

(a) another trustee is appointed to act as pensioneer trustee in place of the trustee, and the appointment of the other trustee takes effect at the same time as the termination;

(b) the trustee has committed a fraudulent breach of trust in relation to the scheme and that is the reason for the termination.]

10

…

Schemes awaiting approval

11

(1) Where at the date of coming into force of these Regulations a scheme which is a small self-administered scheme is in existence and either–

(a) has not yet been submitted to the Board for approval, or

(b) is before the Board for approval,

the Board shall not be prevented from approving it by virtue of section 591 of the Act by reason only that it contains a provision or provisions of a description specified in any of sub-paragraphs (a), (b) and (c) of paragraph (2).

(2) The description of provisions specified in this paragraph is–

(a) a provision which authorises the trustees of the scheme to retain an investment of a description mentioned in sub-paragraph (a), (b) or (c) of regulation 5(1) which is held by them immediately before the day on which these Regulations were made;

(b) a provision which authorises the trustees of the scheme to continue to lend money, or retain shares in an employer or any company associated with that employer, which was being lent or held by them immediately before the day on which these Regulations were made, where at the time the money was first lent or the shares were acquired the aggregate referred to in paragraph (1) of regulation 7 exceeded the figure specified in paragraph (2) of that regulation, but did not exceed the figure specified in paragraph (3) of that regulation, notwithstanding that the loan was made or the shares were acquired during the period of two years from the date on which the scheme was established;

(c) a provision which authorises the trustees of the scheme to sell assets held by them immediately before that day to a member of the scheme or a person connected with him.

Appendix 21

Overseas Lump Sums – Extra Statutory Concession A10

The following information has been published by HMRC with regard tax exemptions on lump sums from overseas schemes:

'Extra Statutory Concession A10 provides an employee with relief from taxation on a lump sum received from an overseas pension scheme to the extent that it relates to overseas service (broadly, to duties undertaken while the individual was not UK resident).

The effect of ESC A10 will continue from 6 April 2006.

The concession will be interpreted in the following ways in the light of the new simplified tax legislation:

- 'overseas retirement benefits scheme' and 'overseas provident fund' will be interpreted as overseas employer financed retirement benefits schemes, as defined in section 393A ITEPA.
- The concession will continue to apply to lump sums received from schemes within section 615(6) ICTA.
- 'relevant benefits' will be defined in accordance with section 393B ITEPA.
- The concession will not apply to any benefits chargeable under Schedule 34 Finance Act 2004.'

The full text of the ESC is shown below:

SE15063 – Non-approved retirement benefits schemes: overseas schemes: Extra Statutory Concession A10: text

'Income Tax is not charged on lump sum relevant benefits receivable by an employee (or by his personal representatives or any dependant of his) from an Overseas Retirement Benefits Scheme or an Overseas Provident Fund where the employee's overseas service comprises

(a) not less than 75 per cent of his total service in that employment; or

(b) the whole of the last 10 years of his service in that employment, where total service exceeds 10 years; or

(c) not less than 50 per cent of his total service in that employment, including any 10 of the last 20 years, where total service exceeds 20 years.

If the employee's overseas service is less than described above, relief from income tax will be given by reducing the amount of the lump sum which would otherwise be chargeable by the same proportion as the overseas service bears to the employee's total service in that employment.

In addition, income tax is not charged on lump sum relevant benefits receivable by an employee (or by his personal representatives or any dependant of his) from any superannuation fund accepted as being within Section 615 ICTA 1988.

For the purposes of this concession, the term 'relevant benefits' has the meaning given in Section 612(1) ICTA 1988 and the term 'overseas service' shall be construed in accordance with the definition of 'foreign service' found at Paragraph 10 Schedule 11 ICTA 1988.'

Notes:

- whether a fund is within section 615 ICTA 1988 is a matter for IR SPSS (Nottingham). See SE15064
- for the definition of 'relevant benefits' see SE15020
- for the definition of 'foreign service' see SE13690
- there is an example of full exemption at example SE15425 and of partial exemption at example SE15426

Appendix 22

Form 1(SF)–Chargeable Events

Inland Revenue

Chargeable Events

Please use these if you write or call. It will help to avoid delay.

Tax reference /

Our reference

Date stamp

Information required under regulation 10 of the Retirement Benefits Schemes (Information Powers) Regulations 1995 (SI 1995 No 3103).

The Administrator, *see note 1*, is required to supply the following information **no later than 30 days** after the end of the tax year in which the event occurs. **Failure to do so may lead to penalties under section 98 Taxes Management Act 1970.** Nil reports are not required.

Send this report directly to the Inland Revenue office dealing with the tax affairs of the scheme. If you do not know where this is (or a scheme file has not yet been set up), please send this form to the Inland Revenue office dealing with the Employer's Corporation Tax or Self Assessment tax affairs.

Please read the notes on page 3 before completing this form. If you report figures relating to more than one member, please attach a breakdown showing each member's refund.

If you do not make this notification within the time limit specified, please provide the reason for the delay.

Employer's name
Employer's address
Postcode

Company Registration number

Scheme name

1(SF) BS 2/05

Tax year ended 5 April 20______	Gross figure £	Tax deducted £	Net figure £	IR office use only
1 Contributions including additional voluntary contributions (plus interest thereon, if any) repaid to employees or former employees during their lifetime **except surplus voluntary contributions.** *See notes 2, 3, 4 and 5.*				IM8130
2 Payments to an employee or their Personal Representatives out of surplus funds arising from employee's voluntary contributions. *See notes 5 and 6.*				
3 Lump sums paid in commutation of entire pension in the following special circumstances. *See notes 2, 4, 5 and 7.* **a.** on the grounds of triviality **b.** in exceptional circumstances of serious ill-health.	**a.** **b.**			M8141
4 Payments to an employer out of funds held for the purposes of the scheme. *See note 8.*				IM8121

Declaration

Please provide the name and address of the Administrator. *See note 1.*

Name
Address
Postcode

Person to whom any enquiries may be sent, if not the Administrator.

Name
Address
Postcode

Signed (by/on behalf of* the Administrator)

* delete as appropriate.

Notes on Completion

1 The 'Administrator' is the trustees or such persons who are appointed by them (section 611AA Income and Corporation Taxes Act 1988 refers).

2 Where the rules allow the Administrator to deduct the amount of the tax payable from the refund or lump sum, enter the full amount available for the employee before any such deduction. But you can ignore any part of the amount available which is withheld to reimburse the employer for

- a 'payment in lieu of contributions' to the National Insurance Fund,
- a State Scheme premium under the Social Security Pensions Act 1975, or
- any financial loss caused by the employee's fraud or negligence.

3 Enter the total of the gross amounts repaid to employees during their lifetime (including any interest).

4 Where relief is claimed on the grounds that the employee's employment was carried on outside the UK give full particulars of all the places where the employment was carried on with dates. Include the amount(s) on which relief is claimed in the totals entered on the return. *See notes 2, 3 and 7* and give details separately.

5 Boxes 1, 2 and 3 apply to approved Free Standing Additional Voluntary Contribution Schemes (FSAVCS), as well as to the employer's main scheme.

6 Where the total funds available to provide benefits are excessive, the surplus, to the extent that it originates from the member's voluntary contributions, may be repaid to the member or the member's estate. Enter the full amount before any deduction of the tax due under section 599A Income and Corporation Taxes Act 1988.

7 Enter the total of the chargeable amounts. The chargeable amount is normally the amount of the commutation payment less –

a. a sum equal to 3/80ths of the employee's average annual remuneration over the last 3 years' service multiplied by the number of years' service (maximum 40) or, if greater,
b. the largest sum which could have been received by way of commutation under the rules of the scheme, apart from the special circumstances. This is on the assumption that any discretion by the Administrator or employer as to the extent to which an employee may commute their pension would have been exercised to give the maximum lump sum consistent with the rules of the scheme.

Attach a computation for each item included in the total where the amount included is less than the full amount payable to the employee in question, for instance where a deduction is made under a or b above. Where, apart from the special circumstances, the benefits under the scheme take the form of a pension and a separate lump sum, rather than a partially commutable pension, restrict the amount deducted by the amount of the separate lump sum. Where it is known that the employee was also a member of another scheme relating to the same employment, give the name(s) of the other scheme(s) because the law prevents relief being given twice in these circumstances.

Note: Where an employee's benefit rights have been subject to a pension sharing order **or** where the rules of a scheme allow for the commutation of the entire pension payable to an ex-spouse from pension credit rights, reference should be made to PN 17.29 & 30.

8 Enter the total of the sums paid or which become due. Any refunds out of pension scheme surpluses should have been notified already to Audit & Pension Schemes Services (APSS), part of IR Savings, Pensions, Share Schemes, but if not already reported enter them in this section. Exclude any amounts which are paid to an employer to reimburse

- a 'payment in lieu of contributions' to the National Insurance Fund,
- a State Scheme premium under the Social Security Pensions Act 1975, or
- any financial loss caused by the employee's fraud or negligence.

Please see the Occupational Pension Schemes Practice Notes IR12 (2001) and the FSAVCS Guidance Notes IR12 (Supplement).

Appendix 23

Form 2(SF)–Chargeable Events

Audit & Pension Schemes Services
Yorke House
Castle Meadow Road
Nottingham
NG2 1BG

Telephone: 0115 974 1600
Fax: 0115 974 1480

To: Audit & Pension Schemes Services
Yorke House
Castle Meadow Road
Nottingham
NG2 1BG

From:

Date: ………/………/………………

Your ref: SF ………/……………………/………

Our ref: ……………………………………

Insurance Companies

Chargeable Events – "Buy-out" Policies

Information required under regulation 11 of the Retirement Benefits Schemes (Information Powers) Regulations 1995 [SI 1995 No 3103].

Insurance companies should only complete this form where any of the events at 1, 2 or 3 occur under a "**buy-out policy**". Chargeable events that occur other than under a "buy-out policy" should be reported separately on a form 1(SF).

An **insurance company**, which is a prescribed person under regulation 3(c), is required to supply the following information **not later than 180 days** after the end of the chargeable period of the insurance company in which the event occurs. **Failure to do so may lead to penalties under section 98 Taxes Management Act 1970. Nil reports are not required.**

Please read the notes on completion before completing this form.

If you do not make notification within the time limit specified, please give the reason for the delay.

2(SF) (2/05)

	Chargeable period ended ………/………/…………	Enter Totals for Period (£)			see note
		Gross Amount	Tax Deducted	Net Amount	
1	Contributions (including interest thereon, if any) repaid to employees or former employees during their lifetime **except surplus voluntary contributions**				1 and 2
2	Lump sums paid in commutation of entire pension in the following special circumstances:– a. on grounds of triviality b. in exceptional circumstances of serious ill-health				1, 2 and 3
3	Payments to an employer out of funds held under a contract for the purposes of providing an annuity				4

Insurance Company	
4	Name and address of Insurer …………………………………………………… …………………………………………………… …………………………………………………… ……………………………………………………

Signed (by or on behalf of the Insurer)

……………………………………………………………………………………

Name in block capitals

……………………………………………………………………………………

Date ………/………/20………

Footnote: See the Occupational Pension Schemes Practice Notes IR12 (2001) and the FSAVCS Guidance Notes IR12 (Supplement)

Notes on Completion

1. Where the rules allow the insurance company to deduct the amount of the tax payable from the refund or lump sum, enter the full amount available for the employee(s) before any such deduction.

2. Where relief is claimed on the grounds that the employee's employment was carried on outside the United Kingdom give full particulars of all the places where the employment was carried on, with dates. Include the amount(s) on which relief is claimed in the totals entered on the return (see notes 1 and 3) and give details separately.

3. Enter the chargeable amount. The chargeable amount is normally the amount of the commutation payment less:

   a. a sum equal to 3/80ths of the employee's average annual remuneration over the last 3 years' service multiplied by the number of years' service (maximum 40); or, if greater,

   b. the largest sum which could have been received by way of commutation under the rules of the scheme, apart from the special circumstances. This is on the assumption that any discretion conferred on the administrator or employer as to the extent to which an employee may commute their pension would have been exercised to give the maximum lump sum consistent with the approval of the scheme.

   Where, apart from the special circumstances (box 2), the benefits under a scheme take the form of a pension and a separate lump sum, rather than a partially commutable pension, restrict the amount deducted by the amount of the separate lump sum. Where it is known that an employee was also a member of another scheme relating to the same employment, separately provide details of the name of the member and the name(s) of the other scheme(s) because the law prevents relief being given twice over in these circumstances.

Note: Where an employee's benefit rights have been subject to a pension sharing order **or** where the rules of a scheme allow for the commutation of the entire pension payable to an ex-spouse from pension credit rights, reference should be made to PN (2001) 17.29-30.

4. Enter the total amount of the sums paid or which became due. Any refund out of pension scheme surpluses should have been notified already to Audit & Pension Schemes Services, part of IR Savings, Pensions, Share Schemes, **but if not already reported enter in this section.**

   You should attach a Schedule showing:-

   - the name(s), address(es) and company registration number(s) of the employer(s) to whom the payment(s) is/are made; and

   - the amount paid to each employer and the date.

5. Boxes 1 and 2 also apply to Free Standing Additional Voluntary Contribution Schemes (FSAVCS).

Footnote: See the Occupational Pension Schemes Practice Notes IR12 (2001) and the FSAVCS Guidance Notes IR12 (Supplement)

Appendix 24

Form PS 7050 for Transfer of Benefits

Audit & Pension Schemes Services
Yorke House
PO Box 62
Castle Meadow Road
Nottingham
NG2 1BG

Telephone: 0115 974 0000
Fax: 0115 974 1480

To: Audit & Pension Schemes Services
Yorke House
PO Box 62
Castle Meadow Road
Nottingham
NG2 1BG

From:

Date:

Your ref: SF ..../...........................

Our ref:

Transfer of Benefits

Information required under regulations 11A or 11B of the Retirement Benefits Schemes (Information Powers) Regulations [SI 1995 No 3103] as amended.

Please read the following before completing this form.

This form is a multi-purpose form. Please use it to:

1. make a statutory report under regulation 11A or 11B of SI 1995 No 3103; or
2. to obtain prior agreement to an individual transfer in accordance with Chapter 10 Practice Notes (2001) (PN).

Where a statutory report is made under SI 1995 No 3103, the report should be completed by:

- reports under regulation 11A – the administrator of the occupational scheme (or the insurance company for a deferred annuity contract – note 1) making the transfer
- reports under regulation 11B – the administrator of the occupational scheme (or the insurance company for a deferred annuity contract – note 1) receiving the transfer.

For a transfer that consists only of pension credits from a pension sharing order please see note 2.

Section A – Use of form. Tick **all** the boxes that apply to you.	
1. Pre Transfer clearance	
☐ The report is to obtain IR SPSS agreement to the transfer before it is made	
☐ It is a transfer to an overseas scheme	
The report is from	
☐ The transferring scheme	☐ The receiving scheme

2. Post Transfer Reports should be made to IR SPSS within 28 days of the date of the transfer.
☐ Regulation 11A – report by transferring scheme ☐ Regulation 11B – report by receiving scheme The transfer is reportable because ☐ single transfer of over £250,000 ☐ 365 day total of transfers is over £250,000 (note 3)

Section B – Details of the Scheme Making the Transfer	
1. Name of Principal Employer / PP Provider / RAC Contract Provider / Insurance Company	....
2. Principal Employer Company Registration Number (CRN) (if appropriate)	....
3. Name of scheme / arrangement	....
4. SF Reference Number	........../................................
5. Type of scheme / arrangement (tick as appropriate) (see note 4) ☐ Occupational Pension Scheme (specify) ☐ Personal Pension Scheme ☐ SSAS ☐ LSAS ☐ Retirement Annuity Contract (RAC) ☐ Fully Insured ☐ Deferred Policy ☐ Other (please specify)	

Section C – Details of the Scheme Receiving the Transfer	
1. Name of Principal Employer / PP Provider / RAC Contract Provider / Insurance Company	....
2. Principal Employer Company Registration Number (CRN) (if appropriate)	....
3. Name of scheme / arrangement	....
4. SF Reference Number	........../................................
5. Name(s) and address(es) of the recipient of the transfer (and in what capacity) (Note: If the scheme trustees, it is sufficient to state as such, and give a named contact and address for any further enquiries)	....
6. Type of scheme / arrangement (tick as appropriate) (see note 4) ☐ Occupational Pension Scheme (specify) ☐ Personal Pension Scheme ☐ SSAS ☐ LSAS ☐ Retirement Annuity Contract (RAC) ☐ Fully Insured ☐ Deferred Policy ☐ Other (please specify)	

Section D – Member Related Details	
1. Name of member	....
2. National Insurance Number (NINO)	......../......../......../......../.....
3. Normal Retirement Date (NRD)	........../......../......................
4. Does the transfer represent the whole of the member's benefits held by the transferring scheme?	☐ Yes ☐ No
5. Are benefits being retained only because they represent contracting-out benefits?	☐ Yes ☐ No ☐ N/A
6. Have benefits been paid to the member or become due for payment in accordance with the scheme rules? (If answer is yes, see note 5)	☐ Yes ☐ No

Section E – Transfer Details	
1. Date of Transfer	........../......../......................
2. Amount of Transfer	£......................................
3. Reason for transfer (continue on a separate sheet if necessary)	....
4. If a Transfer from an OPS or a deferred annuity contract, does the amount of the transfer conform to the limits imposed by PN 10.26?	☐ Yes ☐ No
5. If a transfer to a PP does the member fall within regulation 8(2) of the Personal Pension Schemes (Transfer Payment) Regulations 2001 [SI 2001 No 119]?	☐ Yes – Go to Question 6 ☐ No – Go to Question 7
6. Has the transferring scheme administrator provided a certificate in accordance with regulation 8(3) of [SI 2001 No 119]?	☐ Yes ☐ No
7. What form does the transfer value take?	☐ Cash Value £........... Go to F ☐ Policies Value £........... Go to F ☐ In Specie Value £........... Go to Q8
8. Give a breakdown on a separate sheet of the in specie elements. Please list and value individually any properties and shares that are reportable under regulation 5 of the Retirement Benefits Schemes (Information Powers) Regulations [SI 1995 No 3103] Please note:- 1. it is not permissible to transfer loans in specie; 2. it is not permissible to transfer unlisted shares (not including shares listed on AIM) to a self invested personal pension scheme; and 3. a transfer is a disposal of assets that may need to be reported within 90 days of the transfer in accordance with regulation 5 [SI 1995 No 3103].	

Section F – Declaration
I declare that:- • the information on this form is correct; • I understand that a false declaration may result in (if applicable) a penalty of up to £3000 under section 98 Taxes Management Act 1970 and could result in withdrawal of approval of the schemes involved; and • the transfer has been/will be made in accordance with the rules of the scheme for which I am making this report. Signed .... Name(s) .... Capacity in which signed (see note 6)..........

Notes

1. A "deferred annuity contract" is a policy that does not provide immediate benefits.
2. If the transfer represents only a transfer of pension credits questions D3-D6 and E4-E7 do not need to be completed.
3. A transfer may be reportable because either on its own it is £250,000 or more or the transfer and any other transfer made for the same person in the previous 364 days is £250,000 or more.
4. SSAS = Small Self-administered Scheme LSAS = Large Self-administered Scheme
5. If the benefits have been paid or are due to be paid, the transfer cannot go ahead by virtue of the provisions set out in PN10.22
6. If this notification is being made after the transfer has taken place, the Scheme Administrator (see note 7 below) must sign this form. If the Scheme Administrator is more than one individual, all must sign unless already agreed with IR SPSS, in accordance with paragraph 9 of PSO Update No 47 (issued 24 July 1998).
7. The "Scheme Administrator" will be the trustees or such persons as they appoint (paragraph 2.6 of PN and section 611AA Income and Corporation Taxes Act 1988 refer).

Data Protection

The Inland Revenue is a Data Controller under the Data Protection Act. We hold information for the purposes specified in our notification made to the Data Protection Commissioner, and may use this information for any of them.

We may get information about you from others, or we may give information to them. If we do, it will only be as the law permits to

- check accuracy of information
- prevent or detect crime
- protect public funds.

We may check information we receive about you with what is already in our records. This can include information provided by you as well as others such as other government departments. We will not give information about you to anyone outside the Inland Revenue unless the law permits us to do so.

Appendix 25

Trust and Estate Return SA900

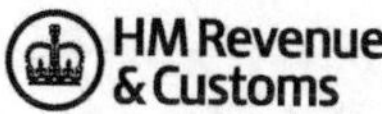

Trust and Estate Tax Return for the year ended 5 April **2006**

Tax reference

Date

HM Revenue & Customs office

Area Director

Telephone

Issue address

For Reference

Please read this page first

The green arrows and instructions will guide you through your Tax Return

*This **Notice** requires you by law to send me a Tax Return, and any documents I ask for, for the year from 6 April 2005 to 5 April 2006, containing details of income and capital gains. I have sent you this paper form to fill in, or you could use:*

- *our Internet service (using 3rd party software) to file your Tax Return online. To register for Self Assessment Online for Trusts go to https://online.inlandrevenue.gov.uk **or***
- *other HM Revenue & Customs approved paper versions.*

Make sure the Tax Return, and any documents I ask for, reach me by:

- *the later of **30 September 2006** and **2 months after the date this notice was given** if you want **me** to calculate the trust or estate's tax, **OR***
- *the later of **31 January 2007** and **3 months after the date this notice was given, at the latest.** Late Returns may attract an initial penalty of £100.*

Make sure your payment of any tax the trust or estate owes reaches me by 31 January 2007. Otherwise, you will have to pay interest, and perhaps a surcharge.

The Trust and Estate Tax Return may be checked. Please remember that there are penalties for supplying false information.

Calculating your tax

You can choose to calculate the trust or estate's tax. But if you do not want to, and providing I receive the Return by 30 September, I will work out the tax for you and I will also let you know if there is tax to pay by 31 January 2007.

***However,** if you file later than 30 September or 2 months after the date this notice was given, see the Tax Calculation Guide (sent with this Return unless I know you have a tax adviser).*

The Trust and Estate Tax Return - your responsibilities

I have sent you pages 1 to 12 of the Tax Return.

You might need other forms - 'supplementary Pages' - if the trust or estate had particular income or capital gains. Use page 3 to check.

*You are responsible for sending me a complete and correct return, but **we** are here to help you get it right.*

Four ways we can help you

- *look at the Trust and Estate Tax Return Guide (sent with this Tax Return, unless I know you have a tax adviser). It should answer most of your questions, **or***
- *go to our website at **www.hmrc.gov.uk or***
- *ring me on the above number - when the office is closed, call our Helpline on **0845 9000 444, or***
- *call in to one of our Enquiry Centres - look under 'HM Revenue & Customs' in the phone book.*

SA900

HMRC 12/05net

INCOME AND CAPITAL GAINS for the year ended 5 April 2006

Step 1 You may not have to answer all the questions in this Tax Return.

Tick if this applies ▼

- see notes on pages 4 and 6 of the Trust and Estate Tax Return Guide

1) **If you are the trustee of a bare trust** (except an unauthorised unit trust), that is, one in which the beneficiary(ies) has/have an immediate and absolute title to both capital and income you can go straight to Question 19 on page 11. ☐

2) **If you are the personal representative of a deceased person,** completing this Tax Return for a period of administration **and all** the points below apply:
   - all the income arose in the UK
   - you do not wish to claim reliefs
   - no annual payments have been made out of capital
   - all income has had tax deducted before you received it (or is UK dividends with tax credit)
   - there are no accrued income charges or reliefs, no income from deeply discounted securities, gilt strips, offshore income gains, or gains on life insurance policies, life annuities or capital redemption policies where no tax is treated as having been paid on the gain.

   Then, **if you have not made any chargeable disposals,** go straight to Question 19 on page 11 ☐

   or, **if you have made chargeable disposals,** answer Questions 5 and 6 at Step 2, Question 8 and then Questions 17 to 22. ☐

3) **If you are the trustee of an interest in possession trust** (one which is exclusively an interest in possession trust), and:
   - no income arose to the trust, **or** ☐
   - you have mandated all the trust income to the beneficiary(ies), **or** ☐
   - all the income arose in the UK and has had tax deducted before you receive it (or is UK dividends with tax credit), **or** ☐
   - you have mandated part of the income to the beneficiary(ies) where the part you have not mandated comprises only income arising in the UK which has had tax deducted before you received it ☐

   and all of the following points apply:
   - the answer will be 'No' in boxes 8.11 and 8.13 of Question 8
   - there are no accrued income charges or reliefs, no income from deeply discounted securities, gilt strips, company buy-backs, offshore income gains, or gains on life insurance policies, life annuities or capital redemption policies
   - you do not wish to claim reliefs (Question 10)
   - no annual payments have been made out of capital (Question 11)
   - no further capital has been added to the settlement (Question 12)
   - no capital payments have been made to or for the benefit of relevant children (see the note on page 6 of the Trust and Estate Tax Return Guide) of the settlor during his/her lifetime (Question 15A)
   - the trust has never been non-resident and has never received any capital from another trust which is, or at any time has been, non-resident (Question 16). ☐

   Then, **if you have not made any chargeable disposals,** go straight to Question 19 on page 11 ☐

   or, **if you have made chargeable disposals,** answer Questions 5 and 6 at Step 2, Question 8 and then Questions 17 to 22.

4) **If you are the trustee of a charitable trust,** and:
   - you are claiming exemption from tax on all your income and gains, you can go straight to Question 7, then Questions 10, 11 and 22, **or**
   - you are claiming exemption from tax on only part of your income and gains, you must complete this Return for any income or gains for which you are not claiming exemption and answer Questions 10 and 11 as appropriate.

5) **In any other cases,** including if you are the trustee of an unauthorised unit trust, you should go to Step 2.

Step 2 Answer Questions 1 to 7 on page 3 to check if you need supplementary Pages to give details of particular income or gains. Pages 8 and 9 of the Trust and Estate Tax Return Guide will help. (Ask the Orderline for a Guide if I haven't sent you one with the Tax Return, and you want one.) If you answer '**Yes**', ask the Orderline for the appropriate supplementary Pages and Notes.

Ring the Orderline on 0845 9000 404 (textphone available) or fax on 0845 9000 604 for any you need (closed Christmas Day, Boxing Day and New Year's Day). Make sure you ask for the supplementary Pages for the Trust and Estate Tax Return.

Or you can go to our website www.hmrc.gov.uk

HMRC 12/05net ■ TRUST AND ESTATE TAX RETURN: PAGE 2

INCOME AND CAPITAL GAINS for the year ended 5 April 2006 *continued*

Make sure you have the supplementary Pages you need and then tick the box below when you have got them

Q1 Did the trust or estate make any profit or loss from a sole trade? *(Read page 8 of the Trust and Estate Tax Return Guide if you are the personal representative of a deceased Name at Lloyd's.)* **Yes** ☐ — *Trust and estate trade* ☐

Q2 Did the trust or estate make any profit or loss or have any other income from a partnership? **Yes** ☐ — *Trust and estate partnership* ☐

Q3 Did the trust or estate receive any rent or other income from land and property in the UK? **Yes** ☐ — *Trust and estate land and property* ☐

Q4 Did the trust or estate receive any income from foreign companies or savings institutions, offshore funds or trusts abroad, land and property abroad, or make gains on foreign life insurance policies? **Yes** ☐

Is the trust or estate claiming relief for foreign tax paid on foreign income or gains, or relief from UK tax under a Double Taxation Agreement? **Yes** ☐ — *Trust and estate foreign* ☐

Q5 Capital gains

- Did the trust or estate dispose of chargeable assets worth more than £34,000 in total? **Yes** ☐

Answer 'Yes' if

- allowable losses are deducted from the chargeable gains made by the trust or estate, which total more than the annual exempt amount before deduction and before taper relief, **or**
- no allowable losses are deducted from the chargeable gains made by the trust or estate and after taper relief the chargeable gains total more than the annual exempt amount, **or**
- you want to make a claim or election for the year. **Yes** ☐

Does this Return include the disposal of assets for either a Trust/Settlement with 'separate funds', or for just one of those separate funds? **Yes** ☐ — *Trust and estate capital gains* ☐
Read page 9 of the Trust and Estate Tax Return Guide.

Q6 Is the trust claiming to be not resident in the UK, or dual resident in the UK and another country for all or part of the year for:

- Income Tax? **Yes** ☐
- Capital Gains Tax? **Yes** ☐ — *Trust and estate non-residence etc* ☐

Q7 Is the trust claiming total or partial exemption from tax because of its charitable status? **Yes** ☐ — *Trust and estate charities* ☐

Q8 *Read pages 10 and 11 of the Trust and Estate Return Guide.*

Are you completing this Tax Return	No	Yes
- for a period of administration?	8.1	8.2
- as the trustee of an unauthorised unit trust?	8.3	8.4
- as the trustee of an employment related trust?	8.5	8.6
- as the trustee of an Heritage Maintenance Fund?	8.7	8.8
Trustees of Funded Unapproved Retirement Benefit Schemes (FURBS): have you provided any non-relevant benefits to any of the scheme's beneficiaries?	8.9	8.10
If you are a trustee,		
- can any settlor (or living settlor's spouse or civil partner) benefit from the capital or income?	8.11	8.12
- are you a participator in an underlying non-resident company (a company that would be a close company if it were resident in the UK)?	8.13	8.14
- is the trust liable to Income Tax at either or both the rate applicable to trusts (40%) or the dividend trust rate (32.5%) on any part of the income or would it be if its income exceeded £500 (for example, it is a discretionary trust)?	8.15	8.16
- has a valid vulnerable beneficiary election been made?	8.17	8.18

Step 3 *Now fill in any supplementary Pages BEFORE answering Questions 9 to 21, as directed.*
Please use blue or black ink to fill in the Trust and Estate Tax Return.
Please do not include pence. Round down income and gains. Round up tax credits and tax deductions. Round to the nearest pound.

Please turn over

INCOME for the year ended 5 April 2006 *continued*

Q9 Did the trust or estate receive any other income not already included on the supplementary Pages? YES [ ] If yes, fill in boxes 9.1 to 9.40 as appropriate.

You may, **if you wish**, not complete some of the boxes in 9.1 to 9.40 in the following circumstances:

a) **If you are the trustee of an interest in possession trust (one which is exclusively an interest in possession trust),** you may exclude income which has had tax deducted before you received it (or is UK dividends with tax credit) unless:

(i) that income has not been mandated to the beneficiary and there is accrued income scheme relief to set against the interest or you are claiming losses against general income, **or**

(ii) its exclusion would make you liable to make a payment on account which would not be due if you included it - see page 11 of the Trust and Estate Tax Calculation Guide concerning payments on account **before** following this guidance.

b) **If you are the trustee of a (non-interest in possession) trust where the income is treated as the settlor's for tax purposes** because the settlor has retained an interest (if in doubt ask the Orderline for *Help Sheet IR270: Trusts and settlements - income treated as the settlor's*) you may exclude income which has had tax deducted before you received it (or is UK dividends with tax credit) unless any of the following apply:

- there is accrued income scheme relief to set against the interest, **or**
- you are claiming reliefs (Question 10) which exceed the untaxed income, **or**
- you are claiming losses against general income, **or**
- the exclusion would make you liable to make payments on account which would not be due if you included it – see page 11 of the Trust and Estate Tax Calculation Guide concerning payments on account **before** following this guidance.

c) **If you are the personal representative of a deceased person** you may exclude income which has had tax deducted before you received it (or is UK dividends with tax credit) unless there is accrued income scheme relief to set against the interest. If the reliefs claimed at Question 10 on page 6 exceed untaxed income, you will need to include estate income that has had tax deducted to ensure a repayment can be calculated.

- Have you received any taxed income (or UK dividends with tax credit) which you have not included in this Trust and Estate Tax Return because (a), (b) or (c) above apply? YES [ ]

■ ***Interest and alternative finance receipts***

- Interest and alternative finance receipts from UK banks and building societies (interest and alternative finance receipts from UK Internet accounts must be included) – *if you have more than one bank or building society etc. account enter **totals** in the boxes.*

	Amount after tax taken off	Tax taken off	Gross amount before tax / Taxable amount
- where **no tax** has been taken off			9.1 £
- where **tax has** been taken off – *the Working Sheet on page 14 of the Guide will help you to fill in boxes 9.2 to 9.4.*	9.2 £	9.3 £	9.4 £
• Interest distributions from UK authorised unit trusts and open-ended investment companies (dividend distributions go in boxes 9.18 to 9.20)	9.5 £	9.6 £	9.7 £
• National Savings & Investments (other than First Option Bonds and Fixed Rate Savings Bonds)			Taxable amount 9.8 £
• National Savings & Investments First Option Bonds and Fixed Rate Savings Bonds	9.9 £	9.10 £	9.11 £
• Other income from UK savings and investments (except dividends)	9.12 £	9.13 £	9.14 £

INCOME for the year ended 5 April 2006 *continued*

■ ***Dividends***

• Dividends and other qualifying distributions from UK companies	Dividend/distribution 9.15 £	Tax credit 9.16 £	Dividend/distribution plus credit 9.17 £
• Dividend distributions from UK authorised unit trusts and open-ended investment companies	Dividend/distribution 9.18 £	Tax credit 9.19 £	Dividend/distribution plus credit 9.20 £
• Stock dividends from UK companies	Dividend 9.21 £	Notional tax 9.22 £	Dividend plus notional tax 9.23 £
• Dividends and other qualifying distributions received by unauthorised unit trusts	Amount of dividend only 9.24 £		
• Scrip dividends received by unauthorised unit trusts	Amount of dividend only 9.25 £		
• Non-qualifying distributions and loans written off	Distribution/loan 9.26 £	Notional tax 9.27 £	Taxable amount 9.28 £

■ ***Gains on UK life insurance policies, life annuities and capital redemption policies***

• on which no tax is treated as paid		Amount of gain 9.29 £
• on which tax is treated as paid	Tax treated as paid 9.30 £	Amount of gain 9.31 £

■ ***Other income***

• Other income	Amount after tax taken off 9.32 £	Tax taken off 9.33 £	Gross amount before tax 9.34 £
		Losses brought forward 9.35 £	Losses used in 2005-06 9.36 £
		2005-06 losses carried forward 9.37 £	
• Deemed income etc. - *see page 20 of the Trust and Estate Tax Return Guide*			Taxable amount 9.38 £
• Company purchase of its own shares		Tax credit 9.39 £	Taxable amount 9.40 £

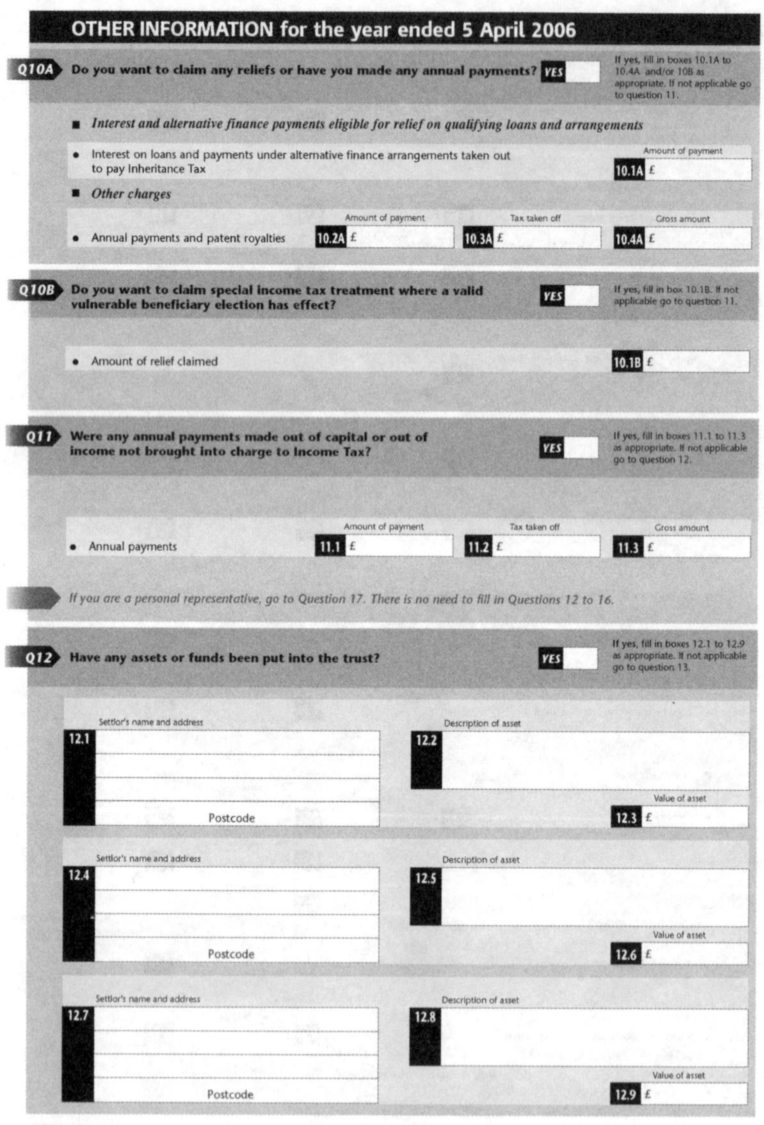

OTHER INFORMATION for the year ended 5 April 2006

Q10A Do you want to claim any reliefs or have you made any annual payments? YES

If yes, fill in boxes 10.1A to 10.4A and/or 10B as appropriate. If not applicable go to question 11.

■ ***Interest and alternative finance payments eligible for relief on qualifying loans and arrangements***

- Interest on loans and payments under alternative finance arrangements taken out to pay Inheritance Tax — Amount of payment **10.1A** £

■ ***Other charges***

	Amount of payment	Tax taken off	Gross amount
• Annual payments and patent royalties	10.2A £	10.3A £	10.4A £

Q10B Do you want to claim special income tax treatment where a valid vulnerable beneficiary election has effect? YES

If yes, fill in box 10.1B. If not applicable go to question 11.

- Amount of relief claimed **10.1B** £

Q11 Were any annual payments made out of capital or out of income not brought into charge to Income Tax? YES

If yes, fill in boxes 11.1 to 11.3 as appropriate. If not applicable go to question 12.

	Amount of payment	Tax taken off	Gross amount
• Annual payments	11.1 £	11.2 £	11.3 £

If you are a personal representative, go to Question 17. There is no need to fill in Questions 12 to 16.

Q12 Have any assets or funds been put into the trust? YES

If yes, fill in boxes 12.1 to 12.9 as appropriate. If not applicable go to question 13.

Settlor's name and address	Description of asset	Value of asset
12.1 Postcode	12.2	12.3 £
12.4 Postcode	12.5	12.6 £
12.7 Postcode	12.8	12.9 £

HMRC 12/05net ■ Trust and Estate Tax Return: Page 6

OTHER INFORMATION for the year ended 5 April 2006

If you ticked box 8.15 in Question 8, on page 3, then you do not need to complete this page - please go to Question 16 on page 9 and carry on filling in the Tax Return.
If you have ticked box 8.16 in Question 8, page 3, complete Questions 13 to 15.

Q13 Is any part of the trust income not liable to tax at the rate applicable to trusts or the dividend trust rate because it falls within one or more of the three categories listed below? YES [ ] If yes, fill in boxes 13.1 to 13.22 below. If not applicable, fill in boxes 13.19 to 13.22.

■ ***Income treated as that of the settlor***

• Amount of income charged at the **10%** rate		13.1 £
• Trust management expenses applicable to the income in box 13.1	13.2 £	
• Amount of income chargeable at the **lower** rate		13.3 £
• Trust management expenses applicable to the income in box 13.3	13.4 £	
• Amount of income chargeable at the **basic** rate		13.5 £
• Trust management expenses applicable to the income in box 13.5	13.6 £	

■ ***Income to beneficiaries whose entitlement is not subject to the trustees' (or any other person's) discretion***

• Amount of income charged at the **10%** rate		13.7 £
• Trust management expenses applicable to the income in box 13.7	13.8 £	
• Amount of income chargeable at the **lower** rate		13.9 £
• Trust management expenses applicable to the income in box 13.9	13.10 £	
• Amount of income chargeable at the **basic** rate		13.11 £
• Trust management expenses applicable to the income in box 13.11	13.12 £	

■ ***Income allocated to specific purposes***

• Amount of income charged at the **10%** rate		13.13 £
• Trust management expenses applicable to the income in box 13.13	13.14 £	
• Amount of income chargeable at the **lower** rate		13.15 £
• Trust management expenses applicable to the income in box 13.15	13.16 £	
• Amount of income chargeable at the **basic** rate		13.17 £
• Trust management expenses applicable to the income in box 13.17	13.18 £	

• Total amount of deductible trust management expenses - *see notes on pages 21 to 24 of the Trust and Estate Tax Return Guide*		13.19 £
• Expenses set against income not liable at the rate applicable to trusts	total of column above 13.20 £	
• Total income not liable to UK Income Tax and not included elsewhere on this Trust and Estate Tax Return (non-resident trusts only)		13.21 £
• Exceptional deductions		13.22 £

OTHER INFORMATION for the year ended 5 April 2006

If you ticked box 8.15 in Question 8, on page 3, then you do not need to complete this page - please go to Question 16 on page 9 and carry on filling in the Tax Return.
If you have ticked box 8.16 in Question 8, page 3, complete Questions 13 to 15.

Q14 **Have discretionary payments of income been made to beneficiaries?** *Trustees of Heritage Maintenance Funds: do not complete these boxes for expenditure on heritage property.*
See notes on page 23 of the Trust and Estate Tax Return Guide before filling in these boxes.

YES ☐ If yes, fill in boxes 14.1 to 14.15 as appropriate. If not applicable, fill in box 14.15 only.

	Name of beneficiary		Net payment	
14.1		14.2	£	☐
14.3		14.4	£	☐
14.5		14.6	£	☐
14.7		14.8	£	☐
14.9		14.10	£	☐
14.11		14.12	£	☐
14.13		14.14	£	☐

Tick the box if the beneficiary was a relevant child of the settlor and the settlor was alive when payment was made.

- Amount, if any, of unused tax pool brought forward from last year (enter '0' if appropriate) **14.15** £

Q15A **Have the trustees made any capital payments to, or for the benefit of, relevant children of the settlor during the settlor's lifetime?**

YES ☐ If yes, fill in box 15.1. If not applicable go to question 15B.

- Total capital payments to relevant children — Amount paid **15.1** £

Q15B **Were there capital transactions between the trustees and the settlors?**

YES ☐ If yes, fill in boxes 15.2 to 15.13 as appropriate. If not applicable go to question 16.

■ ***Capital transactions between the trustees and settlors*** *- read page 25 of the Trust and Estate Tax Return Guide.*

Date	Amount	Name of company (if appropriate)	Registered office
15.2 / /	15.3 £	15.4	15.5 Postcode
15.6 / /	15.7 £	15.8	15.9 Postcode
15.10 / /	15.11 £	15.12	15.13 Postcode

HMRC 12/05net ■ TRUST AND ESTATE TAX RETURN: PAGE 8

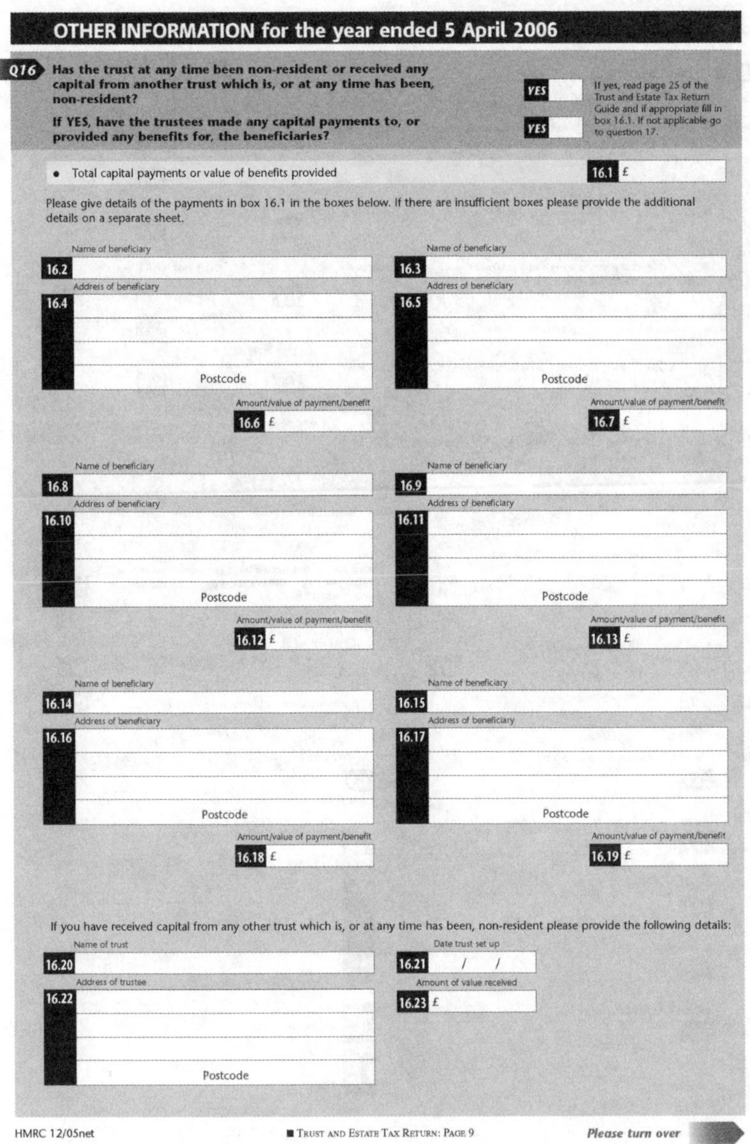

OTHER INFORMATION for the year ended 5 April 2006

Q16 Has the trust at any time been non-resident or received any capital from another trust which is, or at any time has been, non-resident? YES

If YES, have the trustees made any capital payments to, or provided any benefits for, the beneficiaries? YES

If yes, read page 25 of the Trust and Estate Tax Return Guide and if appropriate fill in box 16.1. If not applicable go to question 17.

- Total capital payments or value of benefits provided 16.1 £

Please give details of the payments in box 16.1 in the boxes below. If there are insufficient boxes please provide the additional details on a separate sheet.

Name of beneficiary 16.2 | Name of beneficiary 16.3

Address of beneficiary 16.4 Postcode | Address of beneficiary 16.5 Postcode

Amount/value of payment/benefit 16.6 £ | Amount/value of payment/benefit 16.7 £

Name of beneficiary 16.8 | Name of beneficiary 16.9

Address of beneficiary 16.10 Postcode | Address of beneficiary 16.11 Postcode

Amount/value of payment/benefit 16.12 £ | Amount/value of payment/benefit 16.13 £

Name of beneficiary 16.14 | Name of beneficiary 16.15

Address of beneficiary 16.16 Postcode | Address of beneficiary 16.17 Postcode

Amount/value of payment/benefit 16.18 £ | Amount/value of payment/benefit 16.19 £

If you have received capital from any other trust which is, or at any time has been, non-resident please provide the following details:

Name of trust 16.20 | Date trust set up 16.21 / /

Address of trustee 16.22 Postcode | Amount of value received 16.23 £

HMRC 12/05net ■ TRUST AND ESTATE TAX RETURN: PAGE 9 *Please turn over*

OTHER INFORMATION for the year ended 5 April 2006

Q17 Do you want to calculate the tax? YES

If yes, do it now and then fill in boxes 17.1 to 17.9 below. The *Trust and Estate Tax Calculation Guide* will help you.

- Total tax due for 2005-06 **before** you made any payments on account *(put the amount in brackets if an overpayment)* — 17.1 £
- Tax due for earlier years — 17.2 £
- Tick box 17.3 if you have calculated tax overpaid for earlier years and enter the amount in box 17.4 — 17.3 — 17.4 £
- Tick box 17.5 if you are making a claim to reduce your payments on account, enter your **reduced** payment in box 17.7 and say why in the 'Additional information' box, box 21.11, on page 12 — 17.5

  Tick box 17.6 if you do not need to make payments on account — 17.6
- Your first payment on account for 2006-07 *(include the pence)* — 17.7 £
- Tick box 17.8 if you are claiming a repayment of 2006-07 tax now and enter the amount in box 17.9 — 17.8 — 17.9 £

Q18 Do you want to claim a repayment if the trust or estate has paid too much tax? YES

(If you do not tick 'Yes', or the tax overpaid is below £10, I will use the amount you are owed to reduce the next tax bill.)

If yes, fill in boxes 18.1 to 18.12 as appropriate. If not applicable go to question 19.

Repayments will be sent direct to your bank or building society account. This is the safest and quickest method of payment. If you do not have an account, tick box 18.8A. If you would like repayment to your nominee, tick box 18.2 or 18.8B.

Should the repayment (or payment) be sent:

- to your bank or building society account? *Tick box 18.1 and fill in boxes 18.3 to 18.7* — 18.1

or

- to your nominee's bank or building society account? *Tick box 18.2 and fill in boxes 18.3 to 18.12* — 18.2

- If you do not have a bank or building society account, read the notes on pages 25 and 26, *tick box 18.8A* — 18.8A
- If you would like a cheque to be sent to your nominee, *tick box 18.8B and fill in boxes 18.9 to 18.12* — 18.8B
- If your nominee is your adviser, *tick box 18.9A* — 18.9A

Name of bank or building society — 18.3

Name of account holder — 18.4

Branch sort code — 18.5

Account number — 18.6

Building society reference — 18.7

Adviser's reference for you (if your nominee is your adviser) — 18.9

I authorise

Name of your nominee/adviser — 18.10

Address of nominee/adviser — 18.11

Postcode

to receive on my behalf the amount due

18.12 *This authority must be signed by you. A photocopy of your signature will not do.*

Signature

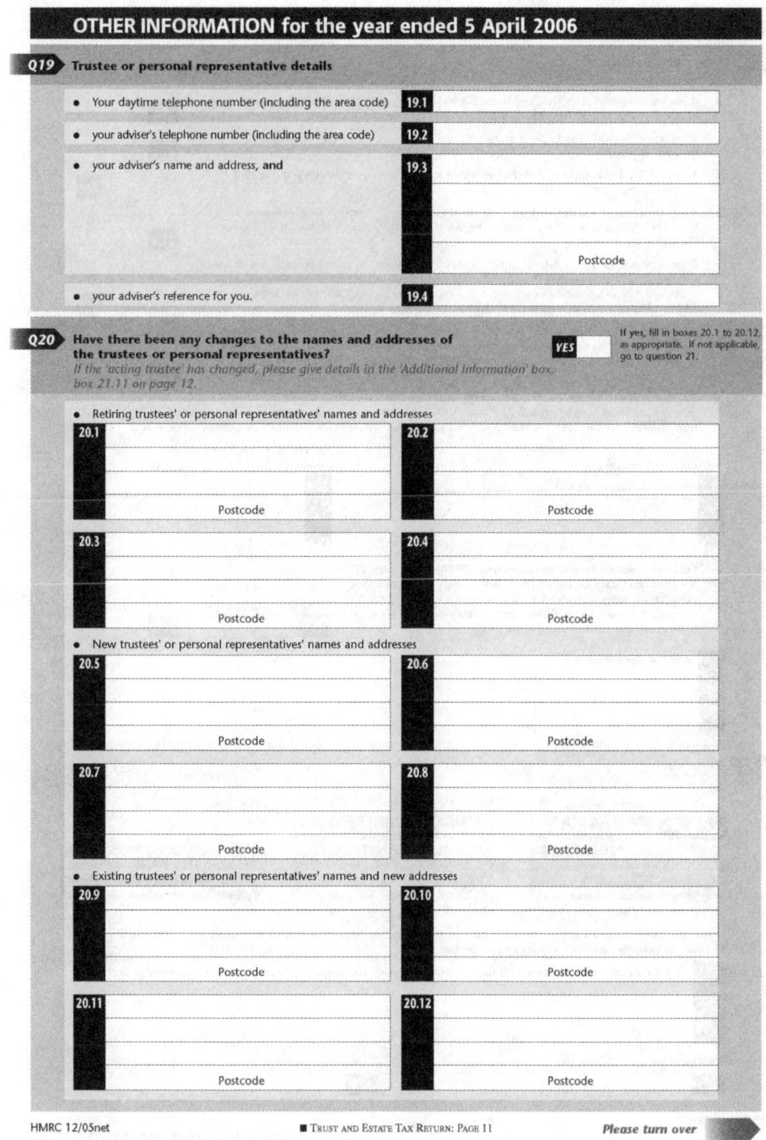

OTHER INFORMATION for the year ended 5 April 2006

Q19 Trustee or personal representative details

- Your daytime telephone number (including the area code) **19.1**
- your adviser's telephone number (including the area code) **19.2**
- your adviser's name and address, **and** **19.3** Postcode
- your adviser's reference for you. **19.4**

Q20 Have there been any changes to the names and addresses of the trustees or personal representatives? **YES**

If the 'acting trustee' has changed, please give details in the 'Additional information' box, box 21.11 on page 12.

If yes, fill in boxes 20.1 to 20.12, as appropriate. If not applicable, go to question 21.

- Retiring trustees' or personal representatives' names and addresses

20.1 Postcode **20.2** Postcode

20.3 Postcode **20.4** Postcode

- New trustees' or personal representatives' names and addresses

20.5 Postcode **20.6** Postcode

20.7 Postcode **20.8** Postcode

- Existing trustees' or personal representatives' names and new addresses

20.9 Postcode **20.10** Postcode

20.11 Postcode **20.12** Postcode

HMRC 12/05net ■ TRUST AND ESTATE TAX RETURN: PAGE 11 *Please turn over*

OTHER INFORMATION for the year ended 5 April 2006

Q21 Other Information

- If you are completing this Trust and Estate Tax Return as a personal representative, please enter in box 21.1 the date of death of the deceased. — **21.1** Date / /
- If the administration period ceased in the year to 5 April 2006, please enter in box 21.2 the date of cessation. — **21.2** Date / /
- Tick box 21.3 if the administration period ceased in the year to 5 April 2006 and there is a continuing trust. — **21.3**
- If you are a trustee and the trust was terminated in the year to 5 April 2006 please enter in box 21.4 the date of termination and, in the 'Additional information' box, box 21.11 below, the reason for termination. — **21.4** Date / /
- If this Trust and Estate Tax Return contains any figures that are provisional because you do not yet have final figures, please tick box 21.5. Page 26 of the Trust and Estate Tax Return Guide explains the circumstances in which provisional figures may be used and asks for some additional information to be provided in box 21.11 below. — **21.5**
- If any 2005-06 tax was refunded directly by the HM Revenue & Customs office, or (personal representatives only) by the Benefits Agency (in Northern Ireland, the Social Security Agency), please enter the amount in box 21.6. Do **not** include any refunds of excessive payments on account or any Gift Aid repayments claimed on form R68(2000). — **21.6** Amount £
- **Disclosure of tax avoidance schemes** – if the trust or estate is a party to one or more disclosable tax avoidance schemes you must complete boxes 21.7 and 21.8. Give details of each scheme (up to 3) on a separate line. If the trust or estate is a party to more than 3 schemes give further details in the 'Additional information' box, box 21.11.

	Scheme reference number		Tax year in which the expected advantage arises - year ended 5 April
21.7		**21.8**	

- **Business Premises Renovation Allowance (BPRA)** - Read page 27 of the Trust and Estate Tax Return Guide before you fill in these boxes. Extract from boxes 1.20 and 3.35, and boxes 1.21 and 3.33 the amounts that relate to any BPRA claims or charges. Enter claims to BPRA in box 21.9 and charges in box 21.10. — **21.9** Capital allowance £ — **21.10** Balancing charge £

21.11 *Additional information*

Q22 Declaration

I have filled in and am sending back to you the following Trust and Estate Tax Return Pages:

1 to 12 of this form	*Trust and estate land and property*	
Trust and estate trade	*Trust and estate foreign*	*Trust and estate non-residence etc*
Trust and estate partnership	*Trust and estate capital gains*	*Trust and estate charities*

Before you send the completed Tax Return back to the HM Revenue & Customs office, you must sign the statement below.

If you give false information or conceal any part of trust or estate income or chargeable gains, you may be liable to financial penalties and/or you may be prosecuted.

22.1 **The information I have given in this Tax Return is correct and complete to the best of my knowledge and belief.**

Signature Date

- Please PRINT your name in box 22.2 — **22.2**
- Enter the capacity in which you are signing — **22.3**

HMRC 12/05net ■ TRUST AND ESTATE TAX RETURN: PAGE 12

Printed in the U.K. by Adare Group R2H 2789 12/05

Appendix 26

Tax Return for Trustees of approved self-administered Pension Schemes SA970

Tax Return for Trustees of approved self-administered Pension Schemes — for the year ended **5 April 2006**

Official use
Tax reference

Date

HM Revenue & Customs office address

Business Director

Telephone

Issue address

For Reference

Please read this page first

The green arrows and instructions will guide you through your Tax Return

This Notice requires you by law to send me a Tax Return, and any documents I ask for, for the year from 6 April 2005 to 5 April 2006. Give details of all your income and, where assets not held for the purposes of the scheme have been disposed of, all your capital gains.
Make sure that your Tax Return, and any documents asked for, reaches me by

- ***30 September 2006 if you want me to calculate the tax (or repayment) due,***

OR

- ***31 January 2007, at the latest, or you will be liable to an automatic penalty.***

Please send a copy of any accounts for the pension scheme for each period of account ending in the year from 6 April 2005 to 5 April 2006 inclusive. If accounts have been prepared, you may, if you wish, complete the Tax Return based on the income received for a twelve month period of account ending in the year from 6 April 2005 to 5 April 2006 inclusive.

If no accounts have been drawn up to a date ending in the year to 5 April 2006 then please send Statements of Assets and Liabilities as at 6 April 2005 and 5 April 2006. Please also include a statement of incomings and outgoings of the Scheme during the year ended 5 April 2006. To comply with this Notice the Return must be sent with a copy of the Pension Scheme accounts or statements of assets and liabilities, incomings and outgoings by 31 January 2007.

Make sure your payment of any tax the Pension Scheme owes reaches me by 31 January, or you will have to pay interest and perhaps a surcharge.

Any Tax Return may be checked. Please remember that there are penalties for supplying false information.

***If you need help** refer to the Pension Scheme Tax Return Guide or ring your HM Revenue & Customs office on the telephone number shown above.*

SA970

Please turn over

Income *for the year ended 5 April 2006*

Step 1

All trustees should answer Questions 1 to 3 **first** to see if any of the supplementary Pages that cover less common situations should be completed. Don't worry if you do not need any. They should only be completed if they apply to your Scheme's circumstances.

The supplementary Pages are available from the Orderline on 0845 9000 404 (fax 0845 9000 604).

If you are calling from outside the UK you can ring the Orderline on the international access code followed by (+44) 161 930 8331 or fax (+44) 161 930 8444. The Orderline is closed on Christmas Day, Boxing Day and New Year's Day.

Or you can go to our website at www.hmrc.gov.uk

If Question 4 applies you will only have to fill in certain questions on this Tax Return; follow the directions in the question.

Questions 5 to 14 on pages 3 and 4 include the common income types and situations that apply to exempt approved self-administered pension schemes.

All trustees must answer Questions 15 to 23.

Q1 Are you claiming all the trustees were Not resident and Not ordinarily resident in the UK for all or part of the year? **YES** ☐

If yes, ask the Orderline for the Non-Residence Pages for the Approved Pension Scheme Tax Return. Complete those Pages and any other Questions that apply.

Q2 Throughout the year ended 5 April 2006 were the assets of the scheme held exclusively for the purposes of the Scheme? **YES** ☐

If not applicable, ask the Orderline for the supplementary Pages 'Income and capital gains from assets not held for the purposes of the Scheme or where a percentage restriction applies'.
Complete those Pages and Questions 10 to 23.

Q3 Have you been notified by HMRC (Savings, Pensions, Share Schemes) (Nottingham), that a restriction applies for 2005-06 so that only a certain percentage of your Scheme's income and gains from assets held for the purposes of the scheme is exempt from tax? **YES** ☐

If yes, enter that percentage ☐ % here and ask the Orderline for the supplementary Pages 'Income and gains from assets not held for the purposes of the Scheme or where a percentage restriction applies'.
Complete those Pages and Questions 10 to 23.

Q4 Throughout the year ended 5 April 2006, and apart from any cash held on deposit and earning interest or alternative finance receipts, were the assets of the scheme held exclusively in funds managed by UK or EU insurance companies, insurance policies or insurance contracts? **YES** ☐

If yes, complete:

- any of the supplementary Pages that apply (Questions 1 to 3)
- Questions 5 and 6
- Questions 15 to 23.

If not applicable, then complete Questions 5 to 23 as appropriate.

Step 2

Please use blue or black ink to fill in the Tax Return and please do not include pence. Round down to the nearest pound, income and capital gains, and round up tax credits and tax deductions.

Fill in any supplementary Pages **before** going on to Step 3.

Income *for the year ended 5 April 2006*

Step 3 Complete pages 3 to 7 only if **all** the income received was from assets held for the purposes of the scheme. If you answer 'Yes' to any question, fill in the relevant boxes. If not applicable, go to the next question.

If you are completing this Return on a 12-month period of account ending in the year from 6 April 2005 to 5 April 2006, you must do so on a consistent basis. If you wish to change from accounting date basis to the strict fiscal basis then the change in basis should not result in there being periods which drop out of account.

Q5 Did you receive interest or alternative finance receipts from which UK Income Tax has not been deducted? YES [ ] — If yes, fill in box 5.1. If not applicable, go to question 6.

- Total income from investments and deposits from which no UK Income Tax was deducted, including income from bank and building societies received gross — **5.1** £

Q6 Did you receive income from which UK Income Tax has been deducted? YES [ ] — If yes, fill in boxes 6.1 to 6.5. If not applicable, go to question 7.

Include all income from investments from which UK Income Tax has been deducted including interest on loans and deposits, bank and building society interest, alternative finance receipts from alternative finance arrangements, interest on UK government securities including those held in the form of bearer bonds, interest from authorised unit trusts and annual payments from unauthorised unit trusts, but not income from UK dividends (this goes in Question 7).

	Amount after tax deducted	Tax deducted	Gross amount before tax
• Total income from investments and deposits from which tax has been deducted	**6.1** £	**6.2** £	**6.3** £

- Tax already reclaimed by the Scheme for the year ended 5 April 2006 **or** for the 12-month period of account ending in the year from 6 April 2005 to 5 April 2006 (if the Return is completed on the accounting date basis) which is included in box 6.2 — **6.4** £
- Tax which has not already been reclaimed at the time this Return is made — *box 6.2 minus box 6.4* — **6.5** £

Q7 Did you receive income from UK Equities? YES [ ] — If yes, fill in box 7.1. If not applicable, go to question 8.

(Do not include any income from which UK Income Tax has been deducted - see Question 6)

- Dividend/distribution — **7.1** £

Q8 Did you receive income from land and property? YES [ ] — If yes, fill in boxes 8.1 to 8.3 as appropriate. If not applicable, go to question 9.

- Income from land and property in the UK — **8.1** £
- Income from land and property outside the UK — **8.2** £
- Tick box 8.3 if box 8.1 and/or box 8.2 have been reduced by enhanced capital allowances for designated environmentally beneficial plant and machinery — **8.3** [ ]

Q9 Did you receive income from overseas investments? YES [ ] — If yes, fill in boxes 9.1 to 9.4. If not applicable, go to question 10.

(Do not include income from stock dividends)

	Net dividend after tax deducted	UK Income Tax deducted
• Income from overseas investments	**9.1** £	**9.2** £

- UK Income Tax already reclaimed by the Scheme for the year ended 5 April 2006 **or** for the 12–month period of account ending in the year from 6 April 2005 to 5 April 2006 (if the Return is completed on the accounting date basis) from overseas investments, which is included in box 9.2 — **9.3** £
- UK Income Tax, which has not already been reclaimed at the time this Return is made — **9.4** £

 Please turn over

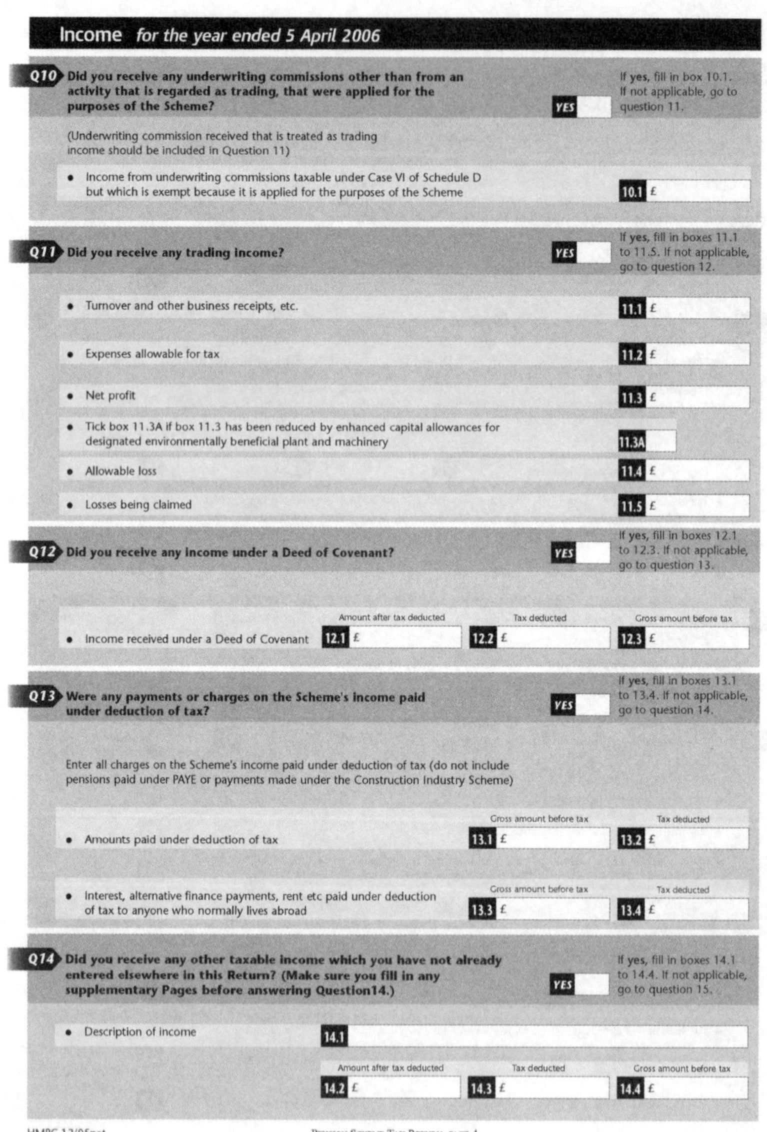

Income *for the year ended 5 April 2006*

Q10 Did you receive any underwriting commissions other than from an activity that is regarded as trading, that were applied for the purposes of the Scheme? YES — If yes, fill in box 10.1. If not applicable, go to question 11.

(Underwriting commission received that is treated as trading income should be included in Question 11)

- Income from underwriting commissions taxable under Case VI of Schedule D but which is exempt because it is applied for the purposes of the Scheme — 10.1 £

Q11 Did you receive any trading income? YES — If yes, fill in boxes 11.1 to 11.5. If not applicable, go to question 12.

- Turnover and other business receipts, etc. — 11.1 £
- Expenses allowable for tax — 11.2 £
- Net profit — 11.3 £
- Tick box 11.3A if box 11.3 has been reduced by enhanced capital allowances for designated environmentally beneficial plant and machinery — 11.3A
- Allowable loss — 11.4 £
- Losses being claimed — 11.5 £

Q12 Did you receive any income under a Deed of Covenant? YES — If yes, fill in boxes 12.1 to 12.3. If not applicable, go to question 13.

	Amount after tax deducted	Tax deducted	Gross amount before tax
• Income received under a Deed of Covenant	12.1 £	12.2 £	12.3 £

Q13 Were any payments or charges on the Scheme's income paid under deduction of tax? YES — If yes, fill in boxes 13.1 to 13.4. If not applicable, go to question 14.

Enter all charges on the Scheme's income paid under deduction of tax (do not include pensions paid under PAYE or payments made under the Construction Industry Scheme)

	Gross amount before tax	Tax deducted
• Amounts paid under deduction of tax	13.1 £	13.2 £
• Interest, alternative finance payments, rent etc paid under deduction of tax to anyone who normally lives abroad	13.3 £	13.4 £

Q14 Did you receive any other taxable income which you have not already entered elsewhere in this Return? (Make sure you fill in any supplementary Pages before answering Question14.) YES — If yes, fill in boxes 14.1 to 14.4. If not applicable, go to question 15.

- Description of income — 14.1

Amount after tax deducted	Tax deducted	Gross amount before tax
14.2 £	14.3 £	14.4 £

HMRC 12/05net — PENSION SCHEME TAX RETURN: PAGE 4

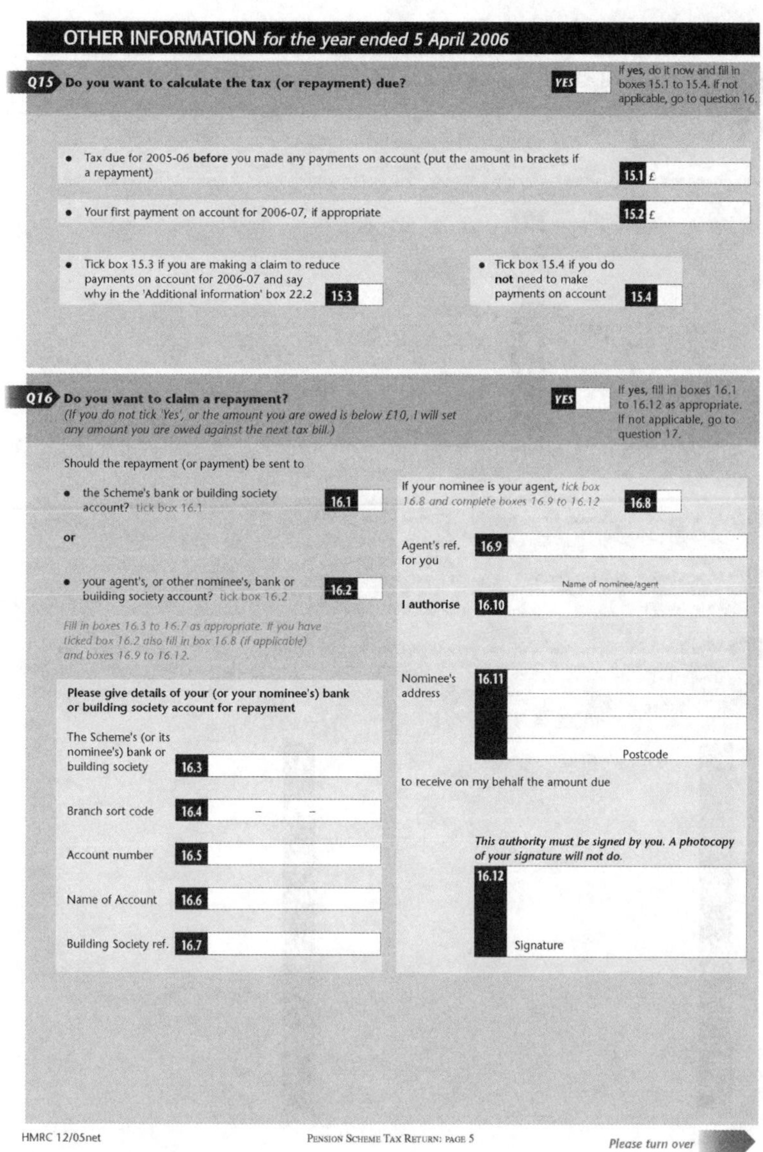

OTHER INFORMATION *for the year ended 5 April 2006*

Q15 Do you want to calculate the tax (or repayment) due? YES

If **yes**, do it now and fill in boxes 15.1 to 15.4. If not applicable, go to question 16.

- Tax due for 2005-06 **before** you made any payments on account (put the amount in brackets if a repayment) 15.1 £
- Your first payment on account for 2006-07, if appropriate 15.2 £
- Tick box 15.3 if you are making a claim to reduce payments on account for 2006-07 and say why in the 'Additional information' box 22.2 15.3
- Tick box 15.4 if you do **not** need to make payments on account 15.4

Q16 Do you want to claim a repayment? YES

(If you do not tick 'Yes', or the amount you are owed is below £10, I will set any amount you are owed against the next tax bill.)

If **yes**, fill in boxes 16.1 to 16.12 as appropriate. If not applicable, go to question 17.

Should the repayment (or payment) be sent to

- the Scheme's bank or building society account? *tick box 16.1* 16.1

or

- your agent's, or other nominee's, bank or building society account? *tick box 16.2* 16.2

Fill in boxes 16.3 to 16.7 as appropriate. If you have ticked box 16.2 also fill in box 16.8 (if applicable) and boxes 16.9 to 16.12.

Please give details of your (or your nominee's) bank or building society account for repayment

The Scheme's (or its nominee's) bank or building society 16.3

Branch sort code 16.4 – –

Account number 16.5

Name of Account 16.6

Building Society ref. 16.7

If your nominee is your agent, *tick box 16.8 and complete boxes 16.9 to 16.12* 16.8

Agent's ref. for you 16.9

I authorise 16.10 Name of nominee/agent

Nominee's address 16.11

Postcode

to receive on my behalf the amount due

This authority must be signed by you. A photocopy of your signature will not do.

16.12

Signature

HMRC 12/05net PENSION SCHEME TAX RETURN: PAGE 5 *Please turn over*

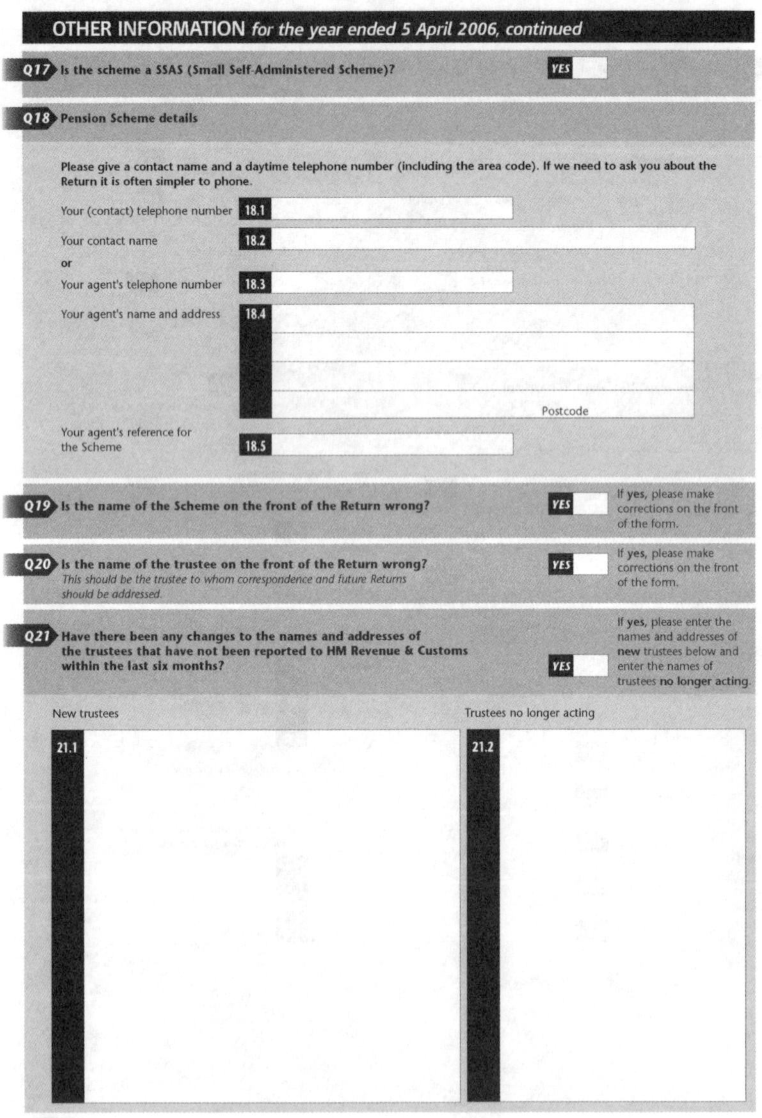

OTHER INFORMATION *for the year ended 5 April 2006, continued*

Q17 Is the scheme a SSAS (Small Self-Administered Scheme)? YES

Q18 Pension Scheme details

Please give a contact name and a daytime telephone number (including the area code). If we need to ask you about the Return it is often simpler to phone.

Your (contact) telephone number 18.1

Your contact name 18.2

or

Your agent's telephone number 18.3

Your agent's name and address 18.4

Postcode

Your agent's reference for the Scheme 18.5

Q19 Is the name of the Scheme on the front of the Return wrong? YES — If **yes**, please make corrections on the front of the form.

Q20 Is the name of the trustee on the front of the Return wrong? YES — If **yes**, please make corrections on the front of the form.
This should be the trustee to whom correspondence and future Returns should be addressed.

Q21 Have there been any changes to the names and addresses of the trustees that have not been reported to HM Revenue & Customs within the last six months? YES — If **yes**, please enter the names and addresses of **new** trustees below and enter the names of trustees **no longer acting**.

New trustees 21.1

Trustees no longer acting 21.2

HMRC 12/05net — Pension Scheme Tax Return: page 6

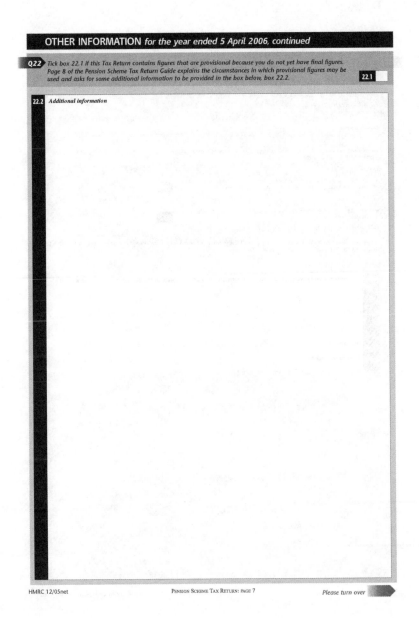

OTHER INFORMATION *for the year ended 5 April 2006, continued*

Q22 *Tick box 22.1 if this Tax Return contains figures that are provisional because you do not yet have final figures. Page 8 of the Pension Scheme Tax Return Guide explains the circumstances in which provisional figures may be used and asks for some additional information to be provided in the box below, box 22.2.* **22.1**

22.2 ***Additional information***

HMRC 12/05net

Please turn over

OTHER INFORMATION *for the year ended 5 April 2006, continued*

Q23 Declaration - you **must** complete this part

I have filled in where required and I am sending back to you the following Pages:

	Tick
Pages 2 to 8 of this Tax Return	
Non-Residence	
Income and gains from assets not held for the purposes of the Scheme or where a percentage restriction applies	

Tick

- box 23.1 if the Tax Return has been completed based on the 12 months accounts ending in the year from 6 April 2005 to 5 April 2006 **23.1**

or

- box 23.2 if the Tax Return has been completed for the 12 months ending on 5 April 2006 **23.2**

Before sending back the completed Tax Return you must sign the statement below.

If you give false information or conceal any part of the Pension Scheme's income or chargeable gains you may be liable to financial penalties and/or you may be prosecuted.

23.3 **The information I have given on this Tax Return is correct and complete to the best of my knowledge and belief.**

Signature of trustee Date

Print name in full here

 Printed in the U.K. by Adare Group R2H 2800 12/05

Appendix 27

Tax Return Guide for Trustees of approved self-administered Pension Schemes SA975

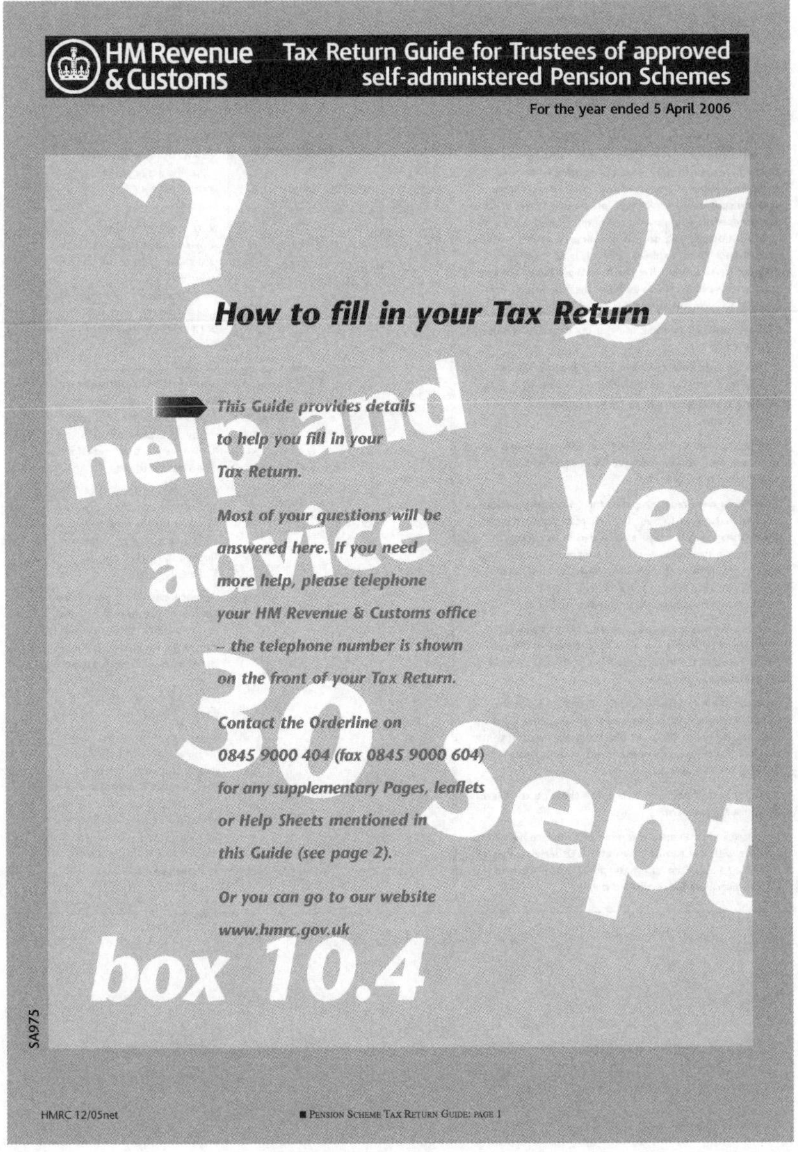

HM Revenue & Customs

Tax Return Guide for Trustees of approved self-administered Pension Schemes

For the year ended 5 April 2006

How to fill in your Tax Return

This Guide provides details to help you fill in your Tax Return.

Most of your questions will be answered here. If you need more help, please telephone your HM Revenue & Customs office – the telephone number is shown on the front of your Tax Return.

Contact the Orderline on 0845 9000 404 (fax 0845 9000 604) for any supplementary Pages, leaflets or Help Sheets mentioned in this Guide (see page 2).

Or you can go to our website www.hmrc.gov.uk

SA975

HMRC 12/05net

■ Pension Scheme Tax Return Guide: page 1

What you have received

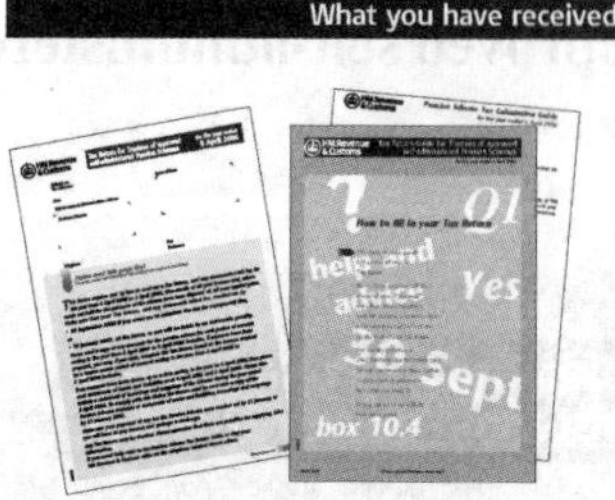

Your Tax Return for Trustees of approved self-administered Pension Schemes asks for details of the Scheme's income and capital gains. It applies to trustees of exempt approved self-administered Schemes and insured schemes with cash on deposit. If the Scheme is neither exempt approved self-administered nor insured with cash on deposit, do not complete this Return. Please send it back to us, explaining why it is not appropriate to your Scheme. With the Tax Return we have sent two guides; this one to help you fill in the Tax Return, and another to help you calculate your tax bill (if you want to).

You are required to complete the Tax Return 2005–06 even if:

- **the Scheme does not have to pay Income Tax or Capital Gains Tax on the income received by it**
- **there is no repayment or further repayment due to the Scheme.**

Completion will not mean that you will have to pay any more tax than you would have had to pay without completing the Tax Return.

If accounts have been prepared for a 12 month period ending in the year to 5 April 2006, you may complete the Return using the figures included in the accounts. If you do so, this method must be adopted on a consistent basis. If you wish to change from the accounting date basis to the strict fiscal basis then the change in basis should not result in there being periods which drop out of account.

If accounts have not been prepared for a 12 month period ending in the year to 5 April 2006, complete the Tax Return for income received in the year ended 5 April 2006.

Trustees of every Scheme get the first 8 pages of the Tax Return. There are supplementary Pages for some types of income and gains. For example, there are Pages if some or all of the Scheme's income is not exempt from Income Tax or Capital Gains Tax.

It is your responsibility to make sure that you complete the right supplementary Pages.

You must send the ones you need to complete back to us on time with the rest of your Return. Otherwise, you will be liable to an initial automatic penalty of £100, and further penalties for continued delay.

What you should do first

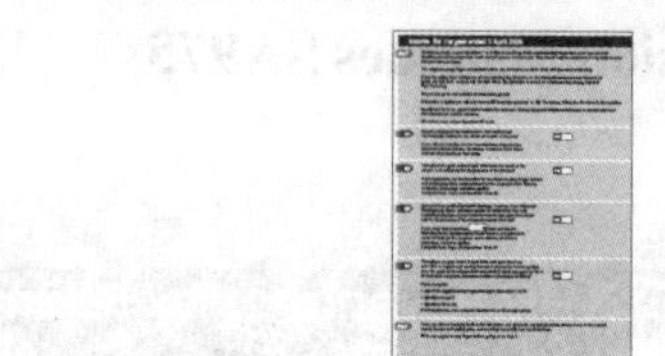

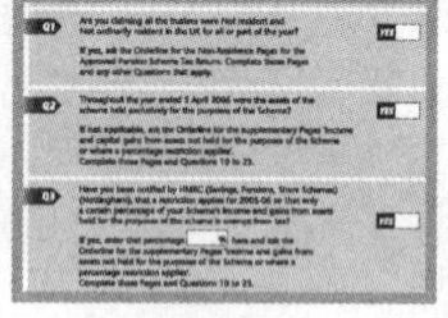

First, fill in page 2 of the Tax Return. This tells you which supplementary Pages you must complete. Pages 4 and 5 of this Guide will help.

Next, if you need any supplementary Pages phone the Orderline. Or go to our website **www.hmrc.gov.uk**
It can provide any of the supplementary Pages, leaflets or Help Sheets mentioned in this Guide.

*The Orderline is open every day (except Christmas Day, Boxing Day and New Year's Day) on **0845 9000 404**. A text phone service is available on this number. Calls are charged at the local rate. You can also order by fax on **0845 9000 604**, or in writing to **PO Box 37, St Austell, PL25 5YN.***

*If you live or work abroad, order using the International Access code followed by **(+44) 161 930 8331** (fax (+44) **161 930 8444**).*

Visit our website for the Internet service at www.hmrc.gov.uk

Decide if you want me to calculate the tax (or repayment) for you. If so, make sure your completed Tax Return reaches me by 30 September 2006. It will save you time and effort if you leave it to me.

If you miss the deadline of 30 September you will need to calculate the tax (or repayment) and make sure your completed Tax Return reaches me by 31 January 2007.

Do not delay doing your Tax Return. You do not have to wait for the deadline shown on the front of the Tax Return. Tackling it earlier means you will have more time to get help if you need it. Sending it earlier does not mean you have to pay tax any sooner.

If you are not sure what to do, please ask for help before you start to fill in your Tax Return. If you have a disability that makes filling in the Return difficult, we will be able to help you complete the form. Please contact your HM Revenue & Customs office, or Enquiry Centre, to talk about this.

What Next

Gather together information about the Scheme's circumstances for 2005–06. For example, if accounts were prepared for a 12 month period ending within the year ended 5 April 2006, you will need these. Whether or not accounts were prepared, you will need any building society statements, dividend vouchers and other financial records. Do not send these with your Tax Return; keep them safe.

You are now ready to fill in your Tax Return. Pages 4 and 5 of this Guide tell you what to do, and the rest of the Guide will help you fill in the boxes. If you need more help, ask us or your tax adviser.

You are responsible for the accuracy of your Tax Return.

If, after sending me your Tax Return, you find that you have made a mistake or any details have changed, then let me know at once. Similarly, you should correct any provisional figures as soon as you can. You will only be penalised if your Tax Return is incorrect through fraud or negligence, or if there is unreasonable delay in providing corrected figures once they are known to you. The penalties can be up to 100% of the difference between the correct tax due and the amount that would have been due on the basis of the figures you returned. You could also be prosecuted.

What HM Revenue & Customs does

When we get your completed Tax Return, we will process it – based on your figures – to work out whether the Scheme owes any tax, and if so how much, or how much we owe you. If we see any obvious mistakes – for example in the arithmetic – we may put them right and tell you what we have done. When we process the Return, we shall only be looking at the Return and documents we requested.

We will send you my calculation of your tax, if you have asked us to do it for you. If you have calculated your tax, we will let you know if it is wrong.

Later, we will send you a Statement. This will explain how to pay any tax due – see the notes on page 10 of this Guide.

In its dealings with you, HM Revenue & Customs is governed by the service commitment set out on page 11 of this Guide. Page 11 also explains how to complain if you are dissatisfied with the way the HM Revenue & Customs handles your tax affairs.

Once your Tax Return has been processed, it may be checked. we have until 31 January 2008 to do this (later if you send your Tax Return late). We may make enquiries about your figures and ask you to send the records from which you took them. We may also check your figures against any details received from other sources, such as your building society or bank.

Read page 10 of this Guide if your Tax Return was delivered to you after 31 July 2006.

KEY DATES AND SUMMARY

2006

You must, by law, have kept all records.

- Failure to do so could give rise to penalties.

April 2006

You receive your Tax Return:

- find your records
- fill in your Return.

30 September 2006

We must have received your completed Tax Return if you want us to:

- calculate your tax in time for the 31 January 2007 payment, if one is due.

31 January 2007

This date is important for three reasons. This is the date by which you **must:**

- let us have your completed Tax Return
- pay the balance of any tax you owe
- pay your first payment on account for the 2006-07 tax year, if appropriate.

You must send us your Tax Return and pay what you owe by this date to avoid automatic penalties and interest.

continued over

Filling in your Tax Return

How to fill in the boxes

Answer all the questions. If you tick 'Yes', fill in the Pages and boxes that apply to you. If the answer is not applicable, go to the next question.

- Write clearly using blue or black ink and only in the spaces provided.
- Use numbers only, when you are asked for amounts.
- Please do not include pence – round down your income and gains to the nearest pound, and round up your tax credits and tax deductions – for example, if building society interest is £3,500.87 after tax has been deducted, enter 3,500 in box 6.1. Round all the boxes, not just totals boxes.
- Do not delay sending your Tax Return just because you do not have all the information you need – see the notes for box 22.1 on page 8 of this Guide.

Amount after tax deducted
6.1 £ 3500

If you need help, look up the question number in the Notes.

Questions Q1 to Q4

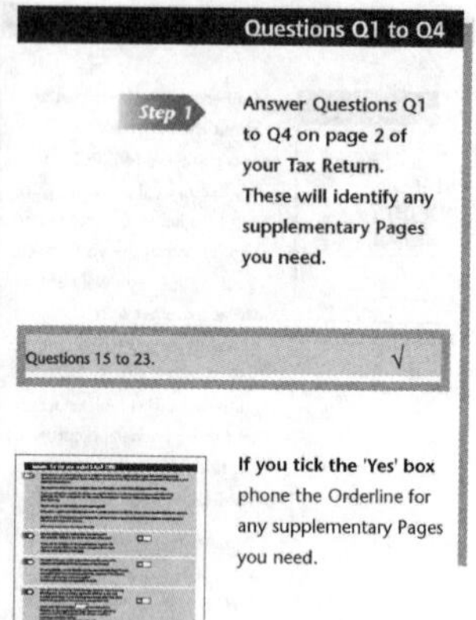

Step 1

Answer Questions Q1 to Q4 on page 2 of your Tax Return. These will identify any supplementary Pages you need.

Questions 15 to 23. √

If you tick the 'Yes' box phone the Orderline for any supplementary Pages you need.

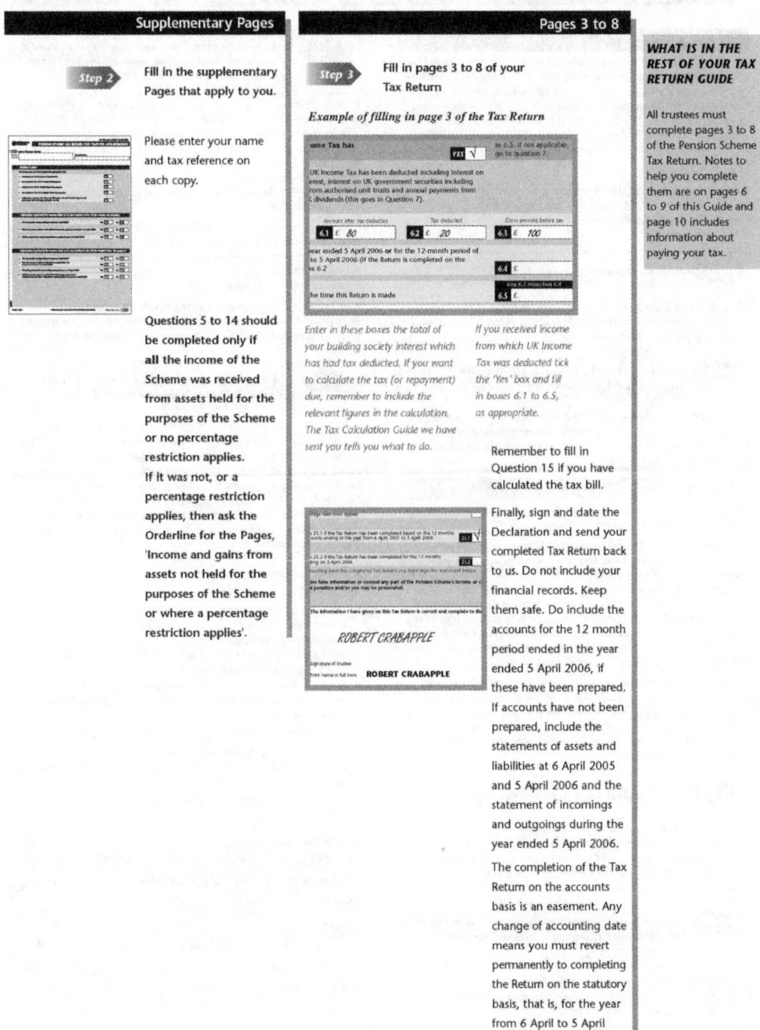

Supplementary Pages

Step 2 **Fill in the supplementary Pages that apply to you.**

Please enter your name and tax reference on each copy.

Questions 5 to 14 should be completed only if all the income of the Scheme was received from assets held for the purposes of the Scheme or no percentage restriction applies. If it was not, or a percentage restriction applies, then ask the Orderline for the Pages, 'Income and gains from assets not held for the purposes of the Scheme or where a percentage restriction applies'.

Pages 3 to 8

Step 3 **Fill in pages 3 to 8 of your Tax Return**

Example of filling in page 3 of the Tax Return

Enter in these boxes the total of your building society interest which has had tax deducted. If you want to calculate the tax (or repayment) due, remember to include the relevant figures in the calculation. The Tax Calculation Guide we have sent you tells you what to do.

If you received income from which UK Income Tax was deducted tick the 'Yes' box and fill in boxes 6.1 to 6.5, as appropriate.

Remember to fill in Question 15 if you have calculated the tax bill.

Finally, sign and date the Declaration and send your completed Tax Return back to us. Do not include your financial records. Keep them safe. Do include the accounts for the 12 month period ended in the year ended 5 April 2006, if these have been prepared. If accounts have not been prepared, include the statements of assets and liabilities at 6 April 2005 and 5 April 2006 and the statement of incomings and outgoings during the year ended 5 April 2006.

The completion of the Tax Return on the accounts basis is an easement. Any change of accounting date means you must revert permanently to completing the Return on the statutory basis, that is, for the year from 6 April to 5 April each year.

WHAT IS IN THE REST OF YOUR TAX RETURN GUIDE

All trustees must complete pages 3 to 8 of the Pension Scheme Tax Return. Notes to help you complete them are on pages 6 to 9 of this Guide and page 10 includes information about paying your tax.

HMRC 12/05net ■ PENSION SCHEME TAX RETURN GUIDE: PAGE 5 continued over

How to fill in your Pension Scheme Tax Return

INTRODUCTION

If a source of income is not taxable and is not specifically asked for on the Tax Return, you do not need to include it on the Tax Return or supplementary Pages. Examples might include contributions received or the proceeds of insurance policies used for the paying of relevant benefits. You do not need to worry because the accounts or statement of income submitted with the Return and which form part of the Return provide the return of this income.

Now fill in the Return.

If you are unsure about the treatment of a certain source of income, you can enter it in the box you think is appropriate and then in the 'Additional information' box on page 7 tell us what you have done and why.

Q1 Non-Residence Pages

Fill in the Non-Residence Pages if you are claiming all the trustees were not resident and not ordinarily resident in the UK for all or part of the year to 5 April 2006.

Q2 Assets not held exclusively for the purposes of the Scheme

If the Scheme's assets were not held exclusively for the purposes of the Scheme, ask the Orderline for the Pages 'Income and gains from assets not held for the purposes of the Scheme or where a percentage restriction applies'.

Assets that are held for the purposes of the scheme

This phrase is used in various places throughout the Tax Return and supplementary Pages.

Approved pension schemes are exempt from Income Tax and Capital Gains Tax on income and gains received from deposits or investments held for the purposes of the Scheme. There is a specific exemption for stock lending fees. There is also an exemption for underwriting commissions where the underlying activity does not fall to be treated as a trading activity. Contracts entered into in the course of dealing in financial futures or traded options are regarded as investments. Any other income and gains that are received are not exempt from Income Tax and Capital Gains Tax.

Assets held by the Trustees of an exempt approved scheme are regarded as held for the purposes of the Scheme so long as, and for as long as, they are held on trust for the purposes, stated in the scheme rules, of providing retirement and death benefits for employees and their families. If the stated purposes are being met, then the exemption is available.

Q3 Notification of a percentage restriction

If HM Revenue & Customs SPSS Nottingham have notified you that a Sch. 22 para 7 Income and Corporation Taxes Act 1988 restriction applies, ask the Orderline for the Pages 'Income and gains from assets not held for the purposes of the Scheme or where a percentage restriction applies'.

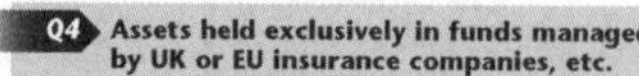

Q4 Assets held exclusively in funds managed by UK or EU insurance companies, etc.

If the Scheme's assets, apart from cash on deposit, were held exclusively in funds managed by UK or European Union insurance companies, policies or contracts, you only need to answer Questions 1 to 6 and Questions 15 to 23.

Q5 Did you receive interest or alternative finance receipts from which UK Income Tax has not been deducted?

From 1 October 2002, a change in the law took effect. From that date onwards, a bank or building society could pay interest to a pension scheme without deducting income tax if they believe the pension scheme to be approved by us. From 6 April 2005 banks and building societies can pay alternative finance receipts without deducting income tax if they believe the pension scheme to be approved by us. The pension scheme thus receives a gross amount of interest or alternative finance receipts.

Only show here interest or alternative finance receipts you have received without tax deducted (gross). Your bank or building society statement or passbook will show you the relevant figures. Add up all the amounts you received gross during 2005–06 for all your accounts and enter the total in box 5.1.

If you received any interest or alternative finance receipts which were paid to you net of income tax, you should show that interest or alternative finance receipt in your reply to Question 6 and not here.

Q6 Did you receive income from which UK Income Tax has been deducted?

Before 1 October 2002, interest on bank and building society accounts was generally paid after lower rate income tax had been deducted. From that date, however, banks and building societies could pay interest to pension schemes without deducting income tax if they believe the pension scheme to be approved by us. From 6 April 2005 banks and building societies can pay alternative finance receipts without deducting income tax if they believe the pension scheme to be approved by us. You may find that the interest or alternative finance receipts you received in 2005–06 were received gross and should therefore not be returned here but at box 5.1 above.

At Question 6, you need to show:

- the total amount of interest or alternative finance receipts you have received from all your accounts during 2005–06 after the deduction of lower rate tax (net) (box 6.1)
- the total amount of tax deducted from that interest or alternative finance receipts (box 6.2), **and**
- the total amount of interest or alternative finance receipts from all your accounts during 2005–06 before tax was deducted (gross) (box 6.3).

You can find the relevant figures on one of the following:

- bank or building society statement or passbook
- certificate of tax deducted provided by the company which pays interest on any loan made by the scheme.

If you do not have all three figures, they can be worked out as follows.

***Either** like this:*

Tax deducted = amount **after tax** x 25%

Statement shows interest of £80 **after tax**

So tax is £80 x 25% = £20

***or** like this:*

Tax deducted = amount **before tax** x 20%

Statement shows interest of £100 **before tax**

So tax is £100 x 20% = £20

How to fill in your Pension Scheme Tax Return

Authorised unit trusts

Income from authorised unit trusts should be entered at Question 7 – unless the certificate of deduction clearly shows Income Tax has been deducted. Generally income from authorised unit trusts does not have Income Tax deducted, but has a tax credit attached which is not reclaimable.

Only the amount of Income Tax deducted that has not already been reclaimed by you at the time this Return is made and for the period covered by this Return is still repayable.

You must not include in any other repayment claim any Income Tax that has been repaid or reclaimed by you (enter such amounts in box 6.4).

If none of the tax in box 6.2 has been reclaimed by you at the time this Return is made, the figure of tax reclaimable now, and to be entered in box 6.5, is the same as that entered in box 6.2.

If, exceptionally, the figure to be entered in box 6.5 is a minus figure and you are calculating the tax (or repayment) due, you will need to take the following action when carrying this figure to the Tax Calculation Working Sheet.

If there is tax available for repayment from box 9.4, deduct the amount shown in box 6.5 from the figure in box 9.4. If the result is a positive figure, enter it in box P23 of the Tax Calculation Working Sheet. If the result is a minus figure, then enter the figure in brackets in box P23.

The deemed distribution element of share buy-backs and dividends from authorised unit trusts should be included in Question 7.

Q7 Did you receive income from UK Equities?

Tax credits from this income are not repayable. You should only enter the amount of the dividend or distribution, ignoring the tax credit.

Include in this question deemed distributions from all share buy-backs.

If the Scheme took up an offer of shares in place of a cash dividend, this is a 'stock' dividend. Your dividend statement should have the 'appropriate amount in cash' on it – this is the amount to include in box 7.1.

Q8 Did you receive income from land and property?

Enter in boxes 8.1 and 8.2 the net income after expenses and deductions, for example, capital allowances, arising from the receipt of income from land and property in 2005–06. This will be the same figure that appears in the Scheme's accounts or statement of income.

Tick box 8.3 if boxes 8.1 and/or 8.2 have been reduced by enhanced capital allowances for spending on designated environmentally beneficial technologies. You will find more information on this type of expenditure in *Help Sheet IR250: Capital allowances and balancing charges in a rental business,* which is available from the Orderline.

Certain forms of income from land and property are regarded as trading income and should be included in Question 11. Such sources of income include the following, although the list is not complete:

- canals and inland navigations and docks
- mines and quarries, including sand pits, gravel pits and brickfields
- rights of markets and fairs, tolls, bridges and ferries.

Overseas tax

If overseas tax was deducted, do not include the income in Question 8 but include it in box 9.1.

Proceeds from disposals of land or property

Gains from the disposal of land or property should be included only if they arose from assets not held for the purposes of the Scheme. In this case, they are appropriate to the 'Income from assets not held for the purposes of the Scheme' supplementary Pages, available from the Orderline.

Q9 Did you receive income from overseas investments?

Include income in box 9.1 even if UK Income Tax has not been deducted.

Income should be converted to sterling at the rate of exchange prevailing when the income arose. If you are unsure of the exchange rate to be applied ask us or your tax adviser.

Q10 Did you receive any underwriting commissions, other than from an activity that is regarded as trading, that were applied for the purposes of the scheme?

Include commissions, other than your own insurance commissions, received from the underwriting of any share issue floated on the Stock Exchange. Where such underwriting commissions are applied to assets held for the purposes of the Scheme, see page 6 of this Guide, then the income is exempt from tax and the amount(s) should be included in box 10.1. An entry in box 10.1 will constitute a valid claim to this exemption. However, if you know that the activity giving rise to the income, or part of it, amounts to trading, do not include that income in box 10.1, but include it or that part of it in box 11.1 at Question 11.

If underwriting commissions were received but were not applied to assets held for the purposes of the Scheme, do not include the income in box 10.1. Instead, ask the Orderline for the 'Income from assets not held for the purposes of the Scheme' supplementary Pages.

Q11 Did you receive any trading income?

If at any time in the year to 5 April 2006 the Scheme carried on a trade, you should attach any trading accounts prepared for the period and complete boxes 11.1 to 11.5. If you need help to arrive at the Scheme's net profit after expenses and deductions, for example, capital allowances, ask us or your tax adviser.

Tick box 11.3A if box 11.3 has been reduced by enhanced capital allowances for spending on designated environmentally beneficial technologies. You will find more information on this type of expenditure in *Help Sheet IR250: Capital allowances and balancing charges in a rental business,* which is available from the Orderline.

The Scheme should have records of all its business transactions. These must be kept until at least 31 January 2012 in case we ask to see them.

Q12 Did you receive any income under a Deed of Covenant?

Enter the total amounts in boxes 12.1 to 12.3. Income Tax deducted from income received from Deeds of Covenant is not repayable.

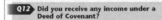

continued over

How to fill in your Pension Scheme Tax Return

Q13 Were any payments or charges on the Scheme's income paid under deduction of tax

Include in boxes 13.1 and 13.2 the total charges on the Scheme's income that were paid under deduction of tax. Do not include the totals of any interest or alternative finance payments or rent etc., paid under deduction of tax to anyone who lives abroad. These payments should be included in boxes 13.3 and 13.4.

Do **not** include payments of pensions made under PAYE, or payments under the Construction Industry Scheme, in any of the boxes in this question.

Q14 Did you receive any other taxable income which you have not already entered elsewhere in this Return?

Only **taxable income** should be entered in Question 14. Enter taxable income of whatever nature that has not been entered elsewhere within this Tax Return. You may wish to refer back to Questions 1 to 4 on page 2 of this Tax Return in case the income is covered in those questions, in which case complete the appropriate Supplementary Pages. An entry in this box automatically gives rise to a tax charge at 40% (the rate of tax applicable to trusts).

Q15 Do you want to calculate the tax (or repayment) due?

Calculating the tax (or repayment) is optional. If you do not tick 'Yes' to this question we shall assume that you want us to calculate the tax for you, therefore you must send the completed Tax Return to us by 30 September 2006. See page 10 of these notes if your Tax Return was issued after 31 July 2006.

If you wish to calculate your tax or repayment, then complete the Working Sheet in the Tax Calculation Guide and copy the figures to Question 15.

We need this information so that we can check that you have got it right.

Q16 Do you want to claim a repayment if the Pension Scheme has paid too much tax?

If you wish to claim a repayment, fill in boxes 16.1 to 16.12 as appropriate. Repayment will be sent direct to you, or your nominee's, bank or building society account. This is the safest and quickest method for the Scheme to receive a repayment. If you do not claim a repayment, one will not be sent to you automatically. Any amount you are owed will be set against your next tax bill.

Note, if you have an amount to pay that is due in the near future (usually within 45 days), then we will generally set off any repayments against this liability. Also, we prefer not to make repayments of small amounts, because of administrative costs. So if the overpaid tax is below £10, we will normally set it against your next tax bill. But if you do not agree with this set-off, please contact us.

Tick box 16.1 if you want the repayment sent to the Scheme's bank or building society account.

Tick box 16.2 if you want the repayment sent to your agent's, or other nominee's, bank or building society account. Fill in boxes 16.3 to 16.7 to give details of your account or, if you want the repayment to go to a nominee, give details of that nominee's account. If you want the repayment to go to your agent, tick box 16.8. Fill in boxes 16.9, 16.10 and 16.11 to give details of your nominee or agent. You must sign box 16.12.

Please note that we reserve the right not to make a repayment to your nominee.

No vouchers are required with this Return.

Q17 to Q21 Pension Scheme details

These questions must be completed. The information will help us keep our records up to date.

Q22 Provisional figures

Do not delay sending your Tax Return just because you do not have all the information you need. You must do your best to obtain the information, but if you cannot provide final figures by the time you need to send back your Return, then provide provisional figures.

Tick box 22.1 and say in the 'Additional information' box, box 22.2:

- which figures are provisional (refer to the appropriate box numbers on the Return).

It would also help us if you say in box 22.2:

- why you could not give final figures, **and**
- an appropriate date on which you expect to give us your final figures.

If you use provisional figures, you must have taken all reasonable steps to get the final figures and ensure that they are sent to us as soon as they are available. You could be charged a penalty if you did not have a good reason for using a provisional figure or you did not take sufficient care to calculate the provisional figure in a reasonable amount. We would not regard pressure of work on either you or your tax adviser, or the complexity of your tax affairs as reasons for using a provisional figure.

You must ensure that any provisional figures you do include are reasonable and take account of all the information available to you.

If you negligently submit a provisional figure which is either inaccurate or unnecessary, you may be liable to a penalty.

Estimates (including valuations)

In some situations you may need to provide an estimated figure or valuation which you do not intend to amend at a later date. Broadly, this will be the case when:

- a valuation is required (for example, of an asset at a certain date for the purposes of calculating Capital Gains Tax liability), **or**
- there is inadequate information to enable you to arrive at a reliable figure (for example, where the records concerned have been lost or destroyed), **or**
- while there is inadequate information to arrive at a precise figure, a reliable estimate can be made.

You should identify any valuations you have used by indicating the figure in the 'Additional information' box on page 7 of your Tax Return, and giving details of the valuation. Do not tick box 22.1.

You should also identify any figures in your Tax Return which may not be very reliable; where appropriate, explain how the figure has been arrived at. If you are including an estimate which, while not a precise figure, is sufficiently reliable to enable you to make an accurate Tax Return, there is no need to make specific reference to it.

You can also use the 'Additional information' box to clarify entries made on the Return. For example, if you are unsure about the treatment of a certain source of income, you can enter it in the box you think is appropriate, then in the 'Additional Information' box give an explanation of what you have done and why.

How to fill in your Pension Scheme Tax Return

Q23 Declaration

Tick the boxes to show which pages of the Tax Return and supplementary Pages you have filled in. Remember to send back:

- the Tax Return, **and**
- any supplementary Pages that you have completed, **and**
- the accounts for a twelve month period ending in the year ended 5 April 2006, **or**
- statements of assets and liabilities at 6 April 2005 and 5 April 2006 and of incomings and outgoings during the year ended 5 April 2006.

Accounts

If accounts have been prepared you may, if you wish, complete the Tax Return based on the accounts period. Tick box 23.1 to indicate if the Tax Return has been completed based on the accounts for the twelve month period of account ending in the year from 6 April 2005 to 5 April 2006. Please send a copy of any accounts for the Scheme with the completed Return. Alternatively tick box 23.2 if the Tax Return has been completed for the 12 months ending on 5 April 2006.

If you have filled in the Tax Return

Sign and date the Return in box 23.3. This must be signed by a trustee of the Scheme who has been nominated by the trustees of the Scheme.

If you have had the Tax Return filled in for you by someone else

If you have had the Tax Return filled in for you by someone else, acting on your behalf, you must still sign the Return yourself to confirm to us that, to the best of your knowledge, it is correct and complete. This applies whether you have paid for the services of an accountant or other tax practitioner, or have simply had help from a friend or relative.

You should always allow sufficient time for checking and signing the Tax Return if it has been completed by someone on your behalf (particularly if you are likely to be abroad near the deadline for sending the Return back to us). Failure to make appropriate arrangements could mean that you miss the deadline and are charged penalties and interest.

notes on Paying your tax begin on page 10

Paying your tax

Your Statement of Account

If we receive your completed Tax Return by 30 September 2006, we will send you a statement showing how much tax you owe us, or we owe you, before any final payment is due on 31 January 2007. It will also explain how to pay.

If we receive your completed Tax Return after 30 September 2006, we cannot guarantee to process it in time to let you know how much to pay on 31 January 2007. This might mean that you have to estimate how much to pay.

We will send you a payslip with either a Statement of Account or a Reminder. If you pay too little, you will have to pay interest (and perhaps a surcharge). If you pay too much and have claimed a repayment, we will repay it with any interest due. If you do not claim a repayment we will set the amount due, plus any interest, against your next tax bill.

If you make payments on account

Some trustees may have to make payments on account. Each payment will normally equal one half of the previous year's tax liability (after taking off tax deducted at source and tax credits on dividends). The payments are due on 31 January in the tax year and 31 July following the tax year.

If you needed to make payments on account for the year to 5 April 2006, we will already have sent you a statement of the first payment on account due by 31 January 2006. We will send you another statement in June or July with details of the second payment on account.

If the payments on account add up to less than you owe for 2005–06, you must pay the difference by 31 January 2007. That amount can be calculated by completing boxes P26 to P28 in the Tax Calculation Guide Working Sheet.

If the payments on account add up to more than the tax bill for 2005–06, we will repay the difference if you have claimed a repayment in Question 16 on your Tax Return, or if not, we will set it against your next tax bill.

When you settle your tax bill for 2005–06 by 31 January 2007, you must also pay any first payment on account for 2006–07. The second payment on account for 2006-07 should be made by 31 July 2007.

If you have asked us to calculate your tax, we will tell you how much to pay on account.

If you are calculating your tax, complete boxes P29 and P30 in the Tax Calculation Guide Working Sheet.

Any Capital Gains Tax included in your 2005-06 tax bill will be excluded from the calculation of your 2006-07 payments on account. If you have asked us to calculate your tax, we will exclude it from the amount we tell you to pay on account. If you are calculating your tax, the calculation excludes Capital Gains Tax when you work through the boxes to calculate your payments on account.

You can make a claim to reduce these payments if you expect your tax bill (net of tax deducted at source and tax credits on dividends) to be lower in 2006–07 than in 2005–06. The Tax Calculation Guide will tell you what to do if you wish to claim to reduce your payments on account. Interest will be charged on late payments on account. For details see 'If you do not pay your tax on time' in the next column.

Ways to pay

You can pay by one of the following methods:

- your bank's internet or telephone banking facility
- BillPay: Debit Card over the internet
- at your bank
- by transfer from an Alliance & Leicester commercial bank account
- at a Post Office
- by post.

Further details of how to pay are given on the back of the Statement of Account, Reminder, or How to Pay leaflet.

You can also visit our website at **www.hmrc.gov.uk/howtopay**

If you do not pay your tax on time

We will charge interest on all late payments from the date the tax becomes due until it is paid. You will have to pay a surcharge on any tax for the year ending 5 April 2006 which is due by 31 January 2007, but is not paid by 28 February 2007.
This surcharge will be:

- 5% of the tax paid late, **and**
- another 5% if the tax is paid later than 31 July 2007.

If you pay too much tax

If you do not claim a repayment, we will take the amount we owe you, plus any interest, off your next tax bill.

If you do claim a repayment by ticking the 'Yes' box in Question 16, we will repay it, plus any interest due on the amount overpaid. Note: if you have an amount to pay that is due in the near future then we will generally set off any repayment against this liability. Also, we would prefer not to make repayments of small amounts (below £10) because of administrative costs. But if you do not agree with these set-offs, please contact your HM Revenue & Customs Office.

If your Tax Return is incorrect

If your Tax Return is incorrect and you have:

- paid too much tax, see 'If you pay too much tax' above, **or**
- not paid enough tax, then we will ask for further tax. We may charge you interest from the original due date, penalties and a surcharge.

If the notice requiring you to make your Tax Return was given after 31 July 2006

If the notice requiring you to make your Tax Return was given on or after 31 July 2006, we must receive it from you:

- within two months of the date the notice was given, if you want us to calculate your tax, **or**
- by the later of 31 January 2007 and three months after the date the notice was given, if you want to calculate the tax.

If the notice requiring you to make your Tax Return was given after 31 October 2006, and you had notified us by 5 October 2006 of income and gains taxable for the year 2005–06, then the tax is due three months after the date the notice was given. In all other cases, the tax is due on 31 January 2007. We will charge interest on any tax paid after the due date. A surcharge of 5% will also be made on any tax still unpaid more than 28 days after the due date.

The notice requiring you to make your Tax Return is 'given' on the day it is delivered to you. We will normally assume, for example, for the purpose of charging automatic penalties for the late submission of your Tax Return, that delivery will have taken place not more than seven days after the date of issue shown on the front of it.

If you have a complaint

Problems can usually be settled most quickly and easily by the office you have been dealing with. You will always be given a contact name or number in any correspondence we send you.

If you cannot settle a matter with the office you have been dealing with, you can write to:

- the Director with overall responsibility for that office or unit, **or**
- if the problem concerns the service you have been given by an Accounts Office, the Director of that Office.

The Director will look into your case and quickly let you know the outcome. For more information about making complaints, please go to **www.hmrc.gov.uk**

If you are still not happy

If the Director has not been able to settle your complaint to your satisfaction, you can ask the Adjudicator to look into it and recommend appropriate action. The Adjudicator is an impartial referee whose recommendations are independent.

The Adjudicator's address is:

The Adjudicator's Office
Haymarket House
28 Haymarket
London
SW1Y 4SP
Telephone: **020 7930 2292** Fax: **020 7930 2298**

The Adjudicator's leaflet AO1 gives information about complaining to the Adjudicator.

Finally, you can ask your MP to refer your case to the independent Parliamentary Commissioner for Administration (usually known as the Ombudsman). The Ombudsman will accept referral from any MP, but you should approach your own MP first. Further information is available from:

The Parliamentary Commissioner for Administration
Millbank Tower
Millbank
London
SW1P 4QP
Telephone: **0845 015 4033** Fax: **020 7217 4160**

Our service commitment to you

HM Revenue & Customs is committed to serving your needs well by

Acting fairly and impartially

We

- treat your affairs in strict confidence, within the law
- want you to receive or pay only the right amount due.

Communicating effectively with you

We aim to provide

- clear and simple forms and guidance
- accurate and complete information in a helpful and appropriate way.

Providing good quality service

We will aim to

- handle your affairs promptly and accurately
- be accessible in ways that aim to meet your need
- keep your costs to the minimum necessary
- be courteous and professional.

Taking responsibility for our service

If you wish to comment or make a complaint we want to hear from you so we can improve our service. We will advise you how to do this.

We can provide a better service if you help us by

- keeping accurate and up to date records
- letting us know if your personal/business circumstances change
- giving us correct and complete information when we ask for it
- paying on time what you should pay.

Privacy and Data Protection

HM Revenue & Customs is a Data Controller under the Data Protection Act 1998. We hold information for the purposes specified in our notification to the Information Commissioner, including the assessment and collection of tax and duties, the payment of benefits and the prevention and detection of crime, and may use this information for any of them .

We may get information about you from others, or we may give information to them. If we do, it will only be as the law permits, to:

- check the accuracy of information
- prevent or detect crime
- protect public funds.

We may check information we receive about you with what is already in our records. This can include information provided by you, as well as by others, such as other government departments or agencies and overseas tax and customs authorities. We will not give information to anyone outside HM Revenue & Customs unless the law permits us to do so. Further information can be found on our website, **www.hmrc.gov.uk**

These notes are for guidance only, and reflect the position at the time of writing. They do not affect any rights of appeal.

Appendix 28

Statement of income from trusts form R185

Inland Revenue

Statement of income from trusts

Trustees: use this form to advise beneficiaries about income payments made under discretion, and income entitlement from trusts. For annuities and other annual payments, use form R185.

Beneficiaries: keep this form and refer to it if making a Tax Return or claiming a tax repayment. The box numbers 7.1 to 7.12 below refer to the box numbers on the *Trusts* page of the Tax Return.

Trustee's declaration

I certify that *(Name and address of beneficiary)*

Full name

Address

Postcode

is a beneficiary of *(name of trust)*

Tax reference of trust

Agent's/Solicitor's reference

The information below is correct

Signature of trustee

Date / /

Discretionary income payment from a trust

I paid income to the beneficiary as follows:

	Net amount	Tax credit at the rate applicable to trusts	Taxable amount	Year ended 5 April
Total payments in tax year *(see Notes 1 and 2 overleaf)*	7.1 £	7.2 £	7.3 £	

Non discretionary Income entitlement under a trust

The beneficiary's income entitlement for year ended 5 April ______ was:

Income taxed at:	Net amount	UK tax or tax credit	Taxable amount	Type of income for a non-resident beneficiary *(see Note 6 overleaf)*
basic rate *(see Note 3 overleaf)*	7.4 £	7.5 £	7.6 £	
lower rate *(see Note 4 overleaf)*	7.7 £	7.8 £	7.9 £	
non-payable dividend rate *(see Note 5 or 11 overleaf)*	7.10 £	7.11 £	7.12 £	

			Taxable amount	Type of income
Untaxed income *(see Note 8 or 12 overleaf)*			£	

	Net amount	UK tax paid	Taxable amount
Foreign income *(see Note 6 or 13 overleaf)*	£	£	£
		Foreign tax paid	
		£	

	Dividend	Notional tax	Dividend + notional tax
Stock/scrip dividends *(see Note 14 overleaf)*	£	£	£

R185(Trust Income) BS6/04

Trustees should read only Notes 1 - 8. Beneficiaries should read only Notes 9 - 14.

Notes for Trustees

1 Boxes 7.1 to 7.3 should be used to record discretionary income payments only. Boxes 7.4 to 7.12 should be used to record non-discretionary income entitlement only.

2 Enter in box 7.1 the actual amount paid, in box 7.2 the amount of tax treated as deducted at the rate applicable to trusts, and in box 7.3 the total of the amounts in boxes 7.1 and 7.2. The rate applicable to trusts is 34% for payments up to 5 April 04, and 40% for payments after that date.

Examples:

Discretionary income payment in tax year 2003-2004:

If the discretionary payment to the beneficiary is £660, enter 660 in box 7.1, 340 in box 7.2, and 1000 in box 7.3.

Discretionary income payment in tax year 2004-2005:

If the discretionary payment to the beneficiary is £600, enter 600 in box 7.1, 400 in box 7.2, and 1000 in box 7.3.

3 Income taxed at the basic rate includes rental income. It does not include interest or dividend income.

4 Income taxed at the lower rate includes savings income such as interest.

5 Income taxed at the dividend rate includes dividends from UK companies.

6 'Foreign tax' is the lower of
- the foreign tax actually withheld
- the amount of tax to which the trust was liable under the terms of a Double Taxation Agreement.

7 If the beneficiary is not resident in the UK, please use the boxes provided to specify the type of income, for example, rent.

8 Use the box on the right to specify the type of income, for example, rent.

Notes for Beneficiaries

9 If you are making a Tax Return, transfer the information from this form to the corresponding boxes on the Tax Return.

10 If you are making a claim for tax repayment, use the information on this form to complete section 6 of form R40.

11 The 10% tax credit on UK dividends is non-payable from tax year 1999-2000. This means that you will be given credit for the 10% against your income, but we will not repay any excess. If you are making a claim on form R40, mark the entry at section 6 for this income 'non-payable'.

12 If you are making a Tax Return, include this income in the pages of your Tax Return dealing with that particular type of income, not the *Trusts* page. For example, if the income is rent, include it in the *Land and Property* pages.

13 If you are making a Tax Return, include this information in the *Foreign* pages of your Tax Return if you are resident in the UK, not the *Trusts* page.

14 If you are making a Tax Return, include this in the scrip dividends boxes of the main Tax Return, not the *Trusts* page.

Appendix 29

Statement of income from estates form R185

Inland Revenue

Statement of income from estates

Executors/administrators: use this form to advise beneficiaries about income from the estate of a deceased person
- for each year during the administration of the estate if a 'sum' is paid to the beneficiary in that year and
- for the year in which the administration of the estate is completed.

Beneficiaries: keep this form and refer to it if making a Tax Return or claiming a tax repayment. The box numbers 7.13 to 7.31 below refer to the box numbers on the *Trusts etc.* page of the Tax Return.

I certify that

(Name and address of beneficiary)

Full name

Address

Postcode

is a beneficiary of the estate of
(Name of deceased person)

Date of death / /

The information below is correct.

Signature of executor or administrator

Date / /

The beneficiary's estate income for the year ended 5 April 20 consisted of the following deemed income:

Income taxed at: *(see Notes 6a to 6f overleaf for tax rates and types of income)*	**Income receivable**	**Tax paid**	**Taxable amount**
basic rate	7.13 £	7.14 £	7.15 £
lower rate	7.16 £	7.17 £	7.18 £
dividend rate	7.19 £	7.20 £	7.21 £
non-repayable basic rate	7.22 £	7.23 £	7.24 £
non-repayable lower rate	7.25 £	7.26 £	7.27 £
non-repayable dividend rate	7.28 £	7.29 £	7.30 £
Total foreign tax for which foreign tax credit relief not claimed		7.31 £	

R185(Estate Income) BS5/03

Notes for Beneficiaries

1 If you normally receive a Tax Return, you should transfer the amounts of income and tax paid shown on the statement overleaf, to the corresponding boxes on the Tax Return, and forward the Tax Return to your Inland Revenue office.

2 If you do not normally receive a Tax Return, you should complete one only if the income you receive from the estate, when added on to any other income, results in you being liable to pay tax at the higher rate.

3 If figures have been entered for tax paid in boxes 7.14, 7.17 or 7.20 overleaf you may be eligible to claim a repayment of the tax paid. If so, use the information from the boxes overleaf to complete section 6 of the R40 claim form. But please note that the tax described overleaf as 'non-repayable' cannot be repaid in any circumstances.

Notes for Executors and Administrators

4 Please prepare a statement on the form overleaf and give it to the beneficiaries of UK estates

- for each year during the administration period in which a *sum* is paid to the beneficiary, and
- for the year in which the administration of the estate is completed.

It should not be given to beneficiaries of a foreign estate as none of the tax will be refundable. A schedule of income and UK/foreign tax credit relief claimable may be provided to beneficiaries of a foreign estate.

5 A 'sum' for this purpose includes cash, assets transferred or appropriated and debts set off or released.

Tax rates and types of income

6a Income taxed at the basic rate includes rental income and profits from a trade. It does not include savings or dividend income.

b Income taxed at the lower rate includes savings income such as interest received.

c Income taxed at the dividend rate includes dividends from foreign companies.

d Income taxed at the non-repayable basic rate relates to gains realised on certain insurance policies.

e Income taxed at the non-repayable lower rate relates to tax years prior to 5 April 1999, and is only relevant if undistributed income is carried forward from 1998–99 or earlier years.

f Income taxed at the non-repayable dividend rate relates to dividends paid on UK shareholdings from 1999–2000 onwards.

7 You can work out the income which each residuary beneficiary should show in their Tax Return by following four steps. For example, for 2002–03 the steps are:

Step 1 Add to any net amount brought forward from 2001–02 the net amount of the beneficiary's share of the residuary income for 2002–03.

Step 2 Compare the net figures in Step 1 with the sum paid to the beneficiary in 2002–03. If the sum paid is greater than or equal to the result of Step 1, then the beneficiary's income is the amount at Step 1 - that is the aggregate income entitlement.

If the sum paid is less than the result of Step 1, the beneficiary's income is the sum paid. The balance of the aggregate income entitlement is carried forward to the next tax year. This will be the whole of the aggregate income entitlement if no distributions were made.

For the final tax year of the administration period, the residuary beneficiary's aggregate income entitlement will be treated as having been distributed in full.

Step 3 The amount to be treated as income in Step 2 is to be treated as paid in the following order of preference:

1. Income bearing basic rate tax.
2. Income bearing lower rate tax.
3. Income bearing dividend rate tax.
4. Income bearing non-repayable basic rate tax.
5. Income bearing non-repayable lower rate tax.
6. Income bearing non-repayable dividend rate tax.

Step 4 Gross up the income in Step 3. Net income taxed at basic rate should be grossed up at the basic rate of tax for the year in which the distribution is made for example, in 2002–2003 the income should be grossed up by multiplying the net income by the fraction 100/78, because the basic rate of tax is 22%.

Appendix 30

Certificate of deduction of income tax form R185

Inland Revenue

Chargeable Events

Please use these if you write or call. It will help to avoid delay.	
Tax reference	/
Our reference	

Date stamp

Information required under regulation 10 of the Retirement Benefits Schemes (Information Powers) Regulations 1995 (SI 1995 No 3103).

The Administrator, *see note 1,* is required to supply the following information **no later than 30 days** after the end of the tax year in which the event occurs. **Failure to do so may lead to penalties under section 98 Taxes Management Act 1970.** Nil reports are not required.

Send this report directly to the Inland Revenue office dealing with the tax affairs of the scheme. If you do not know where this is (or a scheme file has not yet been set up), please send this form to the Inland Revenue office dealing with the Employer's Corporation Tax or Self Assessment tax affairs.

Please read the notes on page 3 before completing this form. If you report figures relating to more than one member, please attach a breakdown showing each member's refund.

If you do not make this notification within the time limit specified, please provide the reason for the delay.

Employer's name
Employer's address
Postcode

Company Registration number

Scheme name

1(SF) BS 2/05

Appendix 31

Specimen Death Benefit Nomination Form

To: The Trustees of [Scheme]

From: [Member]

I wish the following persons to be considered as possible recipients of any lump sum benefits payable on my death.

Name and address	Relationship	Proportion of lump sum

I understand that you have complete discretion under the Scheme provisions as to whom any benefits are paid and that this form is not binding on you in any way.
This nomination supersedes any previous nomination made by myself.

Signature

Name (IN BLOCK CAPITALS)

Date

Appendix 32

The Tax Treatment of Top-Up Schemes

Contents

Part 4 – reporting requirements

Note

These notes are for guidance only and reflect the tax position at the time of writing. It should be borne in mind that they are not binding in law and in a particular case there may be special circumstances which need to be taken into account.

Introduction

Before the 1989 Finance Act, retirement provision by employers had to comply with Inland Revenue tax rules for approved pension schemes. This meant that tax law effectively constrained the total pensions employers could pay to their employees.

The 1989 Act has ensured that employers can now provide whatever retirement benefits they see fit. Tax relief is of course restricted by the maximum benefit limits and the earnings cap, but benefits outside the confines of the tax privileged scheme are unlimited. Non-approved pension schemes give new opportunities and choices to employers which allow them to arrange the retirement package needed to recruit and retain staff.

Employers can now set up non-approved schemes which give flexibility to, for example

- offer a pension greater than the normal two thirds of final salary
- provide a full two-thirds pension even if the normal rules do not allow it – for example, if the employee cannot complete 20 years service with the final employer
- provide lump sum benefits in addition to those allowed under the terms of approved schemes
- give employees who are affected by the earnings cap on tax privileged benefits, pensions and lump sums on earnings above the cap.

But non-approved schemes will not, of course, attract any special tax privileges. And so the purpose of this booklet is to explain in general terms the tax treatment of non-approved pension schemes – which are referred to throughout as "top-up" schemes.

The guidance in this booklet deals only with those social security rules which interact with tax matters – this concerns transfers of pension rights. Any question on how top-up schemes are affected by other Social Security requirements should be sent to the Department of Social Security.

Part 1
Definition of a top-up pension scheme

1.1 What is a Top-up Pension Scheme?

1.1.1 Top-up pension schemes do not have to adopt any particular form. there are no tax rules which govern the structure of schemes, the type of benefits or their amount. These are all matters for employers, employees and their advisers to decide, within the context of general law.

1.1.2 The guidance in this booklet relates only to the tax treatment of schemes which are "retirement benefits schemes" as defined in the Income and Corporation Taxes Act 1988 ("the Taxes Act"). Such schemes will also be subject to other legislation relating to equal treatment, preservation of benefits and so on. These matters are the responsibility of the Department of Social Security to whom any enquiries should be sent.

1.1.3 A retirement benefits scheme is defined in section 611 of the Taxes Act. It means, broadly, a scheme providing benefits for employees or their families which include "relevant benefits" as described in paragraph 1.2.1. The scheme does not have to be set up in any particular way: indeed, a decision to give a relevant benefit on a voluntary basis will be enough to constitute a scheme. More formal arrangements for setting up a scheme may involve a deed, agreement, or other arrangement and it may cover a group of employees or be for just one. For example, a provision in a contract of employment would be enough to establish a retirement benefits scheme.

1.2 Meaning of "relevant benefits"

1.2.1 No matter what form the scheme takes, it is a retirement benefits scheme only if it includes "relevant benefits" among the benefits it gives. Relevant benefits are defined in section 612 of the Taxes Act. They include a pension, lump sum, gratuity or other similar benefit which is, or will be, given

- when a person retires or dies
- in anticipation of retirement
- after a person has retired or died (if the reason for payment is in recognition of past service)

  or

- as compensation for any change in the conditions of a continuing employment.

1.2.2 Disability benefits (whether regular payments or lump sums) are not relevant benefits if they are payable solely because of an employee's death or disablement by accident while employed.

1.2.3 Some schemes which are not intended to be retirement benefits schemes could come within the legislation on top-up schemes. An example is a sick pay scheme which includes a lump sum death in service benefit. On the other hand, redundancy schemes which provide lump sum payments on severance of employment will not normally be affected. This is because redundancy lump sums are payable because of severance of service and not because of retirement or a change in the conditions of a continuing employment.

1.3 Relationship with approved schemes

1.3.1 A tax approved scheme cannot offer non-approvable benefits: they must be kept entirely outside its trust deed and rules. A scheme can only be split into approved and unapproved parts where there are separate classes of employee. For example, where a multi-national employer has a single scheme for its worldwide workforce, it may be possible to approve that part of it covering employees of the UK branch or subsidiary. But only if the types and amounts of benefits payable under the scheme to the UK employers are approvable.

1.3.2 The guidance in this booklet is also relevant to the tax treatment of a scheme, and of payments made to or by it, where its approval is not backdated to commencement, resulting in a period of non-approved status. In such a case the tax privileges that go with approval are available only from the effective date of approval. Prior to that date, the scheme will be treated as a non-approved scheme.

Part 2
Tax treatment of top-up pension schemes

2.1 General

2.1.1 Top-up pension schemes are often referred to as being either

- funded (where money is set aside in advance to meet the benefits promised)
- unfunded (where the promised benefits are met on a pay-as-you-go basis when the employee retires or dies).

In fact, the Taxes Act contains no such distinctions. So although terms like "funded" and "unfunded" are useful labels, they are no more than that. A scheme may combine both approaches (for example, unfunded retirement benefits and funded (insured) death in service benefits).

2.1.2 There are tax consequences when top-up schemes make or receive payments. This Part covers

- the tax treatment of payments to schemes
- the tax treatment of payments by schemes
- the tax treatment of the schemes themselves.

2.2 Tax treatment of payments to schemes

2.2.1 Payments to top-up schemes normally come from contributions by the employer and/or by the employee.

Contributions by the employee

2.2.2 Employee contributions to a top-up scheme are not deductible as an expense in assessing income tax under Schedule E. So where an employee makes direct payment to the scheme no tax relief can be claimed (except on the first £100 each year of premiums paid to secure annuities for a widow and provision for children – section 273 Taxes Act). Where the employer deducts the contributions from pay and passes the money to the top-up scheme, the contributions should come out of taxed income (like, for example, trade union subscriptions and other similar deductions).

2.2.3 As no tax relief is normally due for the contributions, there are no upper or lower limits on the amounts the employee may pay into the scheme. an employee would therefore be better advised to pay additional voluntary contributions, within the normal limits, to a tax approved scheme where that option is available.

Contributions by the employer

2.2.4 Where an employer contributes to a top-up scheme to provide relevant benefits, the contribution counts as the employee's taxable income (section 595(1) Taxes Act). If the scheme is for one employee it is easy to identity the amount chargeable. Where the scheme benefits have been insured, the whole premiums are chargeable to tax. But where the scheme is self-administered, only the contributions used towards providing relevant benefits are chargeable: a tax charge does not arise on separately identifiable contributions which meet the scheme's establishment and administration expenses.

2.2.5 Where an employer pays a contribution for more than one employee, section 595(4) requires the sum to be shared between all of the employees who can benefit from it. The employer, or scheme administrator, should tell the Tax Office how each contribution should be split between the employees. The tax charge will usually be based on these figures.

2.2.6 An employer should notify employees about payments which are chargeable under section 595. *This notice is important and should be retained by the employee*. It may be needed, when benefits become payable, to show that income tax is not payable under section 596A Taxes Act 1988 on all or part of the benefits (see paragraph 2.3.1).

2.2.7 If an employer wants to meet the employee's tax liability on the contributions they may agree on a grossing arrangement: the consent of the local Tax Office is not needed. But, under section 311 Companies Act 1985, it is not lawful for a company to pay a director remuneration free of income tax or varying with the amount of his or her income tax.

2.2.8 Where a grossing arrangement operates, the grossed-up equivalent of the actual chargeable contribution, and the tax figure, should then be included on the employer's pay record (form P11) for the pay period in which the contributions are paid.

Example

A monthly-paid employee is liable to higher rate tax. The employer pays a contribution of £6,000 to a top-up scheme on 6 March. the grossed-up equivalent of the contribution should be included in emoluments, and tax included in tax deducted, for the pay period to 31 March. the employee's top rate of tax is 40%. So the gross contribution, and tax, are

$$\text{£}6,000 \times \frac{100}{60} = \text{£}\,10,000$$

Tax on £10,000 at 40% = £4,000.

2.2.9 Contributions paid by an employer without a grossing arrangement should be notified by the employer at the end of the year to the Tax Office on a form P9D or P11D. The amount of the contribution will then be included in a Schedule E assessment made on the employee who will be asked to pay any resulting tax underpaid.

2.2.10 Benefits in kind can also be chargeable to income tax under section 154 Taxes Act where they are payable to an employee or to members of his or her family or household. But in the case of pensions, lump sums and similar retirement benefits, section 155(4) and Extra Statutory Concession A72 provides exemption from this tax charge. This avoids the possibility of a double charge to tax: once under section 595 and again under section 154.

2.2.11 The borderline between there being a tax charge under section 595 or not can be a fine one. The position will depend upon whether sums have been paid by an employer under a scheme with a view to the provision of benefits for employees. So, for example, payments by an employer to meet the costs of establishing or administering a scheme are not chargeable under section 595. But in other situations the Tax Office will need to consider all the relevant factors before reaching a view.

2.2.12 One example of a borderline case is the creation of a fixed or floating charge on some of the employer's assets. The purpose of such a charge would be to provide security for an unfunded benefit promise. Normally the charge will be called in only if the employer became insolvent or failed to pay the benefits when due. In these cases, the value of the charge would not count as the employee's taxable income when it is created.

2.2.13 On the other hand, if the charge should at any time be called in, that will involve a payment by the employer that could lead to a section 595 charge (even if the employee is then retired or no longer in service). In practice, the tax treatment may depend upon when happens to the funds realised. If they are all paid immediately to the employee, it will often be simpler to charge tax on the benefit paid under section 596A Taxes Act (see paragraph 2.3.1). But where the funds are to be held by trustees on trust until, say, the employee reaches a specified age, then the section 595 tax charge would be applied.

2.2.14 Key man insurance is another difficult area. This insurance is normally used to protect the employer's profits against the loss of a director or other key employee. If used in its conventional form (to protect the employer's profits from the loss of services of a key employee), premiums are not within section 595. But if the insurance contract is part of the arrangements for providing the promised benefits, or to provide security for that promise, then the premiums will be chargeable under section 595(1). The tax treatment in a particular case can be decided by the relevant Tax Office only after seeing the policy and other agreements involved.

2.3 Tax treatment of payments by schemes

2.3.1 The tax treatment of benefits depends on what happened while they accrued. In particular all benefits from a top-up scheme are chargeable to income tax under section 596A Taxes Act unless

- the benefit is chargeable under section 19(1)1 Taxes act (and section 596a does not produce a greater tax liability)

  or

- it can be shown that the benefit is attributable to sums taxed under section 595(1).

Benefits where sums are charged under Section 595

2.3.2 If benefits are paid as lump sums, no tax is chargeable. This is because of the exemptions in section 189(b) Taxes Act (where benefits are paid to the scheme member) or in section 5596A(8) (in other cases). These exemptions apply to benefits payable on retirement or on death.

2.3.3 But pensions and other periodical payments will be chargeable to tax even though they come from sums taxed under section 595(1). In the case of pensions tax will be chargeable under section 19(1) 2 or 3 Taxes Act and where annuities or other annual payments are paid the charge will arise under Case III of Schedule D. In both cases it will be the payer's responsibility to deduct the tax due when making the payment.

2.3.4 If the employee prefers a pension to a lump sum benefit, it will generally be best to give him or her the cash value of the benefits. the money could then be used to buy a life annuity. By arranging matters in this way the annuity will qualify for special tax treatment under which tax is only charged on the income element of each annuity instalment. If the top-up scheme bought the annuity, the whole of each instalment would be taxable.

Benefits where there is no section 595 charge

2.3.5 Pension payments are taxable under section 596A.

2.3.6 Other types of benefit – whether payable on retirement or death, or as lump sums or benefits in kind – are chargeable under section 596A. That section treats the payments made to an individual as Schedule E income. In the case of cash benefits the payer has to deduct and account for tax under PAYE when the payment is made. Where the benefit is not in cash, details should be given by the scheme administrator to the Tax Office within 3 months of its payment.

2.3.7 In some cases an employer might choose to capitalise an unfunded pension promise at retirement and purchase an annuity. But the cost of the annuity would count as the retired employee's taxable income. Also, the annuity would not qualify for the tax relief given for purchased life annuities: the whole of each instalment would be taxable.

2.3.8 Securing benefits in this way could lead to hardship if the employee did not have the cash to meet the tax liability. An alternative would be for the employer to pay the capital value (less income tax under PAYE) to the employee. The balance of the money could then be used to buy the annuity if he or she wished. In this way, the annuity instalments would be taxable only on the income element, not on the whole amount.

2.3.9 Top-up pension schemes are not regulated by tax rules. So payments do not have to be made to the employee or his or her family. For example, the employee could nominate payment to a club or association. These payments would not fit well within a Schedule E charge. Section 596A therefore makes the pension scheme administrator liable to a Case VI, Schedule D tax charge on payments other than to an individual.

2.3.10 There is no statutory provision requiring this tax charge to be deducted from the payments. Authority for doing so should, if needed, be included in the rules or terms of the top-up scheme.

2.3.11 Where the scheme administrator incurs a Case VI Schedule D liability on a payment, the details should be reported to the Tax Office dealing with its affairs. The report, covering all payments of this kind which were made in the accounting period, should be made within 3 months after the end of that period.

2.3.12 Section 596A also taxes benefits in kind which continue after retirement. The measure of the tax charge is on the cash equivalent of the benefit. The cash equivalent is calculated under section 596B according to the type of benefit.

2.3.13 Details of the benefit should be included by the person receiving it on his or her tax return. He or she should be told that if they do not receive a tax return they are legally obliged to tell the Tax Office about the benefit so that it can be assessed.

2.4 Benefits from schemes which formerly were approved

2.4.1 When a retirement benefits scheme ceases to be tax approved, it immediately comes within the tax regime for top-up schemes. Employer contributions payable after tax approval ceases will be chargeable on the members under section 595(1). Lump sum benefits which relate to sums assessed under section 595(1) will be exempt from tax. But any lump sum which relates to the period when the scheme was approved will be chargeable in full under section 596A (even though if the scheme had still been approved, such payments would have been tax exempt).

2.5 Inheritance tax position

2.5.1 It is not possible to give firm guidance on the inheritance tax position since this can only be determined when all the relevant facts about a particular scheme are known. But some general points can be made.

2.5.2 Most top-up schemes (whether funded or unfunded) are likely to be "sponsored superannuation schemes" as defined in section 624 Taxes Act because, even where the employee is charged to income tax under section 595(1), that tax charge does not cover separately identifiable costs of setting up and running the scheme. Where several employers are contributing to a scheme it does not matter whether, or how, participating employers allocate the setting up or administrative costs between themselves as it is the scheme that must bear this cost if it is to qualify as a sponsored superannuation scheme.

2.5.3 For inheritance tax, this means that top-up schemes set up under trust which are also sponsored superannuation schemes will fall within section 151 Inheritance Tax Act 1984. As a result, the normal inheritance tax charges on settled property will not apply. So, for example, benefits paid out under such schemes will be free of any inheritance tax trust charges. there are no special provisions in the Inheritance Tax Act for benefits payable under non-trust arrangements.

2.5.4 Broadly, it is only death benefits that may be liable to inheritance tax. Tax is chargeable if the benefit is expressed to be payable only to the deceased's estate. But commonly, death benefits may be paid at the employer's or scheme administrator's discretion to one or more of a specified group of possible beneficiaries. In these cases inheritance tax will not generally be payable if the employee's estate is excluded from this group.

2.5.5 However, if the employee's estate is included as a possible beneficiary under the discretionary power there may be an inheritance tax gifts with reservation (GWR) charge under section 102 Finance Act 1986. (The provisions outlined in the Inland Revenue press release of 9 July 1986 – which excluded a GWR charge on death benefits under tax approved schemes held on discretionary trusts – do not apply where the scheme is unapproved. "Tax approved schemes" in this context include approved personal pension schemes.)

2.6 Tax treatment of transfer payments

2.6.1 The rules of approved pension schemes do not allow them to make transfer payments to, or accept transfer payments from, an unapproved pension scheme. Benefit rights which have accrued under a top-up scheme may therefore, in practice, be transferred only to another top-up scheme.

2.6.2 There are no tax problems where a cash equivalent is paid between funded schemes. The funds held in the transferring scheme will have accrued from contributions, investment income and gains which have been taxed. For this reason there will not be any tax liability on the transfer payment. and the benefits, when payable, will be subject to the normal tax treatment that applies to funded schemes.

2.6.3 Transfers from a funded scheme of one employer to an otherwise unfunded one of another are also straightforward in tax terms. Once again, the transfer will not itself be a taxable payment. and the benefits derived from the transfer payment will be tax-free if paid as a lump sum, but taxable if paid as pensions. but the unfunded benefits for service with the later employer will all be taxable.

2.6.4 The situation most likely to give rise to complications is transfers from an unfunded scheme. As an unfunded scheme holds no assets, the employer would have to provide the money to pay the cash equivalent, but this would result in a tax liability for the employee under section 595(1) – even if the employee had by then already left service. This may not be an attractive result if the employee did not have the resources to meet the tax liability.

2.7 Income and gains of top-up pension schemes

2.7.1 The tax position of the income and gains of top-up schemes, and the persons chargeable, will depend on the particular structure the scheme takes. A firm ruling on the tax treatment in a particular case can be given by a Tax Office only after considering all the relevant facts. It is therefore possible here to give guidance in only general terms.

2.7.2 Unfunded schemes will not normally have tax complications. the benefit promise will exist on paper, but the scheme will hold no assets. When benefits are due, the employer will at that time provide the funds to pay them and tax liabilities will arise then on the benefits as described in paragraphs 2.3.5 to 2.3.13.

2.7.3 Funded schemes are another matter. In many cases they will be set up under trust (although that is not a tax requirement), and the trustees will be responsible for holding the scheme assets. Some schemes may be wholly insured with premiums paid on insurance contracts. In these cases the trustees will not normally have tax liabilities for those contracts (but see paragraph 3.2.1 to 3.2.4 about the employer's tax position). Any tax due on investment income and gains on the funds which underwrite the contracts will normally be the insurance company's responsibility.

2.7.4 In other cases the scheme may be self-administered. The tax treatment of the income and gains will depend on the particular structure that the scheme takes. Generally, if the scheme is a trust where the trustees have discretion as to the payments to be made or can accumulate surplus income, there will be potential liability to both basic rate and additional rate tax. But, if the only benefits provided by the scheme are "relevant benefits" (see paragraph 1.2.1), it will be exempt from the additional rate tax charge (section 686(2)(c)(i) Taxes Act). The rate of capital gains tax will also normally be restricted to basic rate income tax (section 100 Finance Act 1988). The normal rules for capital gains tax will apply but the trustees will generally be entitled to half the personal annual exemption rather than the full personal exemption (£5,500 for 1991–92).

2.7.5 The "benefit to settlor" rules in Part XV Taxes Act and Schedule 10 Finance act 1988 can apply to top-up pension schemes. But this is not likely to be the case where the structure and operation of a scheme are broadly similar to an approved pension scheme.

2.7.6 Funded self-administered schemes will have to prepare annual accounts and these should be submitted by the scheme's administrator to the scheme's Tax Office so that the appropriate assessments to income tax and capital gains tax may be made.

Part 3
Employer's tax position

3.1 Deductibility of payments

3.1.1 The 1989 Finance Act introduced new rules affecting an employer's right to a deduction for payments to provide non-approved benefits. A right to a deduction now depends on whether those payments are chargeable to tax.

3.1.2 Section 76 Finance Act 1989 disallows the costs incurred by an employer in providing non-approved benefits except where

- the benefits payable under the scheme are taxable

  or

- payments made to provide benefits in future are treated as the scheme member's income under section 595(1).

3.1.3 The section also ties the timing of the deduction to the actual payment of the taxable sums. This prevents an employer claiming a deduction in advance of the payments being chargeable to tax. So, in the case of unfunded schemes, it will not be possible to obtain a deduction for an accounts provision which reflects the liability to pay the future benefits. The deduction will be due only when taxable payments are actually made under the scheme.

3.1.4 Section 76 does not apply to payments made specifically to meet the establishment or running costs of a top-up scheme. Decisions as to whether a deduction is due for these payments are matters for the employer's Tax Office to consider under normal principles.

3.2 Gains on life insurance policies and annuities

3.2.1 The Finance Act 1989 extended the charge on company owned life policies and annuity contracts and on those held on trusts set up by companies.

3.2.2 The company is taxable on any gain made (unless paragraph 3.2.4 – second part – applies). This is, broadly, the difference between the premiums paid and the proceeds. All amounts received from a policy, for example on a partial withdrawal, come into the calculation.

3.2.3 However, in the case of a life policy, the gain on a death is computed by reference to the surrender value of the policy immediately before death. This is particularly important for single policies insuring more than one life ("group policies"). With these, on each death a gain is computed on the surrender value immediately before the death plus all sums paid on earlier deaths. So, instead of using group policies, it will generally be best for each scheme member to have a separate policy. this will ensure that the insurance is individually rated so that liability under section 595 (see paragraph 2.2.4) relates exactly to the premiums paid for the member; the policy benefits can also be tailored more closely to the member's wishes.

3.2.4 Liability arises even on the proceeds received by non-approved pension trusts, but the gain is not charged to tax under these provisions if policy benefits are otherwise chargeable to tax (for example, in the case of Key Man Insurance – see paragraph 2.2.14).

Part 4
Reporting requirements

4.1.1 Section 605(3)(a) Taxes Act requires an employer to report the existence of a top-up scheme to the Revenue. the report should be made to the Tax Office dealing with the employer's accounts.

4.1.2 This notification should be made within 3 months of the date when the scheme first comes into operation for any employee. This means the date a taxable event first arises; for example, the payment of a contribution or a benefit.

4.1.3 So, in the case of a funded scheme with one or more members, the report should be made within 3 months of the scheme being set up. If separate funded schemes are set up for each employee – such as where the benefits are secured by individual insurance policies – the Tax Office should be told about each new scheme.

4.1.4 But with unfunded schemes, no taxation consequences normally arise until benefits become payable. So, no reports will be required until then.

4.1.5 Section 605 also gives the Board of Inland Revenue the power to call for information. In particular

- Section 605(3)(b) requires the employer to comply with a notice requiring details about
  - top-up schemes

  and
  - the employees who benefit under those schemes.
- Section 605(4) places similar duties on the administrator of a top-up scheme.

Appendix 33

HMRC forms and registration procedure

Background – online services

With effect from A-Day the functionality is available for a Scheme Administrator to:

- Register including pre-register for Pension Schemes Online for Scheme Administrators.
- Register new pension schemes.
- Add themselves to a formerly approved pension scheme deemed to be a registered pension scheme.
- Authorise or de-authorise HMRC to deal with a Practitioner acting on their behalf.
- Make a declaration as a Scheme Administrator as required by Section 270 of the Finance Act 2004 including making a declaration as the Scheme Administrator of a Deferred Annuity Contract made on or after 6 April 2006.
- View messages from HMRC on their Pensions Noticeboard.
- Associate new/additional Scheme Administrators to a scheme so they can then add themselves to the scheme.
- View and change their own details.
- View summary details of schemes with which they are linked.
- A Practitioner is able to:
    - Register including pre-register for Pension Schemes Online for Practitioners
    - View messages from HMRC on their Pensions Noticeboard
    - View and change their own details
    - Notify they are no longer acting on behalf of a Scheme Administrator
    - View summary details of schemes with which they are linked.

Pension Scheme Tax Reference Number

On the transfer to the new HMRC database (supporting Pension Schemes Online) the HMRC SF reference of existing approved pension schemes is replaced with a new Pension Scheme Tax Reference (PSTR). The new reference will be in the format NNNNNNNNRC. Character Position 1 – 8 will be numeric, character position 9 will be an 'R', and character position 10 will be a check character. Pension schemes registering on or after 6 April 2006 will also be given a Pension Scheme Tax Reference (PSTR) that follows this format. Pension Schemes set up on or before 5 April 2006 that are approved after 5 April 2006 will be sent their PSTR with their approval letter.

The Scheme Administrator or authorised practitioner of a scheme in existence on 5 April 2006 will thereafter be able to view the PSTR of the pension scheme(s) they are linked with. The PSTR of new pension schemes registered on or after 6 April 2006 will also be viewable by the Scheme Administrator and their authorised Practitioner. If a Scheme Administrator acts for a number of registered pension schemes or a practitioner is authorised to act on behalf of a number of Scheme Administrators of registered pension schemes then they will be able to view a list of the schemes to which they are linked.

Forms

The list of forms for use from A-Day is shown below (the HMRC website link is http://www.hmrc.gov.uk/pensionschemes/tax-simp-draft-forms.htm)

- Registration for tax relief and exemptions
- Registration for relief at source
- Contracting out (Industry wide schemes)
- Contracting out (other schemes)
- Event Report
- Accounting for Tax Return
- Registered Pension Scheme Return
- Protection of Existing Rights
- Enhanced Lifetime Allowance (Pension Credit Rights)
- Enhanced Lifetime Allowance (International)
- Declare as a Scheme Administrator of a Deferred Annuity Contract

Maintenance forms:

- Cessation of Scheme Administrator

- Pre-register as a Scheme Administrator
- Notify Scheme Administrator details
- Change of Scheme Administrator/Practitioner details
- Authorising a Practitioner
- Add Scheme Administrator
- Amend Scheme details

Appendix 34

HMRC Glossary

The following Glossary is to be found in the Registered Pension Schemes Manual on the HMRC website. The reference is RPSM20000000

A

Active member
An individual who has benefits currently accruing for or in respect of that person under one or more arrangements in the pension scheme.

Active membership period
The active membership period

- begins with the date on which benefits first began to accrue to or in respect of the individual under the **registered pension scheme** or, if later, 6 April 2006, and
- ends immediately before the benefit crystallisation event or, if earlier, the date on which benefits cease to accrue under the scheme.

Alternatively secured pension
Payment of income withdrawals direct from a money purchase arrangement to the member of the arrangement (who is aged 75 or over) and that meet the conditions laid down in paragraphs 12 and 13 of Schedule 28 to the Finance Act 2004.

Alternatively secured pension fund
Funds (whether sums or assets) held under a money purchase arrangement that have been 'designated' to provide a scheme member (who is aged 75 or over) with an alternatively secured pension, as identified in paragraph 11 of Schedule 28 to the Finance Act 2004. Once sums or assets have been 'designated' as part of an 'alternatively secured pension fund' any capital growth or income generated from such sums or assets are equally treated as being part of the 'alternatively secured pension fund'. Similarly, where assets are purchased at a later date from such funds, or 'sums' generated by the sale o[f] assets held in such funds, those replacement assets or sums also fall as part of the 'alternatively secured per[sion] fund' (as do any future growth or income generated [by] those assets or sums).

Annual allowance
The annual allowance is such amount, not being le[ss than] the amount for the immediately preceding tax ye[ar, as is] specified by order made by the Treasury.

Annual allowance charge	A charge at the rate of 40% in respect of the amount by which the **total pension input amount** for a tax year in the case of an individual who is a member of one or more **registered pension schemes** exceeds the amount of the **annual allowance** for the tax year.
Annuity protection lump sum death benefit	A lump sum benefit paid following the death of a scheme member who died before age 75 and was in receipt of a either a **lifetime annuity** or **scheme pension** under a **money purchase arrangement**, and which does not exceed the limits imposed through paragraph 16 Schedule 29 Finance Act 2004.
Appropriate date	The earlier of ● a nominated date falling in the tax year immediately after that in which the last pension input period ended, and ● the anniversary of the date on which the period ended.
Arm's length bargain	A normal commercial transaction between two or more persons
Arrangement	A contractual or trust-based arrangement made by or on behalf of a member of a pension scheme under that scheme. A member may have more than one arrangement under a scheme.
Authorised employer payment	Authorised employer payments are ● public service scheme payments, ● authorised surplus payments, ● compensation payments, ● authorised employer loans, ● scheme administration employer payments, and ● any other payment prescribed by Regulations.
Authorised member payment	Authorised member payments are ● pensions that comply with the pension rules in section 165 Finance Act (FA) 2004 or the pension death benefit rules in section 167 FA 2004, ● lump sum payments to comply with the lump sum rule in section 166 FA 2004 or lump sum death benefit rule in section 168 FA 2004, ● recognised transfers that comply with section 169 FA 2004, ● scheme administration member payments, ● payments in accordance with a pension share in order or provision, and ● any other payment prescribed by Regulations.
thorised open-ended stment company	A body incorporated by virtue of regulations under section 262 of the Financial Services and Markets Act 2000 in respect of which an authorisation order is in force under any provision made in such regulations by virtue of subsection (2)(l) of that section.

B

Bank	One of the following • a person within section 840A(1)(b) of the Income and Corporation Taxes Act 1988 (ICTA) (persons other than building societies etc. permitted to accept deposits), or • a body corporate which is a subsidiary or holding company of a person falling within section 840A(1)(b) of ICTA or is a subsidiary of the holding company of such a person (subsidiary and holding company having the meanings in section 736 of the Companies
Basis amount	The basis amount is the base calculation for determining the maximum level of **unsecured pension** or **alternatively secured pension** (and the **dependant** equivalents) payable from a **money purchase arrangement**. The basis amount represents the annual amount of lifetime annuity (or 'relevant annuity') income the **unsecured pension fund** or **alternatively secured funds** (etc) could purchase at the initial calculation and review points.
BCE	Benefit crystallisation event
Benefit crystallisation event	Is a defined event or occurrence that triggers a test of the benefits 'crystallising' at that point against the individual's available **lifetime allowance**. There are eight such events.
Block transfer	The transfer in a single transaction of all the sums and assets held for the purposes of (or representing accrued rights under) the **arrangements** under the **pension scheme** from which the transfer is made, which relate to the member in question and at least one other member of that pension scheme, where before the transfer either the member was not a member of the pension scheme to which the transfer is made, or he has been a member of that pension scheme for no longer than such period as is prescribed by regulations (not laid yet). (Note Paragraph 4C of the Technical Note which appeared on the Inland Revenue website on 16 February 2005 explained that a transfer will still be a block transfer if at the time of the transfer, the member had not been a member of the receiving scheme for more than one year).
Building society	This means a building society within the Building Societies Act 1986.

C

Cash balance arrangement A type of **money purchase arrangement**. An **arrangement** is a cash balance arrangement where the **member** will be provided with **money purchase benefits**, but where the amount that will be available to provide those benefits is not calculated purely by reference to payments made under the arrangement by or on behalf of the member. This means that in a cash balance arrangement, the capital amount available to provide benefits (the member's 'pot') will not derive wholly from any actual contributions (or credits or transfers) made year on year.

For example, the scheme may promise that on retirement, a specified amount will be made available to provide the member with benefits for each year of pensionable service. The specified amount might be an absolute amount, e.g. £5,000 per year of service, or might be a percentage of the member's salary for each relevant year of service. Optionally, the scheme might also guarantee a rate of investment return on the specified amount. The member knows what will go into the promised pot each year (regardless of any contributions actully made) and so can ascertain the amount that accrues in that promised pot each year. It is possible that in a cash balance arrangement the promised pot builds up entirely notionally year by year, being funded only at the end. So, during the build-up phase, the amount in any actual fund held in respect of the member (whether more or less than the amount in the promised pot) is irrelevant. And when benefits ultimately become due, the amount in the promised pot is funded and it is that amount that is used to provide benefits.

In a cash balance arrangement, some of the investment and mortality risk is transferred to the scheme (or, if there is one, the employer); the fact that all or part of the pot is guaranteed or promised means that the promised amount must be made available to provide benefits irrespective of the level of actual funds held.

Chargeable amount The amount that crystallises for **lifetime allowance** at a **benefit crystallisation event** that is not covered by an individual's available lifetime allowance at that time, plus any 'scheme-funded tax payment'. The chargeable amount is the amount on which the **lifetime allowance charge** arises.

Charity lump sum death benefit — A lump sum benefit paid from a **money purchase arrangement** to a charity (as defined in section 506 Income and Corporation Taxes Act 1988) following the death of a scheme member (or a **dependant** of such a member) who is aged 75 or over which meets the conditions of paragraph 18, Schedule 29 to the Finance Act 2004. Such a lump sum cannot be paid where there is still a surviving **dependant** of the member.

D

Deferred member — An individual who has rights under a pension scheme and who is neither an active member, nor a pensioner member.

Defined benefits — Benefits provided under a **pension scheme** that are calculated by reference to earnings or service of the member or any other factor other than by reference to an amount available under the scheme for the provision of benefits to or in respect of that member (so which are not **money purchase** benefits).

Defined benefits arrangement — An **arrangement** other than a **money purchase arrangement** that provides only **defined benefits**. "Defined benefits" are calculated by reference to the earnings or the service of the **member**, or by any other means except by reference to an available amount for the provision of benefits to or in respect of the member, (thus making the definitions of money purchase and defined benefit arrangements mutually exclusive). A defined benefit arrangement is, typically, a 'final salary' scheme, that is, one where the level of benefits paid is calculated by reference to the member's final salary and length of service with the employer. Contributions are often made to such an arrangement, and so there may be a pension fund or pot, but the benefits that may be paid are not calculated by reference to that fund or pot.

Defined benefits lump sum death benefit — A lump sum benefit paid from a **defined benefits arrangement** following the death of the scheme member before the age of 75 (and within two years of that date of death), and as defined in paragraph 13, Schedule 29 to the Finance Act 2004.

Dependant	A person who was married to the member at the date of the member's death is a dependant of the member. A child of the member is a dependant of the member if the child has ● not reached the age of 23, or ● has reached age 23 and, in the opinion of the **scheme administrator**, was at the date of the member's death dependent on the member because of physical or mental impairment. A person who was not married to the member at the date of the member's death and is not a child of the member is a dependant of the member if, in the opinion of the **scheme administrator**, at the date of the member's death the person was financially dependant
Dependants' alternatively secured pension	Payment of income withdrawals direct from a **money purchase arrangement** to a **dependant** of a scheme member who is aged 75 or over, that meets the conditions laid down in paragraphs 26 and 27 of Schedule 28 to the Finance Act 2004.
Dependants' alternatively secured pension fund	Funds (whether sums or assets) held under a **money purchase arrangement** that have been 'designated' after the death of a scheme member to provide a particular **dependant** of that member (who is aged 75 or over) with a **dependants' alternatively secured pension**, as identified in paragraph 25 of Schedule 28 to the Finance Act 2004. Once sums or assets have been 'designated' as part of a 'dependants' alternatively secured pension fund', any capital growth or income generated from such sums or assets are equally treated as being part of the 'dependants' alternatively secured pension fund'. Similarly, where assets are purchased at a later date from such funds, or 'sums' generated by the sale of assets held in such funds, those replacement assets or sums also fall as part of the 'dependants' alternatively secured pension fund' (as do any future growth or income generated by those assets or sums).
Dependants' annuity	An annuity paid by an **insurance company** to a **dependant** of a scheme member following the death of that member that meets the conditions laid down in paragraph 17, Schedule 28 to the Finance Act 2004.
Dependants' scheme pension	A pension paid to a **dependant** of a member of a **registered pension scheme** following the death of that member, the entitlement to which is an absolute entitlement under the scheme and that meets the conditions laid down in paragraph 16, Schedule 28 to the Finance Act 2004.

Dependants' short–term annuity — An annuity contract purchased from a **dependants' unsecured pension fund** held under a **money purchase arrangement** that provides that **dependant** with an income for a term of no more than five years (not reaching to or beyond their 75th birthday), and which meets the conditions imposed through paragraph 20, Schedule 28 to the Finance Act 2004. This definition covers replacement assets purchased after the initial 'designation' from such funds, or any capital growth from or income generated by assets held in the fund (whether held at the time of 'designation' or where replacement assets).

Dependants' unsecured pension — Payments of income withdrawals direct from **a money purchase arrangement**, or income paid from a **dependants' short-term annuity** contract purchased from such an **arrangement**, to a **dependant** (who is aged under 75) of the scheme member who established the **arrangement** and that meets the conditions laid down in paragraph 20 and 23 to 24 of Schedule 28 to the Finance Act 2004.

Dependants' unsecured pension fund — Funds (whether sums or assets) held under a money purchase arrangement that have been 'designated' after the death of a scheme member to provide a particular dependant of that member (who is aged under 75) with a dependants' unsecured pension, as identified in paragraph 22 of Schedule 28 to the Finance Act 2004. Once sums or assets have been 'designated' as part of a 'dependants' unsecured pension fund', any capital growth or income generated from such sums or assets are equally treated as being part of the 'dependants' unsecured pension fund'. Similarly, where assets are purchased at a later date from such funds, or 'sums' generated by the sale of assets held in such funds, those replacement assets or sums also fall as part of the 'dependants' unsecured pension fund' (as do any future growth or income generated by those assets or sums).

E

Employer-financed retirement benefits scheme — This means a scheme for the provision of benefits consisting of or including relevant benefits to or in respect of employees or former employees of an employer. However, neither a registered pension scheme nor a section 615(3) scheme is an employer-financed retirement benefits scheme.

EU member state — Any of the following: Austria, Belgium, Czech Republic, Cyprus, Denmark, Estonia, Finland, France, Germany, Greece, Hungary, Ireland, Italy, Latvia, Lithuania, Luxembourg, Malta, Netherlands, Poland, Portugal, Slovakia, Slovenia, Spain, Sweden, United Kingdom.

European Economic Area (EEA) investment portfolio manager — This means an institution which

- is an EEA firm of the kind mentioned in paragraph 5(a), (b) or (c) of Schedule 3 to the Financial Services and Markets Act 2000 (certain credit and financial institutions), or
- qualifies for authorisation under paragraph 12(1) or 12(2) of that Schedule, or
- has permission under the Financial Services and Markets Act 2000 to manage portfolios of investments.

Ex-spouse — An individual to whom **pension credit** rights have been or are to be allocated following a **pension sharing order**, agreement or equivalent provision.

F

Former approved superannuation fund — Any fund which immediately before 6 April 2006 was an approved superannuation fund for the purposes of section 608 Income and Corporation Taxes Act 1970, that

- has not been approved for the purposes of Chapter 1 Part 14 Income and Corporation Taxes Act 1988 since 5 April 1980, and
- has not received any contributions since 5 April 1980.

FSAVCS — A **registered pension scheme** that was originally approved by the Board before 6 April 2006 as a retirement benefits scheme by virtue of section 591(2)(h) Income and Corporation Taxes Act 1988, established by a pension provider or the trustees of an approved centralised scheme for non-associated employers to which the employer does not contribute and which provides benefits additional to those provided by a scheme to which the employer does contribute.

G

GAD — The Government Actuary's Department.

GAD tables — The Government Actuary's Department Tables on a single life basis.

GMPs — Stands for guaranteed minimum pensions and has the same meaning as in the Pension Schemes Act 1993.

H

Hybrid arrangement

An **arrangement** where only one type of benefit will ultimately be provided, but the type of benefit that will be provided is not known in advance because it will depend on certain given circumstances at the point benefits are drawn.

For example, a hybrid arrangement may provide the member with **other money purchase benefits** based on a pot derived from the contributions that have accrued over time, but subject to a **defined benefit** minimum or underpin. If the benefits proided by the money purchase pot at the point benefits are drawn fall below a certain defined level, for example 1/60ths of final remuneration for every year worked, that higher defined benefit will be provided. So the benefits will be either other money purchase benefits, or defined benefits.

When benefits are drawn, if the benefits actually provided are other money purchase or **cash balance benefits** then the arrangement will become a **money purchase arrangement**. And if the benefits provided are defined benefits then the arrangement will become a **defined benefits arrangement**.

I

Insurance company

Either

- a person who has permission under Part 4 of the Financial Services and Markets Act 2000 to effect or carry out contracts of long-term insurance, or
- a European Economic Area (EEA) firm of the kind mentioned in paragraph 5(d) of Schedule 3 to the Financial Services and Markets Act 2000 (certain direct insurance undertakings) which has permission under paragraph 15 of that Schedule (as a result of qualifying

L

Lifetime allowance

The lifetime allowance is an overall ceiling on the amount of tax privileged pension savings that any one individual can draw. The exact figure will be whatever the 'standard lifetime allowance' for the tax year concerned is or a multiple of this figure where certain circumstances apply.

Lifetime allowance charge A charge to income tax that arises on any chargeable amount generated at a 'benefit crystallisation event'. The rate of charge is either 25% or 55%, depending on whether the 'event' giving rise to the charge was the payment of a lump sum or not. The scheme administrator and member are jointly liable to the charge, except where the chargeable amount arises following the death of the member. Here, the recipient of the payment giving rise to the charge is solely liable.

Lifetime allowance excess lump sum A lump sum benefit paid to a member of a **registered pension scheme** (who is aged under 75) because they have used up their available **lifetime allowance**, and which meets the conditions of paragraph 11 of Schedule 29 to the Finance Act 2004.

Lifetime annuity An annuity contract purchased under a **money purchase arrangement** from an **insurance company** of the member's choosing that provides the member with an income for life, and which meets the conditions imposed through paragraph 3, Schedule 28 to the Finance Act 2004.

M

Market value The market value of an asset held for the purposes of a pension scheme is to be determined in accordance with section 272 of the Taxation of Chargeable Gains Act 1992 and section 278(2) to (4) Finance Act 2004 (where dealing with a right or interest in respect of money lent directly or indirectly to certain parties).

Member An individual who is either an active member, a pensioner member, a deferred member or a pension credit member of a pension scheme.

Money purchase benefits Benefits provided under a pension scheme, the rate or amount of which is calculated by reference to an amount available for the provision of benefits to or in respect of the member (whether the amount so available is calculated by reference to payments made under the scheme by the member or any other person or employer on behalf of the member, or any other factor).

Money purchase arrangement An arrangement is a money purchase arrangement if, at that time, all the benefits that may be provided to or in respect of the member under the arrangement are cash balance or other money purchase benefits.

N

Nominated date

This means

- in the case of a **money purchase arrangement** other than a **cash balance arrangement**, such date as the individual or **scheme administrator** nominates, or
- in the case of any other arrangement, such date as the **scheme administrator** nominates.

O

Occupational pension scheme

A pension scheme established by an employer or employers and having (or capable of having) effect so as to provide benefits to or in respect of any or all of the employees of that employer or employers, or any other employer (whether or not it also has effect so as to provide benefits to or in respect of other persons, or is capable of having such effect).

Other money purchase arrangement

A **money purchase arrangement** other than a **cash balance arrangement**.

An **arrangement** is an other money purchase arrangement where the member will be provided with **money purchase benefits**, and the amount that will be available to provide those benefits is calculated purely by reference to payments made under the arrangement by or on behalf of the **member**. This means that in an other money purchase arrangement the capital amount available to provide benefits (the member's "pot") will derive wholly from actual contributions (or credits or transfers) made year on year.

The **scheme administrator** or trustees may use the payments made under the arrangement to make investments of any kind on behalf of the member (for example, cash on deposit, shares, other investment assets, a life assurance policy on the member's death). As long as the pot ultimately used to provide benefits is wholly derived from the original payments, the arrangement is an other money purchase arrangement. The subsequent investment income and any capital gains are derived from payments made under the arrangement, and they themselves become part of the member's pot.

It is a feature of other money purchase arrangements that the member bears all the investment and mortality risk. The scheme simply pays out whatever benefits the amount in the pot, including the proceeds of all the investments that have been made using the payments into the scheme, will support.

Overseas arrangement active membership period	This is the period beginning with the date on which the benefits first began to accrue to, or in respect of, the individual under the recognised overseas scheme arrangement or, if later, 6 April 2006 and ending immediately before the recognised overseas scheme transfer. If benefits ceased to accrue under the recognised overseas scheme arrangement before the transfer then it is this date on which the overseas arrangement active membership period is treated as ending.
Overseas pension scheme	A **pension scheme** is an overseas pension scheme if it is not a **registered pension scheme** but it is established in a country or territory outside the UK and satisfies the requirements in the Pension Schemes (Categories of Country and Requirements for Recognised Overseas Schemes) Regulations 2004. (Regulations not finalised yet).

P

Pension commencement lump sum	A lump sum benefit paid to a member of a registered pension scheme (who is aged under 75) in connection with an arising entitlement to a pension benefit (other than a short-term annuity contract), and which meets the conditions detailed in paragraphs 1 to 3 of Schedule 29 to the Finance Act 2004.
Pension credit	Pension sharing on divorce was introduced in 1999 under the pension sharing provisions in the Welfare Reform and Pensions Act 1999 (WRPA) and Schedule 10 of the Finance Act 1999. This introduced the 'pension credit' and 'pension debit'. The 'pension debit' is the amount by which the original member's pension is reduced and the 'pension credit' the corresponding amount by which the ex-spouse's pension rights are increased. Section 29 WRPA determines the value of the pension credit to be transferred to the ex-spouse.
Pension credit member	An individual who has rights in a pension scheme which are directly or indirectly attributable to pension credits.
Pension debit	Pension sharing on divorce was introduced in 1999 under the pension sharing provisions in the Welfare Reform and Pensions Act 1999 (WRPA) and Schedule 10 of the Finance Act 1999. This introduced the 'pension credit' and 'pension debit'. The 'pension debit' is the amount by which the original member's pension is reduced and the 'pension credit' the corresponding amount by which the ex-spouse's pension rights are increased.
Pension input amount	The amounts as arrived in accordance with sections 230 to 237 of Finance Act 2004

Pension input period This means

- the period beginning with the **relevant commencement date** and ending with the earlier of a **nominated date** and the anniversary of the **relevant commencement date**, and
- each subsequent period beginning immediately after the end of a period which is a **pension input period** (under either this or the earlier paragraph) and ending with the **appropriate date**.

Pension protection lump sum death benefit A lump sum benefit paid following the death of a scheme member of a **registered pension scheme**, who died before age 75 and was in receipt of a **scheme pension** under a **defined benefits arrangement** and which does not exceed the limits imposed through paragraph 14 of Schedule 29 to the Finance Act 2004.

Pension scheme A pension scheme is a scheme or other arrangements which is comprised in one or more instruments or agreements, having or capable of having effect so as to provide benefits to or in respect of persons on retirement, on death, on having reached a particular age, on the onset of serious ill-health or incapacity or in similar circumstances.

Pension sharing order An order or provision made following the divorce of two individuals as listed in section 28(1) of the Welfare Reform and Pensions Act 1999 (or the Welfare Reform and Pensions (Northern Ireland) Order 1999 (SI 1999/3147)).

Pension year The period the maximum **unsecured pension** and **alternatively secured pension** limits apply to (and the **dependant** equivalents). In the legislation these are referred to as 'unsecured pension years' and 'alternatively secured pension years'. These periods run in consecutive 12-month periods from the point initial entitlement to such pensions actual arise under a **money purchase arrangement**. These periods are set at the point that initial entitlement arise, and cannot be changed from that point onwards (although the pension year the member or **dependant** dies or reaches age 75 will be deemed to end immediately before such an occurrence – these truncated 12-month periods are treated as a whole 12-month period for limit purposes).

Pensioner member A member of a pension scheme who is entitled to the payment of benefits from the scheme **and** who is not an active member.

Personal pension scheme A pension scheme previously approved by the Board of Inland Revenue under section631 Income and Corporation Taxes Act 1988.

Personal representatives In relation to a person who has died, this means (in the UK) persons responsible for administering the estate of the deceased. In a country or territory outside the UK, it means the persons having functions under its law equivalent to those administering the estate of the deceased.

Prescribed occupation Any of the following occupations: Athlete, Badminton Player, Boxer, Cricketer, Cyclist, Dancer, Diver (Saturation, Deep Sea and Free Swimming), Footballer, Golfer, Ice Hockey Player, Jockey – Flat Racing, Jockey – National Hunt, Member of the Reserve Forces, Model, Motor Cycle Rider (Motocross or Road Racing), Motor Racing Driver, Rugby League player, Rugby Union Player, Skier (Downhill), Snooker or Billiards Player, Speedway Rider, Squash Player, Table Tennis Player, Tennis Player (including Real Tennis), Trapeze Artiste, Wrestler.

Property investment LLP A Limited Liability Partnership whose business consists wholly or mainly in the making of investments in land and the principal part of whose income is derived from that business.

Protected rights As defined in regulation 3 of the Personal and Occupational Pension Schemes (Protected Rights) Regulations 1996, but should be read as including safeguarded rights, wherever appropriate.

Public service pension scheme A pension scheme

- established by or under any enactment,
- approved by a relevant governmental or Parliamentary person or body, or
- specified as being a public service pension scheme by a Treasury order.

Q

Qualifying overseas pension scheme An overseas pension scheme is a qualifying overseas pension scheme if it satisfies certain HMRC requirements. The scheme manager must notify HMRC that the scheme is an overseas pension scheme and provide evidence to HMRC where required. The scheme manager must also sign an undertaking to inform HMRC if the scheme ceases to be an overseas pension scheme and comply with any prescribed benefit crystallisation information requirements imposed on the scheme manager by HMRC. The overseas pension scheme must not be excluded by HMRC from being a qualifying overseas pension scheme.

Qualifying recognised overseas pension scheme — A **recognised overseas pension scheme** is a qualifying recognised overseas pension scheme if it satisfies certain HMRC requirements. The scheme manager must notify HMRC that the scheme is a recognised overseas pension scheme and provide evidence to HMRC where required. The scheme manager must also sign an undertaking to inform HMRC if the scheme ceases to be a recognised overseas pension scheme and comply with any prescribed information requirements imposed on the scheme manager by HMRC. The recognised overseas pension scheme must not be excluded by HMRC from being a qualifying recognised overseas pension scheme.

R

Recognised European Economic Area (EEA) collective investment scheme — This means a collective investment scheme (within the meaning given by section 235 of the Financial Services and Markets Act 2000) which is recognised by virtue of section 264 of that Act (schemes constituted in other EEA states).

Recognised overseas pension scheme — A recognised overseas pension scheme is an overseas pension scheme which is established in a country or territory listed in the Pension Schemes (Categories of Country and Requirements for Recognised Overseas Schemes) Regulations (not laid yet). An overseas pension scheme may also be a recognised overseas pension scheme if it is of a description prescribed in those regulations, or if it satisfies any requirements in those regulations. (Regulations not finalised yet).

Recognised transfer — A transfer representing a member's accrued rights under **a registered pension scheme** to another **registered pension scheme** (or, in certain circumstances, to an **insurance company**) or a **qualifying recognised overseas pension scheme**.

Refund of excess contributions lump sum — A lump sum benefit paid to a member of a **registered pension scheme** because they have contributed more to the scheme than they are entitled to tax relief on, and which meets the conditions of paragraph 6, Schedule 29 to the Finance Act 2004.

Registered pension scheme — A **pension scheme** is a registered pension scheme at any time when, either through having applied for registration and been registered by the Inland Revenue, or through acquiring registered status by virtue of being an approved pension scheme on 5 April 2006, it is registered under Chapter 2 of Part 4 of the Finance Act 2004.

Relevant administrator For a **retirement benefits scheme**, former approved superannuation fund or relevant statutory scheme as defined in section 611A Income and Corporation Taxes Act 1988 (ICTA), or a pension scheme treated by HMRC as a relevant statutory scheme, this is the person(s) who is/are the administrator of the pension scheme under section 611A of ICTA.

For a deferred annuity contract where the benefits are provided under one of the types of scheme above, or a retirement annuity, this is the trustee(s) of the pension scheme, or the insurance company which is a party to the contract in which the pension scheme is comprised.

For a Parliamentary pension scheme or fund, this is the trustees of the scheme or fund.

For a **personal pension scheme**, this is the person who is referred to in section 638(1) of the Income and Corporation Taxes Act 1988).

Relevant commencement date This means:

(a) in the case of a **cash balance arrangement** or a **defined benefits arrangement** or a **hybrid arrangement,** the only benefits under which may be cash balance benefits or defined benefits, the date on which rights under the arrangement begin to accrue to or in respect of the individual, or

(b) in the case of a **money purchase arrangement** other than a cash balance arrangement, the first date on which a contribution within section 233(1) of Finance Act 2004 is made, or

(c) in the case of a **hybrid arrangement** not within paragraph (a), whichever is the earlier of the date mentioned in that paragraph and the date mentioned in paragraph (b).

Relevant consolidated contribution A contribution made by way of discharge of any liability incurred by the employer before 6 April 2006 to pay any pension or lump sum to or in respect of the individual.

Relevant overseas individual An individual who either does not qualify for UK relief on contributions paid to a **registered pension scheme** because they are not a "relevant UK individual" as defined in section 178 Finance Act 2004, or an individual who is not employed by a UK resident employer and only qualifies for UK relief on pension contributions because they were resident in the UK both during 5 years immediately before the tax year under consideration and when they became a member of the **registered pension scheme**.

Relevant UK earnings This means

- employment income,
- income which is chargeable under Schedule D and is immediately derived from the carrying on or exercise of a trade, profession or vocation (whether individually or as a partner acting personally in a partnership), and
- income to which section 529 of Income and Corporation Taxes Act 1988 (ICTA) (patent income of an individual in respect of inventions) applies. Relevant UK earnings are to be treated as not being chargeable to income tax if, in accordance with arrangements having effect by virtue of section 788 of ICTA (double taxation agreements), they are not taxable in the United Kingdom.

Relevant UK individual An individual is a relevant UK individual for a tax year if

- the individual has relevant United Kingdom (UK) earnings chargeable to income tax for that year,
- the individual is resident in the UK at some time during that year,
- the individual was resident in the UK both at some time during the five tax years immediately before that year and when the individual became a member of the pension scheme, or
- the individual, or the individual's spouse, has for the tax year general earnings from overseas Crown employment subject to UK tax.

Relievable pension contribution A contribution paid to a **registered pension scheme** by or on behalf of a member of that scheme, unless one or more of the following exceptions applies. A payment is not a relievable contribution if

- the member was aged 75 or over when the contribution was made, or
- the contribution is paid by the member's employer, or
- the payment is an age related rebate or a minimum contribution paid by HMRC to a contracted-out pension scheme under section 42A(3) or section 43 of the Pension Schemes Act 1993 or the corresponding Northern Ireland legislation.

Retirement annuity contract A retirement annuity contract or trust scheme previously approved by the Board under Chapter 3 of Part 14 of Income and Corporation Taxes Act 1988.

Retirement benefit scheme A retirement benefit scheme is any of the following

- a scheme which was approved under Chapter 1 of Part 14 of Income and Corporation Taxes Act (ICTA) 1988;
- a relevant statutory scheme (as defined in s611A ICTA 1988);

- a scheme treated as a relevant statutory scheme; or
- an old code scheme approved under s208 ICTA 1970 that has not received contributions since 5 April 1980.

RPI
Stands for the Retail Price Index, which is the index of retail prices compiled by the Office for National Statistics. Where that index is not published for a relevant month any substitute index or index figures published by the Office for National Statistics may be used. (See section 279 Finance Act 2004.)

S

Scheme administration member payment
Payments made by a **registered pension scheme** to a member, or in respect of a member, for the purposes of administration or management of the scheme.

Scheme administrator
The person(s) appointed in accordance with the **pension scheme** rules to be responsible for the discharge of the functions conferred or imposed on the scheme administrator of the pension scheme by and under Part 4 of Finance Act 2004. This person must be resident in an **EU member state** or in Norway, Liechtenstein or Iceland (EEA states which are not EU states). The person must have made the declarations to HMRC required by section 270(3) Finance Act 2004.

Scheme chargeable payment
Scheme chargeable payments are

- any unauthorised payment by the pension scheme other than a payment that is exempted by section 241(2) Finance Act 2004 from being a scheme chargeable payment (see list below), and
- a payment that the pension scheme is treated as having made and classed as a scheme chargeable payment by secion 183 o 184 Finance Act 2004 because of unauthorised borrowing.

The following unauthorised payments are not scheme chargeable payments.

1 The payment is treated as having been made by section 173 Finance Act 2004 and the asset used to provide the benefit is not a wasting asset as defined in section 44 Taxation of Capital Gains Act 1992.
2 The payment is a compensation payment as defined by section 178 Finance Act 2004.
3 The payment is made to comply with a court order or an order by a person or body with the power to order the making of the payment.
4 The payment is made on the grounds that a court or any such person or body is likely to order (or would be were it asked to do so) the making of the payment.
5 The payment is of a description prescribed by regulations made by HMRC.

Scheme pension — A pension entitlement provided to a member of a **registered pension scheme**, the entitlement to which is an absolute entitlement to a lifetime pension under the scheme that cannot be reduced year on year (except in narrowly defined circumstances) and meets the conditions laid down in paragraph 2 of Schedule 28 to Finance Act 2004.

Section 9 (2B) Rights — Rights derived through section 9(2B) of the Pension Schemes Act 1993.

Secured pension — Either a **lifetime annuity** or **scheme pension**.

Short service refund lump sum — A lump sum benefit paid to a member of an **occupational pension scheme** because they have stopped accruing benefits under the scheme and have less than two years of pensionable service under the scheme, and which meets the conditions of paragraph 5, Schedule 29 to the Finance Act 2004.

Short-term annuity — An annuity contract purchased from a member's **unsecured pension fund** held under a **money purchase arrangement** that provides that member with an **unsecured pension** income for a term of no more than five years (not reaching to or beyond their 75th birthday), and which meets the conditions imposed through paragraph 6, Schedule 28 to the Finance Act 2004.

Sponsoring employer — In relation to an occupational pension scheme means the employer, or any of the employers, to or in respect of any or all of whose employees the pension scheme has, or is capable of having, effect as to provide benefits.

Standard lifetime allowance — The overall ceiling on the amount of tax-privileged savings that any one individual can accumulate over the course of their lifetime without taking any special factors into account that may increase or decrease the tax-privileged ceiling. For the year 2006–07, this amount is £1,500,000. The standard lifetime allowance for following tax years will be specified by an annual order made by the Treasury, and will never be less than the amount for the immediately preceding tax year.

T

Total pension input amount — The aggregation of the **pension input amounts** in respect of each arrangement relating to an individual under a registered pension scheme of which the individual is a member.

Transfer lump sum death benefit	A lump sum benefit paid from a **money purchase arrangement** for the benefit of another member of the same pension scheme following the death of a scheme member (or a **dependant** of such a member), who is aged 75 or over, which meets the conditions of paragraph 19, Schedule 29 to the Finance Act 2004. Such a lump sum cannot be paid where there is still a surviving **dependant** of the member.
Trivial commutation lump sum	A lump sum benefit paid to a member of a **registered pension scheme** (who is aged under 75) because their pension entitlements (under both that scheme and other such schemes) are deemed trivial, and which meets the conditions of paragraphs 7 to 9 of Schedule 29 to the Finance Act 2004.
Trivial commutation lump sum death benefit	A lump sum benefit paid to a **dependant** of a scheme member of a **registered pension scheme** (who died before age 75) because that **dependant's** entitlement under that scheme is deemed trivial, and which meets the conditions of paragraph 20 of Schedule 29 to the Finance Act 2004.

U

Unauthorised employer payment	An unauthorised employer payment is ● a payment by a registered pension scheme that is an occupational pension scheme to or in respect of a sponsoring employer which is not an authorised employer payment, or ● anything which is specifically prescribed as being an unauthorised payment in respect of the member.
Unauthorised member payment	An unauthorised member payment is ● a payment by a registered pension scheme to or in respect of a member of that pension scheme that is not an authorised member payment, or ● anything which is specifically prescribed as being an unauthorised payment in respect of the member.
Unauthorised payments charge	Tax due under section 208 Finance Act 2004 on either **unauthorised member payments** or **unauthorised employer payments**. The rate of tax is 40% of the unauthorised payment.
Unauthorised payments surcharge	Tax due under section 209 Finance Act that is paid in addition to the **unauthorised payments charge**. The tax will be due where total unauthorised payments go over a set limit in a set period of time of no more than 12 months. The rate of tax is 15% of the unauthorised payments.

Uncrystallised funds Funds held in respect of the member under a **money purchase arrangement** that have not as yet been used to provide that member with a benefit under the scheme (so have not crystallised), as defined in paragraph 8(3) of Schedule 28 to the Finance Act 2004. These are defined differently for **cash balance arrangements**. Here it is what funds there would be if the member decided to draw benefits on a particular date not the funds actually held in the cash balance arrangement at that time..

Uncrystallised funds lump sum death benefit A lump sum benefit paid from a **money purchase arrangement** following the death of the scheme member before the age of 75 (and within two years of that date of death) from any **uncrystallised funds** the member held in that **arrangement** at the point of death, and as defined in paragraph 15, Schedule 29 to the Finance Act 2004.

Unit trust scheme manager This means one of the following:

(a) a person who has permission under Part 4 of the Financial Services and Markets Act 2000 to manage unit trust schemes authorised under section 243 of that Act, or

(b) a firm which has permission under paragraph 4 of Schedule 4 to the Financial Services and Markets Act 2000 (as a result of qualifying for authorisation under paragraph of that Schedule; Treaty firms) to manage unit trust schemes authorised under that section.

Unsecured pension Payment of income withdrawals direct from a **money purchase arrangement**, or income paid from a **short-term annuity** contract purchased from such an **arrangement**, to the member of the **arrangement** (who is aged under 75) and that meet the conditions laid down in paragraph 6 and 8 to 10 of Schedule 28 to the Finance Act 2004.

Unsecured pension fund Funds (whether sums or assets) held under **a money purchase arrangement** that have been 'designated' to provide a scheme member (who is aged under 75) with an **unsecured pension**, as identified in paragraph 8 of Schedule 28 to the Finance Act 2004. Once sums or assets have been 'designated' as part of an 'unsecured pension fund' any capital growth or income generated from such sums or assets are equally treated as being part of the 'unsecured pension fund'. Similarly where assets are purchased at a later date from such funds, or 'sums' generated by the sale of assets held in such funds, those replacement assets or sums also fall as part of the 'unsecured pension fund' (as do any future growth or income generated by those assets or sums).

Unsecured pension fund lump sum death benefit A lump sum benefit paid from a **money purchase arrangement** following the death of the scheme member before the age of 75 from any **unsecured pension fund** the member held in that **arrangement** at the point of death, and as defined in paragraph 17, Schedule 29 to the Finance Act 2004.

V

Valuation assumptions The valuation assumptions in relation to a person, benefits and a date are assumptions

(a) if the person has not reached such age (if any) as must have been reached to avoid any reduction in the benefits on account of age, that the person reached that age on the date, and

(b) that the person's right to receive the benefits had not been occasioned by physical or mental impairment.

W

Winding-up lump sum A lump sum benefit paid to a member of an occupational pension scheme because the scheme is being wound-up and their accrued benefits under the scheme are deemed 'trivial', and which meets the conditions of paragraph 10, Schedule 29 to the Finance Act 2004.

Winding-up lump sum death benefit A lump sum benefit paid to a **dependant** of a member of an **occupational pension scheme** because the scheme is being wound-up and their accrued benefits under the scheme are deemed 'trivial', and which meets the conditions of paragraph 21, Schedule 29 to the Finance Act 2004.

Appendix 35

Abbreviations

AVC(s)	–	Additional Voluntary Contribution(s)
CAA	–	Capital Allowances Act 2001
CGT	–	Capital Gains Tax
EC	–	European Commission
ECJ	–	European Courts of Justice
EFRBS	–	Employer-financed retirement benefits scheme
ESC	–	Extra Statutory Concession by the Inland Revenue
EU	–	European Union (formerly European Community)
FA	–	Finance Act
FSA	–	Financial Services Authority–the single regulator from 28 October 1997
FSAVC	–	Free-Standing Additional Voluntary Contributions
FSMA	–	Financial Services and Markets Act 2000
FURBS	–	Funded Unapproved Retirement Benefit Scheme
GAD	–	Government Actuary's Department
GMP	–	Guaranteed Minimum Pension as described in the Pension Schemes Act 1993
GN	–	Actuarial Guidance Note
HMRC	–	Her Majesty's Revenue and Customs
HMRC NICO	–	HMRC National Insurance Contributions Office (formerly Contributions Agency and later NICO)
ICTA 1988	–	Income and Corporation Taxes Act 1988
IHT	–	Inheritance Tax
IHTA 1984	–	Inheritance Tax Act 1984
IORPs	–	Institutions for Occupational Retirement Provision
IPT	–	Insurance Premium Tax
IR SPSS	–	HMRC Savings, Pensions, Share Schemes; including the former PSO (Pension Schemes Office)
ITEPA	–	Income Tax (Earnings and Pensions) Act 2003
MFR	–	Minimum Funding Requirement
NAPF	–	National Association of Pension Funds
NIC(s)	–	National Insurance Contribution(s)
NICO	–	National Insurance Contributions Office
NISPI	–	National Insurance Services to Pensions Industry
OEIC	–	Open-ended Investment Company
PA 1995	–	Pensions Act 1995

AVC(s)	–	Additional Voluntary Contribution(s)
PA 2004	–	Pensions Act 2004
PN(s)	–	Practice Notes issued by the Pension Schemes Office (IR 12). The current version is PN(2001), but PN(1979) is still extant for some schemes.
PSA 1993	–	Pensions Schemes Act 1993
RAS	–	Relief at Source
RPI	–	The Government's Index of Retail Prices
s	–	section
ss	–	Sub-section
Sch	–	Schedule
SERPS	–	State Earnings – Related Pension Scheme
SI	–	Statutory Instrument
SIPPS(s)	–	Self–Invested Personal Pension Scheme(s)
SP	–	Inland Revenue Statement of Practice
SPA	–	State Pension Age (65 for men, 60 for women)
SSA	–	Social Security Act(s)
SSAS(s)	–	Small Self-Administered Scheme(s)
S2P	–	The State Second Pension, which replaced SERPS as a second tier state pension from 6 April 2002
TCGA	–	Taxation of Chargeable Gains Act 1992
TUPE	–	Transfer of Employment (Pension Protection) Regulations 2005 (SI 2005/649)
TMA	–	Taxes Management Act 1970
UK	–	United Kingdom
UURBS	–	Unapproved Unfunded Retirement Benefit Scheme
VAT	–	Value Added Tax
VATA	–	Value Added Tax Act 1994

Appendix 36

Model statutory appointment letter of scheme auditor

Notice of Appointment of Scheme Auditor

In accordance with section 47 of the Pensions Act 1995 and regulation 5 of the Occupational Pension Schemes (Scheme Administration) Regulations 1996, we hereby give you written notice of your appointment as auditors of the XYZ Pension Scheme with effect from the date of your letter of acknowledgment.

In connection with your appointment as scheme auditors, you should take instructions in relation to the audit of the scheme from [name and position] and you should report to [name and position].

Your appointment is initially in respect of the scheme's accounts/auditors' statement about contributions to be prepared as at [insert year end date], the scheme's year end. The scheme's previous auditors were [insert name and address if applicable]. A copy of the previous auditors' statement/declaration on leaving office is attached and we have authorised them to provide information to you as necessary and appropriate.

We confirm that, under section 27 of the Pensions Act 1995, no trustee of the scheme is connected with or is an associate of [auditor name], which would render [auditor firm] ineligible from acting as auditors to the scheme.

We should be grateful if you would write to acknowledge receipt of this notice of appointment and forward your acceptance of this appointment as scheme auditors within one month of the date of this letter.

Yours faithfully

For and on behalf of the Trustees of the XYZ Pension Scheme

Appendix 37

Model statutory acceptance letter of scheme auditor

XYZ Pension Scheme

Notice of Appointment of Scheme Auditor

We write to acknowledge receipt of your notice of appointment dated [date] and hereby accept the appointment as scheme auditor to the XYZ Pension Scheme in accordance with the Occupational Pension Schemes (Scheme Administration) Regulations 1996.

Immediately we become aware of the existence of any conflict of interest to which we are subject in relation to the Scheme, we undertake, as required by the Act, to notify you by informing [name and title], the nominated person to whom we are required to report under the notice of appointment.

Appendix 38

HMRC Guidance 'What will be available from 6 April 2006?'

The requirement to submit all reports and returns of information online to HMRC was postponed to at least six months beyond A-Day, although the registration forms were in place. Details are on the website http://www.hmrc.gov.uk/pensionschemes/tax-simp-draft-forms.htm. The forms are:

Main forms:

- Registration for tax relief and exemptions
- Registration for relief at source
- Contracting out (Industry wide schemes)
- Contracting out (other schemes)
- Event report
- Accounting for tax return
- Registered pension scheme return
- Protection of existing rights
- Enhanced lifetime allowance (pension credit rights)
- Enhanced lifetime allowance (international)
- Declare as a scheme administrator of a deferred annuity contract

Maintenance forms:

- Cessation of scheme administrator
- Pre-register as a scheme administrator
- Notify scheme administrator details
- Change of scheme administrator/practitioner details
- Authorising a practitioner
- Add scheme administrator
- Amend scheme details

Appendix 38

HMRC has published the following Annex, entitled 'What can be done at A-Day':

'The following provides a brief summary of the options you will have at 6 April 2006 (A-Day) for submitting information to HMRC and amending information held by HMRC. Newsletter No 8, set out what will be available online from A-Day and this is reproduced in the table below. The final versions of all the forms noted below will be available on the HMRC Website at A-Day.

Please note you should not submit any forms before A-Day on the draft versions that are currently on the Internet.

Any forms completed before A-Day will be returned as they will not be valid.

Action	Online Form Name	Online form available at A-Day	Who can submit the form online?	Paper Form Name and Number	Paper form available at A-Day	Who can sign the paper form?	Anything else?
1. Use Pension Schemes Online							
Register to use Pension Schemes Online: a) Pre-register to obtain an Activation Token and Scheme Administrator/Practitioner ID.	Register new user	Yes	Only the Scheme Administrator or Practitioner can pre-register themselves	Pre-register as a Scheme Administrator/ Practitioner APSS 161	Yes	Only the Scheme Administrator or Practitioner pre-registering	
b) Complete registration for the online service	Register new user	Yes	Only the Scheme Administrator or Practitioner can complete registration	Not applicable	No	Not applicable	This can only be done online as it requires the user registering to create their password
2. Scheme Registration							
Register a new scheme for tax relief and exemptions	Register a new pension scheme	Yes	Scheme Administrator	Pension Scheme Tax Registration APSS 100	Yes	Scheme Administrator	
Elect to contract out of state second pension.	Elect to contract out	No Proposed release Autumn 06	Scheme Administrator or Practitioner	Registered Pension Schemes -Election to Contract-out APSS 101	Yes	Employer, trustee or person responsible for the day to day management of the scheme	
Elect to contract out of state second pension by industry wide scheme	Elect to contract out	No Proposed release Autumn 06	Scheme Administrator or Practitioner	Registered Pension Schemes -Election to Contract-out for industry wide schemes APSS 102	Yes	Employer, trustee or person responsible for the day to day management of the scheme	
Register to operate relief at source or amend relief at source details	Register for Relief at Source or Amend Relief at Source	No Proposed release Autumn 06	Scheme Administrator or Practitioner	Relief at Source Details APSS 103	Yes	Scheme Administrator or Practitioner	
Send specimen signature(s) authorised to sign repayment claims	Not applicable	No	Not applicable	Relief at Source specimen signatures APSS 103A	Yes	Those authorised to sign repayments of tax relief at source on	This form is optional for providing samples of authorised signatures.

						contributions to registered pension schemes	
Complete single registration form, to register for tax relief and exemptions, elect to contract-out and register to operate at tax relief at source	Register a new scheme	No Proposed release Autumn 06	Scheme Administrator	Pension Scheme Registration APSS 100A	Yes	Scheme Administrator	
Make your declaration as required under Section 270 Finance Act 2004 as the Scheme Administrator of a deferred annuity contract made on or after A-day	Declare as Scheme Administrator for a deferred annuity contract	Yes	Scheme Administrator	Declaration as a Scheme Administrator of a Deferred Annuity Contract scheme APSS 108	Yes	Scheme Administrator	This is only used for deferred annuity contracts made on or after A-day
3. Scheme Administer/Practitioner Maintenance							
Amend your details provided at pre-registration for Pension Schemes Online (see 1 above)	View or amend your details	Yes	The Scheme Administrator or Practitioner whose details are being amended	Change of Scheme Administrator or Practitioner user details APSS 153	Yes	The Scheme Administrator or Practitioner whose details are being amended	
4. Scheme Maintenance							
Amend the scheme name or the establisher/sponsor details or client reference	Amend Scheme Details	No Proposed release Summer 06	Scheme Administrator or Practitioner	Amend Scheme details APSS 152	Yes	Scheme Administrator or Practitioner	
Amend contracting-out details	Not applicable	No	Not applicable	Contracting-out Maintenance APSS 155	Yes	Employer, trustee or person responsible for the day to day management of the scheme	
Scheme Administrator of a pension scheme wishes to authorise HM Revenue & Customs(HMRC) to deal with a Practitioner acting on their behalf .	Practitioner Management	Yes	Scheme Administrator	Authorising a Practitioner APSS 150	Yes	Scheme Administrator	
(a) A Scheme Administrator who was the Administrator of a scheme on 5 April 2006 wishes to have their details recorded on the pension scheme record, or (b) A Scheme Administrator who is appointed on or after A-day (other than the Scheme Administrator of a new deferred annuity contract made on or after A-day) should make their declaration as required under Section 270 Finance Act 2004	Add yourself as Scheme Administrator	Yes	Scheme Administrator	Add Scheme Administrator to a scheme APSS 151	Yes	Scheme Administrator	If the scheme record held by HMRC already shows a Scheme Administrator the known Scheme Administrator will need to associate the new/additional Scheme Administrator before this form can be processed (see below)
The Scheme Administrator recorded against the HMRC record for the pension scheme needs to advise HMRC there is a new/additional Scheme Administrator for the scheme.	Scheme Administrator Management	Yes	Scheme Administrator recorded on the HMRC record for the scheme	Associate Scheme Administrator to scheme APSS 154	Yes	Scheme Administrator recorded on the HMRC record for the scheme	

This is to allow the new/additional Scheme Administrator to add their details to the pension scheme record (this allows them to view pension scheme information) and make their declaration as required under Section 270 Finance Act 2004							
The appointment of a Scheme Administrator of a scheme is terminated they need to report the cessation to HMRC	Scheme Administrator Management	No Proposed release Summer 06	Scheme Administrator that has ceased	Cessation of Scheme Administrator APSS 160	Yes	Scheme Administrator that has ceased	
5. Reporting and returns							
The scheme has wound up this has to be reported to HMRC or The scheme has wound up and there are other events to report to HMRC as well	Event Report	No Proposed release April 07	Scheme Administrator or Practitioner	Event Report APSS 300	Yes	Scheme Administrator	
Claim in-year repayment of tax relief deducted at source from contributions	Not applicable	No	Not applicable	Relief at Source – interim claim APSS 105	Yes	Authorised signatory	Formerly the PP10
Make annual claim for repayment of tax relief deducted at source from contributions	Not applicable	No	Not applicable	Relief at Source – annual claim APSS 106 (Not available until October 2006)	Yes	Authorised signatory	Formerly the PP14
Make annual statistical return	Not applicable	No	Not applicable	Relief at Source – annual statistical return APSS 107 (Not available until October 2006)	Yes and magnetic media	Authorised signatory	Formerly the PP14 (Stats)
6. Enhanced LTA							
Protection of existing rights – Notifications for Primary Protection & Enhanced Protection	To be advised	No Release date to be agreed	Individual or agent	Protection of existing Rights APSS 200	Yes	Individual	Forms can be submitted from 6th April 06 to 5th April 09
Enhanced LTA (Pension credit rights)	To be advised	No Release date to be agreed	Individual or agent	Enhanced Lifetime Allowance (Pension Credit Rights) APSS 201	Yes	Individual	
Enhanced LTA (International)	To be advised	No Release date to be agreed Spring 07	Individual or agent	Enhanced Lifetime Allowance (International) APSS 202	Yes	Individual	
Authorise Scheme Administrator to view LTA Certificate	To be advised	No Release date to be agreed	Individual or agent	Authorise Scheme Administrator to view LTA Certificate APSS 203	Yes	Individual	

Request by Scheme Administrator to view LTA Certificate	To be advised	No Release date to be agreed	Scheme Administrator	Request by Scheme Administrator to view LTA Certificate APSS 209	Yes	Scheme Administrator	
7. International							
Qualifying Overseas Pension Scheme (QOPS) Notification	Not applicable	No	Not applicable	Qualifying Overseas Pension Schemes (QOPS) APSS 250	Yes	Scheme manager	
Qualifying Recognised Overseas Pension Scheme (QROPS) Notification	Not applicable	No	Not applicable	Qualifying Recognised Overseas Pension Scheme (QROPS) APSS 251	Yes	Scheme manager	
Report of benefit crystallisation events	Not applicable	No	Not applicable	Report of benefit crystallisation events APSS 252	Yes	Scheme manager	
Report of payments in respect of relevant members	Not applicable	No	Not applicable	Payments in respect of relevant members APSS 253	Yes	Scheme manager	
Individual's election for a deemed benefit crystallisation event	Not applicable	No	Not applicable	Election for a deemed benefit crystallisation event APSS 254	Yes	Individual	

Scheme Administrator / Practitioner ID

In addition to being required to complete registration for Pension Schemes Online these ID's are used to ensure as far as is possible that information is recorded against the correct record. For this reason many of the forms ask for the Scheme Administrator/Practitioner ID to make the link to the record. It is therefore recommended that if you did not take part in the recent pre-registration exercise you pre-register for Pension Schemes Online (see 1a) in the table above) and obtain a Scheme Administrator/Practitioner ID. For online submissions your user ID and password are linked to your ID (but knowing the ID is not enough to view the record or make submissions. The user ID and password are needed).

Index

[*all references are to paragraph number*]

G

H